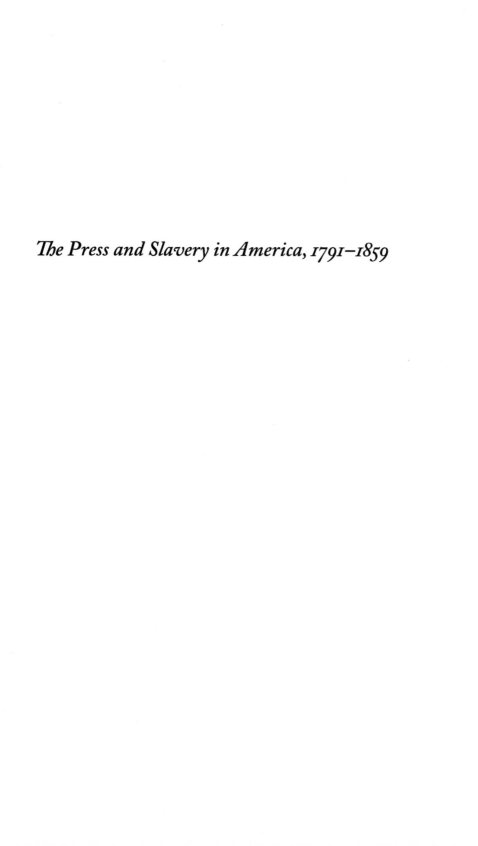

The Press and Slavery in America, 1791–1859

THE PRESS AND SLAVERY IN AMERICA

1791–1859

The Melancholy Effect of Popular Excitement

Brian Gabrial

THE UNIVERSITY OF SOUTH CAROLINA PRESS

Published by the University of South Carolina Press
Columbia, South Carolina 29208

www.sc.edu/uscpress

Manufactured in the United States of America

25 24 23 22 21 20 19 18 17 16
10 9 8 7 6 5 4 3 2 1

Library of Congress Cataloging-in-Publication Data
can be found at http://catalog.loc.gov/.

INBN: 978-1-61117-603-2 (hardcover)
INBN: 978-1-61117-604-9 (ebook)

To Clesta, Esta, and Zona, the Sisters

We should not conclude ... that the function of history is to furnish a record of what man is not, but rather we should regard it as the matrix within which man's essential nature is expressed.

Karl Mannheim, *Ideology and Utopia*

CONTENTS

ILLUSTRATIONS

ACKNOWLEDGMENTS

No work of any length is completed without the help of others, especially friends and family members who lent their support and encouragement along the way. I thank them first. I would also like to single out a few others to whom I am especially indebted. My eternal thanks go to the reference librarians at the University of Minnesota and the New York Public Library for their invaluable assistance in locating secondary and primary sources. I am extremely grateful to Albert Tims and the University of Minnesota's School of Journalism and Mass Communication for providing me with the resources during my sabbatical year to revise the original dissertation that became this book. I must recognize the hard work done by my research assistants Katarina Koleva and Jonathan Montpetit, who spent hours, days, and weeks painstakingly and tirelessly double-checking my sources and footnotes. Finally, I want to acknowledge the significant editorial contribution of my friend and mentor Hazel Dicken-Garcia, whose incisive comments on an earlier draft of this book provided the clarity of structure and emphasis that I believe make this a worthwhile contribution to the study of journalism and race in America.

PREFACE

"Human nature is rarely ever so base as not to love liberty."[1] The historian Joseph Cephas Carroll made that observation about all who fight for freedom. Yet from the moment they landed on American soil, black Americans were not seen as worthy or even capable of having such emotions, and those who did possess them were considered dangerous and threatening to white society. "The negro, once roused to bloodshed, and in possession of arms, is as uncontrollable and irrational as a wild beast."[2] That quote appeared in America's then-largest-circulation newspaper a month after John Brown's 1859 raid sent southern slave owners into spasms of fright and rage. While likely offending today's contemporary readers, the words would have hardly disturbed the sensibilities of most nineteenth-century white newspaper subscribers, who thought such language acceptable, even logical.[3] Yet to reach that degree of acceptance, powerful forces had been working for several centuries to influence European and American thought about black people, creating discourses about race and slavery that normalized their subjugation. In America, as news papers became the preeminent nineteenth-century form of mass communication, reaching previously unsurpassed audiences, their crucial role in disseminating these discourses, which were inseparable, cannot be underestimated, especially in the U.S. antebellum years. This book examines the press's role in informing Americans about slavery and race during those years and the constituted media discourses about them. More specifically the book approaches this examination at points of major crises and disruptions in the slave system, namely when slaves rebelled or conspired to do so, and takes as objects of study news accounts of two slave revolts, two conspiracies, and one raid. All of these events pushed slavery and race discussions into the public sphere, even at times when powerful forces tried to keep them silent.[4]

The historian Helen G. MacDonald once observed, "The press of a country, at one time guides and directs public opinion, at another merely acts as the reflector and registers."[5] In either instance an extensive look at what is contained in past newspapers can help later generations understand the society and culture that created them, helping make sense of then commonly held beliefs contained in discourse. Notably, this book differs from other important contributions about slavery and the press in that its focus is on northern and southern mainstream newspapers and how they informed a general, white readership about slavery when slave troubles occurred. Such events generated important news and opinion about black Americans, a group largely ignored in the mainstream press during the antebellum years. The book also departs from other scholarship in that it systematically examines news content that spans nearly seventy years to identify media discourses that consistently appeared over time and expressed ideas about black Americans, both slave and free. What becomes clear from these newspaper accounts is that when disruptions occurred in the slave system, white authorities took repressive and violent steps to restore the status quo, in this case slavery and its racial hierarchy, and to suppress black Americans in general. What this book cannot be, however, is a comprehensive history of American slavery or race, the press, or the events considered. Instead the focus remains on media discourses about race and slavery in antebellum America, suggesting that those discourses have resonance in contemporary U.S. society.

Those discourses began to shift in the United States as the country neared the Civil War's final break, illustrating how fierce and powerful reactionary responses, which emanated from a powerful class of Americans who demanded slavery's preservation, competed with a growing antislavery voice that articulated strong sentiment to see it end. Such discourses highlight the sustenance that slavery provided the ongoing contest between the country's two dominant strands of political thought, conservative and liberal. Further, as this book explores the genealogies, chronologies, and discontinuities of these discourses, it offers perhaps a new look at the nineteenth-century American press as an elite social institution that ignored, supported, or resisted slavery, a horrific system that left its destructive mark on those American blacks forced to endure its vicious spiritual, psychological, and corporal transgressions.

The Civil War historian Kenneth Stampp has called slavery "America's most profound and vexatious social problem" before the Civil War.[6] It was the great and tragic American paradox, existing in a society founded on an enlightened ideal that asserted "all men are created equal." To compensate for this bizarre dissonance, many of the nation's most powerful and intellectual elites, including newspaper editors and politicians, adhered to a racist ideology that, for a variety of philosophical, religious, and scientific reasons, framed blacks as inferior beings, a rationale that seemed common sense to most white Americans.[7] As a result probably no other constitutionally protected institution damaged the nation's culture and society more as it thrived in an intellectual and philosophical environment that should have killed it.

Despite increasing social and legal protections afforded slavery in the early to mid-nineteenth century, the system with its seemingly harmonious master and slave relationship belied undercurrents of resistance and white fears of it.

"The image of black violence and retribution, drawn not only from Nat Turner but from memories of what had occurred in Santo Domingo [now Haiti], continued to haunt the Southern imagination," the historian George M. Fredrickson has keenly observed.[8] The slave insurrection or the threat of it became a lasting fear among the South's antebellum whites, who lived in lands where blacks often outnumbered whites. The thought of slave rebellion and its ensuing violence, from mysterious late-night fires to open slave defiance, created a constant anxiety that Winthrop Jordan has called "gnawing, gut-wringing" because it presented "an appalling world turned upside down, a crazy nonsense world of black over white."[9] To ease this apprehension and to prevent any form of slave resistance, as Frederickson has noted, "Southern slave owners were extraordinarily careful to maintain absolute control over their 'people' and to quarantine them from any kind of outside influence that might inspire dissatisfaction with their condition."[10] As early as 1710, for example, Virginia colonial governor Alexander Spotswood called for stronger slave laws, cautioning that "all Those who Long to Shake of [*sic*] the fetters of Slavery and as Such an Insurrection would surely be attended with Most Dreadfull Consequences."[11]

In some ways the slave owners' methods succeeded, preventing all but a few dramatic acts of open revolt even in regions where the slaves greatly outnumbered the masters. Short of open rebellion, though, a slave might show discontent by stealing or destroying the master's property, running away, becoming obstinate, malingering, lying, or feigning ignorance.[12] As well, as one historian has argued, many captive Africans brought to North America managed to retain some of their cultural roots, which remained foreign to their white overseers and challenged them and their demands for absolute obedience.[13] Despite increasing repression, captured Africans, almost from the moment they stepped onto North American soil, tried to flee or rebel. The Spanish, who first transported these captives in 1526 to what became the South Carolina coast, could not prevent the escape of several slaves, who found refuge among the native population.[14] Nearly one hundred years passed before other European whites forced African slaves to settle in North America, this time in Virginia.[15] In 1663 the first slave conspiracy in North America was recorded in that colony.[16] The most notable examples of armed slave discontent occurred in South Carolina in 1739,[17] on Louisiana's German Coast in 1811, and in Southampton County, Virginia, in 1831. In addition, toward the end of the eighteenth century there began a slave revolt that eventually expelled the French from Haiti, then known as St. Dominique or Santo Domingo. Its violence imprinted a real and bloody image that defined exactly for white Americans what the words "slave revolt" meant. Equally terrifying to whites were slave conspiracies because they indicated that slaves were not a docile group and that horrific outcomes could occur if the conspiracies succeeded. These conspiracies included one in 1741 in New York, Gabriel Prosser's 1800 conspiracy in Henrico County, Virginia, and the Denmark Vesey conspiracy in 1822 Charleston, South Carolina.

Perhaps the most frightening event of all to slave owners occurred in 1859 when John Brown, a white man, led his quasi-military excursion into Virginia hoping to arm black slaves. After that October raid, the writer of a November 23 *New York Herald* editorial preyed on white fears of black violence by asserting, "The whole history of negro insurrection proves that there is no race of men so brutal and bloody-minded as the negro." Even the *New York Times,* the *Herald*'s antislavery rival, noted in an editorial headlined "The Negro Insurrection," "No man can justify an insurrection of Southern slaves upon any other basis than this—that a better state of society for all concerned would certainly result from it than that which now exists. Anything less than this would not compensate for the slaughter of innocent women and children, the wholesale destruction of property, the infliction of torture, rapine and every imaginable horror, the overthrow of all order, peace and security, and the black and bloody anarchy, which must inevitably attend upon the most successful insurrection of Southern slaves which could possibly take place."[18]

About slavery in the press before the Civil War, the historian Donald Shaw wrote, "News about [it] did not overwhelm other kinds of news," and most discussions about slavery were framed in a regional context.[19] Deep in slave country, slave owners controlled much of the press, silencing perhaps reports of slave trouble so as to impress readers both white and black that they fully controlled their chattel.[20] Such an observation is exemplified by a Richmond, Virginia, newspaper editor's caution to fellow editors after Nat Turner's 1831 revolt not to give slaves "false conceptions of their numbers and capacity, by exhibiting the terror and confusion of the whites, and to induce them to think [revolt] practicable."[21] What can never be known with any certainty, then, is how much real slave resistance occurred on isolated plantations far from towns and cities and their newspaper presses. Regardless of attempts to suppress press content, reports about slave resistance did surface in the nation's newspapers, often appearing as hastily written correspondence or, later, as terse telegraph dispatches sent within hours after troubles surfaced. Those contents concern this book because over time they formed recurring media discourses about race and slavery in America.

Because this book is about discourse, it is important to consider what that means within its context. The media scholar Teun van Dijk has noted that discourse is "a central and manifest cultural and social product in and through which meaning and ideologies are expressed or (re)produced."[22] For van Dijk, journalists as well as other social elites play a crucial role in sustaining a discourse because they "have a primary role in setting the agenda, and hence have considerable influence in defining the terms and the margins of consent and dissent for public debate, in formulating the problems people speak and think about, and especially in controlling the changing systems of norms and values by which ethnic events are evaluated."[23] These media discourses become commonsense ways of looking at public events, signaling larger contexts of meaning and understanding.[24] In this way discourses are inextricably linked to power structures, as Norman Fairclough has argued, with "powerful participants controlling and constraining the contribution of non-power participants."[25] Furthermore, according to Margaret Wetherell and Jonathan Potter, discourse "feeds off the social landscape, the social groups, the material interests already constituted."[26] In antebellum America, the "material interests" of powerful, white southern landowners included slaves-as-property, and maintaining their property required an imperative to maintain slavery.

Over time these media discourses, emerging in news coverage of America's slave troubles, reflected the country's ideological struggles as its sections, each representing legitimate and powerful cultural forces, grappled with and finally divided over slavery. Thus it is important to consider how cultural forces can predispose media discourses to reflect ideas that members of a society can understand and accept. About slaves and other black Americans, these discourses qualified news content in ways that served to marginalize anything seen as threatening to white-controlled slave society or to white people in general. Such would be the case for black Americans, including slave rebels, slaves, and free blacks.

Still, "different and even contradictory" discourses exist and compete for dominance.[27] In America two powerful and competing political discourses— namely conservative and liberal views of the federal government's role in the lives of citizens—have existed since the nation's founding. Before the Civil War, a conservative view held that the federal government had no right to tamper with constitutionally protected slavery, while a liberal, more progressive view came to maintain otherwise. As a result, whenever slave troubles occurred, America's newspaper editors and publishers, depending on their particular ideologies, determined the emphasis that competing discourses had in their newspapers. This book highlights those competing discourses.

This book also tells something about how newspaper technology and journalistic practice changed from the partisan press era to that of the penny press, illustrating their fundamental transformations between 1791 and 1859. As late as 1831 newspaper editors relied on fellow editors to provide "news" about slave troubles, which arrived usually as written correspondence from affected areas. In 1800 and 1831, for example, New York editors had to wait until Virginia newspapers reached them before they could inform readers about Gabriel Prosser's conspiracy and Nat Turner's revolt, respectively. By 1859 northern and southern newspaper editors sent their own reporters to Harper's Ferry[28] and Charlestown to telegraph dispatches for same-day publication. In addition editorial voices about these events had become much clearer by 1859 than they had been in 1831 or earlier.[29] Because journalism practice is not static, with eighteenth- and nineteenth-century practitioners acting mostly in accordance with beliefs shaped by their culture and society, surviving texts cannot be judged by contemporary standards. Consider this caution by Helen MacDonald: "It is not indeed [by] the study of a single newspaper, however influential that newspaper may be, that public opinion can be accurately gauged, for no newspaper is the spokesman of the entire people."[30] Therefore the assertion here is that a nation's newspapers, though differing in opinion and content, can be collectively examined to shed light on how a past, literate public viewed slavery.

Because of the book's scope and purpose, some organizational challenges exist. First, content must reflect on eighteenth- and nineteenth-century ideas about slavery and race for readers to gain an understanding of how white Americans came to think about Africans and how that thought resonated in press accounts. Second, because the book contains a discourse analysis of newspaper content about race and slavery, each case study must be historically grounded and contextualized. Third, the book presents the dominant discourses revealed over time and therefore is separated into two major sections. Part I focuses on slave troubles from 1791 with Santo Domingo to 1800 Virginia with Gabriel Prosser's conspiracy. It continues with the 1811 Louisiana revolt, Denmark Vesey's 1822 conspiracy, and Nat Turner's 1831 revolt—an event that truly stunned the nation—and concludes with John Brown's 1859 raid, which occurred at a moment when a splintered nation could not surmount its cultural and political chasms over slavery. Part I also accounts for the changing nature of the American press and discusses the rising and dangerous sectionalism that surfaced over slavery as the nation expanded.

The case studies examined are notable because they occurred at critical junctures in American history. For example, the starting point is Santo Domingo, where island slaves began a revolt that stunned white Americans still sorting out the birth of their new national government. While not an *American* slave revolt per se, this rebellion became a reference point, creating an intertextual signpost for later troubles. Whenever newspaper content connected this island's revolt to later troubles, it provided readers with instant clarity about what had occurred (or nearly occurred) and what black-on-white violence meant. Nine years later when Gabriel Prosser's slave conspiracy shocked Virginia, it occurred during the hotly contested 1800 presidential race, and much news coverage of the conspiracy was heavily laced with political rancor from Federalist and anti-Federalist camps. The next case study discussed involved the 1811 Louisiana slave revolt, a frightening event that took place on the eve of Louisiana's admission as a state, a time when the young nation's military also contended with Spanish incursions in nearby Florida. In South Carolina the residues of the Missouri Compromise may have spurred Denmark Vesey, a free black man, to act. His eponymous 1822 conspiracy shocked white Charlestonians and led to a strangely repressive period that silenced the city's presses. Of all the troubles to this point, Nat Turner's 1831 revolt can be considered a true media event because of the significant press coverage it generated, despite occurring near the end of the partisan press era, a time when news traveled about as fast as a horse or ship could carry it. After the Nat Turner revolt there was an emergence of fiercely competing discourses about slavery, especially as anti-slavery factions exerted greater pressure on southerners to end it. The final case study concerns John Brown and the clamor following his 1859 Harper's Ferry attack. The volume of news coverage about the raid surpassed anything before concerning slave troubles, and the media discourses embedded in that coverage sharply illustrate the fractured state of the country and the serious threat that slavery then posed to the nation's very survival.

Part 2 of this book focuses on the media discourses that emerged during times of slave troubles, beginning with a discourse about how slavery's enemies were dealt with in newspaper constructions of the slave rebels and others who threatened the institution. These threats created significant media discourse that concerned the panic caused by a consuming, irrational fear of black-on-white violence and the need to right the slave system immediately and to restore order and white control. This discourse about racial panic reveals how any suspected slave trouble led to violent reactionary responses toward slavery's enemies, especially those who were black. A third media discourse identified in the final chapters shows that slavery created extreme sectionalism and destroyed America's founding ideals and civil liberties while severely damaging the national psyche. These discourses suggest a genealogy of how slavery and race were threaded into America's political divide. Of course, if the past's political discordance over American slavery serves as any warning, such extreme political impasses regarding any important issue remain dangerous and destructive to the nation's future.

Before embarking, a question remains: How can an examination of media discourses found in American press coverage of events occurring more than a century and a half ago contribute to an understanding of society today? The historian Edmund Wilson offers a response: "If we would truly understand at the present time the kind of role that our own country is playing, we must go back and try to see objectively what our tendencies and our practice have been in the past."[31] This book claims that this can be partly accomplished by interpreting the discourses rooted in the country's newspapers of the past. Sadly, the penumbra of these discourses about race in America is still evident, as a recent study involving white, Florida residents suggested by noting that they believe black Americans remain "disposed to behaviors that threaten public order."[32] Therefore heeding Wilson's directive is a task worth undertaking and exploring.

✿ Introduction
Racism and Slavery in America

Though in many natural objects, whiteness refiningly enhances beauty, as if imparting some special virtue of its own, whiteness gave, when applied to the human race, the white man ideal mastership over every dusky tribe.

Herman Melville, *Moby-Dick*

Cursed be Canaan: a slave of slaves shall he be to his brothers.

Genesis 9:25

Slavery came to be seen as common sense in antebellum America, and by 1800 race and slavery had merged in national discourse—to discuss slavery was to discuss race.[1] Arguments for slavery's rightness as an American labor system that targeted only black Americans originated with powerful influences that imbued its culture, especially in the South, with ideas about race that social conduits such as the press and popular literature supported and legitimized.[2] These particularly American proslavery ideas rationalized black enslavement and preserved a strange, elite slave power status quo whose political power successfully resisted challenges to it and to slavery, regardless of region.[3] Thus by the end of the eighteenth century, skin color defined slavery, a normalized, paternalistic system that most white Americans viewed as a given and not particularly racist. In fact most slaveholders saw themselves as acting "in the best interests of their dependent beings and for the prosperity and happiness of the world," according to Eugene Genovese.[4] Still, this brand of race-based slavery is set apart from other historical forms of slavery because it condemned one people and their descendants to perpetual bondage, giving them few if any rights.[5]

To justify such treatment in a land reifying the Enlightenment's noble ideas about an individual's essential nature, a racist ideology came to flourish, dominating white American thought about black peoples.[6] So just as powerful philosophical ideas about liberty and equality should have killed slavery, it endured and even thrived. Tragically the slave became "an irrepressible reminder of the systematic violence and exploitation which underlay a society genuinely dedicated to individual freedom and equality of opportunity," according to David Brion Davis.[7] Historical, economic, philosophical, theological, scientific, and legal roots supported a system that locked the African and his or her children into a lifetime of servitude. As this book traces that genealogy, it also explores the thoughts of the nation's intellectual founders who, as Enlightenment thinkers, grappled with slavery's paradoxical existence in the young republic dedicated to the principles of equality and liberty.

A Brief History of Slavery

Slavery existed long before Europeans brought it to North America, where it gained its unique racial quality and "was neither invented by white Europeans nor confined exclusively to black Africans."[8] In ancient Greece, for example, Aristotle viewed slavery as one of many natural states[9] and reasoned, "Authority and subordination are conditions not only inevitable but also expedient."[10] Slavery in ancient cultures was seen, theologically, as punishment for sin or a natural defect or, philosophically, as part of a natural order or a starting point on a divine quest for freedom.[11] Later, Saint Augustine, writing about the general condition of slavery, cautioned, "Slaves be obedient to those who are your earthly masters."[12] Centuries later, however, neither Aristotle nor Augustine would have recognized the institution that the American South nurtured, one that its adherents argued had philosophical, theological, scientific, and (especially) economic justifications.

Slavery's links to economics began almost from the moment the Ottoman Turks closed Black Sea trade routes in 1453, forcing Europeans to look westward to the Americas for exploitation of natural resources and other potential wealth.[13] Initially, Europe's insatiable quest for sugar fueled the American slave trade because the growing and harvesting of sugar cane was labor intensive.[14] As many of the Western Hemisphere's indigenous peoples died of starvation, brutal treatment, or disease, the early Spanish and Portuguese empires replaced them quickly with Africans.[15] Further north in the English colonies, the conditions differed in that the first Africans likely came as indentured servants. Invariably blacks served longer terms of servitude than did their white, English counterparts.[16] For example, a 1652 Rhode Island law stated that "no blacke mankind or white being forced by covenant bond, or otherwise" would "serve any man or his assighnes longer than ten yeares, or untill they come to be twentie four years of age."[17] Yet the southern English colonists came to rely on slavery as southern agricultural economies expanded and demanded cheap, abundant labor. There was a clear belief that white Europeans would need African slaves to settle the vast American landscape, and as Davis has observed, slaves played "a major role in the early development of the New World and in the growth of commercial capitalism."[18] By the end of the eighteenth century, agricultural technologies such as the cotton gin increased slave demand in the South, making short staple cotton an important cash crop. Inevitably, as the sugar and later cotton industries bound slaves to large plantations, the status of black laborers transitioned from indentured servants to permanent slaves.[19]

Over time their changed status "provided the foundation for the English image of the Negro as an inferior creature in England and the colonies," Louis Ruchames has noted.[20]

But it was not only a critical labor shortage in the fields that led to this transition. The black slaves became profitable commodities in their own right. The slave trade was an "immense industry itself," as William Lee Miller has observed, and fundamentally linked to the success of other American agricultural industries such as cotton, rice, indigo, and tobacco.[21] The buying and selling of Africans became a primary form of commerce between Europe and Africa, and, according to Davis: "As Negro labor became indispensable for the Spanish and then Portuguese colonization, European traders and African chieftains slowly built a vast commercial system which brought a profound transformation in African culture and stunted growth of other commerce between Europe and the Dark Continent."[22] Similarly, as Winthrop Jordan has observed, "The everyday buying and selling and deeding and trading of slaves underscored the fact that Negroes, just like horses, were walking pieces of property."[23]

In the English colonies, the buyers and sellers of black people realized that the enslaved Africans-as-commodities had certain advantages: 1) they cost less than European slaves or servants; 2) they were considered docile, social, and conditioned to work in tropical temperatures; 3) they had many natural immunities to "Old World" diseases that America's indigenous groups did not; and 4) they had no powerful European friends.[24] Slave traders and slave owners also promoted the tragic fallacy that Africans were "somehow hardier" beings despite the enormous mortality rate on board slave cargo ships.[25] Except for their skin color, though, most slaves shared little else, had no common language or culture, and were strangers to one another.[26] In addition they had little status under English law that protected white English indentured servants but not them. Considered by the English as isolated, familyless, and cultureless beings, Africans were, as one planter noted in 1772, "fit objects of purchase and sale, transferable like any other goods or chattels."[27] According to Barbara Jeanne Fields, "Africans and Afro-West Indians were thus available for perpetual slavery in a way that English servants were not."[28] Slave owners found that black slaves presented another distinct advantage in that they reproduced themselves. While only 6 percent of the slaves brought to the New World went to North America, the American slave population grew so that by 1825 the United States had 36 percent of all slaves in the Western Hemisphere.[29] In sum, a combination of plantation economics, skin color, and English law proved fateful for African blacks, whose descent from indentured servants to slaves was quick.

Justifying the Black Slave

At the outset skin color justified the enslavement of Africans. To Europeans, and later to Americans, words describing Africans—Negro (Spanish), noir

(French), and black (English)—carried "connotations of gloom, evil, baseness, wretchedness, and misfortune," Davis has noted.[30] In 1748 the French Enlightenment philosopher Baron de Montesquieu wrote, "One cannot get into one's mind that god, who is a very wise being should have put a soul, above all a good soul, in a body that was entirely black."[31] Another European, this one a seventeenth-century English explorer, characterized Africans as "Devils incarnate."[32] White Europeans and their American counterparts came to believe that the Africans' very skin color meant they possessed some innate deficiency that made them vile, dangerous creatures. Such ideas became entrenched in white thought about black people so much that after Denmark Vesey's 1822 conspiracy, *Charleston Times* editor Edwin Clifford Holland wrote, "Let it never be forgotten, that our NEGROES, are truely the *Jacobins* of the country; that they are the *anarchists* and the *domestic enemy; the common enemy of civilized society,* and the barbarians who would, IF THEY COULD, become the DESTROYERS *of our race.*"[33] Still, skin color as a racial characteristic likely did not emerge until the eighteenth century. Before that the term "race" generally applied to animal husbandry or family ancestry.[34] This older notion of race continued from the sixteenth through the late eighteenth centuries until Europeans began exploiting other lands and their peoples. Connecting skin color to ideas about the Europeans' "natural" superiority and power became an expedient rationale to subordinate "lesser" peoples.[35] The concept of racial superiority became acutely important to white Europeans as they "acquired or appropriated" global, colonial power, according to Teun van Dijk, who has observed that racism became a form of reproducible social control, keeping the dominant group, such as the European imperialists, in power.[36] By the eighteenth century's end, race and skin color were linked, justifying European conquest, the elimination of America's aboriginals, and the enslavement of dark-skinned Africans.[37]

Just as skin color became connected to race, so too did slavery. "Slavery was no mere happenstance or slip of the moral conscience, but a pre-meditated, enormously profitable, politically desirable, and religiously sanctioned act, particularly when Christians were not the victims," Philip Perlmutter has observed.[38] Early Christian theologians, for example, accepted the slave condition as a divinely ordained state and the result of God's judgment.[39] In establishing America's first slave systems, the devout Roman Catholic Spanish and Portuguese colonizers found that their theology validated the enslavement of, first, the non-Christian indigenous peoples and, later, the imported African slaves. Christianity in general gave reason for "the subjection of 'backward' peoples to colonial rule for the good of their civilization," and religious instruction taught slaves the proper relationship between "master and slave," Davis wrote.[40]

The Protestant English in North America, following the Spanish and Portuguese precedent, further equated a slave's status and loss of liberty as exemplifying a natural state of sin.[41] They understood skin color (and ancestry) as a "precondition for a system of slavery . . . and all that it implied about God's

curse on [black slaves]," according to Alden T. Vaughn.[42] That "curse," stem-
ming from Genesis, marked black peoples as having the mark of Cain and
suffering the fate of Noah's son Ham. As late as 1859 one southern planter
noted, "It was ordained that the descendants of Ham [blacks] should be the
'servants of servants.'"[43] Many decades earlier the Puritans, who mostly saw no
theological conflict with black slavery, believed that slavery provided a divine
opportunity to bring Christ into blacks' pagan lives.[44] Cotton Mather, in the
1706 tract "The Negro Christianized," argued that the master had a duty to
baptize his African slaves despite a view that their natural state "must be low,
and mean, and abject; a State of Servitude."[45] Another Puritan, Judge Samuel
Sewall, held a more sympathetic view. In his tract "The Selling of Joseph" the
judge reasoned that while blacks did not enjoy a place in Puritan society, "They
ought to be treated with a Respect agreeable."[46] Those words were comparably
more enlightened than those of the slave trader John Saffin, who wrote in "A
Brief and Candid Answer to the Late Printed Sheet Entituled, 'The Selling
of Joseph'" that God "hath set different Orders and Degrees of Men in the
World." Saffin concluded the treatise with the poem "The Negroes Character":

> Cowardly and cruel are those Blacks Innate,
> Prone to Revenge, Imp of inveterate hate.
> He that exasperates them, soon espies
> Mischief and Murder in their very eyes.
> Libidinous, Deceitful, False and Rude,
> The Spume Issue of Ingratitude.[47]

Such notions hardly died out among America's intellectual elites. Decades after
Saffin wrote his words, another New England man, this time a Harvard stu-
dent, argued in 1773 that slavery helped Africans by removing them "from the
state of brutality, wretchedness, and misery . . . to this land of light, humanity,
and Christian knowledge."[48] Despite the influence of the Enlightenment's hu-
manistic ideals on America's political leaders, a common white view still held
blacks and Native Americans as inferior humans lacking intellect, republican
values, and control over their destinies.[49] When it came to nonwhites, these
would represent the entrenched convictions of most white Americans. Years
later Josiah Priest, whose popular writings reached a large readership, in a 1845
treatise asserted simply, "In the bosom of the negro man, the idea of liberty,
freedom, and independence, does not give rise to the same sensations, hopes
and expectations, that it does in the bosom of whites"; according to Priest,
black peoples viewed liberty as a time to engage in "perfect indulgences of
indolence, stupidity, and the animal passions."[50]

Influential European philosophy too denigrated blacks, thinking them low
and base peoples. The great Enlightenment philosophers could not escape
their milieu, holding to racist standards that promoted white superiority.[51] The

influential eighteenth-century Scottish philosopher David Hume, for example, argued in "Of National Characters" that "there are NEGROE slaves dispersed over all of EUROPE, of which none ever discovered any symptoms of ingenuity"; continuing, Hume observed, "In JAMAICA indeed, they talk of one negroe as a man of parts and learning; but 'tis likely he is admired for very slender accomplishments like a parrot, who speaks a few words plainly."[52] Even Enlightenment thinkers holding that the races were more or less equal believed that the environment or some other "unfortunate" factors had somehow debased the mental abilities of nonwhite races.[53] In the United States, Thomas Jefferson's damaging words in *Notes on the State of Virginia* did much to fuel enduring American racist thought: "I advance it therefore as a suspicion only, that the blacks, whether originally a distinct race, or made distinct by time and circumstances, are inferior to the whites in the endowments both of body and mind."[54] Later the famed nineteenth-century American landscape architect Frederick Law Olmsted observed during his travels through the antebellum South that even the poorest, nonslaveholding whites believed themselves better than any black: "from childhood, the one thing in their condition which has made life valuable to the mass of whites has been that the niggers are yet their inferiors."[55]

While Jefferson admitted that his observations lacked scientific proof, other eighteenth- and nineteenth-century rationalists based their notions on "scientific" observations, which bolstered theirs and others' claims of black inferiority.[56] In 1738 the Swedish botanist Carl von Linne, known as Carolus Linnaeus, published his racial classification scheme that attributed certain behavioral qualities to different groups. Whites were described as "Light, lively (active), ingenious" and "Governed by custom." Comparatively, blacks were "Crafty, lazy, negligent" and "Governed by whim (caprice)."[57] The Comte de Buffon argued a decade later in *Histoire naturelle, générale et particuliere* that all races derived from a single (white) race and that environmental changes created racial disparities.[58] This notion of "monogenesis" persisted through the eighteenth century. The German naturalist Johann Friedrich Blumenbach's 1775 "Natural Varieties of Mankind" concluded that nonwhite races were merely "degenerate" versions of the white race.[59] Another influential taxonomy, created by the nineteenth-century French naturalist Georges Cuvier, compared blacks to a "monkey tribe: the hordes of which it consists have always remained in the most complete state of utter barbarism."[60]

This was hardly an original idea. Note, for example, that the English insinuated a "sexual link between Negroes and apes" to bolster a misconception that Africans were "a lewd, lascivious, and wanton people," as Winthrop Jordan observed.[61] In 1798 America a description of blacks appearing in the first American edition of the *Encyclopaedia Britannica* described the Negro as follows: "round cheeks, high cheek-bones, a forehead somewhat elevated, a short, broad, flat nose, thick lips, small ears, ugliness, and irregularity of shape, characterize their external appearance"; "Vices the most notorious seem to be the portion of this unhappy race: idleness, treachery, revenge, cruelty, impudence, stealing, lying, profanity, debauchery, nastiness and intemperance, are said to have extinguished the principles of natural law, and to have silence the reproofs of conscience. They are strangers to every sentiment of compassion, and are an awful example of the corruption of man when left to himself."[62]

The idea of racial "monogenesis" shifted in the nineteenth century to polygenesis, which, according to the nineteenth-century naturalist Dr. Samuel George Morton, supported the idea that different racial groups were scientifically distinct species. Morton claimed that Africans, for example, originated separately from whites "to inhabit" tropical Africa.[63] Proslavery advocates favored such an idea because a claim could then be made that whites were the only "authentic descendants of Adam."[64] As late as 1857 Chief Justice Roger B. Taney suggested this in *Dred Scott v. Sanford,* arguing that the framers of the U.S. Constitution considered Africans "a subordinate race and inferior class of beings, who had been subjugated by the dominant race."[65] Hailing the decision, Dr. John H. Van Evrie of New York said it was "in accord with the natural relations of the races" and "had thus fixed the *status* of the subordinate race *forever.*"[66]

Underlying theories supporting monogenesis and polygenesis was a visceral abhorrence among most whites to the mixing of races. Miscegenation was considered unnatural and a threat to both American civilization and the white race.[67] "The Negro race, from the first, was regarded with disgust, and its union with the whites forbidden under ignominious penalties," Davis has observed.[68] English colonial laws, for example, held that interracial relations were a disgrace to the mother country.[69] In 1743 an item in the *Charleston (S.C.) Gazette* said that a grand jury condemned "THE TOO COMMON PRACTICE of CRIMINAL CONVERSATION with NEGRO and other SLAVE WENCHES IN THIS PROVINCE, as an Enormity and Evil of general Ill-Consequence."[70] More than one hundred years later the *National Era* in the July 7, 1854, edition contained these words, originating from the proslavery periodical *DeBow's Review:* "Our instincts are implanted by nature for wise purposes; they are intended to guard our races from deterioration. It is an abuse of words to call them prejudices. . . . Intermarriage between the white and black races is unnatural, i.e., contrary to the order and design of Providence and fatal to Posterity."[71] Mulatto children born to white women, especially, posed a threat to the "entire system of slavery and white supremacy," according to Abby Ferber.[72] Later the "one-drop" rule of African blood became the standard for determining an individual's blackness and for negating any whiteness, regardless of visible skin color.[73]

The Growing Paradox of Slavery in America

In *Slavery and Human Progress,* David Brion Davis maintains that until about the 1760s "black slavery was generally assumed to be a necessary and 'progressive' institution, accepted or tolerated in cities like Boston, New York, and London that were far removed from the booming peripheral zones of plantation culture" that depended on slave labor.[74] "From about 1700 until shortly after the middle of the 18th Century," Winthrop Jordan wrote, "slaves were imported and worked by white men without effective challenge or even effective questioning of the rationale underlying what had rapidly become an important New World institution."[75] Despite this normalization, from about 1760 through the end of the eighteenth century, tolerance for slavery waned and many southern and northern American political leaders, influenced by the Enlightenment, called it a curse, an evil remnant of British colonialism.

The existence of slavery in America challenged America's intellectual founders, with men such as Franklin and Adams as well as slave owners such as Washington and Jefferson expressing clear antislavery sentiments. For his part, Benjamin Franklin never favored slavery, and his views shifted from a belief in racial inferiority to one that blamed the system itself for debasing Africans. In "Observations Concerning the Increase of Mankind," written in 1751, Franklin expressed these reasons to ban the slave trade in the English colonies: "Why increase the Sons of Africa, by Planting them in America, where we have so fair an Opportunity, by excluding all Blacks and Tawneys, of increasing the lovely White and Red? But perhaps I am partial to the Complexion of my Country, for such partiality is natural to mankind."[76] Franklin reasoned that slaves were too costly, warning that "almost every slave [was] by nature a thief."[77] Thirty-eight years later Franklin's attitude shifted: "Slavery is such an atrocious debasement of human nature," he wrote, "that its very extirpation, if not performed with solicitous care, may sometimes open a source of serious evils." Franklin wrote the following to a Pennsylvania abolition society: "The galling chains that bind his body do also fetter his intellectual faculties, and impair social affections of his heart. Accustomed to move like a mere machine, by the will of a master, reflection is suspended; he has not the power of choice; and reason and conscience have but little influence over his conduct because he is chiefly governed by the passion of fear. He is poor and friendless; perhaps worn out by extreme labor, age and disease."[78] Shortly before his death, Franklin urged the U.S. Congress to "devise means for removing this Inconsistency [slavery] from the Character of the American people."[79] He added that liberty must be restored "to those unhappy Men, who alone, in this land of Freedom, are degraded into perpetual Bondage."

While Franklin, apparently, never reconciled the "inconsistency" of slavery with America's enlightened, revolutionary principles, another influential American leader did. Thomas Jefferson, who was at heart deeply antislavery, accepted the paradox despite his reservations. One Jefferson biographer has said that Jefferson was constantly "oscillating between outright condemnation of slavery as incompatible with republican values and equally outright procrastination when pushed to offer practical remedies to end it."[80] As opposed to slavery as he was, Jefferson did not believe in racial equality, as a 1791 letter to Benjamin Banneker, a free black man, illustrates: "No body wishes more than I do, to see such proofs as you exhibit, that nature has given to our black brethren talents equal to those of the other colours of men; and that the appearance of the want of them, is owing merely to the degraded condition of their existence, both in Africa and America."[81] Four years later Jefferson published his thoughts about slavery and race in *Notes on the State of Virginia,* in which he advocated gradual emancipation because of slavery's "unhappy influence on the manners of our people." He observed, "The whole commerce between master and slave is a perpetual exercise of the boisterous passions, the most unremitting despotism on the one part, and degrading submissions on the other."[82] He feared that the nation would pay the consequences for slavery's injustice: "Indeed I tremble for my country," Jefferson prophetically remarked, "when I reflect that God is just; that his justice cannot sleep forever."[83] For Jefferson, the only solution was to free "these inferior beings" and remove them "beyond the reach" of general white society.[84] While decidedly antislavery, *Notes on the State of Virginia* later served the "positive good" theorists, who used Jefferson's racist ideas to justify their proslavery ideas.[85]

Jefferson's fellow Virginian George Washington wanted to end slavery too, even acknowledging slaves' contributions to the Revolutionary War effort. Slavery embarrassed him. As one biographer has noted, "He seldom uttered the word *slavery,* as if it grated on his conscience, preferring polite euphemisms such as 'servants,' 'Negroes,' 'my people,' or 'my family.'"[86] After the Revolutionary War he refused to surrender slaves who served in the Continental army without first examining "the validity of the [masters'] claim[s]."[87] For Washington, plantation economics and a genuine concern for the welfare of his human property suppressed his personal desire to free them, convinced as he was that bondage at Mount Vernon provided a better life than living free could ever afford.[88] In his last will he did something in death he could not do in life: "Upon the decease of my wife, it is my will and desire that all slaves whom I hold in my own right shall receive their freedom."[89]

Other influential founders such as John Adams consistently called "Negro slavery . . . an evil of colossal magnitude."[90] His good friend Dr. Benjamin Rush helped organize the Pennsylvania Society for Promoting the Abolition of Slavery with a mission to promote the "ABOLITION of SLAVERY and the relief of FREE NEGROES unlawfully held in BONDAGE."[91] In 1773 Rush published "An Address to the Inhabitants of the British Settlements in America, upon Slave-Keeping," which refuted the "mark of Cain" theory and agreed with Franklin that slavery had debased American blacks.[92]

Other Americans were not so tolerant. Richard Nisbet responded to Rush in "Slavery Not Forbidden by Scripture," also printed in 1773. Nisbet argued that blacks "are a much inferior race of men to the whites, in every respect."[93] He added that Africa, "except the small part of it inhabited by those of our own color, is totally overrun with barbarism." Indeed, echoing the later "positive good" theory of slavery, Nisbet offered this slavery defense: "It is, likewise, certain, that these creatures, by being sold to the Europeans, are often saved from the most cruel deaths, or more wretched slavery to their fellow barbarians."[94] Nisbet's view is the one that eventually held sway with southern political leaders as America entered the nineteenth century.

As the great debates over the Constitution raged, James Madison, writing in the *Federalist Papers,* made at least two references to slavery and Africans without using the word "slave." The first came in a discussion about banning the slave trade after 1808: "It ought to be considered as a great point gained in favor of humanity, that a period of 20 years may terminate for ever within these United States, a traffic which has so long and so loudly upbraided the barbarism of modern policy. . . . Happy would it be for the unfortunate Africans if an equal prospect lay before them, of being redeemed from the oppressions of their European brethren!"[95] As a signal to a general antislavery sentiment in the young country, the new Constitution did ban the slave trade.[96] About that, Thomas Jefferson applauded the end to "further participation in those violations of human rights which have been so long continued on the unoffending inhabitants of Africa, and which the morality, the reputation, and the best interests of our country have long been eager to proscribe."[97] (Even earlier, in 1787, the new U.S. Congress banned slavery in the Northwest Territories.) Madison, who called the slave problem a "peculiar one" in Federalist #54, argued that slaves are "inhabitants debased by servitude below the equal level of free inhabitants, which regards the slave as divested of two fifth of the *man.*"[98] So it would be that the Constitution's framers refused to free slaves or even use the words "slave," "Negro," or "African" in the document, referring to slaves only as "three-fifths of all other persons."[99] The framers, who lived in a world "where slavery was a fact of life," the constitutional historian James Bolner Sr. has observed, were willing to be pragmatic and chose compromise over dissension, leaving the unresolved slavery question for future American generations.[100] Simply put, America's post–Revolutionary War leaders claimed America as a white man's country, leaving their descendants with an unresolved social evil. Unfortunately the great compromise over slavery would disintegrate, shattering this creative political enterprise with devastating results.

By the time the new states ratified the Constitution, the cultural and political divide over slavery was beginning to develop, with northern states such as New Hampshire, Massachusetts, Pennsylvania, Connecticut, and Rhode Island abolishing slavery. By 1804 three other states north of Delaware had emancipated slaves or planned to do so.[101] Even Virginia legislators approved a law allowing slave owners, if they so chose, "to free their slaves at their own discretion," according to the historian Joseph Ellis.[102] Ellis also surmised that slavery's abolition in the early years of the Republic was unlikely for several reasons: 1) the new government could not afford to pay slave owners for the large number of slaves living in the South; 2) no acceptable postmanumission plan existed; and 3) a virulently racist ideology had taken root in America.[103]

Noah Webster wrote his 1793 pamphlet "Effects of Slavery, on Morals and Industry" rejecting the idea of black inferiority but recognizing America's (especially southern America's) economic ties to slavery. Webster feared cataclysmic economic and social results if slavery suddenly vanished: "To give freedom at once to almost 700,000 slaves, would reduce perhaps 20,000 families to beggary. It would impoverish the country south of Pennsylvania; all cultivation would probably cease for a time; a famine would ensue; and there would be extreme danger of insurrections which might deluge the country in blood and perhaps depopulate it. . . . The evil has taken such deep root, and is so widely spread in the southern States, that an attempt to eradicate it at a single blow would expose the whole political body to dissolution."[104] Regrettably, slave labor was still profitable by the end of the eighteenth century,[105] and forty-three years after Webster's lament, a South Carolina congressman argued that the government could never afford to pay slave owners for their property, saying flatly, "The thing is impossible."[106]

Slave Control

Of course no amount of economic, philosophical, theological, or scientific debate about their status meant anything within the slave population, which by the 1830s had grown to more than 15 percent of the total U.S. population.[107] In some states, such as South Carolina and Louisiana, the slave population outnumbered whites. To keep such an enslaved population in check, slave owners developed a complicated set of laws and codes to control their slaves. Such legal and extralegal measures prevented what Paul Gordon Lauren has called "challenges to existing social and economic structure and political authority."[108] These codes and laws, which were often brutally harsh, determined punishments and covered everything from slave insubordination to slave insurrections. The codes, according to Jordan, "played a vital role" in maintaining slavery because they affirmed the consensus among whites of "their sense of mastery over their Negro slaves—and over themselves."[109]

Many of the first slave laws dealt with length of servitude for imported African slaves. However, because English law did not protect Africans per se, they became subject to colonial laws that eventually removed from them the possibility of manumission. The following Maryland law appeared in 1663: "All negroes or other slaves within this province, and all negroes and other slaves to be hereafter imported into the province, shall serve *durante vita;* and all children born of any negroe or other slave, shall be slaves as their *fathers* were for the term of their lives."[110] The law, which was later changed to reflect the mother's condition as slave or free, did two things: it protected a master's property rights and perpetuated the labor system.[111] In Louisiana the French established the

Code Noir, decreeing, "Children born of Slave marriages will be slaves" and will belong to "the Masters of the females."[112] So as Genovese has observed, "The South had the only legal slave system in the New World in which the slaves reproduced themselves."[113]

In criminal matters colonial courts held slaves to different standards, regardless of whether they were the perpetrators or victims. For example, it was considered "disgraceful to humanity" if a black person killed a white person,[114] and in general blacks could not testify against whites. A 1705 Virginia law held that any runaway slave could be killed or suffer dismemberment if caught.[115] Virtually all crimes that blacks committed were punishable by death. As to white crimes against blacks, a 1798 North Carolina law illustrated how the courts handled such matters: "whereas ... the killing of a slave, however, wanton, cruel and deliberate, is only punishable in the first instance by imprisonment and paying the value thereof to the owner."[116] The law was not particularly exceptional compared to others in the colonies, and such laws ensured that blacks would bend to the will of white people.[117] Even as late 1861 the Alabama State Supreme Court ruled, "Absolute obedience and subordination to the lawful authority of the master are the duty of the slave."[118] Such judicial rulings and slave laws mitigated whites' fears of slave rebellion and revolt.[119] Legally, then, slaves were placed on a level with brute animals.

Slave codes were designed to restrict daily activities among slaves. Slaves could not, for example, leave their homes after dark without a pass, assemble outside a plantation, meet in groups of more than five without the presence of a white man, hold religious services without a white man present, own a horse or gun, or work in a print shop or drugstore.[120] Other recommendations included restrictions on slave earnings and how much a slave could drink in "dram" shops. The historian Russell Blaine Nye has asserted that the slave codes became harsher as the abolitionist movement grew.[121]

In Charleston, South Carolina, for example, even the manner of slave dress became a concern. Following Denmark Vesey's 1822 conspiracy, an item in the *Charleston Courier* informed readers that a grand jury recommended to the state legislature the regulating of slave dress because "the apparel of persons of color" was "highly destructive to their honesty and industry, and subversive of that subordination which policy requires to be enforced."[122] Thirty-seven years later, after John Brown's raid, the writers to South Carolina newspapers seemed especially focused on controlling the dress of slaves and other blacks. An item signed "MANY VOTERS AND LANDHOLDERS" in the *Courier* said that the regulation of slave dress was of "vital importance not only to our city, but to our state."[123] Similarly, "ANOTHER VOTER" wrote in the October 26 *Charleston Courier*: "The love of dress in the negro may be considered as the parent of all the other vices destroying the virtue of the females, and rendering both sexes insufferably impertinent."[124] The *Courier*'s rival, the *Mercury*, contained the comments of "A Resident and Native" noting that it was evil to let free blacks and slaves choose their dress: "Shall [free blacks and slaves] in silks and laces, promenade our principal thoroughfares, with the arrogance of equals—by their insolent bearing making the modest lady yield the walk, and the poor white woman to feel that to be virtuous and honest gives her place in appearances, below the slaves."[125]

In addition to the laws and codes controlling the slave population, physical punishment or the threat of it further repressed the slave population, subjecting disobedient slaves to the whip or worse. This proved psychologically damaging because of the "arbitrariousness, the caprice, the inhumanity that allowed one man to vent his passions on another," Genovese has observed.[126] Such a heinous system of corporal punishment could only result in deleterious effects on the slave's emotional and psychological makeup. W. E. B. Du Bois articulated this about the slave's predicament: "It was in part psychological, the enforced personal feeling of inferiority, the calling of another Master; the standing with hat in hand. It was the helplessness. It was the defenselessness of family life. It was the submergence below the arbitrary will of any sort of individual. It was without a doubt worse in these vital respects than that which exists today in Europe or America."[127] "The black man, denied personage, was split symbolically into a thing—like commodity and a warm amoral body. . . . The 'good nigger'," Joel Kovel has observed.[128] Years later the psychiatrist/historian Frantz Fanon made this remark about the oppressed aiding the tyrant: "The first thing which the native [slave] learns is to stay in his place, and not to go beyond certain limits."[129] While those comments concerned colonialism's effects on the colonized, they seem apropos to the behavior of the good Negro/ black slave in America.

Still, not all blacks, slave or free, believed that perpetual servitude was the natural state of being for the Negro, believing, as they did, that if whites would not grant them liberty, they would seek it for themselves. What they discovered was that powerful forces abetted by America's strong racist belief in blacks' inferiority would not permit this and would counter with swift, brutal measures to suppress them while ensuring slavery's survival.

THE PRESS AND SLAVE TROUBLES
PART I ❧ IN AMERICA

Slavery had become enshrined in American law and culture by 1800. Despite this, many black Americans refused to accept the idea that their lives (or, if free, the lives of their slave brethren) had little meaning beyond the boundaries of their masters' domains. Among those were people such as Gabriel Prosser, Denmark Vesey, and Nat Turner, who, along with allies such as John Brown, made fateful choices about helping themselves and other slaves strike out for freedom. In due course they all sealed their fates because they could never overcome powerful forces that supported black American slavery as natural and right. Indeed these conspirators and rebels were committing great crimes against the state, and they would pay for their deeds with their lives.

Part I provides a brief look at these events that often stunned white Americans out of a lethargic belief that black Americans did not want nor cherish liberty. It begins with the story of the slave revolt on the island of Santo Domingo because, of all the events, this rebellion elicited a continuing discourse in the newspaper stories about what black violence against white people meant. As these reports with their graphic details about the revolt spread from newspaper to newspaper, they left little doubt about what might happen in slave country if America's black slaves decided to rebel. In fact a newspaper reader would need little explanation what the "horrors of Santo Domingo" meant. Details from newspapers stories about subsequent revolts and conspiracies that culminated in the events at Harper's Ferry then provide a clear view of the situation.

Slavery's proponents also became obsessed with silencing other enemies of slavery who attacked the "peculiar institution" with their words or by their very existence. These enemies included free blacks and abolitionists and their political allies. Slave owners especially feared that "incendiary" words from abolitionist or antislavery factions would also filter down to their slaves and incite them to rebellion. As George Fredrickson asserted in *The Black Image in the White Mind:* "Southern slave owners were extraordinarily careful to maintain absolute control over their 'people' and to quarantine them from any kind of outside influence that might inspire dissatisfaction with their condition" (p. 53). Similarly, Eugene Genovese in *Roll, Jordan, Roll* observed that the slave power controlled the press in the slave South and worked at suppressing news accounts of slave revolts and conspiracies to impress readers—white or black— that the owners fully controlled their human property (p. 50). One Richmond, Virginia, newspaper editor, following Nat Turner's revolt in 1831, cautioned southern colleagues against giving slaves "false conceptions of their numbers and capacity by exhibiting the terror and confusion of the whites and to induce them to think it [revolt] practicable" (Stampp, *Peculiar Institution*, 136).

Still, stories about slave troubles appeared in the nation's newspapers, and imbedded in them are discourses about slavery. These discourses, discussed later in more detail, are situated within the context that created them. Part 1 shows how newspaper content from 1800 to 1831 about Prosser, Louisiana, Vesey, and Turner expressed similar ideas about slavery as being an unfortunate colonial legacy. The nature of these stories also illustrates the nature of an American press that had yet to undergo the technological transformations that would make news mass and instant. By 1859 those changes in the press became apparent in the reports about John Brown's raid at Harper's Ferry. Newspapers had become active news gatherers not mere news collectors. What also emerges with those changes is a sense that the critical alterations in America's political, social, and geographic landscape that had turned a small, Atlantic coastal nation into a vast, increasingly powerful country that stretched from one ocean to the next was now on the verge of splintering in two.

1 ❧ Haiti in 1791, Gabriel Prosser's 1800 Conspiracy, and the 1811 German Coast Slave Revolt

> At reading the following every heart must shudder with horror.
>
> *New York Daily Advertiser*, October 1, 1800

In the late eighteenth and early nineteenth centuries, most Americans learned about the 1791 Haitian slave revolt, Gabriel Prosser's 1800 conspiracy, and the slave revolt that shook Louisiana in 1811 from newspapers that had changed little since the invention of the printing press. Certainly the way American newspaper editors shared news remained the same, with one newspaper's content being reprinted in newspapers in other cities. Importantly, these news accounts most often originated as correspondence from the affected areas. Thus the only information a Boston reader would receive about a slave conspiracy or revolt in Virginia came from a slave owner or the authorities there. Such would be the nature of news in the partisan press era.

As this information was shared and repeated within the country's newspapers, it shaped a way of thinking about slaves, slave rebels, and other black people in America. In other words it formed a discourse. Such discourse concerned the marginalization of slave rebels during the troubles and reflects America's racist ideology that held blacks inferior, unworthy of freedom despite their struggles in an age when such efforts to obtain liberty should have resonated positively with post–Revolutionary War Americans. In each news account the black rebel is always an immediate threat to the white-controlled slave system and is transformed into an objectified thing that must be stopped and destroyed.

Even as late as 1831 and at the time of Nat Turner's revolt, the press "was more closely akin to that which existed fifty years earlier, than it was to the press which would exist a mere thirty years later," according to Henry Irving Tragle.[1] Until technological changes such as rotary presses and manufacturing of cheap paper became common, newspapers between 1791 and 1831 looked much the same—usually four- to six-page broadsheets filled with commercial advertisements and a page or possibly two of "news" content and opinion. Their editors, likely serving as both printers and publishers, relied nearly exclusively on other newspapers for content, editorial or otherwise.[2]

In this partisan press era such content took days, weeks, or even months by ship or horseback to reach other cities and towns. Because these newspapers were relatively expensive to produce, they catered to an elite, literate readership that could pay for them. Often the newspapers were passed along to others and shared within communities.[3] Yet distribution could hardly be considered wide, and as such it cannot be determined with any certainty how many Americans read reports of America's slave troubles or what effect these reports would have had on them. This would be the case for stories about Santo Domingo, Gabriel Prosser, and the German Coast.

Another important facet about newspapers during this period is that rumor and speculation ran rampant in their pages.[4] Citing sources was rare, and editors often printed stories to serve their political sensibilities and allegiances.[5] In addition objectivity as a professional journalistic standard was decades away from development.[6] This meant that nearly all published content during the partisan era of the press contained biases as well as exaggerations. Still, the stories found in these newspapers offer important clues about what happened when slave troubles occurred, and for most readers living far from Santo Domingo, Henrico County, or Louisiana's German Coast, this would have been the only information they would get.

When serious slave troubles erupted, the news items took the form of firsthand narratives written by (white) eyewitnesses, who sent them as correspondences to their local newspaper editors/publishers. From Massachusetts to Pennsylvania to South Carolina, newspaper editors shared these correspondences with one another.[7] On occasion some would send their letters directly to friends, relatives, or newspaper editors located great distances away. Often rich in detail, both exaggerated and real, this information provided insight and perspective on late eighteenth- and early nineteenth-century white American views on slavery and their fellow black Americans.[8] For white readers, regardless of their sympathies for or against slavery, any slave trouble involving black violence against fellow whites meant disaster. In America the first defining event that shook southern slave society to its core took place on an island just off the nation's coast, and the letters sent by frantic whites from French-controlled Santo Domingo (Haiti) spelled out clearly what black-on-white violence truly meant.

Haiti's Slave Revolt

When the Haitian slave revolt began in the summer of 1791, the letters reaching American shores were, as one historian wrote, "received with legitimate terror by the white people of the South."[9] Before 1800 no slave trouble alarmed white Americans more than this rebellion in French-controlled Hispaniola, then referred to as St. Dominique, San Domingo, or Santo Domingo. Years later in news accounts of later slave troubles, the very mention of Haiti in those stories "symbolized how extensive racial disorder might be and served to rally whites to defense of their race and institutions."[10] The whole idea of "Santo Domingo" became a compacted, recurrent intertextual discourse that exploded in newspapers anytime later slave troubles occurred, summarizing immediately for the reader what black-on-white violence meant.

To France, Haiti was the jewel in its colonial crown. To Americans, it was a valuable trading partner, supplying North America with 30 percent of its sugar imports.[11] The revolt began in the summer of 1791 when black slaves, enraged that the French National Assembly broke its promise of freedom, rebelled, killing scores of white men, women, and children.[12] That fall word about the revolt finally reached newspapers in the United States. "INSURRECTION OF NEGROES," read a headline in the *Pennsylvania Journal and Weekly Advertiser* on September 21. Under it was a letter, dated August 26, from a "gentleman at CAPE FRANCOIS" (a major northern port city) who, writing "to his friend in New-York," explained that "an insurrection broke out amongst the Negroes and Mulattoes, and they are now destroying every Person and thing they come across"; the desolate writer added, "There are now eleven Plantations on fire in sight, and where it will end God only knows."[13] Weeks later another letter, dated September 18, reached New York and Boston newspapers, telling readers that the situation had only deteriorated: "The blacks have continued their ravages; they have burnt and destroyed almost every sugar plantation in this part of the island."[14] The writer lamented, "When these devastations will cease, is as uncertain as it was on the first day of the insurrection."[15] From 1791 to 1804 rebelling slaves in disparate groups fought the French and struggled for control of the island. Eventually strong leaders such as Toussaint L'Ouverture and Jean Dessalines expelled their colonial overseers, leading to Haiti's independence in 1804 and making it the second nation in the Western Hemisphere, after the United States, to win independence from a European colonizer.[16]

Of grave concern to southern slaveholders was the influx of island refugees to southern port cities such as Charleston and New Orleans. By 1793 concern mounted as the white population watched "French refugees, many accompanied by their personal slaves" stream into America from the island.[17] Their exodus caused alarm among southern and northern whites who feared that these fleeing blacks, exposed as they were to revolutionary ideas, would infect the local slave population with notions of liberty and freedom. Newspaper content reflected this concern. In 1800, for example, as news of Gabriel Prosser's conspiracy unfolded in Virginia, a letter from Fredericksburg, Virginia, published in the *New York Daily Advertiser* referred to the island and warned that the doctrines of liberty and equality "cannot fail of producing either a general insurrection or a general emancipation."[18] Any slaves with ties to or origin in Haiti could not be trusted, as an excerpt from a South Carolina newspaper warned: "The NEGROES have become very insolent, in so much that the citizens are alarmed, and the militia keep a constant guard. It is said that the St. Domingo negroes have sown these seeds of revolt, and that a magazine has been attempted to be broken open."[19]

So powerful were the Haitian revolt's discursive connections to America's nineteenth-century slave troubles that nearly all later news accounts of them would make reference to it, conflating in a word the dire situation at hand. The "horrors of Santo Domingo" were reflected in the tone and content of an account of Gabriel Prosser's 1800 slave conspiracy. A Virginia newspaper item described how the conspirators had "cutlasses" that would make anyone "shudder with horror at the sight of these instruments of death."[20] Decades later, following John Brown's 1859 raid, a New York newspaper item, alluding to the Haiti and Nat Turner revolts, reminded readers, "No one can think of the possible results of an outbreak of this kind, should it become general, without shuddering, without calling up to his imagination the most terrible scenes of incendiarism, carnage and rape."[21]

Gabriel Prosser's 1800 Conspiracy

It was still a revolutionary time in 1800 America with the government not even a decade old and facing its first real political test: the fall presidential election. It was then that readers learned of Gabriel Prosser's slave conspiracy in Virginia. Raised as he was in an era when Virginia leaders were profoundly shaping the course of the new nation, Prosser understood what the promises of liberty meant and decided, perhaps, that they applied to all men, including him and his fellow slaves. His conspiracy occurred during a period of important changes in the new nation's political landscape and shortly before the contentious 1800 election that resulted in a peaceful transfer of power from John Adams's Federalist Party to the Jeffersonian Republicans. Importantly, this was a period when slavery was not the politically charged issue it would later become, remaining in the minds of most Americans as a social evil with no suitable end solution. Another fact that cannot be ignored is that at the time, Haiti's still-ongoing revolt "remained a powerful symbol of Black liberation" for Virginia slaves, especially for a man such as Gabriel Prosser, according to James Sidbury.[22]

Born in 1776, the same year as the signing of the Declaration of Independence, Prosser grew up on a plantation six miles outside Richmond, Virginia.[23] Given the last name of his owner, Thomas Prosser, the slave seemed to enjoy a favored status on the plantation.[24] It seemed that blacks and whites alike considered him a courageous and intelligent man.[25] Prosser had also become a skilled urban artisan and frequently traveled to Richmond, where he came in contact with free blacks.[26] Certainly he lived at a time when the slave appeared to enjoy modicums of freedom that would later became restricted. During his travels to Richmond, Prosser might have taken advantage of his unrestricted visits to memorize the city streets and landmarks, later using this information when devising his plot.[27] Because Prosser was also literate, he knew of Virginia's Revolutionary War role and what its leaders claimed when they talked about liberty and equality. In brief, he was "American born, literate, probably

Christian, and heavily influenced by the radical political doctrine generated by the American Revolution," according to Walter C. Rucker.[28] According to Douglas Egerton, it is possible that Prosser—a Virginian raised "amid all the heady talk of liberty and natural rights"—assumed that the state's revolutionary legacy should hold meaning for its slaves.[29] As he learned, it did not.

Two other factors may have led Prosser to believe that this was an apropos time to revolt. First, Virginia was still in a state of general disorder following the Revolutionary War. Second, he may have felt that the political battles of the contentious election season would linger, causing further disruptions and distractions and catching an unarmed white population unaware.[30] Prosser was a man of action and believed that he was, in the historian Joseph Cephas Carroll's words, a "child of destiny" who might deliver fellow slaves from bondage.[31]

In the spring of 1800 Prosser and his destiny met as he began forming the plot that included plans to kill his master Thomas.[32] A fellow slave named Jack Bowler (also known as Jack Ditcher) became an important co-conspirator, believing, like his leader, that slaves warranted liberty.[33] Also assisting Prosser were brothers Martin and Solomon as well as John Scott, George Smith, and Sam Bird. Their mission was to deliver slaves from bondage as the Israelites were delivered out of Egypt.[34] Because of Prosser's status as a blacksmith, other slaves gave him the necessary authority to lead the group, and his profession afforded him easy access to a meeting spot where they could talk about their strategy, namely his plantation forge.[35] They kept their plan secret. Later a piece of correspondence in Virginia and Massachusetts newspapers compared their organization to the Freemasons, another secret society of members who took secret oaths, telling readers that the conspirators had one goal: "to obtain their liberty, and to render themselves masters of the country, by murdering all the whites, except white women."[36]

By July the conspiracy's details were known to slaves in six Virginia towns and in "distant parts of the State," according to a later account by Virginia governor James Monroe.[37] Monroe, later informing South Carolina's lieutenant governor of the conspiracy, asserted that the plan "embraced most of the slaves in this city and neighbourhood" and that "knowledge of such a project pervaded other parts, if not the whole of the State."[38] On Saturday, August 30, the uprising was to have begun with a slave army killing all whites, except the French, in a march toward Richmond to seize the town and confiscate its arms, ammunition, food, and money.[39] The French were apparently singled out for exclusion because, as it was later revealed, two Frenchmen, Charles Quersey and Alexander Beddenhurst, implicated in the plot, may have offered assistance, believing as they did in the slaves' revolutionary promise.[40]

Prosser expected fellow slaves who were met along the way to join the insurrection, but this never happened.[41] On the uprising's intended date, two slaves revealed the plans to their master, who notified Governor Monroe. Monroe, who had been suspecting trouble, ordered Virginia cavalry and militia to monitor the roads and watch for suspicious activity among blacks.[42] Despite his concern, Monroe remained reluctant to believe that any real conspiracy was possible until he finally conceded "that a general insurrection of the slaves was contemplated by those who took the lead in the affair."[43]

The exact number of slaves willing to carry out the plan is not certain, but one historian's guess is that a thousand armed slaves waited outside Richmond, although the poor road conditions caused by a fierce thunderstorm had washed out roads, making an attack impossible.[44] James Callender, Thomas Jefferson's scandalmonger and eventual nemesis, learned of events while sitting in a Richmond jail on sedition charges and delivered this account: "Between Prosser's [plantation] and Richmond, there is a place called Brook Swamp which runs across the high road, and over which there was a . . . bridge. By this, the africans [*sic*] were of necessity to pass, and the rain had made the passage impracticable."[45]

Whites' response was twofold: destroy the threat and then contain any ensuing white panic.[46] By September 12 five conspirators had been executed, but Prosser and Jack Bowler had escaped.[47] The local Richmond newspaper, the *Virginia Argus,* on September 12 published word about Gov. James Monroe's offer of a three-hundred-dollar reward for Gabriel's capture. Later two blacks working on a schooner where Prosser took refuge for eleven days recognized the fugitive and reported him to authorities.[48] Prosser was arrested on September 24, returned to Richmond in chains, tried, and hanged on October 7 along with "15 other rebels," who joined twenty-one others already executed for taking part in the conspiracy.[49] About his arrest, details appeared in one Richmond newspaper informing readers that it came about after a "negro boy, formerly of this neighborhood, who being acquainted with the General, very friendly accosted him as he accidentally met with him on the wharf."[50] As described, Prosser showed great strength of character. "On Saturday last," the writer said, "the noted Gabriel arrived here by water under guard, from Norfolk" and "manifested the greatest marks of firmness and composure, shewing [*sic*] not the least disposition to equivocate, or screen himself from justice."[51] According to the account, Prosser denied "the charge of being the first in exciting the insurrection, although he was to have had the chief command." Prosser's refusal to implicate himself seemed an irritation to the writer, who remarked that the captive "was determined to make no confession," adding, "It is to be hoped, that this hardened miscreant, when under condemnation, will reflect more seriously on his situation, and open some circumstances." According to another writer, "The behavior of Gabriel under his misfortunes, was such as might be expected from a mind capable of forming the daring project he had conceived."[52] In the end white "authorities made a bigger spectacle of hanging Gabriel's conspirators," according to Sidbury, than of hanging usual offenders.[53] Perhaps this was to send a strong message to any other slaves contemplating rebellion.

Prosser remained silent during his trial, giving newspaper readers little information about his motives. Gov. James Monroe, who interviewed the slave before his hanging, said, "From what he said to me, he seemed to have made up his mind to die, and to have resolved to say but little on the subject of the conspiracy."[54] Still, one Richmond account, dated October 7, let readers know that the "strongest testimony" convicted Gabriel, who "during his trial appeared extremely uneasy in his mind, as if labouring under the severest oppressions of a guilty conscience."[55] After the pronouncement of his death sentence, "much anxiety and trouble seemed to hang upon his countenance," but Gabriel Prosser did not confess, and "he would make no discoveries." While Prosser was never quoted directly, the newspaper coverage implied something about his strong character by reporting his refusal to cooperate with authorities.[56] All of his fellow conspirators joined their leader in remaining silent, refusing to implicate others.

The Press and Gabriel Prosser

Newspaper accounts of Gabriel Prosser's actions were sparse, but they did appear during the fall of 1800. "A contemporary of the event said the truth of it would never be known," a writer to the *Virginia Herald* remarked in September, "because of the quietus was put upon the Richmond Press in the name of what the officials called prudence."[57] Another item put it this way: "Indeed fear seems to have put an imprimateur on the press."[58] About the information that later surfaced concerning the depth and breadth of the conspiracy, one historian has contended that much of what a newspaper reader in 1800 would have received was so laced with partisan rhetoric that any "reliable evidence on the origins and evolution of the aborted rebellion" is simply too murky to give an accurate representation of what really occurred.[59]

Despite the "quietus" and potential misinformation, northern and southern newspaper readers did learn of the plot, with editors unanimously condemning it. In tone and content items quickly drew connections to Haiti's ongoing slave revolution, as the following excerpt from the *New York Daily Advertiser* indicated: "At reading the following every heart must shudder with horror" to hear of the plan that "was systematically laid, for a general insurrection throughout the state, and the most brutal acts were to have been perpetrated."[60] The "wretches" had "singled out for their barbarity in the massacre" several "respectable characters."

In a Fredericksburg letter dated September 23, New York and Boston readers were given further details about the plot: it was "perfectly organized, generals, captains, etc., etc. appointed," and "one thousand negroes were to have entered the town with fire and sword."[61] They would take weapons from the penitentiary house and money from the treasury, make bread from flour taken from the mill, and hold the bridge "to keep out their enemies." According to the writer, after the slave leader and his followers secured Richmond, they would issue a "proclamation" and invite "negroes from the county and southern states" to their "standard." They hoped that fifty thousand men would join them in a week, as well as "every Frenchman . . . every free negro and mulatto, and many of the most redoubtable democrats in the state." The letter also said that "Gabriel was to have commanded at the seat of government."

Weeks later "An Impartial Statement of the Negro Insurrection" appeared, describing how "a considerable body of slaves would set off on that evening from the Brook . . . for the purpose of massacring all the whites of Richmond, and to cause a general insurrection throughout the state."[62] According to the article, Prosser preferred the Saturday, August 30, date "because all the negroes were noticed for that day," but another conspirator, George, insisted on Sunday because it would be "more convenient for the people of Caroline county" to join and because slaves could enjoy Sunday travel "without suspicion." Once a slave informer revealed the plot, "it was a work of no difficulty to seize the suspected and convey them to Richmond." Assuring white readers that authorities had the situation under control became an important theme and part of the discourse of racial panic that focused on the reestablishment of white control and the slave status quo.[63]

Newspaper references to Gabriel Prosser often made special mention of his servitude, identifying him as "a slave" and "property of Mr. Thomas Prosser, of the county of Henrico."[64] In other instances Prosser might be identified as "general," a rank given to him by his conspiracy group.[65] Perhaps reflecting America's strengthening racist ideology, the published accounts failed to acknowledge the baseness of the slave system. Instead the target for opprobrium was the rebel slave who needed to be held to account for stirring "agitation among the blacks," as one writer argued. Describing him as an "ambitious and insidious fellow," the writer of the following passage likely expressed the views of most whites: "This villain, assuming to himself the appellation of *General*, through his artfulness, has caused some disturbance, having induced many poor, ignorant, and unfortunate creatures to share in his nefarious and horrid design."[66]

An October 14 *Virginia Argus* item noted that Prosser went to his death without providing any further details.[67] The story of Prosser and fellow slave conspirators did not fade in the memory of Virginians. Four years later a Richmond lawyer told an English visitor that one conspirator, who called the trials a "mockery," told him about the motives of the slaves: "I have nothing more to offer than what General Washington would have had to offer, had he been taken by the British and put to trial by them. I have adventured my life in endeavouring to obtain the liberty of my countrymen, and am a willing sacrifice to their cause."[68]

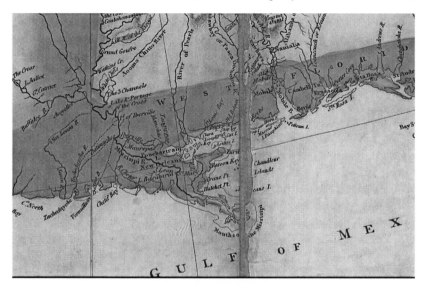

New Orleans and surrounding areas, detail from "Map of the United States of America: With the Contiguous British and Spanish Possessions." Courtesy of the Library of Congress, Geography and Map Division.

The Louisiana (German Coast) Revolt (1811)

The residues of America's revolutionary era were dissolving by the time Louisiana slaves embarked on their futile quest for freedom. While Nat Turner's 1831 slave revolt in Southampton County, Virginia, is considered America's deadliest, the 1811 German Coast slave revolt near New Orleans was, according to one historian, the country's largest.[69] These slaves, who labored under extremely difficult, even horrific conditions, may have had only one goal: to reclaim, as one historian put it, "their humanity from their oppressors."[70] Led by a slave named Charles Deslondes, described as a "mulatto from Santo Domingo,"[71] this revolt took slave owners in the Orleans Territory by surprise and created a tremendous panic among the white population that well understood what had happened in Haiti. In addition these troubles erupted just as members of Congress debated Louisiana's admission to the Union as the eighteenth state.[72] Deslondes may have chosen this time for a revolt because he knew of heightened tensions between Spain and the United States and understood that they might divert the military's attention.

Deslondes began planning the revolt in December 1810, swearing, like Gabriel Prosser before him did, his followers to secrecy.[73] Like Governor Monroe in Virginia, Louisiana's territorial governor W. C. C. Claiborne sensed something afoot north of New Orleans since, in a letter dated January 7, 1811, he requested that U.S. general Wade Hampton provide a military escort for mail carriers because "such part of the Territory ... may be infested by the Brigands."[74] It is not clear if the "Brigands" were slave rebels or the Spanish. The revolt began in January 1811 in St. John's Parish, approximately thirty-six miles north of New Orleans,[75] along an area south of Lake Pontchartrain known as the German Coast—so called because of mid-eighteenth-century German settlements—and involved perhaps three hundred to five hundred slaves, armed with pikes, hoes, and axes, who marched toward New Orleans with the goal of taking it.[76]

The revolt began with an attack on the Manuel André plantation.[77] In a letter dated January 10 to Claiborne, André wrote, "Sir, I have only time to inform you, in the shortest way, of the unfortunate events which have lately happened, and of which I am one of the principal sufferers."[78] In the letter, which appeared in several newspapers, the panicked man explained that his slaves, "an atrocious gang of banditti," attempted to "assassinate" him "by the stroke of an axe" and that his "poor son" had been "ferociously murdered by a horde of brigands."[79] The slaves "marched along the river toward [New Orleans] ... compelling the blacks they met to join their disorderly crew," according to the Louisiana historian Charles Gayarre.[80] In another André account, appearing in the January 17 *Louisiana Gazette* and *New Orleans Daily Advertiser*, the plantation owner said that "the most active, prime slaves, were concerned or joined the poor deluded miscreants."

According to the accounts, as several plantations burned, most panicked whites fled.[81] Eventually two federal militias, one from Baton Rouge and the other from New Orleans, surrounded the rebels and exacted a terrible retribution, hanging black prisoners "on the spot."[82] Another described the scene this way: "Their heads were placed on poles, above and below the city, and along the river as far as the plantations on which the revolt began."[83] Deslondes later surrendered under the flag of truce but was soon executed at the André plantation, the site where the troubles began.[84]

The Press and the Louisiana Revolt

Local newspaper editors published little information about the slave revolt, perhaps because, as one historian surmises, editors feared that negative press accounts would "adversely influence the slave market."[85] While it is true that local newspapers contained little content about the slave revolt, the published accounts that did appear reached other parts of the country and even Europe. A March 25 *Times* of London item, for example, mentioned "a very serious insurrection which had taken place among the negroes, who had set fire to many plantations, and destroyed property to a vast amount."[86]

Louisiana's territorial governor did keep citizens informed by sending messages to local newspapers, as a January 10 *Louisiana Gazette* item, credited to Claiborne, indicated. In it the governor told readers that the "brigands" numbered from "180 to 500." Giving further details, he wrote, "The mischief done is not ascertained—there is, however, reason to apprehend that several of our fellow citizens have been massacred, some dwelling houses burnt and others pillaged." He urged the citizens of New Orleans to "continue their vigilance."[87]

Of all the accounts that appeared in northern and southern newspapers, the most detailed was an item signed by "Z," which originally appeared in the *Louisiana Gazette* on January 17.[88] The writer, again believed to be Manuel André, whose plantation first came under attack,[89] wrote, "It is very difficult to obtain any thing like a correct statement of the damages done by the banditti on the coast." This telling estimated the insurrectionist camp as being possibly "500 strong, and that at least one half of them were armed with muskets and fusils, and the others with sabres and cane knives." According to "Z," the black slaves broke "open sideboards and liquor stores" on the André plantation, "getting half drunk" before their march toward New Orleans.[90] His words recalled the stories from Haiti as he described the ensuing panic: "The road for two or three leagues was crowded with carriages and carts full of people, making their escape from the ravages of the banditti."

Panic became a dominant feature of the newspaper accounts. New York subscribers, for example, might have thought they were reading correspondence from Haiti when they read an "Extract of a Letter from a Gentleman in New Orleans to His Friend in Chester, Pennsylvania," dated January 10.[91] "You cannot easily form an idea of the alarm and confusion that prevailed on the first news of this event," the "gentleman" explained, adding that "many of the inhabitants of this place were sufferers in the insurrection at Cape Francois [Santo Domingo/Haiti]." The writer described how "women and children flocked to the town [New Orleans] for refuge, and every face wore the marks of consternation." Letters dated January 11 from New Orleans appearing in the February 22 *Virginia Argus* gave "an account of a horrid insurrection of the Negroes near there, up the Mississippi" and indicated the murders of "Many whites" and plantations burned.[92]

Despite reports of massacre and destruction, the writer "Z" clarified the damage in his account: "In this melancholy affair," only two white citizens died "by the hands of those brigands, and three dwelling houses burned," and "not a single sugar house nor sugar works were molested."[93] While the loss of whites' lives and property appeared minimal, such was not the case for the rebelling blacks, as the newspaper accounts indicated. As to the exact losses, a January 21 *Louisiana Gazette* item said that "an accurate enumeration was taken . . . of the negroes killed and missing" and indicated sixty-six slaves killed or executed, seventeen still missing, and sixteen others sent to New Orleans for trial.[94]

"Those reported missing," the writer said, "are generally [thought] to be dead in the woods, as many bodies have been seen by the patrols." A March 2 *Newport (R.I.) Mercury* item stated, "About 100 brigands have been killed and hung, and several more would be executed."[95]

Conclusion

Both Gabriel Prosser and Charles Deslondes died in their attempts to overthrow slavery and found no sympathy in the newspaper accounts for their actions. Instead their plans sparked grave concern among the white population remembering Haiti's slave revolt and served to remind those living among black slaves that this human property were not content and might rebel, upend the slave system, and destroy them. As a media discourse with racial determinants, the intertextual nature of Haiti in press accounts contained instant symbolism that defined black-on-white violence. Later this connection would have unfortunate consequences by invigorating proslavery arguments during the antebellum years.[96] Slavery's proponents, in the historian William Sumner Jenkins's words, "continued to use the example of Santo Domingo [Haiti] as the chief objective argument to show the impossibility of emancipation whenever it was proposed within the South or by outsiders."[97] The references to Haiti also propped the arguments of antislavery interests by pointing out the uneasy master-slave relationship: "San Domingo has taught this lesson to the world. Southampton has taught it to the people of this country and this state. Scarcely more insecure are those people who work by day and sleep by night underneath the craters of Vesuvius and Aetna, who are liable to an irruption at any moment of burning lava."[98] For whites living in Henrico County and southern Louisiana, their panicked, heavy-handed responses quelled the success of any Haiti-like event on American shores.

2. Denmark Vesey's 1822 Conspiracy and Nat Turner's 1831 Slave Revolt

What an abandoned set of banditti these cut-throats are!

Richmond Enquirer, August 30, 1831

In the years following the Louisiana revolt, national discussions about slavery failed to generate a suitable solution for ending it. Even before most white Americans knew of Nat Turner or Denmark Vesey, slavery, which had remained mostly a local and state issue following the three-fifths compromise during the Constitutional Convention, burst onto the national stage in 1820 with the Missouri Compromise. Once again it forced national leaders to wrestle with how to maintain slavery and balance political power between slave and free states.[1] The wrangling prompted Thomas Jefferson to compose his oft-quoted "like a fire bell in the night, [it] awakened and filled me with terror."[2] To southerners, the Constitution obligated the federal government to maintain this balance, but others, mainly in the North, were beginning to think otherwise. John Quincy Adams remarked to South Carolina senator John C. Calhoun about the Missouri Compromise and slavery's corrosive effect on the nation, "The discussion of this Missouri question has betrayed the secret of [southerners'] souls."[3] He wrote, "In the abstract, they admit that slavery is an evil, they disclaim all participation in the introduction of it. . . . But when probed to the quick upon it, they show at the bottom of their souls pride and vainglory in their condition of masterdom." The words fell on deaf ears, as years later Calhoun said this about slavery to fellow senators: "We now believe it has been a great blessing to both of the races—the European and African, which, by a mysterious Providence, have been brought together in the Southern section of this Union. The one has greatly improved, and the other has not deteriorated; while, in a political point of view, it has been the great stay of the Union and our free institutions, and one of the main sources of the unbounded prosperity of the whole."[4] Calhoun's words reflected the slave owners' growing sentiment about slavery: that it was not a national evil but a positive good. Regardless, the rhetoric of both men showed America's growing political divide over slavery.

Certainly the burden of slavery on America and its underlying racist ideology affected all blacks, slave and nonslave alike. In the years following the Louisiana revolt, one organization worked to ease that burden on them. While the American Colonization Society (ACS) was seemingly progressive, its goal was to provide a way to rid the country of its free black population as well as encourage the establishment of missions in Africa.[5] While many of its white, northern supporters viewed black people as social deviants like "drunkards" or "infidels,"[6] others, including many Protestant denominations, argued rightly that black people—free or slave—could never enjoy the fruits of liberty in white America: "In every part of the United States, there is a broad and impassible [sic] line of demarcation between every man who has one drop of African blood in his veins, and every other class in the community."[7] That passage is from a Connecticut Colonization Society tract that appeared in the *African Repository* in 1828. Its writer, referring to the one-drop rule that determined a person's racial purity, also observed that racial prejudice against African Americans forced them "by birth to the lowest station in society." It seemed that the humane solution was to repatriate them to Africa, ignoring the reality that these Americans had for generations lived on American soil.

For many, colonization solved the problem that emancipation presented to even the most "enlightened" Americans, namely the creation of a large, free black population. Many colonizationists and abolitionists, for example, expressed concern that slavery had denied blacks a "chance for moral, religious, and intellectual self-development."[8] Therefore they were not fit for U.S. citizenship and would thrive in Africa. Many supporters of the colonization movement, who viewed slavery as an unsound economic policy incompatible with U.S. goals and philosophy, saw colonization as providing a logical resolution.[9] Sen. Henry Clay of Kentucky, for example, favored it because he feared that maintaining slavery would only end in social disaster for the United States.[10] Like Jefferson, Clay feared that blacks would seek violent redress for their "grievances" against white America. With black Americans back in Africa, this would not happen. "All parts of our country have an anxious desire to return the black race to their native land, where they may have freedom unconnected with the white," wrote "a Virginia correspondent" to the *National Intelligencer* in 1822.[11] His views mirrored those of other whites when he suggested that state and federal governments must help colonization efforts if the country "shall ever be exonerated from the ignominious burthen of African slavery." He suggested that state legislatures encourage emigration by passing laws forbidding emancipation unless a slave's former owner provided "written assurance or warrantee, that the subjects of his liberality are willing and consent to emigrate to Africa." Echoing notions of polygenesis, the writer added, "Nature having made a distinction between the two races, the wish of this country is, the distinction may ever remain, which can only be insured by a distant and permanent separation."

However, the main target of the ACS remained the country's free black population, who lived marginal lives in America, regardless of region. In cities with a large, free black population, the ACS offered a seemingly fair alternative

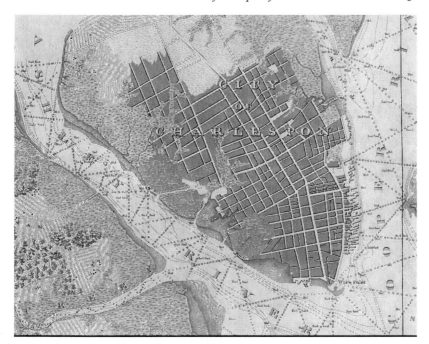

Charleston, South Carolina, circa 1823, detail from "Charleston Harbour and the Adjacent Coast and Country, South Carolina. Surveyed at Intervals in 1823, 1824, and 1825." Courtesy of the Library of Congress, Geography and Map Division.

to this life in America. Charleston was one such city. In August 1822, after the Vesey conspiracy unraveled, the *Courier*'s readers found this positive suggestion in a *New York National Advocate* item: "This is a favorable experiment, and may lay the foundation of important benefits to this country, by relieving us from a surplus population of Blacks. Policy and humanity unite to urge every encouragement, nationality and individually, in promoting the emigration of people of color."[12] The writer noted, "Several persons of color, who visited Africa" found the area (Sierra Leone) "a suitable place for a permanent residence" and were going to take their families back with them. To white Charlestonians still fearful of what their large populations of free blacks and slaves might do, this idea might have resonance.[13]

The Vesey Plot (1822)

Eleven years after the Louisiana revolt and nearly twenty-two years after Gabriel Prosser's conspiracy in Henrico County, Denmark Vesey's insurrection plot stunned Charleston, South Carolina's white community. The facts of the

conspiracy still remain shrouded in mystery, with at least two historians asserting that it may be a historian's fantasy. In 1964 Richard C. Wade challenged the
accuracy of the "Official Report of the Trials of Sundry Negroes," concluding
that white hysteria led to the deaths of innocent Charleston blacks as well as
the free black man Denmark Vesey.[14] Thirty-five years later Michael P. Johnson
reexamined the existing trial records and the "Official Report" and argued that
"almost all historians have failed to exercise due caution in reading the testimony of witnesses recorded by the conspiracy court."[15] Johnson observed that
the court and its intimidated witnesses might have created the "conspiracy"
that led to the deaths of innocent men. Despite this, other historians, such as
David Robertson, have argued that Denmark Vesey conceived "the most elab-
orate and well-planned slave insurrection in the history of the United States."[16]
One possible reason that details of the Vesey conspiracy remain murky is, as in
Gabriel Prosser's plot, the local press tightly controlled information, giving few
details to readers and hoping to keep them from, especially, the city's literate
blacks.[17]

According to what is assumed to have occurred, Vesey, who worked as a carpenter in Charleston, and his coconspirators planned to burn the city starting
on July 14, Bastille Day.[18] His goal was to free slaves and to create an "African
identity" for slaves whose cultural heritage had been lost on the Middle Passage.[19] In addition, according to Walter Rucker, Vesey used his knowledge of
"pan-African cultural phenomena and intercultural connections to his advantage" to remind his followers of their origins and their common ancestry.[20] This
free black man likely understood that he and other blacks in Charleston had a
distinct advantage. According to the 1820 census, the area had more blacks than
whites, giving Charleston the largest concentration of blacks in the United
States.[21] In all, there were 12,652 slaves to 10,653 whites and 3,615 free blacks,
including Vesey.[22] Many of those blacks had retained their African cultural
identities, no doubt causing some consternation among whites.[23]

In terms of design and leaders, the 1822 plot had similarities to the 1800 plot.
As in Prosser's plan, conspirators chose Sunday because slaves would not be so
closely supervised. As in the earlier plot, a fellow slave revealed it to authorities,
who began arresting conspirators and eventually executed Vesey on July 2, 1822.
Vesey, like Prosser, lived in a city that remained "immersed in the politics of
revolution and liberation," which may have influenced its black people.[24] In
addition Vesey likely knew about both Prosser's deeds and the Haitian revolt
and, according to Edward Pearson, "appeared determined to emulate the violence of Saint Dominique's black Jacobins[,] perhaps seeing himself as another
Toussaint L'Ouverture"[25]

James Hamilton's *Account of the Late Intended Insurrection among a Portion
of the Blacks in This City*, published in August 1822, provided much of what is
known about Denmark Vesey, the plot, and how "near" to success he came to
carrying out designs similar to the "bloody events of San Domingo."[26] The

pamphlet arrived weeks after the conspiracy had been revealed and its participants eliminated. In the preface Hamilton, who was the city's intendant, or
mayor, wrote that "a full publication of the prominent circumstances of the late
commotion, [is] the most judicious course, as suppression might assume the
appearance of timidity or injustice." He observed that the execution of thirty-
five blacks involved in the plot served as a lesson to "a *certain* portion of our
population [free blacks]" and added that "there is nothing they are bad enough
to do, that we are not powerful enough to punish."[27]

According to Hamilton's version of events, a Revolutionary War naval captain named Vesey picked up a fourteen-year-old slave in St. Thomas in 1781, and
the teenager's "beauty, alertness, and intelligence" charmed him so much so that
he gave the boy his last name and the first name "Telemaque," later corrupted
into Denmark.[28] Except for a single brief separation, the slave belonged to the
captain for twenty years until Denmark Vesey won a lottery and bought his
freedom for six hundred dollars, which was, according to Hamilton, "much
less than his real value."[29] The now free Vesey worked as a carpenter, and like
Gabriel Prosser, "among the people of color he was always looked up to with
respect and awe," according to Carroll.[30]

By 1822 Vesey was about fifty-five years old and had become a learned man
and bilingual.[31] Hamilton described him as a man of "passions," "ungovernable
and savage," "impetuous and domineering," assailing his character by asserting
that he treated his several wives and children with "haughty and capricious
cruelty."[32] About Vesey's motives related to the plot, Hamilton said that he
possessed a "malignant hatred of the whites, and inordinate lust of power and
booty."[33]

Whoever the real Vesey was, this free black man, like Gabriel Prosser before
him (and Nat Turner and John Brown after), couched his argument for a slave
insurrection in "theological and secular" appeals to the rights of man.[34] "When
not at his workbench, Vesey devoted every available moment to exploring the
mysteries of the Old Testament," Douglas Egerton has observed, noting that
Vesey "became the master . . . of 'all those parts of the Scriptures' that dealt with
servitude, and he could 'readily quote them, to prove that slavery was contrary
to the laws of God.'"[35]

While hatred of whites may have motivated Vesey, the slaves he tried to free
thought that Vesey had more lofty reasons that echoed the "Spirit of 1776." One
slave involved in the conspiracy said that Vesey told him, "We are free, but the
white people here won't let us be so; and the only way is, to raise up and fight
the whites."[36] Another testified that Vesey felt that "the negroes' situation was
so bad that he did not know how they could endure it—and was astonished
that they did not rise and fend for themselves."[37] This slave, named Frank, said
that Vesey told him "the negroes were living such an abominable life, they
ought to rise."[38] Jesse, a third slave, concurred, adding that Vesey had accused
whites of depriving blacks of their "rights and privileges" and told him that

slaves could overcome their oppression if they were as "unanimous and coura-geous, as the St. Domingo people were."[39]

In December 1821 Vesey began enlisting conspirators. According to the of-ficial "Narrative of the Conspiracy and Intended Insurrection . . . ," Vesey held frequent meetings of the conspirators at his house and plotted to secure money and arms.[40] His closest aides included Gov. Thomas Bennett's slave Rolla, a man considered brave and self-possessed; Peter Poyas, described as resolute and cautious;[41] Gullah Jack (Pritchard), a slave who practiced "witchcraft";[42] and Monday Gell, a discreet man of intelligence.[43] Vesey did not want to enlist house servants in the plot, believing them too loyal to their masters.[44] Thus a combination of Old Testament promise, the rights laid out in the Declaration of Independence, the success of Haitian slaves, and Gullah Jack's knowledge of the "magical practices of Atlantic Africa" proved an irresistible lure for many slaves.[45]

By mid-June 1822 the conspirators had amassed 250 "pike heads and bayo-nets" as well as hundreds of daggers, and they had identified the location of the city's arms and ammunition. What they did not know was that weeks earlier, on May 30, a frightened slave who had been contacted by one of the conspir-ators had revealed the plot to his master.[46] Authorities arrested the contact, who then confessed that the plot "was very extensive, embracing an indiscrim-inate massacre of the whites."[47] When Charleston authorities, initially slow to respond, learned that "the explosion" was to begin on June 16, they initiated arrests at midnight, including Vesey's.[48]

Shortly a "Court of Magistrates and Freeholders" convened and tried those charged with "*attempting to raise an insurrection among the Blacks against the Whites.*"[49] The *New York Evening Post* referred to members of the court as "gen-tlemen of the highest respectability."[50] According to the "Official Report of the Trial of Sundry Negroes, Charged with an Attempt to Raise an Insurrection in the State of South-Carolina," the trials were closed to the public.[51] The court stipulated that slaves' testimonies had to be made in the presence of the slaves' masters or attorneys and that corroborating testimony was necessary, and slaves were severely hampered in their abilities to defend themselves.[52]

In Charleston the writer of the unsigned June 21 *Courier* editorial "Melan-choly Effect of Popular Excitement" feared that authorities would be too quick to condemn innocent slaves. In juxtaposing the current crisis with a story of a wrongly accused and executed slave, the writer—supposedly Governor Ben-nett's brother-in-law William Johnson—suggested that the coerced testimony of slaves would provide false information and diminish the magistrates' abilities to judge the cases brought before the court. He cautioned against an increasing mob mentality in the white community.[53]

The editorial created a sensation in Charleston. On June 29 the *Couri-er*'s editor A. S. Willington, perhaps wishing to deflect criticism directed at him, acknowledged that "a gentleman whose standing in society is of such a commanding character" had brought the editorial to his office and that he had read it over "in a very hasty manner" and printed it. He emphasized that he would not "voluntarily admit into the *Courier*, a publication tending, in the remotest degree, to wound the feelings of any one in the community." "As an act of justice" to readers, Willington wrote that "Melancholy Effect" "contained an insinuation that the Court, under the influence of popular prejudice, was capable of committing perjury and murder," and he accused its author of arrogance for implying that he "possessed sounder judgement, deeper penetration, and firmer nerves, than the rest of his fellow citizens." Concluding his communication, the editor said that despite the author's insinuation of injustice, the "Injured and defamed" court must continue the trials.[54]

During the trial Gullah Jack, described as seemingly "untouched by the influences of civilized life," would stare with a "malignant glance" at witnesses appearing against him. Upon sentencing, the court told him that "all the powers of darkness" that he enlisted in his "wicked designs" would not save him from the "cold and silent grave:"[55] "Your boasted charms have not preserved yourself, and of course could not protect others.—'Your altars and your Gods have sunk together in the dust.' The airy spectres, conjured by you, have been chased away by the superior light of Truth, and you stand exposed, the miserable and deluded victim of offended Justice."[56] Vesey, finally brought before the court on June 27 after his arrest at the home of one of his wives, maintained his innocence. "Several witnesses," however, confirmed Vesey's "*atrocious* guilt," according to Hamilton, noting that "it was said, [Vesey] had spoken of [the plot] for upwards of four years" and that "all the channels of communication and intelligence are traced back to him."[57] The magistrates determined Vesey's guilt for "animating and encouraging the timid, by the hopes of prospects of success; removing the scruples of the religious, by the grossest prostitution and perversion of the sacred oracles, and inflaming and confirming the resolute, by all the savage fascinations of blood and booty."[58] The court sentenced Vesey and five others to die on Tuesday, July 2. Judge Lionel Kennedy said this to Vesey after sentencing: "Your professed design was to trample on all laws, human and divine; to riot in blood, outrage, rapine, and conflagration, and to introduce anarchy and confusion in their most horrid forms. Your life has become, therefore, a just and necessary sacrifice, at the shrine of Justice."[59] No record of Vesey's response exists.

Like John Brown would later do, Vesey is said to have complained that he "had not had a fair trial, [and] that his accusers had not been brought before him."[60] But Hamilton's account countered that "no cruel vindictive or barbarous modes of punishment" were used and that the court acted with "enlightened humanity" toward the conspirators who had singled out whites for "murder, rapine and conflagration, in their most savage forms."[61] Like the accused in Prosser's conspiracy, those involved in Vesey's plot "mutually supported each other, and died obedient to the stern and emphatic injunction of their Comrade (Peter Poyas): "Do not open your lips! Die silent, as you shall see me do!" Vesey is said to have told others on trial to "die like men."[62] In drawing another connection to Haiti, Hamilton's report noted that Vesey never revealed the extent of help the conspirators were supposed to receive from the island's blacks.[63] In all, authorities arrested 131 participants, executed 35, and exiled another 37. The court found the remaining 67 not guilty.[64] Still, unease within Charleston's white community lasted for months.[65]

The Press and the Vesey Conspiracy

Except for brief, official items, little substantive information about the plot or the trials appeared in the country's newspapers during the summer of 1822. All the local newspapers would print were items giving information about the court proceedings. The *Charleston Courier*, for example, first noted on June 29 that the "Court of Magistrates and Freeholders" had "convened for the trial of sundry persons of color, charged with an attempt to raise an Insurrection." Another, June 29 notice briefly described Vesey's conviction and execution.[66] A month later a July 27 *Courier* item listed the names of twenty-two slaves to be executed and said that "their bodies [are] to be delivered to the surgeons for dissection, if requested."[67] The slaves were identified as property, and according to an August account in the *Newport (R.I.) Mercury*, seventy to eighty slaves and others had been "confined" because of "the Negro Plot."[68] An August 9 *Courier* notified readers in one item that said the court had "adjourned," thus signaling the end of the proceedings.[69]

The sparse information coming out of Charleston from its newspapers may have prompted this observation in the August 3 *National Intelligencer:* "The newspapers at Charleston have been necessarily silent on this subject, pending the investigation and the trials." The silence in the local press seemed all the more conspicuous given the number of slaves hanged as a result of the plot and trials. About Vesey, the conspiracy's leader, newspaper readers learned little. A June 29 *Courier*, for example, merely noted that the Court of the Magistrates found "Denmark Vesey, a Free Black man" guilty,[70] and on July 3 the following item provided a few, although brief, details: "DENMARK Vesey, (a free black man) ROLLA, Batteau, NED, PETER, and JESSE, (slaves) convicted of an attempt to raise an insurrection in this State, were executed, pursuant to sentence, yesterday morning between the hours of 6 and 8 o'clock."[71]

While Charleston newspapers were silent about the troubles, editors in other cities were not, publishing more about Vesey and his conspiracy. New York and Richmond subscribers read the "faithful account of the rise and progress of the late contemplated rebellion of the blacks in Charleston" in their newspapers. An article headlined "The Negro Plot" in the *New York Evening Post* began, "As you will have heard, ere this reaches you of a conspiracy in this place of the blacks against the whites" and continued with the information that "some faithful blacks" brought the conspiracy to the attention of the city "Intendant," who informed the city council. Council members kept the circumstances quiet until "they apprehended a number of suspicious slaves, as well as many whose guilt was beyond suspicion."[72] The article pronounced, "No one I believe, of the citizens, ever thought that the blacks could possibly succeed, were they ready to begin to put their nefarious designs into execution, but that they would take some lives and this would be but a signal for a general massacre of the poor devils." The writer described it as an "infernal plot" with the goal to "set fire to the city in different places." In Newport, Rhode Island, an August 3 *Mercury* item described how the conspirators had devised a plan that "appears to have been well digested": "They intended to have provided themselves with passes so as to deceive the guard and place themselves at certain parts of the city," where "an indiscriminate massacre was to commence on all whites appearing in the streets, and particularly to prevent any company to form."[73]

In addition to these reports, Governor Bennett supplied further conspiracy details in late August to newspapers outside of Charleston. He noted that he had "entered with much reluctance" to reveal details of the conspiracy but that he must inform the public "to counteract the number of gross and idle reports, actively and extensively circulated, and producing a general anxiety and alarm."[74] According to Bennett's account, published in the August 24 *National Intelligencer* and the *Richmond Enquirer* six days later, a servant, "prompted by attachment to his master," revealed "that he had been requested to give assent and subscribe his name to a list of persons already engaged in the conspiracy." The governor called any idea of the plot's success "folly or madness": "Servility long continued debases the mind, and abstracts it from that energy of character, which is fitted to great exploits." Readers also learned from the governor that Vesey was "a free negro" who had been "arrested on the 21st, and on the 22nd put on his trial." Bennett had no doubt that Vesey "was unquestionably the instigator and chief of this plot," adding that the court had "positive proof of his guilt," which "grew out of the confession of one of the convicts."

Like Haiti's revolt and Prosser's plot, the Vesey conspiracy remained in the national consciousness throughout the antebellum years, long after white authorities had hanged its leaders. In 1859 following John Brown's raid, Boston readers were reminded of these past slave troubles when an item in the November 14 *Boston Evening Transcript* noted, "The late Harper's Ferry affair has revived the recollection of previous plots to produce insurrections among the slaves in Southern States."[75] About Vesey, the writer recalled that the "Charleston Plot, in 1822" was "known to the Secretary of War," and its "ringleader . . . bore the name of Denmark Vesey," who "devised one of the most diabolical plots of blood and murder that ever stained the annals of insurrection." Two years later Thomas Wentworth Higginson, the noted abolitionist and supporter of John Brown, published his version of the Vesey plot in the *Atlantic Monthly*, noting about Vesey that he made the slaves of Charleston realize "to a full consciousness of their own condition" and perhaps giving them a hope that they might be able to change that condition.[76]

Slavery under Pressure

In the nine years between Vesey's Charleston conspiracy and Nat Turner's uprising in Southampton, Virginia, the pressure to end slavery increased at home and abroad.[77] In the United States antislavery movements were growing, and slavery was being boxed in. Across the southern border the Republic of Mexico banned slavery, and to the north Great Britain's Parliament passed the Slavery Abolition Act of 1833, making Canada free land. At home slavery's opponents were becoming increasingly vocal and hostile. In the North the appearance of Benjamin Lundy's abolitionist newspaper *Genius of Universal Emancipation* in 1821, the publication of David Walker's influential *Appeal, in Four Articles: Together with a Preamble, to the Coloured Citizens of the World, but in Particular, and Very Expressly, to Those of the United States of America*, and William Lloyd Garrison's *Liberator* in 1831 put the slave power on notice that slavery would no longer be tolerated in America. Still, slavery's powerful advocates thought otherwise and pushed back with considerable political and rhetorical might.

David Walker began distributing his tract in 1829, and his words challenged slavery's proponents and called on slaves to work toward its demise. Walker's *Appeal* "smoked and blazed with black militance, with religious and revolutionary zeal," as Stephen B. Oates has described it.[78] The pamphlet introduced "subversive ideas" into slave culture and stimulated "increased efforts of the slaves to communicate among themselves and to extend their networks," according to Peter Hinks.[79] In tone and substance, Walker's words stoked fear and outrage in slave country, and southern authorities called for its immediate suppression and the arrest of anyone possessing it. In Georgia, for example, authorities quarantined black sailors on ships coming into the state's harbors because they were thought to carry copies of the pamphlet.[80]

By the late 1820s Walker was a prominent black activist living in Boston and acting as the principal Boston agent of *Freedom's Journal*, the first African American newspaper, which began in 1827.[81] When *Appeal* appeared in September 1829, it stirred immediate sensation in Boston because of the strong rhetoric harshly criticizing Thomas Jefferson's assertion about blacks' inferiority in *Notes on the State of Virginia*. Urging blacks everywhere to "contradict or confirm" Jefferson's words "by your own actions,"[82] Walker quoted Jefferson's Declaration of Independence to counter the former president's claims: "We hold these truths to be self evident—that ALL men are created EQUAL."[83] By 1831 Walker was dead of a mysterious, undisclosed lung ailment, possibly tuberculosis.[84]

Walker's *Appeal* particularly disturbed southern whites for its call for slave resistance. Throughout the South rumors consistently surfaced about abolitionists secretly conveying the tract into slave quarters. This possibility concerned the *Richmond Enquirer* editor enough for him to warn on January 28, 1830, that a "systematic design has been formed for circulating these pamphlets clandestinely among our coloured population."[85] To mitigate the possibility that it might fall into slaves' hands, Virginia legislators passed a law in April 1831, only months before Turner's uprising, forbidding slaves' literacy.[86] Just how extensive the *Appeal*'s eventual reach was in the South is unclear, but the Underground Railroad and patterns of "communal reading" among slaves may have spread its message. That message, like Gabriel Prosser's and Denmark Vesey's, suggested a link between blacks' resistance and religious retribution: "O Americans! Americans!! I call God—I call angels—I call men, to witness, that your DESTRUCTION *is at hand,* and will be speedily consummated unless you REPENT."[87] (John Brown would later echo similar sentiments.)

Walker's impassioned call to correct social injustice with violence compelled some abolitionists to express concern. The editor Benjamin Lundy, for example, said he believed that *Appeal* would "injure" the cause of slaves, calling it a "daring, inflammatory publication" and heaping "the broadest seal of condemnation upon it."[88] Even the firebrand William Lloyd Garrison called it a "most injudicious publication,"[89] deeming its call for armed self-defense and resistance too radical.[90] Regardless, Garrison gave *Appeal* extensive coverage in the *Liberator* and called Walker one of the "great inspirational leaders for African Americans."[91] About slave resistance, though, Garrison wrote in the first edition of the *Liberator* on January 8, 1831, "We say, that the possibility of a bloody insurrection at the South fills us with dismay; and we avow, too, as plainly, that if any people were ever justified in throwing off the yoke of their tyrants, the slaves are that people."[92]

Appearing eight months before Nat Turner's revolt, the *Liberator*'s launch brought a new editorial voice that radically challenged slavery.[93] While most antislavery groups favored gradual emancipation or colonization, William Lloyd Garrison called slavery "one of the strongholds of the devil."[94] He and like-minded abolitionists such as Lydia Maria Child, author of *An Appeal in Favor of That Class of Americans Called Africans,* blamed slavery for the degraded state of blacks. Their radical views stirred fierce opposition from some white, antislavery groups, according to Russell Blaine Nye, because those groups feared integration, equality, and amalgamation of the races.[95]

Like Walker's *Appeal,* the *Liberator* received universal condemnation from powerful southern slave owners who considered it a crime to bring it into the South. Not to be intimidated, Garrison enraged them when, after Turner's revolt, he wrote on September 3, 1831, "The first step of the earthquake, which is ultimately to shake down the fabric of oppression, leaving not one stone upon the other, has been made. The first drops of blood, which are but the prelude to a deluge from the gathering clouds, have fallen."[96] Garrison exhorted, "The blood of millions of her sons cries aloud for redress! IMMEDIATE EMANCIPATION can alone save her from the vengeance of Heaven, and cancel the debt of ages!" Southerners accused Garrison of inciting Turner. With Garrison and his ilk in mind, Virginia governor John Floyd wrote to South Carolina governor James Hamilton on November 19, 1831, that "Yankee pedlars and traders" had brought their incendiary message and "spirit of insubordination" to the slaves.[97] Floyd, citing Garrison and Walker specifically, wrote, "Often from the pulpits [of black preachers] these pamphlets and papers were read, followed by the incendiary publications of Walker, Garrison, and Knapp of Boston," and he continued, "I am fully convinced that every black preacher, in the whole country east of the Blue Ridge, was in [on] the secret, that the plans as published by those northern prints were adopted and acted upon by them." The governor's angry accusations had little justification because the *Liberator*'s influence in the South and the North remained small due to its limited circulation and, in Oates's words, "most Northerners spurned the abolitionist movement itself as sinister and potentially destructive."[98]

Nat Turner's Revolt (1831)

While it is not certain that Walker's *Appeal* or Garrison's *Liberator* influenced Nat Turner, it is certain that his revolt in the late summer of 1831 struck terror deep in the heart of slave country. "In one desperate blow [it] smashed the prevailing stereotype of master-slave relations in the Old South," Oates wrote, by forcing "whites to confront a grim and dreaded reality" of slave insurrection.[99] The shocking massacre of white families heightened whites' fears and increased the slave power's fierce rhetoric that black slaves were violent brutes needing slavery's strict regimen to check their passions.

Born in the same year that Gabriel Prosser's conspiracy shook Richmond, Nat Turner grew up seventy miles to the southeast in Southampton County, a tidewater area with a population of about 60 percent slaves and 40 percent whites.[100] His mother named him Nathaniel, meaning "gift of God," and by some accounts tried to kill him to keep him from a slave's life.[101] Like Prosser and Vesey before him, Turner showed remarkable intelligence, and in his "Confession" as told to Thomas Gray on November 1, 1831, he said he did not recall "learning the alphabet" but that he acquired reading "with the most perfect ease."[102] Turner was likely aware of Denmark Vesey and other slave conspirators and knew of the growing abolition movement.[103]

Benjamin Turner, Nat's first master, encouraged his slave to read and study the Bible.[104] Despite his great intelligence, the twelve-year-old was forced to work as a common field hand, sparking a long-standing resentment against the system's intrinsic injustice.[105] According to his "Confession," Turner said that

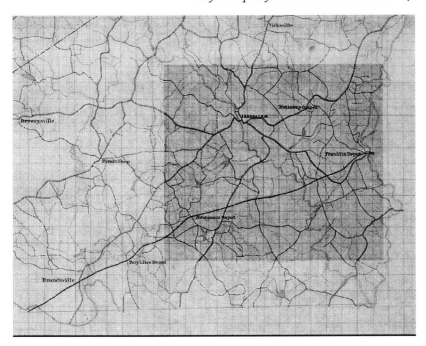

Southampton, Virginia, and surrounding counties, circa 1867, detail from "Sussex, Southampton Counties, Virginia." Courtesy of the Library of Congress, Geography and Map Division.

he had too much intelligence and could "never be of any service to any one as a slave."[106] Also like Prosser, Turner studied the Bible, cultivating an image of a prophet, and he once baptized a white man, thus earning great respect from fellow slaves.[107] He ran away once from the plantation because a "Spirit" directed him to do so. Turner eventually married. He and his wife had three children but lived apart on separate plantations.[108]

In Gray's account from Turner, the slave spoke of having visions compelling him to act against slavery: "I saw white spirits and black spirits engaged in battle, and the sun was darkened—the thunder rolled in the Heavens, and blood flowed in streams—and I heard a voice saying, 'Such is your luck, such you are called to see, and let it come rough or smooth, you must surely bare it.'"[109]

One vision on May 12, 1828, he said, changed his life: "I heard a loud noise in the heavens, and the spirit instantly appeared to me and said the serpent was loosened, and Christ had laid down the yoke he had borne for the sins of men, and that I should take it on and fight against the serpent, for the time was fast approaching when the first should be last and the last should be first."[110] In February 1831 Turner interpreted an eclipse as a "sign" to begin the work to seek freedom. Taking four slaves—Hark, Nelson, Henry, and Sam—into his confidence, he gave them military titles, and he became "General" Nat.[111] Perhaps as a symbolic act, the original plan was to attack whites on July 4. That plan was postponed.

Turner then received another sign—an atmospheric disturbance—on August 13, setting things in motion for Sunday, August 21. Like slave rebels before him, he chose a Sunday, knowing that the "whites would be tired and lulled after a day of visiting and driving," according to Oates.[112] Turner expected other plantation slaves to join in the simple plan to annihilate every white person in their path, push toward the town of Jerusalem to collect stored arms, and make an escape into the nearby Dismal Swamp, where the slaves could establish a stronghold.

In the early morning hours of August 22 at the home of Joseph Travis, Turner's then master, the killings began. To avoid notice, the killers used axes instead of guns to slay the sleeping victims.[113] From farm to farm they moved, methodically killing and often decapitating those caught.[114] According to Turner's confession, "A general destruction of property and search for money and ammunition, always succeeded the murders."[115] Here is Turner's description of Catherine Whitehead's murder: "As I came round to the door I saw Will pulling Mrs. Whitehead out of the house, and at the step he nearly severed her head from her body, with his broad axe."[116] Word of the massacres spread quickly, and by mid-morning a local militia had mounted a swift course of retaliation. The news also spread white panic, especially in the nearby towns of Norfolk and Petersburg, forcing Virginia governor John Floyd to send more help and to request federal troops.[117]

Turner's efforts found initial success as more slaves joined him and his "army," but these new recruits fled as the militia, bent on revenge, approached.[118] Of course not all slaves joined the slave rebels. One slave woman, for example, saved the life of her mistress, and at one farm slaves fought off the advancing insurrectionists.[119]

White retaliation was extreme. One slave, Albert Waller, was strung up and riddled with bullets to serve as an example. Elsewhere the militia killed innocent black men, women, and children and in one instance decapitated fifteen blacks and put their heads on pikes for all to see.[120] Such extreme reaction repulsed the commander in charge, who called for an end to the atrocities, saying that they were "never looked upon but with horror by any but savages."[121] The commander added, "This course of proceeding dignified the rebel and the assassin with the sanctity of martyrdom, and confounds the difference that morality and religion makes between the ruffian and the brave and the honorable." In a final confrontation at a bridge near Jerusalem, Turner's men were caught, were killed, or escaped. Turner fled.[122]

Judicial retribution came swiftly too. The courts rapidly convened to try and execute captured insurrectionists. In all, about sixty whites and an estimated two hundred blacks died during the revolt.[123] As for Turner, he evaded capture for two months but was finally caught on October 30 near his former home, the Travis farm.[124] Upon sentencing, the judge blamed him for misleading the "poor misguided wretches" and, according to Gray's account, ordered him to "be hung by the neck until you are dead! dead! dead! And may the Lord have mercy on your soul."[125] Turner met the noose on November 11, and his body was given to surgeons for dissection.[126]

The Press and the Turner Revolt

While 1831 newspaper editors still depended on eyewitness accounts, written as hasty correspondences sent to their offices, their newspapers, in comparison to those reporting the Prosser, Louisiana, or Vesey events, published far more extensive information about what happened in Southampton County.[127] Report after report dispensed graphic accounts of Turner's deeds. Clearly no "quietus" or "silence" of the press existed as it had in 1800 or 1822. "In the greatest haste, I write you a few lines," a writer from Belfield in Greenville County wrote on August 24.[128] The letter, published in the August 30 *Richmond Enquirer* and other newspapers, said, "I can merely say that we are all in arms and in great excitement on account of the insurrection, which broke out on Sunday night." Turner and his men had "commenced by murdering a family, taking their arms and horses, and pushing on to the next house with all possible speed, where they massacred every white, even to the infant in the cradle." Another writer, whose August 23 correspondence appeared in the Richmond paper, expressed shock: "These events have burst unexpectedly upon us . . . —No one has dreamed of any such event happening in any part of Virginia."[129] The firsthand account explained that "several white families had been destroyed" and that "a considerable military force might be required to subdue the disturbers." As to the story's veracity, the *Enquirer* editor noted that his newspaper had not as yet received "authentic" reports, adding that if the claims were proven true, "these wretches will rue the day on which they broke loose upon the neighboring population . . . —Dearly will they pay for their madness and their misdeeds."

Among the white inhabitants, the idea that such an unexpected turn of events could occur seemed incomprehensible. As one Jerusalem woman noted in her letter, "The oldest inhabitants of our county, have never experienced such a distressing time."[130] For the white community, the worst of social catastrophes had occurred and their fears of black brutality were now reified. Containing the Haitian revolt's imagery, an extract from a letter to the *Norfolk Herald* in the August 30 *Richmond Enquirer* described "a state of confusion" and how a "Mr. Williams" heard the cries of Catherine Whitehead and then found her "butchered with an axe" and her son's "head severed from his body."[131] He later found his own family murdered. A Smithfield man wrote in a letter dated August 24 that Nat Turner and his men "have committed some horrid acts of murder and butchery in their march, upon women and children."[132] Similarly an extract from a Belfield letter in the *Enquirer* that day informed readers that the heads of innocent victims had been "severed from their bodies."

Turner and his men were described in only the most extreme terms in the newspaper coverage. As more details emerged, an August 30 *Enquirer* column headlined "THE BANDITTI" contained item after item of correspondence that noted the "horrible ferocity of these monsters," calling them a "parcel of bloodthirsty wolves rushing down from the Alps; or, rather like the former incursion of the Indians upon the white settlements" and referring to them as "misguided wretches."[133] Northern newspaper editors relied on these stories, especially those from Norfolk and Richmond. Readers in Boston, for example, learned from a *Richmond Compiler* item about the "wretches who have contrived this thing," who were described as "mad—infatuated—deceived by some artful knaves, or stimulated by their miscalculating passions."[134] It concluded that "ruin must return on their own heads; they must fall certain sacrifices to their own folly and infatuation." In Richmond and New York newspaper subscribers read one account from Norfolk noting that the group had been "bent on plunder; but, having steeped their hands in human sacrifice, became infuriated, and, like bloodhounds, pursued the game of murder in mere wanton sport!!!"[135] These "marauders," the account continued, "pressed all the men of their own race whom they fell in with to join them on pain of death."

A Richmond writer described how Turner and another slave named "Moore" convinced three or four slaves to join them, increasing the group to "15 others."[136] The writer guessed that through begging or "threats," Turner and Moore convinced twenty slaves to join the insurrection. But the writer added, "We cannot say how long they were organizing themselves." After commencing, the "slaughter" became "indiscriminate"; the group "went from house to house" and "drank ardent spirits." However, Turner discouraged this, fearing that his "party should become too much intoxicated to carry out their murderous career."[137] A writer to the *Richmond Compiler* claimed that the insurgents got drunk on "Black Jack" and that drinking or fatigue made them pause "in their murderous career."[138]

Like initial published accounts from 1811 Louisiana, varied reports about the number of white people murdered appeared. One letter from Jerusalem dated August 24 in the August 30 *Enquirer* told readers, "The negroes, about fifteen miles above this place, have massacred from 50 to 75 women and children, and some 8 or 10 men. Every house, room and corner in this place is full of women and children, driven from home, who had to take the wood, until they could get to this place."[139] Other items put the number of victims between thirty and eighty.[140] Another letter from Jerusalem noted forty killed, "most of them, women and children." This information was carried to newspapers in the North. One report, dated August 25 from Southampton, in the September 3 *Newport (R.I.) Mercury* said that about seventy white persons were murdered and that one of the "ringleaders" had been shot and "mortally wounded."[141] As to the disputed numbers, a writer to the *Richmond Compiler* cautioned, "There are reports in abundance—but where are the facts to be relied on? A thing is stated at one moment—the next, it is confirmed—and then again it is contradicted."[142] Perhaps wishing to assure nervous white readers, the writer called many reports "gross exaggerations," noting that "our colored population were never more tranquil." Still, the writer added that "for the sake of prudent precaution, every preparation, was made for a strong patrol to scour the city in the course of the night."

Unlike the scant information readers learned from newspapers about Gabriel Prosser, Charles Deslondes, and Denmark Vesey, they learned much about Turner. One item described him as "an old grey headed man" who had been caught.[143] When it was clear that "General" Nat had vanished, questions arose about his background and motives. A writer from Belfield wrote on August 24, 1831, asking, "Who is this Nat. Turner?—Where is he from?"[144] In a proclamation published in the newspapers, Virginia governor Floyd offered a five-hundred-dollar reward for Turner, with an official description: "NAT is between 30 and 35 years old, 5 feet 6 or 8 inches high, weighs between 150 and 160 lbs. rather bright complexion, but not a mulatto, broad shoulders, large flat nose, large eyes, broad flat feet, rather knock-kneed, walks brisk and active, hair on top of the head very thin, no beard, except on the upper lip, and the top of the chin, a scar on one of this temples, also one on the back of his neck, a large knot on one of the bones of his right arm, near the wrist, produced by a blow."[145] The August 31 *New York Evening Post,* citing the Richmond newspapers, published this information: "The story of the leader said to be shot down near Jerusalem, is said to be contradicted. It is suggested that he is a negro from North Carolina, and his name has been quoted, we know not on what authority to be that of Nathaniel Turner."

The descriptions about Nat Turner were extensive, frequently mentioning his religious fervor and identifying him as a preacher or false prophet. They dominated newspaper constructions of him, framing Turner in a way so as to marginalize him and his goals. An *Enquirer* item described him in this fashion: "A fanatic preacher by the name of Nat. Turner (Gen. Nat Turner!) who had been taught to read and write, and permitted to go about preaching in the country, was at the bottom of this infernal brigandage. He was artful, impudent and vindictive, without any cause or provocation, that could be assigned.—He was the slave of Mr. Travis."[146] He was also called, in a *Richmond Whig* item, "a slave, a preacher, and pretended prophet" and the "most remorseless of the executioners."[147]

Turner managed to evade capture for more than two months, during which time newspaper articles tracked reported sightings or rumors of his capture. One report from Baltimore said that a man held in the city jail had come from the "South on a horse, which he had stolen at Washington City"; he was thought at first to be Turner.[148] Days later a Richmond newspaper identified the man as a horse thief and urged readers, "Keep a good look out for Nat Turner—The description in the Governor's Proclamation points the hue and cry by proper marks to his person."[149] The October 4 *Richmond Enquirer* contained an erroneous *Norfolk Herald* account headlined "Reported Capture of Nat, the Insurgent"; to his credit, the editor wrote that the story had not been verified.[150] On October 18 *Enquirer* readers learned about the arrest of a "negro named Billy," who was thought to be one of Turner's men, noting, "It was generally suspected that Nat had been in the neighborhood for several days." Others surmised that Turner escaped to Ohio with some "free negroes." Another said that he "drowned in attempting to cross New River, and believing it will be some satisfaction to the public to know that the [wretch] has been punished by the justice of the Deity for his offense."[151]

As authorities closed in on Turner, they kept newspaper readers abreast of the search. The October 27 *Maryland Gazette,* for example, reported that "NAT TURNER" had been spotted in the woods near Jerusalem and "600 persons" were "in pursuit." The November 1 *New York Evening Post* said that Turner's "cave had been discovered on the estate of his master," and there was little "doubt" he would be caught in Southampton. Three days later news of Turner's capture broke with the headline "Gen. Nat. Turner Apprehended!" in the November 4 *Richmond Enquirer.* The story described how Turner was discovered at "the very scene of his atrocities" and did not resist with "any degree of courage."[152] The editor added, "We shall attempt to obtain as accurate an account as possible, of the conduct of this murderous Bandit. We shall place it upon record—in order, that if any future historian should hereafter paint him incorrectly." (This editorial comment, discussed later, was meant to counter an error-filled account of Gabriel Prosser's arrest that appeared in an Albany, New York, newspaper during that time.)

The *Norfolk Herald* and the *Petersburg Intelligencer* supplied many of the details of Turner's arrest for other newspapers. A man by the name of William Clark provided this information for the *Petersburg Intelligencer:* "The prisoner [Turner] . . . submissively laid himself on the ground . . . not making the least resistance."[153] Clark said that Turner seemed "indeed, one of the most miserable objects he ever beheld—dejected, emaciated and ragged." The Norfolk paper added that the "news of his capture spread so rapidly, that in less than an hour a hundred persons had collected."[154] It was feared that the mob's "feelings on beholding the blood-stained monster" would make it difficult for Turner to "be conveyed alive to Jerusalem." When news reached the town, the citizens "fired guns for joy at his arrest."[155] A November 1 letter from Southampton described the captured fugitive as of a "darker hue, and his eyes, though large, are not prominent—they are very long, deeply seated in his head, and have rather a sinister expression."[156] The November 8 *Richmond Enquirer* editorial, headlined "THE BANDIT-TAKEN!," called Turner "a wild fanatic or gross imposter" lacking "a single quality of a Hero or a General" and described him as being "without spirit, without courage, and without sagacity."

After his capture, Turner's religious fanaticism again became the focus of the newspaper coverage. Although he was never directly quoted, New York and Richmond readers gained fresh insight from a *Norfolk Herald* article saying that Turner spoke freely "in his confessions," which showed "the wildest superstition and fanaticism" that motivated him and "the circle of the few ignorant wretches whom he had seduced by his artifices to join him."[157] The article explained that Turner "still pretends that he is a prophet, and relates a number of revelations which he says he has had, from which he was induced to believe that he could succeed in conquering the *county of Southampton!* (what miserable ignorance!) as the white people did in the revolution." The writer would not repeat Turner's "profanities in comparing his pretended prophesies with passages in the Holy Scriptures," arguing that these proved Turner's insanity. Another item, however, would say that Turner "evinced great intelligence and much shrewdness of intellect, answering every question clearly and distinctly, and without confusion or prevarication."[158] Perhaps written with a white readership in mind, it noted that Turner admitted he acted as a "coward" under the "influence of fanaticism" and was "now convinced that he has done wrong, and advises all other Negroes not follow his example."

It seems, however, that once Virginia authorities had Turner safely in their hands, the local newspapers appeared to show little interest in his trial or hanging. The November 8 *Richmond Enquirer*, for example, reported that the editor had been "informed by a gentleman from Southampton, that Nat Turner, the leader of the late insurrection in that county[,] was tried on Saturday last." The informer said that the "testimony was clear and conclusive as to [Turner's] guilt, and he will be hung on Friday next."[159]

Like Prosser and Vesey before him, Turner, according to press accounts, kept a stoic demeanor in the face of impending death. According to the *Norfolk Herald*, Turner "betrayed no emotion"; he "last appeared to be utterly reckless of the awful fate that awaited him," and he "even hurried the executioner in the performance of his duty!" According to the item "NAT TURNER" in the November 14 *Norfolk Herald*, he was "launched into eternity" with "few people to see him hanged." From a *Petersburg Intelligencer* item, the November 22 *Richmond Enquirer* reported that Turner "exhibited the utmost composure throughout the whole ceremony." He "declined availing himself of the privilege" of addressing the crowd. "His body after death, was given over to the surgeons for dissection."

Unlike Prosser's, Deslondes's, and Vesey's, Turner's voice lived on after his death in Gray's published "Confessions."[160] On November 26 a *Boston Evening Transcript* item headlined "CONFESSIONS OF NAT TURNER" quoted the *New York Mercantile Advertiser* editor as saying he read the confession and it made him "shudder at the recital of so many cold hearted butcheries." According to the editor, Gray's pamphlet described how Turner "in a religious phrenzy [*sic*] deemed himself commissioned by Heaven to perform some great work." The writer observed that "the spirit of fanaticism among a sect of ignorant blacks, spread consternation over a wide extent of country and robbed fifty-five innocent persons of their lives." When the *Richmond Enquirer* reported on the publication on December 4, it said that the "Confession," which "professes to give from the Bandit's own lips, the circumstances which formed him a leader and a fanatic," would make the "blood run cold." This writer condemned Gray for "one defect" in "style," saying that the words credited to Turner were "far superior to what Nat Turner could have employed—Portions of [the pamphlet] are even eloquently and classically expressed." Echoing Thomas Jefferson's assertion about black inferiority, this reviewer noted that besides creating "doubt over its authenticity," Gray's pamphlet gave "the Bandit a character for intelligence which he does not deserve." The writer, concluding that the pamphlet "is deeply interesting!," said, "It ought to warn Garretson [*sic*] and the other fanatics of the North how [southerners] meddle with these weak wretches."

Conclusion

What happened in Southampton County, Virginia, in 1831, as in the case of the Haiti revolt, remained locked in the nation's memory. Turner's deeds "haunted Southern whites," and his name became "a symbol of black terror and violent retribution."[161] Fears of another "Nat Turner" resulted in insurrection panics throughout the South, with the most significant occurring in 1856 in parts of Tennessee and Texas. In Texas a slave conspiracy involved Mexicans as well as black slaves.[162] In Tennessee a slave woman claimed to know of a November plot by slaves to revolt on election day when white men would be out voting at the polls.[163] As Nye has observed, these and other insurrection panics in Virginia, South Carolina, Louisiana, Kentucky, and Mississippi resulted in the torture and hanging of many innocent blacks.[164] The *New York Herald* reported years later, in 1859, "The lash was freely applied to extort confessions."[165] This fright caused white panic whenever slave troubles surfaced and gave rhetorical ammunition to America's slave owners, resulting in the continued repression of slave and free blacks. Turner's murderous acts as well as the publication of David Walker's *Appeal* kept southern whites' fears burning while cementing in their minds slavery as an important cultural good tied to states' and property rights.

3 ❧ Slavery, the Press, and America's Transformation, 1831–59

The historian Russell Blaine Nye has observed that neither "the institution of slavery nor its abolition became an important issue in the United States" until the 1830s.[1] In the decades following the Turner revolt the nation wrestled with an exponential growth that transformed it from a small nation bounded by a mountain range and an ocean to a vast geography lying between the Atlantic and Pacific Oceans. In the years after the Turner revolt, nine additional states joined the Union's other twenty-four states and the District of Columbia. Not surprisingly, "in a country with the extent and the physical diversity of the United States, regional differentials necessarily existed," the late David M. Potter observed.[2] The most striking of these "differentials" was slavery, which split the country into free and slave/North and South, and forced national leaders to maintain the tenuous balance of the political power between free and slave states. The post-Turner years also witnessed an ideological shift in the South over slavery: it was no longer considered an embarrassing relic of the colonial past but rather was seen as an integral part of the region's cultural identity, mattering greatly to its powerful politicians and newspaper editors.

Americans had always struggled with slavery's paradox, and the country had factions long opposed to it. Long before the Constitutional Convention, Quakers held firm, long-standing antislavery beliefs, and they initiated antislavery societies in the eighteenth century.[3] It is worth noting that holding antislavery views did not mean promoting racial equality.[4] In the early nineteenth century, an explosive growth of antislavery societies occurred, with more thirteen hundred formed by 1838. Not surprisingly this included the South, where by 1827 the number of antislavery organizations in slave states outnumbered those in the free states by at least four to one.[5] Up to the Civil War, antislavery sentiment remained in the South, especially in the border states and western Virginia.[6]

In the North, American newspaper content began reflecting these sectional differences over slavery. During the time of slave troubles discussed earlier, for example, northern editorial content expressed a general sentiment of support for southerners, including sympathy or mild criticism of slavery. That changed in the decades after Nat Turner, when antislavery ideas found a mainstream place in American newspapers, especially in cities such as New York and Boston. After the Southampton murders, for example, an August 29, 1831, *Boston Evening Transcript* item called them "an awful warning" and said that "a day of tremendous retribution approaches" if slavery did not end: "Let our Southern Brethren do more to enlighten their slaves and they will do much to protect themselves. Let them introduce, a system of gradual amelioration and emancipation. . . . Slavery in this country, cannot exist forever, and they who feel its curse fall heaviest, should surely not be the last to attempt a remedy for the evil."[7] In the post-Turner years, the abolitionist press—always a marginalized editorial voice in America—grew with the launch of publications such as the *National Anti-Slavery Standard*, the *National Era*, and the *Liberator*.[8] Joining them were the more powerful mainstream newspapers, for example the *New York Times* and Horace Greeley's *New York Tribune*, which, although not abolitionist, were staunchly against the spread of slavery in America.

One solution to the country's race/slavery problems was the colonization movement, considered progressive at the time. In 1831 the writer of a *Boston Evening Transcript* item expressed sympathy for southerners' "peculiar" problem: "We feel much commiseration for those who own this species of property, and cannot cultivate their lands without it."[9] In the writer's estimation, once the government paid the national debt, it could furnish the American Colonization Society with money and ships to "relieve our beloved country from as many of its colored population as possible." Colonizing black peoples back to Africa seemed a reasonable option in a racist culture that could not imagine black persons as having much potential to contribute to white America.

Of course its supporters viewed the main focus of the colonization movement as a solution for the problem of free blacks living in white America. In Virginia the writer "Appomattox" described himself and other Virginians in a *Richmond Enquirer* item as "warm" friends of the Colonization Society.[10] He said that the "public sentiment" embraced the "necessity of getting rid, as speedily as possible" of the free people of color, noting that emigration to Canada or "Hayti" would not work: "A negro nation in Hayti, and a negro tribe in Canada, would be very undesirable neighbours." The expense of moving free blacks "to a territory west of [the Rocky] [M]ountains would be intolerable," so the only appropriate location seemed to be Liberia, where "a free, and happy, and virtuous community may grow; and all that is required of our people is, to transport our free colored population thither." In Liberia "the institutions of religion and of elementary literature, spring up," "agriculture thrives," and "high wages" abound. Another southern editorial read, "Those of them who deserve to be free, cannot hesitate a moment to avail themselves of the generous aid of the Colonization Society, to emigrate for Liberia. For the rest, we see no ultimate step but compulsion."[11] Another southerner, while keeping an antislavery tone, expressed bluntly what should be done about blacks in America: "The sentiment is gaining ground in Virginia, that the whole African race ought to be removed from among us.—Many people feel unwilling to die and leave their posterity exposed to all the ills which from the existence of slavery in our State, they have themselves so long felt."[12] The editorial concluded that "the evil [slaves]" should be taken away.[13]

Growing Abolitionism

By 1831 the antislavery movement had developed a more radical wing that demanded the immediate end to slavery. These abolitionists, most prominent among them being the editor William Lloyd Garrison of the *Liberator*, caught the attention of slave owners and editors, who blamed them for inciting slaves to rebel. At the height of the post-Turner panic, for example, the writer of a "letter from Wilmington" (North Carolina) observed that there were "few, very few" abolitionists, but the "fanatics of the North" were nearly succeeding "in producing a state of things fraught with the most dreadful consequences to the miserable beings whose condition they wish to better."[14] A writer who signed his letter as "OLD VIRGINIA" said that "our good brethren of the North" who had spoken about "freedom" and "the injustice and cruelty" of southern slavery must share some of the responsibility for Turner's revolt.[15] Louisiana's governor blamed the slave troubles on "imprudent propagandists, and the false philanthropy of a certain class of persons styling themselves the friends of the blacks."[16] Abolitionists, he said, were the slaves'"greatest enemies." An editorial signed "One of the People" in the vehemently proslavery *Charleston Mercury* blamed Turner's massacre on both the "Colonization Societies and abolition philanthropy."[17]

Despite such rhetoric, some emancipation schemes gained traction after the Turner revolt, especially in Virginia. During the 1831–32 winter, state politicians discussed ideas for freeing slaves. Even Gov. John Floyd considered freeing Virginia slaves by executive order: "Before I leave this Government," he wrote in his diary on November 21, 1831, "I will have contrived to have a law passed gradually abolishing slavery in this State, or at all events to begin the work by prohibiting slavery on the West side of the Blue Ridge Mountains."[18] Yet by February 4 of the next year, readers of the *Richmond Enquirer* learned that the "debates in the House of Delegates . . . have been terminated" after the adoption of a resolution that deemed it "inexpedient to make any legislative enactments at present, for the abolition of Slavery."[19] Thus the governor and others abandoned their emancipation schemes, and the South entered a period when slavery's defenders became the dominant voices politically and culturally.[20]

Another factor may have increased pressure on the South and further prompted a reactionary stance among slaveholders. Shortly after the emancipation schemes failed in Virginia, Great Britain's Parliament voted to free its colonial slaves in 1833, making the vast Canadian expanse to the north free territory and free from the hands of U.S. slave-catching authorities. As Parliament's discussion over emancipating slaves in its colonies reached American newspapers, one writer to the *American Spectator* remarked that the situation in Great Britain differed from that in America. In the editorial "SLAVERY ABOLITIONISTS," the writer argued, "To attempt to bully and irritate the sanguine people of the South to an act [abolition] which in its very nature must be voluntary, will prove quite as idle, as it is inconsistent with decorum."[21] Still, this antislavery action by the nineteenth century's most powerful nation had to increase the South's growing geographic and moral isolation over its "peculiar institution." In addition a reinvigorated antislavery movement in the North and parts of the South added to that isolation.[22] So, as Potter has observed, "as the abolitionists grew abusive, the South became increasingly defensive."[23] All of this manifested in reactionary times when southern authorities took repressive measures to curb the civil liberties of blacks and of the press.

Liberty and a Dangerous Population

In the 1830s abolitionist newspapers and antislavery tracts greatly concerned slave owners, who feared that they gave slaves unrealistic ideas about freedom. To prevent such literature from falling into slaves' hands, the South entered an exceptionally dark period designed both to prohibit abolitionist materials from filtering south and to control tightly its slave population.[24] Eight months before Nat Turner's revolt, for example, a petition from the citizens of Hanover County sent to the General Assembly of Virginia highlighted this concern: "It is by the expectation of liberty, and by that alone, that they [slaves] can be rendered a dangerous population."[25] Four years later U.S. postmaster general Amos Kendell gave local postmasters the power to decide how to handle "incendiary" material coming south.[26] In many instances state statutes called for fines or imprisonment for anyone receiving abolitionist materials. Notably the North hardly welcomed abolitionists or their literature in the 1830s, and mob violence assaulted them and silenced their presses.[27] The 1837 murder of Elijah Lovejoy in Alton, Illinois, serves as an exemplar of how dangerous inflamed emotions swirling about slavery and the power of the press had become.[28]

Abolitionists, however, took no caution and flooded Congress with antislavery petitions protesting the brutal suppression of blacks following the Vesey conspiracy and the Turner rampage.[29] This outraged southern politicians, leading to South Carolinian Henry Pinckney's proposed gag rule that said all such petitions "on the subject of slavery, or the abolition of slavery, shall, without being either printed or referred, be laid on the table and . . . no further action shall be had thereon."[30] It passed in May 1836. John Quincy Adams, an antislavery man but not an abolitionist, led the fight in Congress against the rule, which was overturned eight years later.[31] Increasing southern inflexibility over slavery bolstered arguments by northern abolitionists, who identified the "gag rule" with the slave power's "subversion of civil liberties."[32] The powerful proslavery view became further entrenched, employing persuasive rhetorical argument that to a racist, white American would ring logically true.

"Slavery—the Bond of Union throughout the World"

Suppression or violence was not the only means to counter antislavery thought. The idea that slavery was beneficial to American society, while always an undercurrent in Americans' proslavery thought, gained renewed vigor and prominence after the Turner revolt, becoming a powerful weapon in the slave oligarch's racist arsenal.[33] Called the "positive good theory," it grew out of slave owners' internal fears of slave insurrection and reaction to the external pressures created by the growing antislavery and abolitionist sentiments. The theory rested on the supposition that slaves needed masters to act as loving but firm parents.[34] Without the master-slave relationship, as slave advocates argued, blacks became, at best, dissolute ne'er-do-wells or, at worst, crazed, "bloodthirsty savages."[35] America's underlying racist ideology spurred these ideas that reinvigorated attitudes about Negroes, both free and slave, as "inferior" and "a menace." While they magnified a worldview about the rightness of slavery as natural and progressive, they perpetuated the slaveholders' (and other white Americans') belief that it was their Christian duty and burden to care for African slaves whose very existence depended on paternalism.[36] A Charleston, South Carolina, pastor put it this way: "*The relation itself is moral. . . .* Our slaves are our solemn trust and while we have a right to use and direct their labors, we are bound to feed, clothe, and protect them."[37]

In 1829 the *Charleston Courier* published South Carolina governor Stephen D. Miller's words that first articulated the "positive good" idea: "*Slavery is not a national evil; on the contrary, it is a national benefit.*"[38] All of this rested on the idea that, as another South Carolina governor put it six years later, blacks were "inferior to millions of the human race."[39] However, it would be Professor Thomas R. Dew of William and Mary College, writing *Review of the Debates in the Virginia Legislature of 1831 and 1832,* who offered the most influential and widely accepted definition of the theory: 1) slavery was a necessary stage of human development; 2) southern life depended on it; and 3) blacks were ill-prepared for freedom and could not succeed as free persons in a prejudiced white society that "would degrade them to the condition of slaves."[40] Dew argued that the African was used to being in a state of servitude to whites.[41]

Of course newspaper readers were exposed to such ideas. One early expression of the "positive good theory" in newspapers surfaced in 1822 after the Vesey conspiracy. A letter from a Charleston "gentleman" to his Boston friend, published in the October 3 *Maryland Gazette,* called slaves a "labouring class," adding that "colour is an insurmountable barrier to actual equality," with "negroes" being a "degraded cast."[42] In the North, the writer claimed, "a vast proportion of blacks live in idleness and support themselves by plunder," but "a slave in the Southern states enjoys perfect freedom from the cares of life" with food, shelter, and clothing provided. The slave did not have to worry about his future, and "his labour is light." Concluding, the gentleman argued, "It would thus be taking from them protection of a kind master to liberate the blacks."

Richard Colfax in his 1833 pamphlet *Evidence against the Views of the Abolitionists, Consisting of Physical and Moral Proofs of the Natural Inferiority of the Negroes* argued that "the Negroes, whether physically or morally considered, are so inferior as to resemble the brute creation as nearly they do the white species, . . . *no alteration of their present social condition would be productive of the least benefit to them,* inasmuch as no change of their nature can be expected to result therefrom."[43] Colfax was not alone.

While the nation's founders may have thought of slavery as an evil remnant of British colonialism, positive-good theorists dismissed that idea. In 1833 the *Charleston Courier* editor challenged a Boston editor's assumption that southerners still regarded slavery as a curse: "On the contrary they hold it to be absolutely necessary to the proper cultivation of the soil, and to be the great source of their prosperity, wealth and happiness. . . . Nor do the people of the South deem slavery 'a curse' to the Negroes themselves—it exists with us in a mild and parental form."[44] Whereas the *Richmond Examiner* editor called slavery "a dark and growing evil" in 1832, the newspaper's editor by 1855 referred to it as "a natural and necessary and hitherto universal hub, element, or institution of society."[45]

Southern newspaper editors were not the theory's only advocates. In *Cotton Is King and Proslavery Arguments* (1860), E. N. Elliott, president of Mississippi's Planters College, asserted the system's paternalistic and reciprocally beneficial nature: "Slavery is the duty and obligation of the slave to labor for the mutual benefit of both master and slave, under a warrant to the slave of protection, and a comfortable subsistence, under all circumstances."[46] The theory's adherents also contended that southern slaves had better lives than free workers in northern and European factories. After Turner's revolt, a Charleston, South Carolina, writer observed that a free state such as New York had a ratio of "41 whites to one negro," but incarcerated blacks made up a much higher proportion of the state's prison population; the writer argued, "Such are the blessings of emancipation."[47] Compare that to an editorial twenty-eight years later in the *New Orleans Daily Picayune.* Headlined "MASSACHUSETTS HUMANITARIANS," it criticized the abolitionists for letting poor white laborers starve to death while complaining about southern slavery—which, the editor argued, produced "happy, cheerful, well-fed, well-clothed and comparatively independent" black men.[48] The editor said, "Deliver us from such charity as passes by the desolation and death that blot the fame for kindness and love of humanity in our Northern cities."

The South had now identified slavery as an integral part of its culture and adopted a "proslavery doctrine as a matter of creed," according to Potter.[49] As the South's antislavery movement died, it began, in Potter's words, "to formulate a doctrine that slavery was permanent, morally right, and socially desirable."[50] States' rights advocates led by South Carolina senator John C. Calhoun defended slavery in Congress, while southerners such as James H. Hammond called slavery the "greatest of all the great blessings which a kind providence has bestowed."[51] By 1859 and John Brown's raid, slavery as a positive good became cemented in most northern and southern whites' thought. Even an antislavery *New York Times* editorial published on October 20, referring to Harper's Ferry as "The Negro Insurrection," suggested the same: "Who believes for a moment," the writer argued, "that the enfranchised negroes of the Southern States if they were to throw off their chains to-morrow, could possibly inaugurate a state of society better than that in which they now exist?"[52]

However, southern editors pushed the argument to new, irrational limits. A November 29 *Richmond Enquirer* headline announced, "Slavery—the Bond of Union throughout the World." "Trade binds the world together, and feeds and clothes Christendom," the writer averred, "but slavery sustains trade, and therefore, *slavery is the true bond of nations throughout the world!*"[53] Black people, according to the writer, thrived in the southern climate and agrarian lifestyle: "We find negroes illy adapted for commerce, trade, the mechanic arts, manufactures, &c." The editor put it this way: "The Southern slave is the happiest of human laborers; the best treated, the best cared for, the least inclined to be rebellious, and the least willing to exchange his comfortable condition as a servant for that of a desperate and starving so-called freeman." Another *Richmond Enquirer* editorial, while blaming northern failure to enforce the (1850) Fugitive Slave Act for precipitating John Brown's actions, added, "If the negroes of Harper's Ferry did not rally to the black standard, and enlist in the 'irrepressible conflict,' it was because non-intervention had already rendered them free, and they were unwilling to risk the consequences of a conflict where the benefits it could confer, if successful, were no greater than those already enjoyed."[54]

To southern slave owners, their way of life became defined by a racist, romantic notion of a chivalric culture that included slavery. For them slavery was simply a states' rights issue, not a moral one. The following words by a southern writer, which appeared in the *Charleston Mercury* on November 7, 1854, expressed a belief in slavery as the "foundation" of southern life and culture and a fear of its demise: "The owner and the non-owner will fall, side by side, beneath the general ruin. . . . When the foundation crumbles the superstructure must follow."[55] As argued, slavery was, in Nye's words, "of vital necessity to the safety of the life as well as the civilization of the Southern white man."[56] Even though only a small elite sector of southern society could afford to own slaves, many southern whites believed their very skin color made them members of this "ruling class" and that they had a right to own black persons.[57]

From Negro to "Nigger"

While the "positive good theory" provided a seemingly logical argument for maintaining slavery, another rhetorical choice contained in a single word powerful, marginalizing properties. The highly pejorative word "nigger," which never appeared in southern or northern newspaper coverage of earlier slave troubles, appeared frequently in newspapers by 1859, targeting black people and slavery's enemies (for example, abolitionists and the antislavery Republican Party and its members).[58]

The use of the word "nigger" along with the increasingly vocal denigration of blacks in public venues such as newspapers became easy ways for proslavery advocates to maintain white superiority. In one instance the November 16, 1859, *Charleston Mercury* headlined a *Richmond Examiner* article as "Nigger Churches." While informing readers about a "bill about to be introduced in the legislature of South Carolina concerning a distinctive style of dress for niggers," the writer asked, "Where did all the fine attire with which Sambo and Dinah were attired come from?" Another Charleston newspaper item, from its New York correspondent who signed off as "Pink," reported that there was "quite a stir in Africa," a reference to a fire in a section of town where free blacks lived.[59] As the correspondent described, "Some of the darkies I saw to-day . . . were almost white with fear." A *Mercury* item headlined "Where Are We Drifting To?" preceded an editorial supporting slavery as necessary because blacks were "naturally indolent" and they "waste the greater part of their time in idleness and dissipation, and are compelled to resort to unlawful means to procure their wages."[60] The November 22 *Richmond Enquirer* reported peace and quiet in the city and added this about the city's faithful black population while reserving the use of the word "nigger" for white abolitionists: "Indeed, as proof of how abolition doings are regarded by our colored population, we may state that a large number of them sent to our city's Mayor, and asked permission to be armed and sent to fight against the Northern *'niggers* [emphasis added],' who want to come 'fooling in this State.'"[61] Such overtly racist language was not the sole purview of the southern press. In the North, America's largest circulation newspaper, the *New York Herald,* ran this headline on November 21, 1859: "Nigger Capacity for Self Government." The headline drew readers' attention to an article about Haiti's constant upheaval after independence and the argument that black peoples were not fit for a life with liberty: "The fact is, that the negro has not, and never can have, the capacity to understand the difference between a despotic and a representative system of government. He comprehends only the arguments of a brute force."[62]

The *Herald* used the word "nigger" to disparage John Brown and other abolitionists as well. An October 28, 1859, *New York Herald* headline announced "The Exposure of the Nigger Worshipping Insurrectionists." The writer accused leading antislavery men such as New York governor William Seward or abolitionists such as Gerrit Smith and Joshua Giddings of inciting the Harper's Ferry raid: "They are morally, if not legally, as guilty in the eyes of the country and of the world as are the unfortunate men now on trial for their lives at Charlestown." A *Herald* editorial in the November 3 *Charleston Mercury* reminded readers of the Kansas troubles approximately five years earlier: "There is no doubt that both the nigger-worshippers of the North and the nigger-drivers of the South got up the fights in Kansas and committed many lawless acts."[63] The *Charleston Mercury* editor called John Brown "a vagabond" and "that meanest of the species, a 'nigger thief.'"[64] The word was used as a useful political smear too, as the item "A Calm Southern Appeal" in the *Richmond Enquirer* indicated. Originally from the *New York Express,* it labeled the New York governor a "political nigger," adding that he "now has the monopoly of the nigger here [New York], and runs him as a monopoly, election day."[65]

The Growing Political Stalemate

By the late 1840s the nation stretched from ocean to ocean, and national discussions focused, again, on balancing the number of slave and free states. The Wilmot Proviso of 1848, though intended to protect "free labor" and not slaves, did suggest a slavery ban in the territories gained during the Mexican War. Although Congress failed to pass the act, its members engaged in inflammatory debates, leading to the Compromise of 1850 and the Fugitive Slave Act as well as the 1854 Kansas-Nebraska Act, which embraced the idea of "popular sovereignty." While white politicians worked with piecemeal plans to appease southerners who fiercely defended slavery, the U.S. Supreme Court issued its own coup de grâce to slaves in 1857. In the *Dred Scott* decision, justices denied citizenship to them. While a victory for the slave owner, it would only fuel greater sectional and political dissension and deemed the long-standing Missouri Compromise null and void.[66]

Thus in this decade before the Civil War, chaos dominated the political landscape as Americans witnessed the death of the Whig Party and the birth in 1854 of the new, antislavery Republican Party, whose leaders advanced a "slave power" thesis contending that southern, slave-owning elites had controlled America's destiny for too long by demanding slavery's expansion into new territories.[67] Southerners feared that this new political threat would be less willing to compromise with the dominant Democratic Party. To them, Republicans advocated an antisouthern ideology, supporting a belief that the "South was a world apart from the North."[68] Compromise was not an option.

America's Changing Newspapers

Coinciding with America's changing political and geographic landscapes in the post–Nat Turner era were significant changes in the business of making newspapers. "Many institutions were drastically altered after 1830 but none more than the press," the historians Edwin and Michael Emery wrote.[69] On the eve of the American Civil War, the orator Edward Everett said, "The newspaper press of the U.S. is, for good or evil, the most powerful influence that acts on the public mind,—the most powerful in itself."[70] Newspapers had become by 1860 "the most popular form of literature available to Southerners—or to all Americans, for that matter," according to Donald Reynolds.[71] "Virtually all observers remarked on the pervasiveness of the American press, which was wedded, in their minds, to a direct, potent influence on thought processes and opinions," Dicken-Garcia has observed.[72]

Up to the 1830s the press, hardly an industry, had remained largely technologically static, serving primarily as expensive, political organs or commercial sheets for educated elites.[73] That changed with the introductions of the double cylinder steam press and the availability of cheap paper, which made daily newspapers possible and affordable.[74] Newspaper content too changed when in 1844 the telegraph made news "instant," leading to the creation of the first wire service four years later. All of this innovation encouraged newspaper readers to seek only the latest information.[75] When news of John Brown's raid broke, the *Daily National Intelligencer* editor noted on October 18, 1859, that Washingtonians clamored for the very latest intelligence from Harper's Ferry: "The bulletin boards of the telegraph and newspaper offices were beset the greater part of the day by seekers after the 'latest intelligence,' and they and the public could but be happy in right speedily hearing that the most groundless and irrational outbreak on record was so soon and effectually, and, we may add, mercifully put down." Telegraph use also became a marketing tool for many newspapers, as this excerpt from an October 20, 1859, *Charleston Courier* item illustrates: "The telegraphic advices we this day give—*obtained at great expense* [emphasis added],—will inform our readers that the surviving prisoners have to some degree made the revelations which alone could demand any postponement of punishment."

Yet the national division between North and South had become so pronounced by 1859, some southerners feared that the technology was being used as a northern political weapon. A November 25 *Richmond Enquirer* item, for example, warned city readers that "reliable Virginians in New York City" had observed that a majority of the telegraph operators, agents, and reporters were "of Black Republican and abolition tendencies, and contribute to giv[ing] a false coloring to everything" concerning events in Virginia. Four days later Charlestonians would read the *Mercury* editorial "Military Aid to Virginia," which said that "those in possession of the telegraph were in league to ridicule the South and make us a laughing stock to ourselves and before the world."

During the period after the Nat Turner revolt there was also a shift in news content from, according to Dicken-Garcia, "an orientation to groups—parties, elites, the commercial class—to the individual," in which news "became event oriented."[76] Following the emergence of the penny press, appearing first with Benjamin Day's *Sun* in 1833 and followed by James Gordon Bennett's influential *New York Herald* in 1835, there was an editorial change in that newspapers would "pursue policies" that their advertisers (and politicians) did not necessary like.[77] The penny newspapers pushed "news" into a new realm of timely and local issues that were of human interest and often highly sensational.[78] This content evolution turned journalists into active rather than passive collectors of information.[79] By the time of the Civil War, some considered journalism a profession.[80] Still, the technological changes that transformed the northern press by 1850 had not affected the southern press to the same degree.[81] The South simply did not have as many newspapers, and by 1860 its newspaper circulation amounted to only about 11 percent of the national circulation.[82]

In addition newspaper editors became prominent voices in their publications. As the slavery debate intensified, their positions became clear to readers. Robert Barnwell Rhett, editor of the *Charleston Mercury*, for example, became known as the "father of secession." He along with many other fellow southern newspapers editors supported an ongoing "intellectual blockade" involving any discussion about slavery, hewing "to a narrowly ideological line emphasizing resistance" to what they saw as a growing northern hegemony, according to the historian Carl Osthaus.[83] While not an ally of men such as Rhett, James Gordon Bennett used his large-circulation *New York Herald* to lend a sympathetic editorial ear to the conservative, southern arguments, antagonizing Republicans and abolitionists along the way. Eventually southern fire-eating papers such as the *Mercury* conflated the Republican Party with abolitionism and viewed as inevitable the "irrepressible conflict"—a term coined by Republican senator William Seward in 1858—between slave and free societies.[84] Still, powerful antislavery Republican editors such as Horace Greeley of the *New York Tribune* and to a lesser extent Henry Raymond of the *New York Times* increasingly spoke out against slavery's effects on the national character.[85]

Conclusion

For a variety of reasons, the division over slavery was magnified after Nat Turner. For one, northern public opinion shifted, prompted in part by the increasing antislavery sentiment. As well the increasingly vocal abolitionist movement—with men such as William Lloyd Garrison leading the way—heightened awareness among northerners about slavery's brutalities. While most white northerners may not have liked what abolitionists said, they believed that the

First Amendment and "popular sovereignty" protected such publications and speech.[86] The nation also struggled with the futile, decades-long failure by its political leaders to deal with slavery, transforming it from a regional issue into a national one focused on states' rights. Abetting that position were southern editors and Democratic politicians who relentlessly defended slavery as a positive good, linking it existentially to the South's cultural, economic, and social fabrics. In response northern public opinion began to shift away from sympathy about slavery to exasperation over southern intransigence.

In addition changes in America's press, both technological and editorial, made newspapers powerful tools for disseminating information and influential editorial positions. The telegraph made news instant, and by 1859 what happened at Harper's Ferry became an inescapable "media" event. Sectionalism finally tore away the nation's *e pluribus unum* spirit. When John Brown took his men into slave territory in the fall of 1859, Thomas Jefferson's silent fire bell finally rang, and slavery became, as Potter wrote, "a catalyst of all sectional antagonisms, political, economic, and cultural"[87] between the North and the South. The two regions, which had generally respected their cultural differences that emphasized different social values and ways of life, had reached their nadir of political compatibility, and newspaper content reflected the depth of this low point.[88]

4. John Brown's "Greatest or Principal Object"

"There is an unbroken chain of sentiment and purpose from Moses of the Jews to John Brown of America, to the untutored Gabriel, and the Denmark Veseys, Nat Turners and Madisons, Washingtons of the Southern American States," wrote Osborne P. Anderson, an African American member of John Brown's party who escaped after the Harper's Ferry raid.[1] That purpose, that "unbroken chain of sentiment," according to Anderson, was to end slavery. For Brown, his sole intent on going to Harper's Ferry was to arm slaves so that they could free themselves, and after a lifetime of despising slavery, he convinced himself that he must act on God's behalf. To slaveholders, the fact that a white man would help slaves revolt only magnified the shock of Brown's October raid into Harper's Ferry because they had lulled themselves into thinking—despite what had happened in Southampton County—that their slaves enjoyed their lives and would be incapable of rising on their own.[2] Another scholar put it this way: "John Brown charismatically violated the sensibilities of mid-nineteenth century America in a dramatic raid on a prosperous nation divided by notions of liberty, personal rights, race, and morality."[3]

John Brown was perhaps "the most psychologically complex and personally wayward" of the white emancipationists, often acting in contrary fashion, according to Bertram Wyatt-Brown.[4] Years after John Brown was hanged in Virginia, W. E. B. Du Bois observed about him, "To him the world was a mighty drama. God was an actor in the play and so was John Brown. But just what his part was to be his soul in the long agony of years tried to know, and ever and again the chilling doubt assailed him lest he be unworthy of his place or had missed the call."[5]

Although a general pacifist, Brown came to renounce the then-in-vogue concept of "moral suasion," which advocated debate, not violence, as the means to end slavery. Concluding that moral suasion could not end it, Brown opted for extreme measures, even murder. As he remarked to Frederick Douglass twelve years before Harper's Ferry, "Slavery was a state of war."[6] By rejecting moral suasion, he transformed into what the historian Ken Chowder has called the "Father of American Terrorism."[7] Yet throughout most of his life Brown, a failure at almost every personal and business endeavor, found clear direction in his antislavery crusade, which became a strange mix of self-righteousness and a suppressed penchant for violence combined with a depressive personality. These psychological and social ingredients compelled John Brown toward a final reckoning with slavery.[8]

Like Nat Turner, Brown had a vision, an epiphany that he referred to as his "greatest or principal object." Perhaps it was his disgust with Elijah Lovejoy's murder that inspired Brown to decide two years later in 1839 to turn the "dark mysterious tragedy of life"—the fight to end slavery—into his life's work.[9] He spelled out that goal in a letter to his brother Frederick, writing that he needed "to devise some means whereby I might do something in a practical way for my poor fellow-men who are in bondage."[10] Even with this new focus, Brown remained largely on the margins of the abolition movement until 1856, when he led his band into Kansas and murdered proslavery residents near Pottawatomie Creek. Ironically this violent act turned Brown into a cult figure among the very abolitionists who had so long preferred moral suasion. To the rest of the nation, he became known by his nickname "Osawatomie Brown" or "Old Osawatomie."[11]

Some historians have noted that Brown's violent actions imbued the northern abolitionist movement with important, nineteenth-century notions of manliness. Such ideas, important as they were to a culture that, in the historian Daniel C. Littlefield's words, "equated boldness and heroic violence with masculinity,"[12] silenced the proslavery ideologues who ridiculed the antislavery movement as too womanly. Brown would become the movement's eventual martyr, a role that he relished and even worked to create.[13] While unlikely, it has been suggested that Brown deliberately failed at Harper's Ferry so that his trial and hanging would become public spectacles, thereby enlarging his martyr status.[14] Regardless, to antislavery forces, Brown was a saint, but to proslavery forces, he was a murderous fanatic. One thing was clear: his Harper's Ferry deeds revealed how slavery deeply split the nation.

John Brown, who could trace his descendants to the Mayflower, was born in 1800, a year that had "the shudder of Haiti" running "through all the Americas" along with the fresh memory of Gabriel Prosser's foiled "formidable uprising in Virginia," as Du Bois observed.[15] He grew up in an antislavery household and learned from his father to detest slavery.[16] Yet, "Old Osawatomie" Brown endured a hardscrabble life, losing his mother at an early age and then his first wife, who died giving birth to a son, who also died.[17] His financial losses and failures too sapped his emotional reserve while forcing great hardships on his family. Despite this, he once paid a fine rather than serve in the military, and he remained a pacifist until his Kansas years.[18]

Unlike many of his contemporaries, Brown believed in racial equality, shocking a church congregation once by giving the family pew to the town's free blacks, a population for whom he felt great sympathy.[19] Later he convinced the New York abolitionist and philanthropist Gerrit Smith to donate land and money to establish a colony of "Negroes" in upstate New York, a place to which he moved his family in 1848.[20] According to Osborne Anderson, "No hateful prejudice dared intrude its ugly self—no ghost of distinction found space to enter" at the Kennedy Farm in Maryland where Brown planned his Harper's Ferry raid during the summer of 1859.[21] In planning the 1859 raid, Brown gave "commissions" to black recruits even though they lacked military training.[22]

"Osawatomie Brown"

By the mid-1850s the push for popular sovereignty made Kansas the center of the slavery battle, transforming Brown into a "religious revolutionary."[23] He arrived in 1855 just as Missouri's "border ruffians" sacked the town of Lawrence, and he soon concluded that he needed to act. "All the frustrations of a hard, ill-fated life without purpose or meaning," according to Wyatt-Brown, "without stability or rooted-ness burst forth in his savage midnight attack in 1856 on some unarmed proslavery farmers near Lawrence—The Pottawatomie Massacre."[24] Brown gave direct orders to those who used broadswords to hack the five men to death.[25] To him, the murders were "just, necessary, and God-inspired"—like Nat Turner's justification for murder in 1831 Virginia.[26] Years later, though, Jason Brown recalled that his father told him he did not partake in the killings but "approved" of them.[27]

With a national persona now fully shaped, Brown put his "greatest or principal object" into practice, freeing slaves wherever possible, despite the means.[28] Before Harper's Ferry, Brown committed a daring raid into Missouri in December 1858, killing the owner of eleven slaves and leading them to freedom in Canada.[29] Upon his return to the United States, Brown resumed speaking and fund-raising activities and his close association with the so-called "secret six."[30] Brown pressured this small group of wealthy East Coast abolitionists—Thomas Wentworth Higginson, Gerrit Smith, Franklin Sanborn, George Luther Stearns, Samuel Gridley Howe, and the Reverend Theodore Parker—for money and support.[31] The men were "well organized, meticulous, and circumspect . . . so unlike the carelessly organized Brown," according to Edward J. Renehan Jr.[32] Brown never divulged their names after Harper's Ferry, and they never admitted their involvement, despite the incriminating letters found after the raid and indicating their support. In his testimony to the Senate panel investigating Harper's Ferry, George Luther Stearns called Brown "the representative man of this century, as Washington was of the last."[33]

By the summer of 1859 Brown was ready for battle and selected an old Maryland farmstead near Harper's Ferry to encamp. By July the band, which consisted of sixteen whites and five blacks, had some two hundred Sharpe's rifles plus a thousand pikes and two hundred revolvers from various sources.[34] John Cook, one of Brown's men, who were now known as the soldiers of the

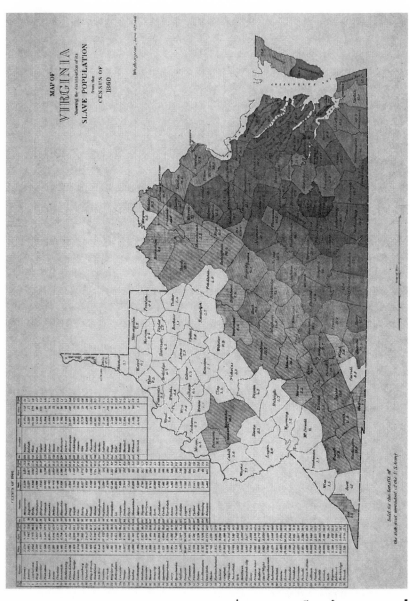

Virginia's slave population 1860, detail from "Map of Virginia: Showing the Distribution of Its Slave Population from the Census of 1860." Courtesy of the Library of Congress, Geography and Map Division.

"Provisional Government," had been living in the area for a year and had married a local woman.[35] During that summer the group spent time in Bible study and reading the training publication "Manual of the Patriotic Volunteer," written by Hugh Forbes, a British military man who became their military strategist.[36] As it turned out, Forbes would implicate the secret six in a *New York Herald* article published ten days after the raid began, explaining, "Some abolitionists of good judgment insisted strongly that I should make Brown desist from his projects, which they considered would prove fatal to the anti-slavery cause."[37] The newspaper scooped the competition the following day, telling readers the latest details of this "Well-Matured Plan."[38] For the most part, Brown's men kept out of sight to avoid raising suspicion, and Brown assumed the alias "Isaac Smith."[39]

Upon his return from a fund-raising mission, Brown decided to strike out for Harper's Ferry two days later on Sunday, October 16. That morning Brown read a passage from the Bible about the slaves' condition. Then the men waited until night to move. According to Anderson, Brown told his men, "You all know how dear life is to you, and how dear life is to your friends. And in remembering that consider that the lives of others are as dear to them as yours are to you."[40] Shortly thereafter, "the invasion thus silently commenced, was as silently conducted, none of the inhabitants having been aroused," the Senate's investigation later noted.[41]

While Brown assumed that some fighting would take place, the main goal was to evade and resist capture.[42] Initially some of the men managed to secure the railroad bridge into town while others cut telegraph lines and took captives, to whom Brown made his plans clear. "We are Abolitionists from the North," Brown told the armory master, "come to take and release your slaves; our organization is large, and must succeed."[43] He continued, "I suffered much in Kansas and expect to suffer here, in the cause of human freedom. Slaveholders I regard as robbers and murderers; and I have sworn to abolish slavery and liberate my fellow-men."

While Brown demanded the secrecy of his plan, someone had sent an anonymous letter to Secretary of War John B. Floyd—the son of John Floyd, Virginia's governor at the time of Nat Turner's revolt—warning him of the raid.[44] Floyd ignored the letter because he "was constantly receiving anonymous communications" and thought it a hoax by a Brown sympathizer.[45] Newspapers later published the letter, which originated from Cincinnati and was dated August 20, 1859: "I have lately received information," the letter said, "of a movement of so great importance that I feel it to be my duty to impart it to you without delay."[46] The writer identified John Brown and the place of attack, predicting that Brown would "arm the negroes and strike the blow in a few weeks; so that whatever is done must be done at once." The editor of the *Charleston Courier* wrote, expressing his frustration, "[Floyd] will be expected to give some reasons for his neglect of that warning."[47] Floyd later testified that the details in the letter confused him because they referred to an armory in Maryland, not Virginia, adding, "I was satisfied in my own mind that a scheme of such wickedness and outrage could not be entertained by any citizens of the United States."[48]

News of the raid broke once passengers on a Baltimore and Ohio train that Brown's party had stopped finally reached their destinations. In a letter dated October 17, John A. Garrett, president of the Baltimore and Ohio Railroad, exaggerating the extent of it, informed Virginia governor Henry Wise that "an insurrection of seven hundred and fifty (750) whites and blacks ... [is] reported to be busy in taking slaves from their owners."[49] According to the Senate's investigation, as soon as Harper's Ferry events became known, "the citizens assembled, hurriedly enrolled themselves into military bands, and with such arms as they could find, proceeded to the Ferry."[50]

Brown departed from his original plan by ordering the town to be taken.[51] While intending no deaths, Brown's men killed a hotel porter by the name of Heywood Shepherd, who was black. It was with some irony, then, that a black man died for failing to obey orders to stop. Osborne Anderson later justified the murder, writing that no one knew if Heywood was "white or colored, but his movements were such as to justify the sentinels in shooting him, as he would not stop when commanded."[52] Coincidentally, the first among Brown's men to die was also a black man, Dangerfield Newby. The former slave joined Brown hoping to buy his wife's freedom and to rescue her from a master who planned to sell her down south. Panic ensued as the events unfolded, with Brown's men also shooting the town's mayor.

Local militia and federal troops ultimately repelled Brown's small band and cornered those still living, including John Brown and his captives, in the armory's engine house.[53] Throughout October 17 the gunfight grew fierce. Captain Dangerfield, an armory clerk taken prisoner, described the fight from inside the armory: "Then commenced a terrible firing from without, at every point from which the windows could be seen, and in a few minutes every window was shattered, hundreds of balls came through the doors."[54] He said that Brown was "as brave as a man could be, and sensible upon all subjects except slavery." The white captives, including a distant relative of George Washington, were never mistreated and received Brown's protection during the storming of the engine house. Eventually, Bvt. Lt. Col. Robert E. Lee, who had arrived with U.S. Marines, ordered his second in command, J. E. B. Stuart, to demand Brown's unconditional surrender.[55]

Brown refused unless guaranteed safe passage from Harper's Ferry. Richmond readers learned from an October 28 *Enquirer* item what Brown supposedly said: "In consideration of all my men, whether living or dead, or wounded ... we will then take our prisoners and cross the Potomac bridge, a little beyond which we will set them at liberty."[56] After Brown's refusal, a final assault began with marines breaking down the engine house doors. Brown has been quoted as telling his men, "Men! Be cool! Don't waste your powder and shot! Take aim, and make every shot count!"[57] One account described the final moments: an officer "sprang about twelve feet" at the old man and "gave [Brown] an under-thrust of his sword, striking him about midway the body and, raising him completely from the ground."[58] The thrust did not kill Old Osawatomie.

A little more than forty-eight hours after Brown left the Kennedy Farm, his great plan reached finality at Harper's Ferry, and according to the later Senate report, "It resulted in the murder of three most respectable citizens of the State of Virginia without cause, and in the like murder of an unoffending free negro."[59] One marine also died. Among the raiders, eleven died, including two of John Brown's sons. Townspeople reacted so violently to the raid that one of Brown's men, William Thompson, was dragged out of the town's hotel, beaten, shot in the head, and tossed over a bridge. The body of another of Brown's men, William Henry Leeman, was used for target practice as it floated in the Shenandoah River.[60] The body of Dangerfield Newby, the first of Brown's men to die, lay in the street and was subjected to "shocking indignities,—his ears were sliced off for souvenirs," according to Villard.[61]

The Press and Harper's Ferry

Once the nation's newspapers got wind of the story, Harper's Ferry and John Brown dominated press coverage for weeks to come. This was so much the case that by November 6 an editorial in James Gordon Bennett's overtly racist *New York Herald* said that readers "have had too much Brown. They object to Brown. They say Brown has become a bore."[62] In a tone of exasperation regarding the state of the nation's affairs, the editorial flatly asked, "Is there nothing else in the world, we are asked, but the irrepressible conflict [over slavery]? Are we to be continually bored to death with niggers and politicians?" Even an editorial in the antislavery *New York Times* on November 11 said, "Most readers are heartily sick of the Old Brown's enterprise" and added further that "the Virginia Press has kept us so well supplied with intelligence about the plot and its ramifications, that we really have not stomach for another syllable."[63]

Changes in newspaper technology made news of the raid instant. Similar to the "breaking news" practice in contemporary journalism, the facts surrounding the events at Harper's Ferry would be sorted out eventually, but many early reports contained erroneous, exaggerated, or unsubstantiated information about the raid's scope and magnitude. As soon as telegraph dispatches reached newspaper editors, they rushed them to print and sent correspondents dashing to northern Virginia. Hourly dispatches from the Associated Press (AP), based on what passengers and crew on the Baltimore and Ohio train saw at Harper's Ferry, provided many early details, noting the frightening possibility that this was truly a slave insurrection. One wire report in the *New York Herald* told readers that "a negro insurrection of a formidable character, headed by white men, is in active operation."[64] An AP dispatch dated October 17 in the October 18 *Richmond Enquirer* read, "The band is composed of a gang of about 250 whites, followed by a band of negroes who are fighting with them."[65]

Some of the first dispatches implied that the whole affair was a labor dispute "caused by the failure of the contractors on the government dam to pay the employees, who number several hundred, and have pressed the negros into their service."[66] Because so many conflicting reports appeared in the same newspaper editions, editors warned readers not to believe everything they read. The *Enquirer's* editor, for one, called the wire reports from Baltimore "improbable" and commented that they "should be received with great caution until confirmed."[67]

Initial eyewitness accounts told of armed slaves and much slave participation. This concerned southern editors, who along with Virginia authorities made particular note that blacks were neither instigators nor willing members of Brown's band. The October 18 *Charleston Mercury* reported on the "serious outbreak" where "negros, led on by some infuriated abolitionists, have been *forced* [emphasis added] to co-operate." The concerned *Enquirer's* editor informed white readers, "Dispatches received at the Railroad Office say, that the affair is greatly exaggerated . . . that the negroes have nothing to do with it."[68] An item in the October 19 *New York Tribune* began with these words: "A most extraordinary telegraphic bulletin startled the whole country yesterday." Following was the information that "negroes are not abundant in that part of Virginia [and] no Abolitionists were ever known to peep in that quarter," and the item concluded, "We believe the nature of the affair must be grossly misapprehended."

Still, Osborne Anderson claimed that the southern press deliberately reported that blacks appeared frightened or failed to aid Brown. Disputing this, he claimed that a "proper per centage of colored men" were killed or executed.[69] Further he asserted, "The Virginians may well conceal their losses, and Southern chivalry may hide its brazen head, for their boasted bravery was well tested that day, and in no way to their advantage."[70] While the debate over the degree of slave participation remains unsettled, Brown's biographer Oswald Garrison Villard, the journalist grandson of William Lloyd Garrison, would add only that "the negro population" seemed "unaffected by the raid," which likely "went far toward reassuring the South" that "their greatest fear of a bloody slave insurrection did not happen."[71]

While initial reports bordered on the breathlessly sensational, two newspapers, the *Baltimore Sun* and the *Baltimore American*, provided perhaps the most reliable narratives for southern and northern readers. The *Baltimore American* reported this about Brown's intentions: "The sole object of the attempt was to give the negroes freedom, and Captain Brown had represented that as soon as they seized the Armory the negroes would flock to them by thousands. . . . He believed that the freeing of the negroes was a proper purpose, one for which he would sacrifice his life."[72] The *Baltimore Sun* reported Harper's Ferry as a town in panic once the fighting began: "Women and children ran shrieking in every direction, but when they learned that the soldiers were their protectors they took courage, and did good service in the way of preparing refreshments and attending the wounded."[73]

The editorial response, especially by the southern press, was notably harsh once the abolitionist connection emerged. The October 19 *Mercury* referred to the raid as "this bloody outbreak" and as a "concerted movement of abolitionists and their black victims."[74] The following day in the *Charleston Courier,* an editorial called the raid "matured plans of malevolence and mischief" guided by "malignant and fanatical agents."[75] An editorial headlined "The Conspiracy at Harper's Ferry" in the *Daily National Intelligencer* described the "outbreak" as coming "without any premonition and roused by no provocation," adding that it "appears to have been a phrenzied movement" and asserting that "there will be no sympathy entertained in any part of the land" for Brown and his men.[76] On October 21 the newspaper noted in the editorial "The Tragedy and Its Moral" that the raid's participants were "fanatical desperadoes" engaged in a "quixotic enterprise": "It seems indeed difficult to reconcile the conduct of the infatuated conspirators with any supposition of the insanity, though the method betrayed in their madness sufficiently attests the guiding presence of a rationality adequate to the adaption of means to an end."[77] It blamed events on the intensifying sectionalism between the North and the South over slavery.

The pro-Democratic, conservative *New York Herald* on October 18 referred to the events as a "Negro Insurrection," linking them to the New York abolitionist Gerrit Smith, who only that past August had written that insurrection was "a terrible remedy for terrible wrong" but that no other recourse seemed available.[78] The newspaper asked, "Is this the first act in that programme?" The following day the paper referred to John Brown as "that notorious Kansas free State abolition madman."[79] Another editorial in the newspaper that day targeted "that demagogue" Republican leader William H. Seward for inciting the raid with his "Irrepressible Conflict" speech at Rochester, which firmly stated that slave and free societies could not coexist.[80] Seward's speech also came under heavy criticism in an October 21 editorial in the *Enquirer* headlined "The Harper's Ferry Riot—Its Moral and Consequences," which averred, "The irrepressible conflict was initiated at Harper's Ferry, and though there, for the time suppressed, yet no man is able to say when or where it will begin again or where it will end."[81]

The initial editorial response in other northern newspapers elicited similar reactions, with their editors reserving little sympathy for Brown or his men. The October 19 *Boston Evening Transcript,* for example, reported that the insurrection was "an insane and villainous scheme, from first to last," adding that "Capt. Brown and his confederates, whose lives will pay or have paid the forfeit for their desperate attempt at revolution, will meet with little sympathy at the north."[82] Horace Greeley's pro-Republican, antislavery *New York Tribune* reported new details of the "INSURRECTION AT HARPER'S FERRY" on October 19, and in a subsequent editorial called it a "deplorable affair" and "the work of a madman." Greeley asserted, "There will be enough to heap execration on the memory of these mistaken men." He then added this biting, antisouthern, antislavery commentary: "We leave this work to the fit hands and tongues of those who regard the fundamental axioms of the Declaration of Independence as 'glittering generalities.'" William Cullen Bryant's *New York Evening Post*, also an antislavery newspaper, noted in an October 18 editorial that slaveholders may have "greatly exaggerated the extent of the danger."[83] Identifying Brown as the leader of the "fanatical enterprise," the editorial recalled the horrors of the Nat Turner and Haiti riots: "No one can think of the possible results of an outbreak of this kind, should it become general, without shuddering, without calling up to his imagination the most terrible scenes of incendiarism, carnage and rape." Although observing that these slaves appeared "too ignorant and stupid" to take part in the insurrection, the editorial added, "There are yet thousands able and willing to strike for their emancipation." With words that must have antagonized and frightened the slave power, it observed, "It has been impossible to keep them in entire ignorance of the blessings of freedom. . . . the fugitive slaves of the North have found means of communicating with their old comrades; the abolitionists have spoken to them by pictures, if not by language; demonic orators have told them falsely that the entire North was engaged in a crusade against the South for the sake of the slaves."

The severely wounded Brown and his surviving men were quickly taken to nearby Charlestown, Virginia (now West Virginia), to be held for trial. Despite assurances of impartial proceedings, Judge Richard Parker's words in the October 25 *Enquirer* indicated that would be unlikely: "I will not permit myself to give expression to any of those feelings which at once spring up in every breast when reflecting upon the enormity of the guilt in which those are involved who invade by force a peaceful, unsuspecting portion of our community, raise the standard of insurrection amongst us, and shoot down without mercy Virginia citizens defending Virginia soil against their invasion."[84] The State of Virginia charged Brown with treason, conspiracy to incite slave insurrection, and murder—all capital crimes (even though Brown and his men had been living in Maryland and committed the raid on federal property).[85] Thus it is not surprising that an editorial in the October 24 *Herald* rightly acknowledged, "No criminal trial has taken place in this country within the last half century that approached in point of national importance" that of John Brown's upcoming trial at Charlestown: "With one half of the Union the question involved is of life and death: with the entire republic it is a question of national existence."[86]

From Madman to Martyr
John Brown's Transformation in the Northern Antislavery Press

Unlike Gabriel Prosser, Denmark Vesey, or Nat Turner, who were black and had little access to the press, John Brown, a white man, sought and was given the media spotlight. He reveled in his antislavery martyr persona, perhaps believing that gaining lasting glory would, as Wyatt-Brown has suggested, "extinguish the many debits and sins of his career."[1] Newspaper editors noticed his fervor. A *Chicago Press and Tribune* sketch of Brown said, "[Brown] seems to have been laboring under a religious hallucination to the effect that he was the appointed instrument of the Almighty for putting an end to human slavery."[2] Thus, Brown transformed himself into a heroic symbol for abolitionists and Republicans—once they stopped apologizing for his crimes.

Before his trial Old Osawatomie seized the opportunity to reach a national audience with his antislavery views, understanding that they now had enhanced value.[3] Shortly after his arrest at Harper's Ferry, Brown, still covered in his own blood, spoke willingly to Ohio congressman Clement Vallandigham, Virginia congressman Charles Faulkner, Virginia senator James Mason, and Gov. Henry Wise about his purpose at Harper's Ferry. Newspapers, both northern and southern, quickly published all or parts of the October 19 interview. The *Herald* reporter described Brown as "fifty-five years of age, rather small sized, with keen and restless gray eyes and a grizzly beard and hair. He is a wiry, active man, and should the slightest chance for an escape be afforded, there is no doubt that he will yet give his captors much trouble."[4] The reporter said that Brown's hair was "matted and tangled" and his "face, hands and clothes" were "smeared with blood." Yet, Brown talked "freely, fluently and cheerfully, without the slightest manifestation of fear or uneasiness, evidently weighing well his words, and possessing a good command of language."

When Mason asked Brown to justify the raid, Brown replied, "I think, my friend, you are guilty of a great wrong against God and humanity" and "I think I did right, and that others will do right who interfere with you."[5] Brown admitted to Vallandigham that he did not expect a slave uprising and that he believed he failed because, out of concern for slaves, he waited too long to escape. The old man criticized soldiers for wounding him after his surrender,

John Brown. Courtesy
of the Library of Congress,
Prints and Photographs Division.

claiming that he was not an "incendiary or ruffian" and that he had come only
to "aid" slaves "suffering under a great wrong." He then warned, "You had better,
all you people of the South, prepare yourselves for a settlement of this question
[slavery]." During the interview Wise demanded to know who financed the
raid, but Brown kept silent, as Prosser and Vesey had before him.[6] "Old Brown"
admitted, however, to plotting the raid "as far back as 1856," saying he had mis-
takenly believed that three thousand to five thousand men would assist him.

One witness, Capt. John Dangerfield, an armory clerk, said that Brown answered the questions as well as any lawyer, noting, "Governor Wise was astonished at the answers he received from Brown."[7] Such tenacity from Brown
earned the begrudging respect from some in the southern press who viewed
Brown as manly, which to them was a high nineteenth-century virtue. "There
is an acuteness, intelligence, caution and deliberation manifested in all his

replies," the *Charleston Mercury's* observed, "that is utterly inconsistent with the idea that he was bereft, as some say, of his senses, and that he was not the crafty, audacious, reckless and criminal agent of men and parties as crafty, daring, desperate and guilty as himself."[8] A *Richmond Enquirer* item, although headlined "Old Brown a Common Thief—Statement of a Virginia Senator," cited Mason's praise for Brown's "boldness [and] daring."[9] In the senator's view, those qualities were actually serving others who may have manipulated Brown for his "unscrupulousness," targeting him "as a fit instrument for carrying out the hellish designs of men too cowardly to execute their own base schemes."

Some northern editors expressed outrage that such an interview took place, with one *New York Evening Post* headline announcing "Torturing the Dying for Political Capital."[10] Quoting the editor of the *Detroit Tribune*, it described the interview as "one of the most disgusting sights that has ever been witnessed in the country." The editor added that "these ghouls [Wise, Mason, Vallandigham] stepped in between the grave and its victims, to extort from them some expression that might be turned to political advantage."

Despite the grudging respect accorded Brown, he generally found little sympathy in the southern press or from the *New York Herald,* both of which emphasized his violent past and blamed the antislavery movement for his Harper's Ferry actions. The *Herald* called Brown that "insane Kansas abolitionist" and "notorious Kansas shrieker."[11] The *Enquirer* was especially relentless in its attacks on Brown and his supporters and published excerpts of a New York letter that called the old man "one of the blackest hearted scoundrels unwhipped of justice."[12] A *Cleveland Democrat* item in the *Enquirer* put it this way: "A bolder or a worse man than that same Ossawattomie [*sic*] Brown the world never knew. Fanatic to the highest degree."[13] This writer accused Brown's supporters of giving him "confidence" and deluding him into thinking that he would be supported "in whatever he might do against the men of the South."[14]

The press found its natural dramatis personae in the guises of Brown and Virginia's Henry Wise. Their adversarial relationship symbolized in many respects the differences between antislavery northern and proslavery southern views. Both men intuitively understood that the magnitude of press coverage served their interests. Shortly after the assault on the engine house, Brown said to Wise, who had rushed to the scene, "Well, Governor, I suppose you think me a depraved criminal. Well, sir, we have our opinions of each other."[15] For his part, Wise said this about Brown: "And they are themselves mistaken who take [Brown] to be a madman. He is a bundle of the best nerves I ever saw, cut and thrust, and bleeding and in bonds. He is a man of clear head of courage, fortitude and simple ingeniousness. He is cool, collected and indomitable."[16] Stressing that Brown was not insane, the governor called Brown "the gamest man I ever saw."[17]

For southern Democrats, Henry Wise was the "man for the time and place."[18] He represented them by "virtue of both public position and erratic zealotry," the historian Richard Hinton has observed.[19] Wise's political organ, the *Richmond Enquirer,* consistently praised the governor's actions in handling the affair and for bravely withstanding supposed threats against him, as this editorial on November 4, two days after a jury convicted Brown, indicated: "The Governor of Virginia, whose energetic patriotic and prudent conduct in regard to the Harper's Ferry outrage commands universal approval, is in the daily receipt of a large number of letters from Abolitionists in various States, threatening his life, threatening an attempt to rescue old Brown, and threatening the renewal of like attempts to those of Brown."[20] Wise, true to the ideals of southern chivalric tradition, which held high the virtue of courage in the face of danger, sharply criticized the Harper's Ferry citizens for the panic that overtook them during the raid and for allowing "fourteen white ruffians and five negroes" to control a United States arsenal. According to the October 25 *New York Tribune,* the people of Harper's Ferry were "indignant at the language employed by Governor Wise."

Later, as Brown awaited execution, Wise kept a tight rein on Charlestown activities, perhaps believing that Brown meant business when he warned the governor and all southerners to prepare for a "settlement" of the slavery issue.[21] However, *New York Tribune* editor Horace Greeley viewed this as being deliberately heavy-handed and politically motivated: "The fact that Gov. Wise's term of office is just about to expire ... tends to explain the tremendous flourish made by him over the Harper's Ferry affair, his marching and countermarching, his hastening from Richmond to Charlestown, and from Charlestown to Richmond, his calling out of troops, his letter-writing, and his speech-making, and his evident determination to ride this hobby to death."[22] About Wise's excessive military buildup in Charlestown, the editor of the *New York Evening Post* composed this sarcastic play on words: "An old John is Osawatomie Brown, a correspondent suggests that old Wise should be called What-an-ass-omie Wise."[23]

The Press and John Brown's Trial and Execution

From arrest to hanging, it took Virginia authorities just over six weeks to dispatch with the problem of John Brown. "Many northerners interpreted the hasty actions of the Virginia authorities in trying and executing Brown," the historian Paul Finkelman has observed, "as another example of Southern injustice," while southerners saw it as an appropriate response to a "dangerous man whose goal was to destroy their entire society."[24] The rapidity of Brown's trial angered antislavery northern editors, who faulted the Virginia judiciary for its seeming eagerness to dispose of Brown. An October 25 *New York Tribune* editorial criticized the court's quick action, saying that the prisoners "have no defense" and that the question of jurisdiction was not properly settled: "It is a rule of the criminal law, that a man shall be tried in the county where the act charged was done."[25] The editorial urged a change of venue. A November 1 *Boston Evening Transcript* editorial argued, "Some of the best legal minds of this section of the country aver that the State of Virginia has no right to try Brown and his confederates."[26]

During the trial newspaper stories explained how Brown had to be carried into the courtroom, where he rested on a cot to hear the proceedings.[27] The Associated Press, which provided daily coverage from Charlestown, described the scene in this fashion: "The jailer was ordered to bring Brown into Court. He found him in bed, from which he declared himself unable to rise. He was accordingly brought into Court on a cot. The prisoner laid most of the time with his eyes closed, and the counterpane drawn up close to his chin." Brown did not challenge the selection of his jurors, and his trial began on October 27, a week after his arrest, with cannons, in Hinton's words, "trained on the courthouse."[28] On the trial's second day, the AP reported, "Brown was brought in walking, and laid down on his cot at full length within the bar. He looked considerably better, the swelling having left his eyes." For a newspaper that exhibited such demonstrable editorial fury over the raid, it seemed odd that the *Richmond Enquirer* published no trial updates until November 1.

As Virginia authorities proceeded against Brown, he intuitively knew that the nation's newspapers would print his every word.[29] After the grand jury handed up its indictments, the still-recovering Brown boldly and in dramatic fashion told the courtroom, "Virginians, I did not ask for any quarter at the time I was taken. I did not ask to have my life spared."[30] Brown wondered, since he believed that Virginia would not give him a fair trial, why not immediately execute him? "I beg for no mockery of a trial," he asserted, and he closed with an insult to Virginia chivalry: "I have now little to ask, other than that I may not be foolishly insulted only as cowardly barbarians insult those who fall into their power." According to the AP, as he pleaded with Judge Parker to grant a short delay, he stated, "I do not intend to detain the Court, but barely wish to say, as I have been promised a fair trial, that I am not now in circumstance that enable me to attend a trial, owing to the state of my health."[31] Telling Parker that his "severe wound in the back, or rather in one kidney, which enfeebles me very much" had affected his hearing, Brown said that he "merely" was asking, "as the saying is, [that] 'the devil may have his dues,' no more." On the third day Brown again asked for a fair trial: "I have discovered notwithstanding all the assurances I have received of a fair trial, nothing like a fair trial is to be given me, as it would seem."[32] According to Brown, he could not call witnesses because his money had been taken when he was "sacked and stabbed" at the engine house. After speaking, "Brown then lay down again, drew his blanket over him and closed his eyes, and appeared to sink in tranquil slumber."

On October 31 Charlestown jurors took less than an hour to find John Brown guilty. Then on November 2 the judge sentenced him to death and gave him another chance to speak. According to the AP dispatch, "Mr. Brown immediately rose, and in a clear, distinct voice" denied everything except for his "design" to "free slaves."[33] The AP reporter would soon telegraph across the country that as Brown spoke, "perfect quiet prevailed." Brown said, "I see a book kissed, which I suppose to be the Bible, or at least the New Testament, which teaches me that all things whatsoever I would that men should do to me, I should do even so to them." Brown continued, "It teaches me, further, to remember them that are in bonds, as bound with them. Now, if it is deemed necessary that I should forfeit my life for the furtherance of the ends of justice, and mingle my blood further with the blood of my children, and with blood of millions in this slave country—whose rights are disregarded by wicked, cruel and unjust enactments, I say let it be done." For his national audience, thanks to the press, Brown had put Virginia and the rest of the slave South on trial with him.

Except for the *Herald,* Brown's speeches and courtroom demeanor seemed to change the tenor of the northern, antislavery press, which had presented a mixed image of Brown, beginning a media transformation of him from madman to martyr. A *Boston Evening Transcript* editorial, while calling Brown "misguided and unfortunate," said that even those without sympathy for him "are deeply moved by his undaunted pluck and martyr spirit."[34] Similarly a November 5 *New York Tribune* excerpt read, "[Brown] is really a man of imposing appearance, and neither his tattered garments, the rents in which were caused by sword-thrusts, nor his scarred face, can detract from the manliness of his [illegible]. He is always composed, and every trace of disquietude has left him." The *Enquirer*'s editor would have none of it and dismissed Brown's verbal theatrics by calling him a "humbler" follower of the Republican Party merely reciting words from its abolitionist "orators."[35]

As northern editorial sympathy grew, some expressed concern that Brown did not fully comprehend what he faced. A November 3 *New York Times* editorial questioned Brown's understanding of the crimes against him and expressed a worry that his execution would only cause greater trouble: "We own [*sic*] ourselves at a loss to see in what way the execution of such a man can be so brought about that it may not be converted to the inflammatory purposes of sectional partisans with whom John Brown has plainly nothing in common; and who will be as eager to make him a profitable martyr when dead, as they are to repudiate him while he still lives."[36] Some members of the southern press too believed that killing Brown would turn him into a hallowed symbol for the antislavery cause. On November 16 an editorial in the *New Orleans Daily Picayune* cautioned, for example, that if "John Brown is executed, we are warned that a great sympathy will grow up in the North; that he will be made a hero and a martyr."[37] Sympathetic northerners would hold up, as the editorial continued, "the Ossawattamie [*sic*] ruffian, murderer and robber, as worthy to be ranked with the noblest victims to freedom, and canonized as a saint and martyr."

As time passed, some northern editors turned on Virginia authorities for their handling of the affair and on their fellow southern editors for their shrill tone. An October 24 *New York Times* editorial referred to the "mad ravings of some portions of the Virginia Press ... which resemble an Indian war-whoop."[38] The following day another *New York Times* item, while calling Brown's crimes "the most heinous which can be committed against a community," cautioned against southern editors' "ferocious tone," which might transform Brown and his men into "martyrs" and "screen their enterprise from the just detestation and abhorrence which it everywhere inspires."[39]

Virginia authorities' alacrity to get rid of Brown also elicited greater sympathy for him in the antislavery press. In the October 28 *New York Tribune,* an editorial attacked "Judicial assiduity in Virginia" for "trying a wounded, sick, and suffering man in his bed."[40] The editorial condemned this "kind of legal Clinique," which was "new in this country, but not unknown, long ago, in the amiable tribunals of the middle ages." The editorial continued, "Yes! The Virginians must make the most of Brown. We hope the old man will have the decency to live until he can be made away with properly." Likewise readers of the *New York Times* learned that this "arraignment of a sufferer, stretched on his bed of pain, before a Civil Court, in a time of profound peace, is an anomaly which it will be very difficult to justify."[41]

On Halloween the headline "THE HASTE TO HANG OLD BROWN" appeared in the *New York Evening Post,* with its subsequent editorial asserting, "Of all the circumstances attending the strange affair at Harper's Ferry, one of the most discreditable to the parties on either side is the haste which is made to put an end to the life of the poor maimed lunatic Brown."[42] The editorial applauded Brown for his "calmest courage, the most unflinching resolution, the most perfect presence of mind." The next day an editorial in the newspaper dripped with sarcasm as it noted, "It was a great piece of forbearance to allow those mutilated prisoners a trial at all; and such a trial was hurried through at railroad speed."[43] An editorial in the *Boston Evening Transcript* called "the course pursued at the trial of Old Brown a disgrace to the civilization of the age."[44] The editorial's writer asked, "Can any one read his simple, touching, and yet plucky appeal for a delay without a tear?"

Editorials in southern newspapers and the *New York Herald* remained steadfast in the face of criticism, defending Virginia's actions and their correspondents' work. An October 25 *Herald* editorial referred to the people at Charlestown as "men of honor and intelligence, free from bias and prejudice ... uninfluenced by fear," who "certainly" had "no sympathies with the fanatics who got up the outbreak."[45] In the South editors went on the defensive. A November 4 editorial in the *Charleston Courier* said, "The Evening Post and journals of the Black-Brown Republican stripe are sadly annoyed and disappointed because Brown has received a full, fair and patient trial." The writer asserted, "We invite the attention of the Post, and all other white-washing friends of Brown, to the facts which will be given in a few days concerning his doings in Kansas."

As they awaited Brown's execution, newspapers reported on his activities and his many guests, most notably his wife and northern abolitionists such as Lydia Maria Child, and the northern antislavery press published several of the man's letters. What may have struck some newspaper readers was the growing idealization of Brown in print. Two days before the execution, the *Tribune's* Charlestown correspondent described a noble Brown preparing for death: "In all his conversation Brown showed the utmost gentleness and tranquility, and a quiet courtesy withal, that contrasted rather strongly with the bearing of some of his visitors. He repeated that he was in every way reconciled to his destiny, and spoke cheerfully of what was to come upon him."[46] "During the month before he was hanged, Brown struck such a heroic pose that nearly everybody who saw him was impressed," the historian Stephen Oates has said; "even Southerners who hated him had to concede that he was a spirited old man who was not afraid to die."[47]

On execution day Brown arose at dawn, read the Bible, wrote a note to his wife, and prepared a last will and testament.[48] The *Herald* editor noted the following day that Brown "exhibited the same fortitude that has characterized his demeanor since the day of his capture at Harper's Ferry in the heat of battle, with the victims of his violence lying lifeless around him."[49] Reminiscent of the manner in which Gabriel Prosser and Denmark Vesey spoke to their men, Brown, according to a reporter at Charlestown, told two of his men, Copeland and Green, "to stand up like men and not betray their friends."[50] Brown then said goodbye to the other prisoners. When he reached the door and saw the number of armed guards, he said, "I had no idea that Gov. Wise considered my execution so important."[51] In a colorful but fabricated postexecution account in the December 5 *New York Tribune,* the correspondent described the scene: "The prisoner sat upon the box which contained his coffin, [and] although pale from confinement seemed strong."[52] As he sat in the wagon pulled by "two white horses," Brown remarked, "This is a beautiful country." The following stirring words are what the *Tribune's* correspondent wrote during Brown's final moments at the jailhouse: "As he stepped out of the door a black woman, with her little child in arms, stood near his way. The twain were of the despised race, for whose emancipation and elevation to the dignity of children of God, he was about to lay down his life. . . . He stopped for a moment in his course, stooped over and, with the tenderness of one whose love is as broad as the brotherhood of man, kissed it affectionately." The incident described, while sure to stir the emotions of Brown's supporters, did not happen, as Andrew Hunter, Brown's prosecuting attorney, later explained: "That whole story about his kissing a negro child as he went out of the jail is utterly and absolutely false from beginning to end. . . . Nothing of the kind occurred—nothing of the sort could have occurred. He was surrounded by soldiers, and no negro could get access to him."[53] The *Herald* correspondent described a more likely scenario, saying that Brown was the first person to reach the top of the scaffold and that "he was swung off at fifteen minutes past eleven."[54]

By the December 2 hanging, the media transformation of Brown in the northern antislavery press from madman to martyr was complete. A Boston editorial called the Harper's Ferry events "reckless" and "foolish" but said that Brown's "offence is that of risking his life for the welfare of strangers, and those of an outlawed race."[55] The previous day an *Evening Post* editorial said that "Brown's ends were in themselves just and generous; but his methods of obtaining them were misguided and foolish"; it continued, "Virginia brands Old Brown as a wretch; the opinion of the South execrates him; but conscience reverses their decision; and history, forgetting the errors of his judgment in the contemplation of his unfaltering courage, of his dignified and manly deportment in the face of death, and of the nobleness of his alms, will record his name among those of its martyrs and heroes."[56] According to an *Evening Post* editorial headlined "The Execution and Its Effects," Americans should admire Brown's "heroism," "fortitude," and "hatred of oppression": "The death of a criminal on the gallows of whom half the nation speaks tenderly, and whose last hours the prayers and fastings of many thousands of sincere religious men have sought to hallow is certainly not an incident to be dismissed with newspaper paragraphs. It is an event in our national history which warrants every thoughtful man amongst us in pondering over it deeply."[57]

A December 2 *New York Times* editorial comment referred to Brown as "the hero, the victim, the martyr, the murderer." A separate editorial in the same edition called it "strange and sad" that Brown's execution required "five thousand soldiers" in one part of the country while in another "the bells of churches will be tolling, and the voices of Christian congregations lifted" to honor Brown.[58] A sympathetic Horace Greeley wrote in his *New York Tribune* on December 3, the day after the execution, "Slavery has killed John Brown." Greeley asserted, "Thirty Millions of Americans—including the Four or Five Millions of Slaves—are talking and thinking of John Brown—of his daring, his purpose, his defeat, and his death." The editor concluded, "History will accord an honored niche to Old John Brown." The man's death did little to assuage the feelings of southern slave owners. Editorials in their newspapers following the execution suggested that all that had happened—from Harper's Ferry to John Brown's execution—was nothing more than a cautionary tale, and they warned southerners to brace themselves against the growing abolitionist menace.[59]

"'Tis Done" was the headline for a December 6 *Richmond Enquirer* editorial in which the editor wrote, "Virginia has vindicated her outraged laws by the execution of John Brown, the leader of the Harper's Ferry raid." Citing "Demoniac Letters" to Governor Wise asking for Brown's pardon, the writer expressed the belief that they only exemplified the "demoniac spirit that prevails among Northern men—not all—God Forbid, but those whose morbid appetites for blood have been whetted by the stimulating influences of the prayers and saint-like doctrines preached by the [noted abolitionists] Beechers and Cheevers and other such presumptuous servants of God." On the day following the execution, an editorial comment in the *Charleston Courier* warned against future insurrections in Virginia: "If there should be found upon the soil of Virginia those who would dare to attempt to defeat the ends of justice, we are confident that the strong arms and stout hearts of the yeomanry and military of that ancient Commonwealth would quickly crush those who may be engaged in it."[60] On December 1 a *New Orleans Daily Picayune* editorial likewise noted, "There is no doubt that John Brown will die bravely. Courage on the scaffold is the trait of men of his physical organization, and his rugged habits of living, whether they be saints or criminals."[61] The editorial called northern abolitionists' hatred of slavery "moral treason" while backhandedly praising Brown by calling it "treason without his courage, his frenzy without his nerve." In the end it would be Brown's final message to the nation—in the form of a note dated December 2 and handed to a jailer as he left for the scaffold—that proved the most prophetic: "I John Brown am now quite *certain* that the crimes of this *guilty land; will* never be purged *away* but with Blood. I had *as I now think: vainly* flattered myself that without *very much* bloodshed; it might be done."[62]

Conclusion

John Brown, the once marginalized abolitionist figure, suddenly found himself in the eye of a media storm over Harper's Ferry. Over nearly seven weeks of news coverage, he remained a dangerous and deluded abolitionist's pawn in the southern press. In the North, especially among the New York and Boston antislavery editors, he morphed into a hero for the cause. Such divergent views of a single man indicated how divisive slavery had become in the United States. Southerners, with their economic, political, and cultural interests at stake, could not countenance any sympathy for Brown, a man who threatened these interests (as did others like him). As the newspaper coverage suggested, their harsh, reactionary measures taken against Brown in the form of a quick trial and execution only prompted some northern editors to criticize sharply those actions and to drop any pretense of having sympathy for what happened at Harper's Ferry.

PART II ⚹ MEDIA DISCOURSES ABOUT SLAVERY

It took generations for American slavery to develop into its unique, self-perpetuating brand of human bondage. And, once the United States achieved nationhood, its political leadership failed to resolve the inherently tragic problem that slavery posed to the country, pushing it toward crisis. For some black Americans and their white allies this left them with little recourse except to attempt to throw off the bonds of slavery. When this occurred, the nation's newspapers gave notice, informing mostly white readers about the troubles and about other black Americans, who had no voice in national public affairs. Adding to all of this was the changing nature of newspapers, both in technology and in content, transitioning from the partisan press era to the age of the penny press and becoming a true mass medium. By 1859, because of the telegraph, it was instant. All this occurred as the United States transformed from a relatively small, postcolonial nation to one encompassing huge amounts of land.

As the news content from 1800, 1811, 1822, and 1831 revealed, national discussions about slavery remained fairly united in the view that it was a base system and a tragic leftover from colonial days. In the years following Nat Turner's revolt and as the nation grew, southern society came under increasing pressure to end slavery, prompting reactionary responses from that region that became blaring defenses of slavery, an institution now firmly imbedded in the fabric of southern agricultural and cultural life. As a result of these defenses, southern elites and their conservative Democratic supporters, including newspaper editors, were helping to move the United States toward a state of political intransigence over the South's peculiar institution.

Part 2 of this book moves from that general history and contextualization about American slavery, slave revolts, and slave conspiracies to an examination of the media discourses that emerged about them and about black Americans in general. The discourse of slavery's enemies constructed slave rebels and their abettors as threats to slavery and, by extension, the state. Following that a significant and complex media discourse involved an all-consuming, irrational fear that white people had regarding the potential or real violence that black people could inflict on them. Such fears had their grounding in the stories about panicked whites fleeing from Santo Domingo (Haiti) after the start of its 1791 slave revolt. This discourse of racial panic also possessed a notable feature in that it always indicated how any slave trouble triggered immediate and severe responses from the white community to destroy slavery's enemy, maintain the institution, and preserve the racial hierarchy. A third media discourse, that of slavery as a threat to the nation, placed slavery within the context of a national discussion in which extreme sectionalism began to dominate the talk about slavery, and the diminution of America's cherished ideals concerning basic civil liberties became an acceptable choice among conservatives to silence any threat to slavery. This damage eventually became irreparable.

It is worth considering again a general definition of "discourse" as involving political and ideological practices that bind societies together and help their members gain meaning about the world around them. As an ideological practice, a discourse, as Fairclough puts it in *Discourse and Social Change,* "constitutes, naturalizes, sustains and changes significations of the world from diverse positions in power relations" (67). Discourse is revealed through the stories we tell one another. Often, but not always, the powerful determine how those stories get generated and which of those stories get told time and again. Fairclough has identified three constraints in power relationships that discourse reveals: 1) content constraints about what was said and done; 2) relational constraints between those entering into discourse; and 3) subject restraints, which concern the position a person occupies (see Fairclough, *Language and Power,* 46). As it concerned slavery—an agricultural labor system that relied on a class of enslaved workers to sustain it—it benefited (primarily) an elite group of white Americans whose political influence came to dominate the political landscape and represent a conservative view of states' and property rights in the United States. Yet, another group of elites with their long-standing antislavery views became more vocal about their opposition to slavery. In both cases, among those elites were newspaper editors who selected story content for their readers and who, in the decades long after the Constitutional Convention, came to the defense or condemnation of slavery.

Thus as America's political, geographic, and cultural landscape began to change in the decades before the Civil War, two diverging political ideologies— one representing the conservative, proslavery view and the other a progressive, antislavery stance—began to compete. Over time the emphases that these two views had in newspaper content signaled the shifting and competing discourses about slavery. Whereas the conservative view remained steadfast in support of slavery, the competing, antislavery view, one that found its place in powerful northern newspapers, transitioned from a grudging tolerance for slavery to outright hostility toward it.

In considering media discourses from the past, it must be remembered that in general, eighteenth- and nineteenth-century newspapers were edited by white men for white readers, so it is not particularly surprisingly that they reflected discourses holding to America's racist ideology that marginalized and demeaned African American blacks, both free and slave. The stories contained in those pages, while disconcerting to a present-day reader, would have made sense to white Americans who, for a variety of theological, philosophical, and scientific reasons, had come to view black peoples as inferior and incapable of enjoying the fruits of liberty. For decades after the Revolutionary War, members of America's most powerful political class were slave owners who controlled or at least influenced the southern (and to some extent the northern) press. In addition these elites had strong cultural and especially economic interests in maintaining slavery despite the increasing moral pressures to end it. Their cultural and economic interests were vested in property rights and racially motivated to keep black people as inferior beings. Therefore media discourses reflected those ideas and their underlying racist ideology. It is also worth remembering that these media discourses were constituted by white men and seldom concerned those most affected by slavery, namely black slaves and other black Americans, whose voices were almost always silent in the mainstream press and in the talk about slavery.

6 ❧ Dealing with Slavery's Enemies

In antebellum America the black slave rebel was always an enemy who, because of his race and actions, represented a serious internal threat to the strict social order that slavery created. Another enemy of slavery, this one representing an external threat, was the white person who helped slaves in their fight for freedom. While the black rebel was considered especially dangerous, the external, white enemy represented something far worse because this person had betrayed his or her race, an act that was considered beyond the pale in slave society. Another enemy class, free blacks, became a target just by their very existence in slave society: they were individuals considered grotesque social anomalies and lived on the margins in both slave and free societies.

Throughout the antebellum years, members of America's slave-owning class enjoyed cultural, political, and economic power that translated into the power to guide, direct, and control social discourse. For decades after the Revolutionary War, their views aligned with those of most Americans who agreed that any violent threats to slavery could be considered threats to the nation's well-being, keeping in mind that the Constitution protected slavery. Still, an underlying antislavery discourse always existed in the country and gained momentum in the early years of the nineteenth century, putting pressure on the institution and its supporters, who reacted strongly against slavery's enemies, regardless of the degree of opposition. Certainly the slave rebel was always a threat to slavery and to the social order. In 1800, 1811, 1822, and 1831 this enemy was always black. By 1859 and John Brown's raid, slavery's enemies became external threats in the guise of abolitionists. The white abolitionist had replaced the black rebel as the true enemy. By the time Brown died, slavery's supporters had enlarged their list of enemies to include any antislavery voice, including the young Republican Party and the editors and politicians who supported it. To the proslavery factions, the enemies of slavery were simply enemies of the state.

The media discourse on "slavery's enemies" was informed by concepts from psychology and sociology that suggested the enemy was not created by chance but rather served vested social interests, in this instance those of America's powerful slave-owning elites. The political psychologist Vamik D. Volkan has suggested that "people actually use and 'need' enemies as external stabilizers of their sense of identity and inner control" and that they serve as a negative reflection of themselves and provide them with a "heroic" sense of self.[1] Put another way, enemies form communal bonds among people. In creating the enemy class, the enemy must be identified and its negative qualities legitimized through cultural and social conduits such as the mass media. Once created, they, as Robert W. Rieber and Robert J. Kelly have noted, "occupy a specific position" in that social structure "that is fashioned to evoke responses that dehumanize."[2] Over time, though, what defines an enemy can shift, and enemies can be reimagined and reconstituted.[3] Nations, for example, often construct new enemies as former ones are vanquished and eliminated.[4] Still, once enemies become part of a communal consciousness (and status quo), they require little intellectual, psychological, or sociological effort to maintain their status. Destroying them becomes an imperative. Such was the case for slavery's enemies.

To construct enemies, the focus must be on their noxious qualities, which include racial, linguistic, religious, cultural, ethnic, and physical attributes that become repellent to a public conditioned to understand how different these enemies are from them and how dangerous these enemies are to their safety and well-being.[5] To make this construction work, the enemy must be objectified so as to lose human qualities and become a threatening "thing" worthy of destruction.[6] Such ideas become central in understanding the discourse of slavery's enemies and how they manifested in the discourse found in newspapers. Invariably the southern slave-owning elites, whether consciously or not, worked to construct the black slave rebels and the later abolitionists as enemies and existential threats to their way of life and to white America.[7] During slave troubles between 1800 and 1859, America's newspapers reflected this discourse and constructed slave enemies as 1) religious fanatics; 2) betrayers of race, which included whites who directly abetted the slave rebels, such as the abolitionists and other antislavery whites; or 3) social anomalies, namely free black persons living in slave society.

The Enemy as Religious Fanatic

Within the discourse of slavery's enemies, one element that would have made sense to most nineteenth-century newspaper readers involved religion. Because nineteenth-century America was a deeply Christian nation composed of primarily Protestant denominations, it seems that clues for what had occurred would suggest religion (or some corruption of Christianity) had played a role in precipitating the trouble. This seemed logical because slave owners and other whites who had already relied on religious rationales to justify slavery's rightness would seek similar rationales as easy explanations for slaves' behavior, believing that slaves would not have acted without this powerful influence on them. Therefore it followed that the slave rebels had devised corrupt and debased versions of Christian doctrine to convince other slaves to follow their path. Seeking a religious explanation for slave troubles allowed slavery's advocates to ignore the systemic violence inflicted on black people and to perpetuate their strange brand of cognitive dissonance about slavery in America.

During the partisan press era especially, the coverage of Prosser, Vesey, and Turner connected religion as superstition or fanaticism to the slave rebels, considering it a major contributor to their actions. In *The River Flows On: Black Resistance, Culture, and Identity Formation in Early America*, Walter C. Rucker forcefully points out that the black rebel slaves, such as Prosser, Vesey, and Turner, used religion to influence slaves but that this religion was not necessarily based on Christian ideas. Rucker argues that slave rebels had knowledge of their African religious heritage, including its "folkloric traditions," which survived the passage to America and helped them in their attempts at resistance to slavery.[8] This amalgamation of African traditions, passing as Christian ones, would certainly raise alarm among a white, Christian population who likely viewed them as merely corrupted versions of their own ideas of what Christianity was supposed to be. In the later case of John Brown, his religious fanaticism had strong Christian roots that were nurtured by his abolitionist influences.

Gabriel Prosser was likely a Christian who used his ancestral traditions and recruited followers who could spiritually influence other slaves to his advantage.[9] Regardless the newspaper accounts ignored the African connections, instead warning that dangerous Christian religious influences affected the slaves. After the revelations of his conspiracy appeared, a letter dated September 23, 1859, in the October 1 *New York Daily Advertiser* identified this influence when the writer urged caution in the "pulpits" about preaching ideas of liberty "without any sort of reserve."[10] A September 20 letter in the *Massachusetts Spy* and the *Virginia Argus* said that religion or superstition may have led to the conspiracy's failure, noting that on the night the rebellion was to commence, Gabriel's brother Martin—who "was acquainted with the Holy Scriptures"— told conspirators that "their cause was similar to that of the Israelites who had escaped from the Egyptians; and that, if their cause was good, God would help them and give strength to one hundred of them, to destroy a thousand of their enemies, etc."[11] The writer told readers that the plan failed because "terror spread among them" after "a tremendous thunder storm which took place about the time when the negroes assembled." He asserted that the superstitious slaves deemed it "a judgment from Heaven."

The discourse of slavery's enemies, as it concerned religion, also indicated that certain organized religious organizations adversely affected the black slaves' minds. Stories about them gained special prominence in news coverage of Vesey's 1822 conspiracy in Charleston. Here the link was made between the slave rebel and the city's African Methodist Episcopal (AME) Church, which was increasingly viewed as a growing menace within Charleston's white community. "Though mostly African in outlook, members of the African Methodist Episcopal (A.M.E.) churches in Charleston," according to Rucker, "not only identified in a positive way with the African past, they also identified with a denomination that supported resistance to white racism and oppression."[12] Certainly the AME Church would pose a distinct threat for its strange brand of Christianity with African roots and for encouraging church members to resist slavery. Five years earlier, for example, city leaders made clear their intolerance for the church by ordering the arrest of 469 members of the AME, fearing they fomented antislavery thought.[13] After the 1822 trials, Charleston's mayor James Hamilton, who blamed "religious fanaticism" for the plot, observed that a "majority" of conspirators "belonged to the African Church."[14] An item in the October 3 *Maryland Gazette* was an "Extract of a letter to a gentleman in Boston," dated August 19 from Charleston.[15] In it the gentleman specifically condemned the AME Church for its suspected role in the plot. He reasoned that the slaves had "no reason to rebel" and that these "deluded creatures" suffered "partly from religious fanaticism." The writer observed, "With scarce an exception" the participants were "methodists who had seceded from the white methodists." According to him, the plot had proved "satisfactorily that religion, in the hands of the ignorant and uninstructed, is the fruitful source of delusions."

After the Vesey conspiracy, if newspapers did not specifically target the AME Church, their items still connected religion to the rebellion. The August 3 *Newport (R.I.) Mercury* said, "Religion and superstition were used by the more cunning to delude the incredulous Africans in the plot."[16] The writer commented that one participant, Gullah Jack, performed "witchcraft" on his misguided followers. Thirty-seven years after Vesey's death and following the Harper's Ferry raid, a December 1, 1859, item in James Gordon Bennett's *New York Herald* reminded readers of the Charleston plot and referred to Vesey as "the chief and prime mover of the conspiracy" (something 1822 Charleston newspapers had not). This story warned readers of the dangers of religious manipulation, accusing Vesey of convincing his followers to conspire against whites by "*removing the scruples of the religious by the gravest perversion of the Scriptures, and influencing the bold by all the savage fascinations of blood, beauty, and booty.*"[17]

Decades before those words in the *Herald* appeared, anyone reading accounts about Nat Turner in 1831 would have considered him a religious zealot claiming to have had visions and to be a prophet. In the coverage he was constructed as a deluded and murderous fanatic. The writer of a *Richmond Whig* item appearing in the September 7 *National Intelligencer* described Turner as a "shrewd fellow, [who] reads, writes, and preaches; and by various artifices had acquired great influence over the minds of the wretched beings whom he has led into destruction."[18] Calling him a "fanatic" who counted on divine intervention and "concocted" his plan "under the cloak of religion," this writer concluded that he wanted "revenge against the whites, as the enslavers of himself and his race." Trial testimony noted that Turner "had been for some time mediating this plan of mischief" and sought to control the minds of "his more ignorant comrades."[19]

Ignoring slavery as a possible cause of his actions, the newspaper focused on Nat Turner's religious fanaticism in its rationalization of his horrific deeds to white readers. A Jerusalem writer, whose letter appeared in the *New York Evening Post,* called him "a preacher and prophet" among the slaves, adding that Turner was "stimulated exclusively by fanatical revenge, and perhaps misled by some hallucination of his imagined spirit of prophecy."[20] Turner was seen as manipulating followers through the power of religion, and local Richmond newspapers profiled him as a "fellow, of the deepest cunning, who for years has been endeavoring to acquire an influence over the minds of these deluded wretches."[21] The writer said that the literate Turner hoped "to operate upon the superstitious hopes and fears of others." Readers of the September 12 *New York Evening Post* found a "letter from Southampton" that corrected an error about Turner's legitimate religious credentials: "Nat. Turner is very improperly represented to be a Baptist preacher. I wish you to see the Editors of your papers on this subject, and say to them, that, that account from the best information I can obtain, is an entire mistake. He never was a member of the Baptist or any other Church; he assumed that character of his own accord and has been for several years one of those fanatical scoundrels, that pretended to be divinely inspired, of bad character, and never countenanced, except by very few of his deluded black associates. To give this explanation, is an act of justice, to which I am sure they will readily accord."[22] A writer living near Southampton observed that Turner pretended "to be divinely inspired" and that "he announced to the Blacks, that he should baptize himself on a particular day, and that whilst in the water, a dove would descend from Heaven and perch on his head."[23] The writer, who was from Jerusalem, described Turner as using "every means in his power, to acquire an ascendancy over the minds of the slaves . . . he used all the arts familiar to such pretenders to deceive, delude, and overawe their minds."

Because white readers would not countenance any sympathetic view of Turner or his religious beliefs, newspaper stories invariably constructed him as a radical and dangerous fanatic. A *Richmond Compiler* item in the October 10 *New York Evening Post* read, "Nat has been a long time a fanatic as well as imposter."[24] The author expressed outrage that Turner had the "impiety to declare himself inferior to Jesus Christ alone!" He "never belonged to any established church," yet he "attempted to pass himself off as an inspired prophet." A letter from Southampton dated November 1 said about Turner, "A more gloomy fanatic you have never heard of" who provided "with great candour, a history of the operations of his mind for many years past," speaking of "the signs he saw; the spirit he conversed with; of his prayers, failings, and watchings, and of his supernatural powers and gifts, in curing diseases, controlling the weather, etc."[25]

Like the accusations against the AME during Vesey's conspiracy, the discourse of slavery's enemies at the time of Nat Turner held black churches accountable for alienating slaves' affections. For its October 18, 1831, edition, the *Richmond Enquirer* resurrected an 1825 item from the *Southern Religious Telegraph* in which the writer claimed that "ignorant preachers" injured "religion" by using their influence for self-serving purposes: "It is most obvious to the careful observer that [slaves] are withdrawing more and more from those ministrations where they can learn the true character of Christianity; and insist, with increasing pertinacity, on holding meetings in their own way, and having preachers of their own color."[26] The writer continued, "The preachers among them, although extremely ignorant (often unable to read a verse in the Bible, or a line in the hymn-book) are frequently shrewd, cunning men. They see what influence misdirected religious feeling gives them over their brethren, and they take advantage of it—many of them feel their importance and assume the part of men of great consequence."

After Turner's death, the discourse of slavery's enemies continued to construct him as a religious fanatic. One *Richmond Enquirer* item referred to "this murderous banditti," attacking his character for "calling himself a Prophet, and pretending to receive immediate revelations from Heaven."[27] In the writer's view, "true religion," as practiced by white people and advocating the maintenance of slavery, "has its seat in the heart, and has the effect of subduing all these horrid, natural passions and inclinations." Instead of holding to true religious practice, Turner and his men gave themselves up to the "natural lusts and passions of their depraved and wicked hearts." An editorial comment in the *Enquirer* urged the suppression of religious freedom among slaves, saying that the "case of Nat Turner warns us [that] no black-man ought to be permitted to turn a Preacher through the country. The law must be enforced—or the tragedy of Southampton appeals to us in vain."[28]

Even though Nat Turner was black and John Brown white (and also considered a betrayer of his race), they shared similar treatment in how newspapers reinforced ideas about their religious fanaticism. As in the case of Turner, Brown's religious inclinations dominated constructions of him in both northern and southern newspapers. "[Brown] says he has had rifles leveled at him, knives at his throat," the October 27 *New York Tribune* reported, adding that he "has made no confession; but, on the contrary, says he has full confidence in the goodness of God, and is confident that he will rescue him from the perils that surround him: and his life in as great peril as it now is, but that God has always been at his side. He knows God is with him, and fears nothing."[29]

The *Enquirer*, as well as the rest of the southern press, could not countenance Brown's religious justification for the raid and considered him, rather than a fanatic, a deluded victim of abolitionism. On November 1 the *Richmond Enquirer* reported, "Brown still cherishes the idea that the Lord will release him."[30] A later editorial in the November 4 *Enquirer* said, "If Brown is a crazed fanatic, irresponsible either in morals or law, there are yet guilty parties. He is then the agent of wicked principals."[31] Three weeks later another item in the Richmond newspaper claimed that Brown "refuses to receive any ministers who countenance slavery, telling them to go home and read their Bibles."[32] Another quote had Brown saying to a proslavery minister paying him a visit, "My dear sir, you know nothing of Christianity."[33] Such an admonition would have shocked the sensibilities of a white slaveholder or anyone else who used the Bible to justify slavery.

The media constructions of Brown's "monomania" and sanity as being affected by his religious fervor were divided along geographic lines. For Gov. Henry Wise and his southern newspaper editor allies, Brown needed to be sane so that he could be executed without offending anyone's conscience or violating Virginia law. To a sympathetic northern press, proving Brown insane would save him from the noose.[34] Early on, Governor Wise may have intended to inculcate opinions of Brown's sanity when he pronounced after his interview that Brown was no "madman" but rather the "best bundle of nerves I ever saw." Wise's comments deflected the insanity argument and protected "Virginia's honor," as the historian Robert McGlone has argued.[35] Ironically members of the abolition movement also attested to Brown's sanity, preferring to think of him as a "Puritan warrior" rather than a fanatic.[36] Brown ultimately rejected any insanity defense: "I am perfectly unconscious of insanity, and I reject, so far as I am capable, any attempts to interfere in my behalf on that score."[37]

The Enemy as Betrayer of Race

Because John Brown was a white man who led an invasion into slave territory, his was the most unconscionable act to the white southerner. It was one thing for slaves to rebel but quite another for a white man to help them. This betrayer of race construction reveals another discursive level used when slave troubles occurred and is another element of the discourse of slavery's enemies. Just as white elites, newspaper editors, and politicians blamed misguided or corrupt religious influences as affecting the slave rebels, they also suggested that white involvement must be a plausible cause of slave rebellion. Believing as they did in Negro inferiority, these elites could not believe that blacks were intelligent or courageous enough to devise successful rebellion schemes, so abetting white collaborators made sense to them. Therefore any aid given to rebelling or escaping slaves was deemed a violation of the social order. In one instance during the sentencing of a white man caught helping an escaping slave, a South Carolina judge referred to white abolitionists, arguing that any help given a slave seeking freedom only served to harm society: "Slaves are capable of being seduced, swerved from the allegiance to their masters; capable of evil purposes as well as good. . . . When, therefore, you or any other person shall succeed in corrupting a slave, in swerving him from allegiance, what have you done but turn loose an enemy to society in its very bosom."[38]

Of all the events considered, with the exception of John Brown's plot, newspaper items about Gabriel Prosser's conspiracy most often contained suggestions of white involvement, especially of the French. Prosser and his fellow conspirators might have known about the Adams administration's troubled relations with France and hoped for, as Herbert Aptheker has suggested, "assistance from France once their own rebellion was well under way."[39] Still, these accounts also reflected the partisan-press-era bias that was often politically motivated to damage the reputations of the Federalists or the anti-Federalists, especially during the contentious 1800 election, when the Prosser conspiracy unfolded. Any French involvement in the conspiracy would have been terribly embarrassing to Virginia's governor James Monroe—a Jeffersonian Republican—who belonged to a party strongly favoring ties to France.[40]

Details about the conspiracy in the pro-Federalist newspapers, when referring to white involvement, frequently made a French connection that would serve the political goals of the Adams Federalist administration. The Federalists blamed the 1800 conspiracy on anti-Federalist Jeffersonian Democrats' "French babble" with their constant call for "Equality, Fraternity and Human Rights," according to Joseph Cephas Carroll.[41] The pro-Federalist Philadelphia, New York, and Massachusetts newspapers, for example, contained one item, dated September 16, 1800, from Richmond warning that "the French principle of Liberty and Equality has been infused into the minds of the negroes, and that the incautious and intemperate use of these words by some whites amongst us, have inspired them with hopes of success."[42]

Other anti-French items appeared. A letter from Fredericksburg noted, "It is very certain, however, from all that has been discovered, that this dreadful conspiracy originates with some vile French jacobins, aided and abetted by some of our own profligate and abandoned democracts [sic]."[43] The letter said that conspirators hoped fifty thousand men would join them in a week, adding that it was learned at the trials that "two Frenchmen planned the plot" and that "in the general massacre of white males . . . , not a Frenchman was to be touched." Similarly an item from the *Richmond Gazette* of September 16 in Philadelphia, New York, and Massachusetts newspapers implicated "two . . . terrible Frenchmen," whom the writer said, "are yet unknown."[44] The *Philadelphia Gazette* editor added that the two Frenchmen intended "to spread murder and desolation throughout southern states" and to proceed "on a system of the most extensive ruin," whereby some of the "unhappy people of the southern States" would be sacrificed.

On September 24 the pro-Federalist *Philadelphia Gazette* editor made a more sweeping statement about the connections between the slave conspirators and the Jeffersonian Republicans, suggesting that the success of these blacks to achieve their goals would (perhaps) "effect a revolution in the administration," a clear anti-Federalist aim. However, the editor argued that even if the "blacks . . . were to break the 'Lilliputian ties' of bondage, by the indiscriminate murder of the whites, and . . . then erect a republic for themselves," their political power would be nil and of no use to the anti-Federalists. Holding to a nineteenth-century racist view of blacks, the editor reasoned, "The jacobins [blacks] are, politically speaking, 'hewers of wood, and drawers of water': the blacks are slaves to the planters." They could never enjoy (nor master) political power, he emphasized.[45]

In the discourse of slavery's enemies, another linkage of whites abetting slave rebels at the time of the 1800 conspiracy appeared in an interesting item about James Callender, Thomas Jefferson's paid scandalmonger and later critic.[46] The content also served political ends. "An Extract of a Letter from Washington" in the September 25, 1800, *Philadelphia Gazette* asserted that the anti-Federalist Callender's "artfully written hand-bills" inspired the "rising of the negroes." The writer said he hoped that "all the *people* of that city begin to think they were wrong in their designs against Federalism." Richmond citizens should focus on the "busy designing Foreigners [French] who have lately come among us," according to the writer.[47] As he sat in a Richmond jail on sedition charges, Callender responded in a letter dated October 3 to the *Virginia Argus.* Attacking "Andrew Brown," the editor of the Philadelphia newspaper, he wrote, "It is needless to tell any person in Richmond, that every syllable of the above story is a direct lie," adding, "I have long known Andrew Brown as a very zealous partizan of the present [Adams] administration; but it did not occur to me, that he was capable of baseness like this."[48] Callender said that "something has been said respecting French people of colour," but "if an idea so murderous, as that of promoting an African conspiracy can have entered into the head of any white man, he must have been a Federalist. An insurrection, at the present critical moment, by the negroes of the southern states, would have thrown everything into confusion, and consequently, it was to have prevented the choice of electors in the whole or greater part of the States to the South of the Potomac. Such a disaster must have tended directly to injure the interest of Mr. Jefferson, and to promote the slender possibility of Mr. Adams." Callender added that he did not believe "any white person whatever was concerned in the business" but that if a white man had a part in the conspiracy, only someone such as "Alexander Hamilton, the theoretical incendiary of Pittsbourg [*sic*], and the grand Patriarch of American calamities," could have been behind it.[49]

After Turner's revolt, early reports suggested white involvement too. A *New York Journal of Commerce* item claimed that the insurrectionists consisted of "eight negroes and two whites."[50] Later a *Journal of Commerce* item in the September 2 *Boston Evening Transcript* and headlined "INSURRECTION IN VIRGINIA" stated, "Any whites who might be involved must be "monsters in human shape, undoubtedly." Those thoughts echoed an earlier report in the August 29 *New*

York Evening Post that said "two white men" might be involved.[51] The writer stated, "We earnestly hope it is not true. If desperate men from among the whites, with the advantages of knowledge and intelligence belonging to their cast, are to stir up the slaves of the southern states to rebellion, to give them an organization, and to direct their movements, the situation of the planters in those parts where the slave population is largest is more unsafe than has yet been dreamed of." Such language shows the belief that whites might have been capable of such plots and that if so, they were a dangerous lot indeed.

While the accusations that appeared in the press after Prosser's conspiracy were deeply partisan, later stories about slave troubles that involved white connections, especially abolitionists, identified them as betrayers of their race. After the Vesey conspiracy collapsed, one item suggested that while abolitionists per se were not to blame, their ways of thinking should be held to account.[52] In "Extract of a Letter to a Gentleman in Boston" in the October 3 *Maryland Gazette,* the writer said the conspiracy sprang "partly from the instigation of base incendiaries, who form a pretended humanity."[53] According to the writer, these "base incendiaries" who interfered "in our domestic concerns, actually planned and concerted to desolate our city with conflagration, rapine and indiscriminate murder."

By 1859 slave owners had come to despise abolitionists, viewing them as enemies of the state in the Harper's Ferry aftermath. After John Brown, editorials expressing intense hatred of abolitionists and their supporters seared southern newspaper pages. Ten days after Virginia militia and federal troops secured the engine house and took John Brown into custody, a *Philadelphia Press* item in the *Charleston Mercury* said that Brown's raid represented slavery's natural outcome and abolitionists' work: "The dragon's teeth which have been so profusely sown, have sprung up and are bearing their natural fruit."[54] Despite the fact that most northerners were not abolitionists,[55] much southern newspaper coverage conflated abolitionism with antislavery sentiment, implicating sympathizers such as the Republican Party and editors such as Horace Greeley in the raid.

The abolitionist cause found no sanction in the southern press, in which editorials universally portrayed them as marauding brutes who, as the *Charleston Courier* editor noted, "would have rejoiced to see children murdered, women abused and rivers of blood flowing."[56] Later a piece of correspondence from a writer who signed his piece "Squatter" described abolitionists as "resolute, determined, and utterly unscrupulous" and warned *Courier* readers, "The South will have to gird up her loins to meet an enemy so powerful and so insidious."[57] A *New Orleans Daily Picayune* writer called Brown's men "desperadoes" who belonged to the "extreme section of the Abolition party," but he also warned that they were the "vanguard" of such a movement.[58]

Southern editors and politicians appeared certain that abolitionists had a role in the planning and execution of the Harper's Ferry raid and were planning more attacks. The editorial "NEGROPHILLISM—ITS EFFECTS" in the *Richmond Enquirer* made the claim, "Northern negrophillism has supplanted patriotism, not only throughout Abolition ranks, but has invaded, to some extent, the Northern Democracy."[59] The writer called abolition a "loathsome disease" that had "corrupted public sentiment" and become "destructive to public interest . . . [and] under its debasing and degrading influence, conservative [proslavery] men have kept away from the polls, fanatics become mad men, and public journals seem to have lost not only their distinctive political principles, but even their balance of common sense." An October 22 *New Orleans Daily Picayune* editorial read, "This Harper's Ferry insurrection is the reduction of [abolitionists'] principles to action. What is meant by 'irrepressible conflict between free and slave labor,' is now explained."[60] Three days later an editorial in the paper accused abolitionists and their publications of being responsible for the assault on Virginia's soil: "If we are to live together in kindness, the temper and practices which have incited the disorders must be changed, and those who indulge in them or countenance them, and to whose rash teaching the insane excesses are distinctly traceable as their sources, must be rebuked by public opinion."[61]

The discourse of slavery's enemies surfaced in the talk about prominent northern abolitionists whom southern editors targeted. Their anger was not without some justification, especially after authorities confiscated letters at the Kennedy farm addressed to Brown from men such as Gerrit Smith and Frederick Douglass as well as *New York Tribune* editor Horace Greeley. Greeley's cross-town rival James Gordon Bennett, a fierce Democratic Party loyalist and southern sympathizer, relished Greeley's connection. Bennett used the *Herald*'s pages to condemn Greeley, the Republican Party, and its leaders. Shortly after Brown's raid, one editorial referred to Republican senator William Seward as that "demagogue" and held him responsible for the raid, the "first overt act in the great drama of national disruption."[62] The genesis for Bennett's vitriol stemmed from Seward's "irrepressible conflict" speech, given a year earlier, which argued among other things the following: "It is an irrepressible conflict between opposing and enduring forces, and it means that the United States must and will, sooner or later, become, entirely a slaveholding nation or entirely a free labor nation."[63] In Bennett's view, such words incited unstable men such as Brown: "The immediate moral, and the immediate legal responsibility for the bloody affair at Harper's Ferry rests, we believe upon W. H. Seward and his teachings of incessant war upon slavery; for is not Seward the great Apollo of the republican party, and was not Brown only one of its faithful instruments in his 'Kansas work'?"[64]

The southern, Democratic press seized the chance to condemn Seward and his ilk. The editor of the *Richmond Enquirer,* borrowing Seward's phrase, wrote on October 21 that the "irrepressible conflict was initiated at Harper's Ferry, and though there, for the time suppressed, yet no man is able to say when or where it will begin again or where it will end."[65] A *Charleston Mercury* item urged Charlestonians to remember Seward's speech: "It should be understood at the South as exposing the ends sought by Black Republicans. It indicates the future of troubles we may expect under its auspices."[66] An item in the *Washington Constitution*, the Buchanan administration's political organ, connected Seward's "irrepressible conflict" doctrine to the Harper's Ferry raid.[67] In Seward's defense (and as an indication of a competing discourse about slavery) an *Albany Journal* editorial in the *New York Times* titled "An Opposition View. Who Encourages Insurrection?" said that the Democrats' and slaveholders' lies pushed John Brown to action: "Curses, like chickens," the writer noted, "come home to roost."[68]

Seward was just one target. An October 20 *New York Herald* item said that "other papers" found at the Kennedy farm implicated "Gerrit Smith, Joshua R. Giddings, Fred. Douglas, and other abolitionists and black republicans."[69] Ten days later an editorial urged President James Buchanan to "proceed to this business of extirpating this Harper's Ferry treason to the very roots," including arresting the men "who instigated, aided and encouraged 'Old Brown.'"[70]

Because of an incriminating note found at the Maryland farmhouse, Greeley was especially on the receiving end of southerners' as well as Bennett's ire. Dated April 30, 1859, the note was addressed from Greeley to John Kagi, one of Brown's men who would be killed at Harper's Ferry. In it Greeley mentioned a check sent for forty-one dollars "for seven letters from Kansas and two from Ohio."[71] The *New York Herald* extrapolated from that information that Greeley had paid Kagi to be a "correspondent of the *Tribune*." Of course Greeley denied complicity, dismissing allegations that he was somehow involved with the raid: "Don't they work that Harper's Ferry *placer* industriously?" he asked.[72] He continued, "They actually found a memorandum of Old Brown's, importing that he had once mailed $3 for THE N.Y. TRIBUNE." Greeley called this accusation of guilt by association "desperate" and "scoundrelly." His *Tribune* addressed calls for his extradition to Virginia by letting his readers know that he would be in Washington, D.C., and would gladly "step over at his own proper cost to Alexandria or any convenient point in Virginia and be examined at length" to answer any questions "concerning John Brown and his colleagues in the recent affair at Harper's Ferry."[73]

In the South editors wanted to see these enemies of slavery pay for their alleged crimes. In the October 30 *New Orleans Daily Picayune*, the editor made a "solemn appeal" to the people of the North, saying that John Brown's raid should serve as a lesson about what they owe "to the South, to the constitution, and to our common country, in its dealings with the Harper's Ferry rioters, and their counsellors, abettors and teachers."[74] Richmond editors demanded extradition for punishment of implicated abolitionists despite their denials of involvement.[75] Richmond readers learned from an October 27 *Enquirer* item "that correspondence found on Brown" showed that the "conspiracy extended throughout portions of Ohio, New York, New England, and some towns in Pennsylvania" and implicated leading abolitionists.

The *Richmond Enquirer* was particularly adamant about who shared guilt in the Brown affair. The November 1 edition said, "William H. Seward, John P. Hale, Joshua R. Giddings, Gerrit Smith and Horace Greeley, have all been more or less implicated. . . . These men are the leaders, the thinkers and the mainstay of Black Republicanism."[76] Likewise an editorial from the *Richmond Dispatch* in the November 3 *Charleston Mercury* said that leading northern abolitionists would not admit their role in the Harper's Ferry raid: "Oh! yes, they all deny it, now that it has failed. Greeley, Hale, Sanborne, Howe—every one of them will deny it; for treason is a very ugly thing." The *New Orleans Daily Picayune* editors accused the "Black Republicans" and their leaders, especially Seward, of complicity in the affair: "If the effects of the recent futile and abortive effort to carry into execution the teachings of fanaticism and sectionalism shall be to demonstrate to the teachers their own folly, ineptitude and wickedness, the events which have recently created so much excitement will not have been entirely without their use; and 'out of the nettle, danger,' we shall perhaps have 'plucked the flower, safety.'"[77] Another *Picayune* editorial urged that any coconspirators be arrested and tried for that "which the instincts of justice and humanity cry out for rigorous punishment."[78] In Charleston the *Courier's* editor suggested that the governors of New York, Connecticut, Pennsylvania, Massachusetts, and Ohio turn these conspirators over to Virginia authorities.[79]

One abolitionist who figured prominently in the discourse of slavery's enemies was New York's Gerrit Smith. He remained in the crosshairs of the proslavery press that constantly identified him as a Brown collaborator.[80] According to a *Herald* item in the October 22 *Charleston Mercury,* Smith had shifted from "moral suasion" to a call for general slave insurrection after writing an August letter that seemed to advocate slave resistance.[81] Smith "is fully aware of his complicity with the treason, and perhaps would chivalrously avow his share of the responsibility," another *New York Herald* editorial asserted, "if he were not silenced by the certain knowledge that his disclosure would involve others more criminal than himself."[82]

In New Orleans a *Picayune* editorial called Smith "naturally vain and obstinate" and stated the belief that as Smith's mental health began to deteriorate under the public pressure, it was because "he began early to think himself called to regulate the affairs of others, and to undertake the radical reform of society."[83] As southern editors called for Smith's extradition to Virginia, they attacked the "manliness" of abolitionists in general: "I think the idea of GERRITT [*sic*] SMITH being taken to Virginia for trial has struck greater terror in the marrow-bones of the cowardly Abolitionists who applaud but dare not go to the assistance of Old Brown and his deluded followers."[84]

Pro-Republican newspaper editors, instead of creating a counter or competing discourse to defend Smith, took stances that distanced the Republican

Party from him, for example calling it an "untrue assertion" that he was a member of the Republican Party.[85] Greeley and other pro-Republican editors also defended the party against the aspersions leveled against it in connection with Brown, and on October 24 Greeley reminded *Tribune* readers that the Republican Party held the same slavery sentiments as "those entertained by Washington, Patrick Henry, Jefferson, and all the great Southern leaders in the war of the Revolution."[86] As for John Brown's view of the Republican Party, according to his later biographer James Redpath, "He despised the Republican Party" for its timid stance on slavery.[87]

As noted, the pressure on Smith became so great after the Harper's Ferry raid that he was institutionalized for "insanity." He was, however, sane enough to enlist his brother-in-law in destroying the letters implicating him in the Harper's Ferry raid.[88] Despite his situation, the relentless press attacks in the proslavery newspapers continued against this enemy of slavery.[89] Charleston readers learned from an interview with a person who visited Smith shortly before his confinement that he was highly agitated and asked that "the guilty parties in the wretched and bloody outrage be delivered up to the law, be they whom they may."[90]

Though black, Frederick Douglass received similar treatment in the proslavery press. As readers learned, government men were looking at "this eloquent colored man" "for explanations regarding the recent emeute [uprising] at Harper's Ferry."[91] Douglass addressed the charges in "Letter from Frederick Douglass," dated October 31, from Canada West. The letter appeared in northern newspapers and noted Douglass's words, "The taking of Harper's Ferry was a measure never encouraged by my word or by my vote, at any time or place."[92]

In New York a November 5 *Evening Post* item said that Douglass had left for England on a speaking tour to keep out of harm's way. Yet the defiant Douglass wrote in his note of departure, "I am guilty of neither element of treason. The American government refuses to shelter the negro under its protecting wing, and makes him an outlaw. The government is therefore quite unreasonable and inconsistent." While reporting Douglass's leave, the *Charleston Courier* added this piece of advice: "*Fred* would do well to flee further."[93] The writer said, "It is possible that his complicity in the Harper's Ferry outrages may justify an indictment for an offence embraced in extradition treaties with Great Britain." Sure to recall unpleasant memories for the former slave, a *New York Herald* item in the November 8 *Richmond Enquirer* reminded readers, "The Black Douglas[s], having had some experience in his early life of the pleasures of Southern society . . . has packed up his carpet bag and started for the Canadas."[94]

To be sure, some antislavery newspapers found the language about slavery's enemies too inflammatory and suggested a competing discourse to counter it. In a *New York Times* item headlined "Too Much Zeal," the editor said that northerners would not stand for "sweeping accusations of treason against Northern public men of standing and character."[95] A *New York Evening Post* editorial headlined "Virginia's Bounty on Assassination" reported that Governor Wise and the *Richmond Enquirer* were wrong in supporting a reward that offered a ten-thousand-dollar bounty for a northern politician [Joshua Giddings] delivered "dead or alive."[96] The *Boston Evening Transcript* editor blamed "Virginia Fanaticism" for the continued use of such harsh language.[97] "We dare you, then, to indict them or some one of them, and let us have your charges sifted to the bottom!," a November 2 *New York Tribune* editorial read.[98] The editorial challenged Virginia authorities: "How will you dodge this demand! The eyes of the country are upon you!"

Some northern editors viewed southern hostility as a desperate ploy by southern politicians to retain their power and influence. In a play on Seward's words, the headline "The Irrepressible Terror" appeared in the *Boston Evening Transcript*. Below that headline the editor claimed that southern party leaders, fearing decreasing national influence, worked on "exciting the fears and inflaming the passions of the South."[99] This competing discourse had much to do with a view that the proslavery faction had become so intransigent as to imperil the nation's political and social well-being. To those holding antislavery views, especially those New York Republican editors, the real enemy of the state was becoming southern inflexibility over slavery.

The Enemy as Free Blacks

Free blacks, because their very existence in a slave society represented a perversion of the social order, came to be seen as an especially troublesome population for slave owners who feared that their presence negatively influenced the servile population. They were the natural enemies of slavery, and the discourse of slavery's enemies consistently reflected this idea. Yet they also had no civil rights in America and lived on its margins. In *North of Slavery*, Leon Litwack notes, "Politicians, white Democrats, Whigs, or Republicans, openly and blatantly professed their allegiance to the principles of white supremacy; indeed, they tried to outdo each other in declarations of loyalty to the ante bellum American Way of Life and its common assumption that this was a white man's country in which the Negro had no political voice and only a prescribed social and economic role."[100] After Vesey's conspiracy and Turner's revolt, free blacks became special targets, with news items sounding calls to get rid of them. Edwin Clifford Holland, editor of the *Charleston Times*, for example, said this about free blacks: "We look upon the existence of our FREE BLACKS among us, as the greatest and most deplorable evil with which we are unhappily afflicted."[101] An item in the August 2, 1822, *Richmond Enquirer* warned, "The plan of insurrection was perhaps wider in its means and more desolating in its objects than it was in Virginia." It connected the Vesey plot to Prosser's conspiracy while urging stronger laws to control blacks, especially free blacks, so that "our fair fields shall not be sprinkled with blood." A concerned "Native Citizen" wrote in a series of correspondence "To the Members of the Legislature," published in the November 20 and 29 *Charleston Courier,* that the state is heading toward the same fate as Haiti unless free blacks are expelled. In the November 20 excerpt, he asserted, "The *free people of color,* intoxicated by a change from that state of order and subjection, to one of entire self control: no idea of modest medium, no demeanor corresponding to their situation is exhibited; they disregard the restraints of law; and yielding to the impulse of rude and savage feelings." (Such racist ideas also served to justify American slavery.) Later the writer suggested, "Banishment is a terror painful to the ear, but soft and consoling when compared with *treason, insurrection* and *murder.*"[102] About free blacks, the writer said, "A dismissal by law, from your State, of those who cannot have civil rights, and who have already in their liberation had more than true policy would warrant, cannot be called banished."

After Turner, the newspaper accounts reflected a growing sentiment to expel or control this group of black Americans. For example, a letter from Raleigh, North Carolina, in the September 24, 1831, *Newport (R.I.) Mercury* said, "Yesterday, every free negro in the city without exception, was arrested, and underwent an examination before the Committee of Vigilance constituted at our town meeting." Furthermore, "Those who could not give a satisfactory account of their mode of subsistence, were either imprisoned for the moment or ordered to leave the place forthwith."[103] Nearly a month later a item headlined "For the Enquirer Free People of Color" in the October 21 *Richmond Enquirer* and signed "Appomattox" observed, "The indications of public sentiment from every part of the commonwealth show that the people are deeply impressed with the necessity of getting rid, as speedily as possible, of the free people of color."

Conclusion

In this discussion of the discourse of slavery's enemies, three dominant classes of enemies appeared, with one focusing on the black rebel as a religious fanatic, a second on the enemy as a betrayer of race, and a third that concerned the free black as the natural enemy of slavery. Certainly the pool of slavery's enemies, as reflected in the newspaper discourse, had enlarged to such an extent that by 1859 it encompassed anyone expressing antislavery sentiment, thus amplifying the media discourse. From 1800 to 1859 the discourse always identified the black rebel as an enemy of the social order and the state. Yet because of racist nineteenth-century attitudes that held blacks as inferior, white elites may have found it difficult to accept the black rebel as possessing the necessary cunning and intelligence to carry out a revolt and looked for other rationales and abettors. In 1800, 1822, and 1831 religious fanaticism, which included black churches, became pivots around which these causal elements existed. (About the 1811 Louisiana revolt, this media discourse was not significantly identified; instead the enemy remained the black slave rebel who had been influenced by the Haitian revolt.) Later the enemies of slavery became abolitionists and their sympathizers, which by 1859 included newspaper editors and Republicans and anyone else possessing remotely antislavery sentiments. Yet a counterdiscourse emerged in the antislavery press that challenged assumptions about slavery's enemies, especially as it concerned the white man named John Brown and his supporters. In addition free blacks in America came to represent enemies of slavery simply because, in antebellum America, their skin was black and they were not slaves.

7 ❧ A Racial Panic

"The whole history of negro insurrection proves that there is no race of men so brutal and bloody-minded as the negro," read an editorial in the November 23, 1859, *New York Herald* after John Brown's raid.[1] "The negro, once roused to bloodshed, and in possession of arms, is as uncontrollable and irrational as a wild beast." Such racist language, shaped by centuries of religious, philosophical, and scientific thought, likely aligned with the views of nineteenth-century, white newspaper readers, whose fears of black violence against them had firm grounding in the terrifying survivor narratives from Haiti that appeared in 1791 newspapers. George Fredrickson observes in *The Black Image in the White Mind*, "The image of black violence and retribution, drawn not only from Nat Turner, but from memories of what had occurred in Santo Domingo . . . continued to haunt the Southern imagination."[2] Such fright put a psychological stranglehold on slave society, with masters knowing full well that no amount of coercion—physical, psychological, or legal—could control all slaves all the time. It forced them into a constant state of vigilance regarding their slaves, so that when slaves did rebel or plot against their white overseers, these social fears only became magnified. It is not surprising, therefore, that within slave country the thought of slave insurrection or its potential was enough to elicit an extreme panicked reaction among the white population. Fears of racial violence permeated the antebellum years. For whites, such fears remained emotionally and frighteningly real, and whenever slave troubles occurred, they were met by severe and reactionary responses.

Newspaper content from Prosser's 1800 conspiracy through the John Brown rebellion illustrated that any slave revolt meant social catastrophe to members of a white society that feared the attendant "horrors of Santo Domingo." While specific details of events between 1800 and 1859 vary, the desperate and frightened tone in newspaper content remained strikingly consistent with intertextual links drawn to past troubles as well as (and especially) the terrifying connections to Haiti. Because these events always concerned black people, the resulting media discourse has been labeled "the discourse of racial panic."[3]

Theoretically the discourse of racial panic suggests a moral panic framework that implies social elites manipulate media during crisis periods to maintain a power structure.[4] The underlying foundation of a moral panic is a social fear that can have long standing in a society.[5] As the sociologist Kenneth Thompson has noted, when moral panics form, these social threats are identified (usually in the media), causing public concern that signals authorities to use possibly excessive and repressive measures to diminish or eliminate the threat.[6] These notions were key because white, southern slave owners as social elites wanted to preserve their economic and cultural interests.[7] In antebellum America, slaves taking violent action against this white-controlled power structure broke moral boundaries that delimited their social standing and threatened that structure. Because newspapers often relied on elite sources for "official" information, they became integral contributors in magnifying or diminishing threats of black violence.[8] According to Siân Nicholas and Tom O'Malley, "Panics of this sort also raise the question of why they can occur, in particular what conditions need to exist in order for them to emerge. It is this . . . which links them to the idea of social fear, or underlying anxieties about a range of issues which are then played out in the media . . . the key issue is *the role of the media*."[9] Thus between 1800 and 1831 the primary sources of information about slave troubles rested solely with those in power, namely slave owners and other, sympathetic whites. When the news of John Brown's raid broke, the news sources became more varied but still remained elite and predominantly white. In identifying this discourse, the content used language that expressed a tone of great alarm about the unfolding disaster, suggesting always a "worst-case scenario" whereby the black enemy of slavery, the slave rebel, or his abettors (such as John Brown) had one goal: to massacre white people.

The discourse of racial panic comprised two components. The first involved a media discourse that illustrated the racial fear that white people had of blacks and the potential violence black peoples could unleash. This fear was highlighted by the immediate and panicked responses to the slave troubles. Expressions of these fears coursed through newspaper content, regardless of time or event. The second component concerned a return to a status quo whereby white authorities took necessary action to destroy slavery's enemies to right the slave system's racial hierarchy and to restore social order. The following examination provides the details that newspaper readers found in their pages when trouble-making, black slaves initiated revolts or conspiracies. It continues with a look at how the black threat transformed into a white one in the form of abolitionists. In any case, the trouble presented a frightening outcome for slave owners.

Reacting to Slavery's Enemies

Beginning with Gabriel Prosser's conspiracy, the discourse of racial panic was reflected immediately in the correspondence received from Henrico County and mirrored the language found in the letters from 1791 Haiti. One *New York Daily Advertiser* item, for example, began, "At reading the following every heart must shudder with horror."[10] The writer explained to readers how the "plan was systematically laid, for a general insurrection throughout the state, and the most brutal acts were to have been perpetrated." The former Revolutionary War Patriot Isaiah Thomas published in his *Massachusetts Spy* an account about the "conspiracy of the negroes," referring to Prosser's "diabolical plot" and noting "that the ground for public alarm was extremely serious."[11] The story in Thomas's newspaper explained the dire situation, saying that Prosser and his followers had planned to take over the penitentiary house, where "the magazine of arms, &c." were "deposited," and that a rainstorm had "rendered the water-courses impassible on the evening fixed on for the execution of their scheme." The writer observed, "It is hardly possible to say how extensive and how terrible might have been its consequences."

In the *Virginia Argus* as well as the *Massachusetts Spy,* correspondence explained how "a considerable body of slaves would set off on the evening from the Brook . . . for the purpose of massacring all the whites of Richmond, and to cause a general insurrection throughout the state," enlisting the "negroes of the town in the plot" to murder their "masters."[12] Similar information in the *New York Daily Advertiser*'s September 22 edition laid out the slaves' intention to commence the "undistinguished massacre of the whites" that "was to have taken place without regard to age or sex."[13] As the news spread, so too did whites' fears of black violence—so much so that "even in Boston fears are experienced and measures of prevention adopted," as one New York newspaper noted for subscribers.[14]

The connections to Haiti were drawn even more clearly in the correspondence written during the 1811 Louisiana German Coast slave revolt. A letter "from a Gentlemen at New Orleans, to a Member of Congress, Dated January 11, 1811" appearing in the *New York Evening Post* made the desperate situation perfectly clear: "We began on Wednesday last to have a miniature representation of the *horrors of St. Domingo* [emphasis added]."[15] He described how once the news "56 miles" upriver reached New Orleans, "a procession of carriages, waggons [*sic*] and carts, filled with women and children began and continued until night." They brought with them "the most terrible account" of what was happening as well as "flying reports of murders and burning houses. . . . Last night the whole city was up in great alarms." Subscribers also found stark details of the ensuing panic in the newspaper item signed "Z" in the January 17, 1811, *Louisiana Gazette:* "The road for two or three leagues was crowded with carriages and carts full of people, making their escape from the ravages of the banditti—negroes, half naked, up to their knees in mud with large packages on their heads driving along towards the city."[16] Because slaves and free blacks outnumbered whites in New Orleans, the words "horrors of St. Domingo" had special resonance because many of those who fled the island went to Louisiana.

Thus these fresh memories of what happened in Haiti only intensified racial fears among whites.[17]

Other, similarly toned stories appeared, such as the words of the frantic plantation owner Manuel André, who supplied much of what readers learned about the revolt. His story echoed the stories from panicked white people fleeing Haiti twenty years earlier. In a letter dated January 10 to New Orleans territorial governor William C. C. Claiborne, André wrote, "Sir, I have only time to inform you, in the shortest way, of the unfortunate events which have lately happened," telling Claiborne, his father-in-law, that slaves, "an atrocious gang of banditti," attempted to "assassinate" him "by the stroke of an axe."[18] He explained how his "poor son" had been "ferociously murdered by a hord [*sic*] of brigands." This graphic description found its way into newspapers across the nation.

Eleven years later, when the sporadic reports about Vesey's conspiracy appeared in Charleston's newspapers, the stories indicated the disaster that would have befallen the city's white citizens had the plot succeeded. An August 3 *Newport (R.I.) Mercury* item, for example, told readers that "an indiscriminate massacre . . . on all whites appearing in the streets" nearly took place at the hands of the black rebels.[19] An item from the *Charleston Gazette* that appeared in the *National Intelligencer* noted how twenty-eight accused conspirators had been justifiably hanged for their crimes against Charleston's white citizens: "When the investigation and labours attendant on such a state of things shall have ceased and when Justice shall be satisfied, and our city restored to its wonted tranquility—a succinct account of the whole transaction shall be given to the world. It will bring to view a scheme of wildness and of wickedness."[20] The item added, "Those (they were but few) who at first thought we had no cause for alarm, must be overwhelmed with conviction to the contrary." Because the Vesey plot never unfolded, the Charleston accounts only suggested the worst possible outcome if this conspiracy had achieved fruition. What can be discerned from these published accounts is that a fright spread among panicked whites. According to Robert S. Starobin, "The whole white community seemed gripped by fear for over two months and the panic persisted through the fall legislative session."[21] In sum, the "melancholy effect of popular excitement" in 1822 Charleston fueled racial fears of whites against blacks.

In comparison to Prosser's, Louisiana's, or Vesey's disturbances, Nat Turner's revolt became more of a national media event, generating significant, almost daily, newspaper coverage of what happened in Southampton County. In that coverage the terrifying stories from surviving whites encountering the rebels took local whites by surprise. The editor of the *Enquirer* wrote to readers on August 26, 1831, "These events have burst unexpectedly upon us. No one has dreamed of any such event happening in any part of Virginia."[22] His words echoed those of Manuel André, who in 1811 had described "the unfortunate events which have lately happened" along Louisiana's German Coast near his plantation.

In 1831 Virginia, a letter dated August 24 from a Belfield in Greenville County contained the words of a frantic writer: "I can merely say that we are all in arms and in great excitement on account of the insurrection, which broke out on Sunday night."[23] The letter, appearing in the August 30 *Richmond Enquirer*, described how Turner and his men "commenced by murdering a family, taking their arms and horses, and pushing on to the next house with all possible speed, where they massacred every white, even to the infant in the cradle."[24] Another letter, dated August 24, this time from Jerusalem, described the chaos: "The negroes, about fifteen miles above the place, have massacred from 50 to 75 women and children, and some 8 or 10 men. Every house, room and corner in this place is full of women and children, driven from home, who had to take [to] the wood[s], until they could get to this place."[25] A *Norfolk Herald* item headlined "Insurrection in Southampton County" in both the *Richmond Enquirer* and the *New York Evening Post* on August 30 described how Turner's group had been "bent on plunder; but having steeped their hands in human sacrifice, became infuriated, and, like bloodhounds, pursued the game of murder in mere wanton sport!"[26] Like the correspondence from Haiti, such descriptions would present a frightening scenario for any white reader, especially those living among slaves.

The discourse of racial panic with its expressions of fear of black violence suggested another recurring theme: that of sexual violence against white women. During the 1822 trials of suspected Vesey conspirators, Governor Bennett's slave Rolla's testimony likely shocked white listeners when he is reported to have said in the courtroom, "When we have done with the men we know what to do with the women."[27] His words likely stirred reaction from the white community. A Charleston letter dated June 23 from a woman writing to her cousin noted that after the slaughter of white men and old women began, "we poor devils were to have been reserved to fill their Harams [*sic*]—horrible."[28] Another Charleston writer claimed that once the slave Rolla had killed his master, Governor Bennett, "his reward was to be Miss B. the Governor's daughter—the very thought made my blood recoil in my veins."[29]

This theme of sexual violence also figures in the Turner and Brown accounts. In 1831 the *New York Evening Post* editor said that he had "received in this city from Virginia" letters that "give revolting details of the excesses committed," adding that the "treatment of some of the females who came into their power was horrid in the extreme, and will not bear repeating."[30] Another 1831 story, this from a "venerable negro woman," described the murder of Mrs. Vaughn, who "begged for her life" and pleaded with Turner's men "to take every thing she had."[31] They shot her dead, and as the writer who related the story noted, "It is difficult for the imagination to conceive a situation so truly horrible awful as that in which unfortunate ladies were placed"; he added that "instant death was the *least* [emphasis added] they could expect!" Weeks after Harper's Ferry, this rape theme emerged in a *Baltimore Exchange* item in the *Charleston Courier*. Headlined "Abolition Philanthropy," it claimed that according to a slave woman, one of Brown's men, Aaron Stevens, "entered her cabin, and seized her, threw her upon the bed and attempted to violate her person."[32] The writer wryly observed that "'free love' was one form of liberty tendered to the slaves of the South, and that 'beauty and booty' was the watchword of the liberators." In this case the perpetrators changed from black slave rebels to white abolitionists.

As the story about Stevens suggested, following John Brown's raid, the expressions of fear about the rebelling black slaves were replaced in 1859 with ones that illustrated an irrational fear of abolitionists. Fueling these fears that led to a southern panic was a barrage of unsubstantiated newspaper reports about further abolitionist plots. It must be remembered, though, that beneath the surface of this social anxiety was the deeply attached fear that these marauders would successfully arm black slaves, who would then set out on a path of racially motivated murder and general mayhem.

The daily newspaper reports from Harper's Ferry and Charlestown kept readers informed about the widespread panic gripping northern Virginia and indeed the entire South.[33] The early stories immediately set a predicable tone. On October 18, 1859, a dispatch in the *Richmond Enquirer* claimed, "The insurgents numbered 200 whites and blacks and had full possession of the U.S. Armory. They are commanded or rather led by a man named Anderson who lately arrived at Harper's Ferry."[34] Another dispatch indicated the involvement of between five hundred and seven hundred invaders, adding, "The insurgents have been taking persons from this side of the river (Maryland), tieing them and carrying them off for slaves." Still another reported that "the bridge across the Potomac was filled with insurgents, all armed. . . . Men were seen in every quarter with muskets and bayonets, who arrested every citizen and pressed them into service, including many negroes." These early stories magnified the threat, which to slave society had become real.

Even after Brown's arrest and trial, the panic in Virginia would not subside, as it was often fueled by further clarion calls of misinformation in the press. In one example, a November 18 *Richmond Enquirer* item told Virginia readers about the "Alarming Intelligence" that Governor Wise had received and that was linked to some "anonymous communications," warning that abolitionists "intended raids" along the Virginia and Kentucky borders. Amid increasing fears that these interlopers were mounting a final effort to rescue John Brown, Virginia authorities tightened security in Charlestown as John Brown awaited his hanging. The governor increased the troop strength in Charlestown and ordered women and children kept at a distance.[35]

In Virginia, as the newspapers recounted, every stranger became a suspected abolitionist. A *Baltimore Sun* item in the *Richmond Enquirer* explained that

"Charlestown and the surrounding region remains under strict military surveillance" and added, "All stragglers and strangers are required to give a good account of themselves. A daguerreotypist, with his fan, and a soap and medicine pedlar, were very properly ordered out of town yesterday."[36] In the *Enquirer* the words in letters of "reliable persons, *with names attached*" informed the city's readers of rescue plots aimed at freeing Brown.[37] One of the letters, apparently originating from Pennsylvania, claimed that a "lawless band of fanatical abolitionists and Black Republicans," called "The Noble Sons of liberty," had five hundred supporters and planned to enter Charlestown and "demand the release of that old villain, John Brown."

The reaction in some northern newspapers to the Virginia panic was to ridicule the state, with editors deeming the overreaction to the raid as unreasonable. As a result another competing discourse surfaced, one that was notably less sympathetic than any past news items from 1800, 1811, 1822, or even 1831 had been. "The Anti-Pedler Panic in Virginia" in the *New York Evening Post* noted, "The troops have been called out against an imaginary expedition to rescue the famous captain of Harper's Ferry."[38] Ten days later the November 28 *New York Times* headlined two news reports as "New-Yorkers Warned Away from South Carolina" and "Another Pernicious Peddler." Beneath the headline of the latter, it explained that "the Virginians have caught another of those pestilent peddlers, who fret the lives out of the chivalry."

When the unexplained burning of a wheat stack sent the people of Charlestown into another panic, the *New York Evening Post* editor simply could not resist chiding Virginians in the item "Apples and Hay Stacks": "The Virginians are evidently going daft; old John Brown has addled them. . . . Their terror exaggerates the slightest occurrences. If that poor old prisoner only coughs in his solitary cell, they think it is a pistol shot and fly to arms."[39] Greeley's *New York Tribune* that day referenced the "burning wheatstack" affair, making this comment: "He [John Brown] seems to have infected the good people of Virginia with a delusion as great as his own. It seems to be impossible for them to get over the terror which his bold seizure of Harper's Ferry inspired."[40] However, the editorial took on a more serious tone when it alluded to the tragic 1741 New York slave conspiracy that left many innocent blacks dead: "The present panic which prevails in Virginia calls to mind the bloody delusion with which this City of New-York was visited a hundred years and more ago, and at the bottom of which, then as now, lay the terror of negro insurrections." Even the usually proslavery *New York Herald* had a November 22 editorial that observed, "The people of Virginia appear to be the easy victims of some practical jokes in their midsts."[41] After noting how "the bewilderment assumes a variety of shapes," the editorial continued: "While making every allowance for the natural exasperation of the people of Virginia at seeing their State invaded by a band of crazy desperadoes, we cannot but regret that their excitement and alarm should have carried them so far as to subject them to ridicule."

Conclusion

The discourse of racial panic was focused on the initial and panicked white response to the black threat and then later on the abolitionist threat to slavery. In newspaper coverage that spanned fifty-seven years of slave troubles, this discourse gained expression that reflected the heightened state of fear of racial violence against whites. This media discourse descended from newspaper accounts that appeared at the time of Haiti's slave revolt, and it certainly was fed by a long history that weaved into those accounts the negative attributes that white people assigned to darker-skinned people. Newspaper reports reinforced the negative attributes while informing whites what black slave violence meant for them. These discursive residues imbued all later newspaper accounts of slave troubles. So insistent were these fears of racial violence that they consumed white, especially southern, society throughout the antebellum years and, arguably, up to the present day.

8 ❧ Maintaining Slavery

News content regarding slave revolts and conspiracies reflected an important element of the discourse of racial panic that suggested racial fears would rapidly spread through white communities whenever slave troubles occurred. Newspaper stories also reflected the severe responses that white authorities had to the threats to slavery so that system/institution would be maintained. These responses included an often violent disregard for the humanity of either slaves or abolitionists and often culminated in actions that suppressed them, despite the lives lost, so that order could be restored as quickly as possible. Regardless of specific events, newspaper correspondence and other stories consistently reflected a pattern, indicating that the preservation of the slave status quo was an imperative for the white community. An examination of the newspaper content revealed that three thematic elements defined this reactionary response to maintain slavery against its enemies: 1) the trouble had been quelled in the harshest ways; 2) loyal slaves acted with fealty toward their masters and the slave system; and 3) subsequent actions further repressed blacks or their allies following the troubles.

The discourse of slavery's enemies identified the black slave rebels and their abettors as dire threats to southern racial social order. They became objectified and dehumanized to the extent that their elimination seemed sanctioned and necessary. This is key to understanding the element of the discourse of racial panic discussed here. To people reading accounts about what happened to these human threats against slavery, the violent acts of retribution would have seemed essential.[1]

Destroying Slavery's Enemies

Whenever slave troubles occurred, the immediate response was to eliminate the threat. This was true for all the slave troubles from 1800 through 1859. It seemed that just as quickly as stories about the rebellions or conspiracies emerged, other stories would note that tranquillity had been restored. Despite the sparseness of partisan-era newspaper content concerning Prosser's and Vesey's conspiracies and the Louisiana revolt, the stories universally indicated that these threats had been dealt with and eliminated. As the historian James Sidbury has observed about Gabriel Prosser's conspiracy, whites' response was to crush it and contain any white panic.[2] Sidbury's observation can be applied to any slave trouble.

In 1811 Louisiana newspapers provided details about the white brutality inflicted on the black rebels, and one account indicated that "upwards of one hundred" of the slave insurrectionists "have been killed and hung, and more will be executed."[3] In addition the quick restoration of social order figured heavily in news items from Louisiana. The editor of the *Newport Mercury,* for example, paraphrased the *New-Orleans Gazette* in telling readers that "the strongest assurances of the complete restoration of tranquility throughout that territory" were being made.[4] As the stories spread to newspapers outside Louisiana, an unsigned account taken from a New Orleans newspaper explained that federal troops under the command of Gen. Wade Hampton had foiled the "mature plan . . . arranged by the blacks," assuring white readers that the "danger appears to be at an end."[5] A January 11 account in the newspaper said that "troops continue to kill and capture the fugitives," noting that "in a few days the planters can with safety return to their frms [*sic*]."[6] This story also identified the "leader of the miscreants" as Charles [Deslondes], "a yellow fellow, the property of Andre." Little about Deslondes was ever written about in the newspapers. While it is not possible to know with certainty how a white reader would have reacted to this news, it would seem that any reader, living in an area where black people outnumbered whites, would welcome these assurances that the black slave threat had been eliminated.

After the Vesey conspiracy, short news items in local newspapers informed white Charlestonians that those involved in the conspiracy had been arrested or hanged and that order had been restored. The writer of the "faithful account of the rise and progress of the late contemplated rebellion of the blacks in Charleston" likely had this in mind when he suggested that white authorities would have immediately suppressed any slave trouble had it actually taken place: "No one I believe, of the citizens, ever thought that the blacks could possibly succeed, were they ready to begin to put their nefarious designs into execution, but that they would take some lives—and this would be but a signal for a general massacre of the poor devils."[7]

The Turner revolt generated a much greater volume of news content, and invariably when reports reached newspaper editors, they told tales of brutal, authoritative responses to deal with the blacks. Items in the August 26, 1831, *Richmond Enquirer,* for example, informed Virginia readers that the "spirits" of the insurgents "are broken" and that "any further danger from them is by this time over."[8] "Now that their rampage has been stopped," one writer observed, "their object seems now to be to skulk."[9] An official notice dated August 28 and published in the local newspapers declared that all insurgents had been taken "except Nat Turner the leader, after whom there is a warm pursuit."[10] Weeks later, on September 30, a *Richmond Enquirer* item from a writer in Jerusalem stated with a degree of finality that "the insurrection was effectually and completely suppressed by the citizens of the county."[11]

After the Louisiana and Turner revolts, the necessity to maintain the slave system and control the black population in other parts of the South seemed an apparent reaction to these troubles. When, for example, "intelligence" of the events in Louisiana reached Natchez, Mississippi, Governor Holmes of Mississippi ordered "strong militia patrols throughout the territory."[12] After Turner, white slave society was in a heightened state of fear and looking for slaves who might be planning similar acts. This is suggested by an item from a Fayetteville, North Carolina, newspaper published in the *Richmond Enquirer,* which said that while there had been "no overt act" of insurrection, a "number of slaves" had been "implicated" and "two of the principal actors have been shot."[13] Similarly an account in the September 28 *National Intelligencer* said that twenty-five blacks were in a Sampson County jail and thirty were in the Duplin County jail, and it explained that "examinations [were] going on" and that "a terrible example will be made to deter others from imitating the conduct of these deluded wretches."[14] About the suspected North Carolina conspiracy, a *Wilmington Recorder* item in the October 4 *Richmond Enquirer* reported that "four of the *ringleaders*" had been found guilty of "the frightful disclosures . . . which now agitate the public mind."[15] The Wilmington writer called them "monsters in human shape," adding that their executions were necessary: "If ever stern necessity required a prompt and vigourous course in making pubic examples, this *necessarily exists* in our country."

Newspaper stories about white brutality against black slave rebels illustrated objectification of the enemies that made them fit for destruction. About Prosser's and Vesey's conspiracies, readers understood from the small newspaper notices that the courts had exacted legal revenge to dispense with the troublemakers. However, when black slaves actually revolted, stories about their complete annihilation dominated news content. A New Orleans man writing to his Pennsylvania friend described this scene of white revenge: "One negro was killed after he became a prisoner, for what reason I know not, unless to gratify the revengeful feelings of the planter,—they turned him loose in a lane and shot him as he ran—A few of the whites were wounded."[16] According to the historian Thomas M. Thompson, "numerous uncounted bodies remained scattered through the woods, victims of a shooting spree that continued until no other suspected blacks could be found in the vicinity."[17]

In Manuel André's January 10 letter to Governor Claiborne, he explained that as soon as his troops came upon the insurrectionists, "we rushed upon their troops, of whom we made considerable slaughter."[18] In the letter he justified the response, arguing, "We must make a great example . . . [and] destroy the remainder of those brigands." Surviving slave rebels found little mercy in the hands of their white captors: "The wretches sent to New Orleans were immediately tried and convicted. As it was intended to make a warning example of them, their heads were placed on high poles above and below the city, along the river, as far as the plantation on which the revolt began."[19] A similarly gruesome retribution story appeared in the March 2 *Cincinnati Western Spy*, where a Natchez writer explained how "the levee" was "ornamented with poles, on which are placed numbers of the heads of these unfortunate wretches."[20] Governor Claiborne rationalized such actions in a January 16 letter: "It is just and I believe absolutely essential to our future safety that a proper and great example should be made of the guilty."[21] Like the stories from Louisiana, those about Turner's revolt described the excessive force used against the slave enemies, leaving many innocent black men, women, and children dead. In one instance a slave named Albert Waller was strung up and riddled with bullets to serve as an example for other blacks, and in another instance a cavalry decapitated fifteen blacks and put their heads on pikes for all to see.[22]

By 1859 slavery's enemies were no longer black rebels but abolitionist invaders, and stories about white revenge taken against them were equally dramatic and gruesome. A *Baltimore American* correspondent described what the white people of Harper's Ferry did to one of John Brown's men after he had been shot: "The body of one of Brown's party, shot in the river the previous day, was dislodged from the rock on which it fell and came floating down. As it passed down toward the bridge, it was made the target for probably a hundred shots, and must have been thoroughly riddled with balls."[23] A *Baltimore Sun* report that was widely distributed across the country contained a disturbing account of the nonchalant attitude the town's citizens had toward the body of Dangerfield Newby, who lay dead in the street: "Nearly the first object visible after passing the bridge was a dead negro lying outside the pavement with an ugly gash in his throat, and other wounds. No one seemed to notice him particularly more than any other dead animal."[24]

To be sure, some stories indicated that some whites regretted such retaliation against these threats to slavery, but these sentiments were expressed as a caution against whites acting like black rebels or Indians. For example, thirteen days after the start of the 1811 Louisiana revolt, the writer of a *Louisiana Gazette* item dated January 21, 1811, said, "We are sorry to learn that a ferocious sanguinary disposition marked the character of some of the [white] inhabitants."[25] According to the writer, "Civilized man ought to remember well his standing, and never let himself sink down to a level with a savage; our laws are summary enough and let them govern." Similarly, after Denmark Vesey's conspiracy, a contrite editorial in the August 2, 1822, *Richmond Enquirer* expressed that "until some remedy shall be provided for the evils by which we are cursed," judges and legislators must adhere to the laws to control those "elements of our Society" to prevent "fatal explosions." The writer, assuming a paternalistic posture, supposed that unnecessarily repressing slaves once the troubles ended could result in greater social harm: "We must take care, that all the traces of refinement shall not be swept away—that our fair fields shall not be sprinkled with blood; and a howling ignorance shall not usurp the place of the means of civilization." In suppressing the Turner revolt, the commander in charge issued an order calling for an end to white-on-black atrocities, saying that such behavior was "never looked upon but with horror by any but savages. This course of proceeding dignified the rebel and the assassin with the sanctity of martyrdom, and confounds the difference that morality and religion makes between the ruffian and the brave and honorable."[26]

The Loyal Slave and the Good Negro Discourse

In identifying the loyal slave in newspaper stories, two key ideas were considered. The first indicated that slaves did not participate in the insurrectionary plans or the revolts and that the threat was not serious. In an important way these stories tended to counter the racial panic stories discussed earlier. Stories about this lack of slave participation appeared with regularity. The second key idea was called "the good Negro discourse," which surfaced in stories about loyal slaves acting in the defense of their oppressors. Taken together, these stories assured white readers about the rightness of the slave system, and they appeared most often in the reports about Turner's revolt and the Harper's Ferry raid and support an assertion that blacks would be incapable of wanting to strike out for liberty and in fact did not want to be free.

After Turner, subscribers far from the troubles may have been led to believe that revolt, although serious, did not involve many slaves. In New York one item headlined "THE INSURRECTION IN VIRGINIA" in the *Evening Post* of September 2, 1831, described the "disturbance among the negroes" as being "confined to a number of *runaway slaves*, in and about Dismal Swamp," adding that it was not a "concerted plan."[27] Another indicated that the number of "banditti" had been magnified and, more importantly, "there is no appearance of concert among the slaves—nothing that can deserve the name of insurrection, which it was originally denominated."[28] Shortly after the outbreak, a *New York Evening Post* item pointedly noted, "There is very little dissatisfaction among the slaves generally."[29] An extract of a letter from Jerusalem in the *Richmond Enquirer* said that Turner and his men forced the runaways they caught to join the revolt.[30] The Richmond newspaper quoted the *Albany Argus* editor as saying, "Very few of the slaves could be induced to join them; and such as did do so, were chiefly coerced into participation." The Albany editor commented, "It is creditable to the mass of that population that they not only refused to become participants in the horrible barbarities ... but were in many instances prompt in the defense of the employers."[31] These words were sure to allay whites' fears.

Stories about the lack of slave participation also figured in early reports following Brown's raid. The first AP dispatches reported that blacks were neither leading the invasion nor willing participants. As a Baltimore dispatch in the *Richmond Enquirer* said, "A gentlemen just arrived from Harper's Ferry, thinks the negroes have only participated in the outbreak on compulsion" and that "negroes have nothing to do with it."[32] The October 21 Richmond newspaper contained "authentic details" about the "insurrection at Harper's Ferry": "Several slaves were found in the room with the insurrectionists, but it is not believed that they were there willingly. Indeed, Brown's expectations as to the slaves running to him were entirely disappointed. None seem to have come to him willingly, and in most cases they were forced to desert their masters. But one instance in which a slave made a public appearance with arms in his hands is related. A negro who had been sharply used by one of the town people, when he found he had a pike in his hand, used his 'brief authority' to arrest the citizen and have him taken to the Armory."[33] Likewise, following the Brown raid an editorial in the *Richmond Enquirer* seemed quick to point out that "the Harper Ferry *emeute* failed by a mistaken idea of the temperament of Virginia slaves."[34] An October 22 *New Orleans Daily Picayune* editorial noted the "ridiculousness of the attempt" of this "insanest fanaticism" and said, "Even the slaves of the South would not join in such an insurrection, though it were not immediately crushed out. As in the time of the Revolution, [slaves] would be a source of strength in most of our fruitful and prosperous districts."[35] Similarly a writer to a Charleston newspaper made clear that this was "not an insurrection": "The slaves had no part nor lot in the matter, except in so far as some of them were forced to take part by the menaces of 'old Brown' and the fourteen white men under his command."[36] According to the writer, "The Southern slave is the happiest of human laborers; the best treated, the best cared for, the least inclined to rebellion."

Later, expressions of slaves' loyalty were stressed in much of the southern newspaper coverage of the Harper's Ferry raid. Under the headline "The True Lesson," a New Orleans newspaper reported that it was a "total failure" and "not a negro insurrection at all" because Brown and his men found slaves "unshakenly faithful."[37] Both Charleston newspapers published items pointing out that while John Brown's men armed some slaves and told them to "start for Harper's Ferry," the slaves instead "showed [the owner] the arms, told her what they had done, and went to work as usual."[38]

Southern political figures such as Gov. Henry Wise and Sen. James Mason too stressed slaves' loyalty in their public speeches and letters following the raid. Mason, whose letter appeared in the October 28 *Richmond Enquirer,* asserted that this was not an insurrection because "not a slave escaped or attempted to escape during the tumult" and "it is certain that the only emotion evinced by [slaves] was of alarm and terror, and their only refuge sought at their masters' homes."[39] In a speech shortly after his return from Harper's Ferry to Richmond, Governor Wise said that Virginia slaves' refusal to join Brown was the "only consolation" he had "to offer" Virginians "in this disgrace" of Harper's

Ferry.[40] According to Wise, "the faithful slaves refused to take up arms against their masters, and those which were taken by force from their happy homes deserted their liberators as soon as they could dare to make the attempt." Wise said that John Brown was ignorant of "the patriarchal relations" between masters and slaves and of the "bonds of affection and common interest" that existed between them.[41]

The Good Negro Discourse

Just as stories about the lack of slave participation diminished the threat and figured into the news content about slave troubles, so too did stories about loyal slaves who helped their masters, forming the good Negro discourse. These stories informed white readers about good slaves who despised slavery's enemies and supported those who would oppress them (that is, their white masters). For many white readers, such a discourse supported the logic of slavery's status quo and its racial hierarchy.

Several items about Gabriel Prosser's and Denmark Vesey's conspiracies reported that slaves revealed the plans to white authorities. In 1800, for example, a *Massachusetts Spy* story headlined "An Impartial Statement of the Negro Insurrection" said that a Negro, "terrified with the thought of the danger to which he was about to expose himself," told his master about the conspiracy.[42] The writer, who attended the trial, noted that "a young Negro of 18, named Ben" Woolfolk gave testimony against his fellow conspirators and received a pardon. After Prosser escaped, newspaper readers learned that a black slave had turned him in to authorities: "The discovery [of Prosser] was fortunately made by a negro boy, formerly of this neighborhood, who being acquainted with the General, very friendly accosted him, as he accidentally met with [him] on the wharf."[43] After his capture, a Norfolk article published in other newspapers explained how an "immense" crowd "flocked to behold the now harmless and inoffensive general," adding, "what is a little singular, the exultation of his black brethren was not less apparent than that of the whites."[44] The writer asserted, "If they truly felt all that was expressed by the countenance and the tongue, Gabriel could not deserve a greater punishment than to be delivered into their hands." As the writer reasoned, the crowd understood that Prosser's actions "had drawn down on them greater rigor than formerly, and their resentment was naturally directed to him as the cause."

In South Carolina after the Vesey conspiracy came to light, a "faithful account of the rise and progress of the late contemplated rebellion of the blacks in Charleston" in the *Richmond Enquirer* and the item "The Negro Plot" in the *New York Evening Post* reflected on the trouble, telling readers, "As you will have heard ere this reaches you of a conspiracy of the blacks against the whites, some faithful blacks" brought the conspiracy to the attention of the city "Intendant."[45] City leaders kept quiet about the conspiracy until "they apprehended a number of suspicious slaves, as well as many whose guilt was beyond suspicion." Shortly after those stories appeared, South Carolina governor Thomas Bennett assured white citizens that "a servant prompted by attachment to his master" revealed the conspiracy to authorities, who took immediate action.[46]

The good Negro discourse appeared in many items about Turner's revolt. The October 29, 1831, *National Intelligencer*, for example, reported that a group of Maryland free blacks had made several resolutions, among them that black insurrectionists "have no cause to induce us to join in or try to excite others to an insurrection." They pledged "to make it known immediately to the white people of the neighborhood" information about anyone conspiring to insurrection. Likewise a *Richmond Compiler* story in a New York newspaper provided the details about the trial of a slave woman accused of taking part in Nat Turner's revolt and juxtaposed that story with another about a slave who had saved her white mistress when the "bloodhounds" broke into her home.[47] Both Richmond and New York newspapers contained an August 27 *Norfolk Herald* account that said the slaves were "well affected and even faithful to their employers" after the revolt and described what happened when Turner's men reached "Dr. Blount's" farm: when the "black demons of slaughter" got there "with the full purpose of murdering him and his family," they were repulsed by "the Doctor's own servants, who resolutely opposed their entrance, declaring that they would lose every drop of blood in defense of their master and his family."[48] A *Richmond Compiler* item in the papers said that Blount, "who was very ill with the gout," armed his slaves, "who nobly and gallantly stood by him."[49] This item contained an editorial comment that applauded the slaves' actions. Surely other white readers did the same.

After the 1859 Harper's Ferry raid, southern newspapers consistently published accounts of blacks offering help to whites or refusing to take part. The difference here, though, is that enemies of slavery were abolitionists, not slave rebels. Differing slightly from news reports of slaves' loyalty were accounts of blacks—free or slave—wanting to maintain slave society. For example, an item in the October 22 *Daily National Intelligencer* headlined "Loyalty of Free Colored People" explained that "when the excitement on the subject of the Harper's Ferry insurrection was at its highest," shortly after news reached Washington, D.C., free blacks offered to help the Georgetown mayor "in any service in which he might see fit to employ them in the preservation of the public order and peace."[50] A *Richmond Whig* item reprinted in the November 24, 1859, *New York Times* told of a "free man of color" who offered his services and the services of "colored friends" to the Charlestown mayor.[51] "If any fighting was to be done, in behalf of Old Virginny and the white folks," the man was quoted as saying, "they would do their best. If not, they would be willing to accompany the troops in the capacity of body servants, and shave them, and wash their clothes, and black their boots, or ado anything else that might [be] wanting of them." Another *Whig* editorial, this one in the October 26 *Charleston*

Courier, gave an additional example of the good Negro discourse: "Even in the event of a civil war between the North and South, we for one, should be greatly surprised and amazed if the slave did not constitute a willing and efficient body-guard for the defence and protection of the white families of the South."[52]

As panic about feared abolitionist rescues of John Brown peaked in Charlestown, a *Baltimore Sun* article in a New York newspaper explained how a slave, with his master's approval, "volunteered last week, and proceeded to Charlestown, declaring that he was a 'bent on' having a 'shot at an Abolitionist.'"[53] The November 12 *Charleston Mercury* reported that after buying his freedom, another slave had found previously encouraging abolitionists to be cold and unhelpful. The former slave "wept like a child, lamented that he had ever left his former master, said that he was 'no Abolitionist'—that they had deceived him."[54] This, the writer asserted, was an example of "abolition 'philanthropy'" that coaxed "unwitting slaves" to leave their masters and then ran them "away over the 'underground railroads.'"

Unlike the news coverage of earlier plots and revolts, the editorial voices concerning the good Negro discourse after John Brown began showing distinct breaks in pro- and antislavery arguments. The lack of slaves rushing to Brown's standard rationalized slavery's rightness to white southern readers, as is indicated in a letter from "A Small Slaveholder" in the November 8 *Richmond Enquirer.*[55] It called the invasion a "Yankee riot," and about slavery, the writer asked, "Is not this an evidence, proof strong as Holy Writ, that the institution is of God—Patriarchal in its character, and which can never be overthrown, except through our own folly and dereliction of duty?" The *New Orleans Daily Picayune* editor said that one effect of the Harper's Ferry raid "was to confirm what has been [southerners'] faith in the stability of their institutions and the loyalty of their slaves, against all sources of internal disturbances," and the raid also confirmed that slave owners could repel an "external attack."[56]

The conservative and proslavery *New York Herald* attributed the lack of slave participation at Harper's Ferry to slaves' "very correct appreciation of the misnamed advantages of Northern freedom," adding, "They know very well that all this mock philanthropy exerts itself merely to run them off from their comfortable Southern homes to leave them to starve in the cold and inhospitable wilderness of Canada."[57] The *Herald* editor defended southern "patriarchal servitude," which, he argued, benefited blacks: "From birth the negro is in close and intimate contact with the white man. His childhood is cared for, his youth is constructed in some useful labor." Similarly a *Richmond Whig* editorial in the *Charleston Courier* argued that the "slaves of the South are content with their lot, peaceably disposed, loyal to their masters and hate a meddling Northern intruder with a perfect hatred. Let them [abolitionists] remember this truth, too, that the chief unhappiness of Southern slaves is produced by fear of the Abolitionists . . . that the Abolitionist will, some time or other, and some how or other, forcibly abduct them from their humane masters and comfortable homes, and take them to the free North or to Canada!"[58]

While southern editors and their proslavery allies linked slave loyalty to slavery as a "positive good," northern antislavery editors began to stress an opposing discourse about the lack of slave participation. Shortly after John Brown's raid, an October 18 *New York Evening Post* editorial said that "many of them [slaves], it is true, are too ignorant and stupid to take any effective part in an insurrection, [and] others, too, are profoundly attached to their masters or their families; but these excepted, there are yet thousands able and willing to strike for their emancipation."[59] In the October 27 *New York Times,* one writer argued that the lack of slave participation had nothing to do with slave loyalty but rather was based on self-preservation: "So that on the showing of Harper's Ferry itself, the Africans of the district held back from Brown not because they loved Virginia more but because they loved Louisiana less. They turned their backs on the North Star, not because they would not gladly have followed its liberating light, but because they did not believe it to be the North Star at all."[60] The *New York Times* editor cautioned "Southern friends" that they might be a "trifle hasty" in assuming that slaves did not wish to join John Brown. An excerpt from a *National Era* article in the November 3 *New York Times* asserted, "It would be a fatal mistake to infer that the negroes have no desire to be free, because they remained passive at Harper's Ferry. They know their own strength too well in that vicinity to rush upon destruction as did Brown and his conspirators."[61] The writer then asked, "But *suppose the same thing happened in South Carolina, where there are two negroes to one white person; does anyone believe that they would have remained quiet spectators?*" To these antislavery northern editors and writers, it was not surprising that slaves and free blacks failed to participate in the raid as Brown had hoped. The Reverend J. S. Martin, in a December sermon, expressed that blacks would not likely join a party of whites unless they were certain that there was "a perfect demonstration that the white man [was] their friend—a demonstration bathed in blood."[62]

Repressing Future Slave Enemies

The newspaper stories about slave trouble always gave details about how white authorities had destroyed slavery's enemies and restored order. They also gave example after example of the lack of slave participation, or the good Negro discourse, explaining that loyal slaves maintained the slave system by abetting their masters and by failing to enlist in the rebel cause. The third element of maintaining slavery against its enemies, an essential component of the discourse of racial panic, involved taking steps to make sure no new troubles occurred. Preventing the black population from engaging in ways to undermine slavery became important for white authorities, and this meant taking necessary steps to ensure this outcome. While few stories in the 1800 newspapers reflected these about Prosser's conspiracy, historians have noted three major changes that affected slaves' lives: 1) the white population became wary of its slave population, calling for the enactment of an 1801 law restricting the movement of slaves and free blacks; 2) a public guard began patrolling Richmond; and 3) Gov. James Monroe conferred with the federal administration about colonizing free Negroes and other dangerous slaves out of the state.[63] Also there were public calls for authorities to restrict the means by which slaves could communicate with one another. For example, the writer of a *Norfolk Herald* item in the October 7, 1800, *Virginia Argus* reasoned, "To those who have resided in St. Domingo it is well known that the negroes at the Cape kept up their communications with the plantations by means of sky rockets," and therefore "the firing of sky rockets is both dangerous and improper" and should be stopped.[64]

In 1811 Louisiana, newspaper editors kept readers abreast of the necessity to increase white patrols in New Orleans and surrounding areas. As Governor Claiborne said, "The inhabitants of New-Orleans and its vicinity will continue their vigilance. It is considered essential to our safety."[65] Other items noted, "Patroles [*sic*] night and day were ordered at New Orleans."[66] Stronger measures of control included those found in a newspaper notice that said, "All the carbarets [*sic*] were ordered closed, and no male negro was allowed to be in the streets after dark."[67] Thirty-one years later, after Turner, a writer to the September 30, 1831, *Richmond Enquirer* called for the "rigid enforcement of laws, regulating this class of our population."

As white abolitionists replaced black rebels as the enemies after the Harper's Ferry raid, newspapers were filled with accounts about actions taken against anyone expressing abolitionist sympathies. It became evident that slavery's proponents were willing to disregard civil liberties to maintain slavery. As the *Daily National Intelligencer* reported, when three "merchants of Cincinnati" were "heard to express themselves quite freely in relation to Brown, and exhibited their sympathy for him and his family," "a spy of Gov. Wise" reported it, and upon their arrival at Harper's Ferry, "the volunteers entered with loaded muskets and carried the men away."[68] A *Norfolk Herald* item headlined "Free Speech in Virginia" in the November 22 *New York Evening Post* reported that a Virginia grand jury indicted a man for saying that "John Brown was a good man, and was fighting a good cause, and did nothing but what any honest man would do." The *Enquirer* too published the story, claiming that the man used "seditious language calculated to incite insurrection."[69]

Northern newspaper editors paid attention to what was happening in Virginia and to the crackdown on civil liberties, informing their readers, as the *Tribune*'s Charlestown correspondent did, that "martial [law] holds sway": "The examination of strangers is never relaxed. The surveillance is uninterrupted from the time they arrive until they leave. If they stay too long, it is popularly decided that they mean no good, and if they stay but a very short time, every one is satisfied that they mean very ill."[70] Readers of the November 17 *New*

York Times learned from a Richmond newspaper how unwelcome strangers had become: "The truth is, we have no longer any use for the vagabond tourists or itinerant peddlers, of unknown character, who have heretofore found free counsel among us."[71] Readers both north and south came to understand that Virginia authorities continued with draconian measures to ensure order and to make sure no abolitionists infiltrated the perimeter of security surrounding John Brown. In Charlestown readers discovered that the mayor had issued a proclamation that "there should not be longer permitted to remain in our town or county, any stranger who cannot give a satisfactory account of himself."[72]

As a sign of the growing divide over slavery, many of New York's antislavery editors criticized these repressive acts. Whereas during the earlier slave troubles newspaper content, regardless of region, seemed to express a universal condemnation of the slave rebel and support for any means necessary to maintain slave society, by 1859 that tone had significantly shifted in these northern antislavery presses. This created a competing discourse that suggested the southern status quo had gone too far. A November 21 *New York Times* editorial observed, "Everything said or done concerning Slavery startles the community into instant terror."[73] A month earlier an editorial headlined "The South and the Insurrection" remarked that southern prohibitions on free speech about abolition did more harm than good: "We reproach and denounce [southerners] for their hostility to free discussion [of slavery], for excluding anti-slavery publications, for their suspicion of tourists and travelers from the Northern States, and for the violent and lawless vengeance with which they resent any attempt to interfere with their slaves at home. But there is evident reason for this. They live in the midst of the most fearful perils which can haunt the social life of any community. They are in the power of the slaves who surround them."[74] Horace Greeley's *New York Tribune* on October 26 criticized the Virginia court for refusing to "allow anyone to see or converse with Brown, fearing that he would say that which might, by being published, inflame the slaves against their masters."

Conclusion

In newspaper reports about America's slave troubles, stories about maintaining the slave status quo became important elements of the discourse of racial panic, which indicated whites' fears of blacks' violence against them. As presented in the newspaper content, the idea that the slave system endured and the slave enemy was vanquished seemed natural and right. Any other outcome would have seemed ludicrous, given that the slave enemy was also an enemy of the state and the racial and social order. In racist nineteenth-century America, the white population, even those living far from slave country, would have found assurances that authorities had taken appropriate, usually excessive, steps to quell the potential or real violence and that the black population had refused to act, when the opportunity arose, to destroy slavery. Certainly the fate of black slaves was of little consequence in these stories. What had changed by the time of John Brown's raid is that the enemy of slavery transformed from the black rebel to white abolitionists. They and their sympathizers, real or imagined, were targeted in the conservative, proslavery press as dangerous and un-American. Of course, in all of this, the primary beneficiary of maintaining slavery was America's powerful slave-owning class.

9 ❦ Slavery Divides the Nation

Up to this point the discourse of slavery's enemies and the discourse of racial panic concerned whites' reactions to the slave rebels. But over time another important discourse took shape in the news content about slavery during slave troubles: the discourse of slavery as a threat to the nation. This media discourse signaled the growing political divide over slavery and how it imperiled the country's future. It also illustrated how slavery began to decay and destroy cherished American values. As such, this discourse paid attention to two primary aspects: 1) the growing divide over slavery, leading to talk about secession to maintain it; and 2) the disregard for cherished American civil liberties, especially concerning association, speech, and press. The focus here is on the first element and the notable shift in editorial tone in the southern press that went from apologetic expressions over slavery to hostility toward any criticism of it. In the northern press a shift occurred as well, but here the shift can be seen in content that once expressed sympathy and support for southerners and now expressed sheer exasperation over their animus and intractability over any discussion about slavery.

From Sectionalism to Secessionism: Slavery Destroys the American Spirit of Unity

While newspaper coverage of Gabriel Prosser, Denmark Vesey, and Nat Turner always suggested sectional differences between the North and the South over slavery, those differences magnified, becoming irreconcilable by 1859. The United States from birth was a nation of distinct regions, each with its own economic, social, and political culture. In New England and the Middle Colonies, the vision of America that existed emphasized "ambition and progress" and eventually laid the foundation for independence and nationhood. In the South, colonists slowly accepted this northern position, eventually providing—through leaders such as Washington, Jefferson, and Madison—the intellectual power and military know-how to separate from England and create a new nation. Yet despite their significant contributions, many southerners saw northern cultural ways as at "odds with Southern life," especially as they concerned slavery.[1] Eventually, as time passed further away from the Revolutionary War and the Constitutional Convention, the South nurtured its distinct brand of nationalism, which rested upon the maintenance of its slave-supported culture.[2] As slavery became the South's defining feature, both culturally and economically, it became, in the view of many—convinced as most southerners were by their elite slave-owning brethren—something worth preserving at all costs, even the Union's destruction.[3] By the 1850s slavery's intimate connections to southern life became so compelling that slave owners came to view any attacks on its "peculiar institution" as assaults on the South in general.[4] As the panics following John Brown's raid suggested, many southerners, newspaper editors included, simply understood themselves to be "under siege" by antislavery proponents, especially the abolitionists.[5] Of course reaching this level of understanding took decades of political failure at the national level in dealing with the tragedy of American slavery.

When slave troubles occurred, beginning with Gabriel Prosser's 1800 conspiracy, newspaper content reflected the talk about slavery and its place in America. This talk also turned on what it meant to be an American in the North or the South. Much of this definition depended on how one interpreted the meaning of the nation's sacred documents, the Declaration of Independence and the Constitution. Over time these interpretations and how they related to slavery created two valid but antagonistic views of Americanism.[6] Of course all of this discussion meant little to the African American, who throughout this early national period, according to George Dangerfield, "was almost voiceless in American history."[7] So by 1859 two equally powerful views vied for supremacy in U.S. political thought, views that rested on the role of the central government, on property rights, and on the survival of the nation. Simply put, slavery had become an enormously complex and insurmountable burden on Americans, especially black Americans.

Southern intransigence over slavery began forming long before Harper's Ferry. Following the 1822 Vesey conspiracy, South Carolina governor Thomas Bennett's message appearing in the December 11, 1822, *Charleston Courier* apologetically suggested that slavery, as a social vexation, would remain uniquely American and concluded that "the period has long passed by, when a corrective may have been applied" because "the institution is established—the evil is entailed." Implying that the nation's best minds had failed to find a solution, he wrote, "The treasures of learning, the gifts of ingenuity, and the stores of experience, have been exhausted, in the fruitless search of a practicable remedy." Bennett urged masters to be kind to their slaves, adding, "The world will cease to chide us for evils we did not originate, and cannot remedy."[8]

Bennett's comments appear reflective of the Era of Good Feelings—a period from about 1816 to 1840 when it seemed that everyone was a "Jeffersonian Republican"—when talk about slavery and its connection to sectionalism was more restrained. Still, references to the 1820 Missouri Compromise, which forced slavery discussions into the public sphere long after the Constitution's framers created the original compromise to preserve it, surfaced in 1822. Oddly, the nation's second great slavery debate after the constitutional compromise may have spurred the rebel Denmark Vesey, convinced, as he may have been, that Congress had already emancipated the slaves.[9] One Charlestonian, in a letter dated August 13, 1822, to President James Monroe, coincidentally Virginia's governor during Gabriel Prosser's plot, said, "The discussion of the Missouri question at Washington, among other evils, produced this [Vesey's] plot."[10] Governor Bennett wrote at the time that "speeches of the oppositionists in Congress to the admission of Missouri" fueled one conspirator's aspirations and "gave a serious and imposing effect to his machinations."[11] The words appeared in the nation's newspapers, as did the following observation by another writer in the August 31 *National Intelligencer:* "We are sorry to see that a discussion of the hateful 'Missouri question' is likely to be revived, in consequence of the allusion to its supposed effect in promoting the late servile insurrection in South Carolina." He added, "No one ever supposed, nor have the public authorities or prints of Charleston most remotely suggested, that the speeches in Congress were *intended* to produce such an effect." The negative references to the contentious admission of Missouri suggest that slavery was something better kept quiet about and that the careful balance worked out should not be discussed again for fear it would tip and the compromise would unravel.

The nation's cultural makeup became an important point in the essay "NORTH AND SOUTH," originally from the *Boston Recorder* and appearing in the November 15 *Charleston Courier.* In it the northern observer took a mediating stance, charging that citizens in the nation's two sections had failed to communicate properly about slavery. He observed that some fellow northerners "condemn the late proceedings of the people of Charleston as unlawful, unjust and cruel; who contemplate all the horrors of the intended insurrection without one sympathetic emotion, and who extend their indifference to the peace and safety of all their southern brethren." The writer continued, "They view them as answerable for the existence and all the evils of slavery, and of course deserving the judgments of heaven." Accordingly the writer observed about slavery's critics that they possessed "limited knowledge of facts, and [are] unjust and unchristian." Surely such words would appeal to a southern reader. In describing southern attitudes about northerners, the writer said, "There are those in the south who consider the northern people as mean, ignorant and depraved" and "devoid of every generous feeling; hypocritical in their professions of morality and religion; selfish in all their political measures, and devising plans to deprive them of their property, or to involve them in difficulty." In a conciliatory tone, the writer urged Americans to "view the different States as forming but different parts of one great and happy nation, that will ever rejoice in the suppression of internal commotion, and repel hostile invasion."[12]

In November 1822 a "Soldier and a Patriot of the Revolution" from Charleston wrote a series of "Reflections" about the Vesey conspiracy and pressed the "Legislative body" and other authorities to "adopt such measures as their wisdom and patriotism can devise, to prevent forever the recurrence of such enormities."[13] The soldier, likely Thomas Pinckney, perhaps wrestling with slavery's roots on American soil, observed that it "is an evil entailed upon us by our former British rulers" but is enmeshed in the southern agricultural economy.[14] After that acknowledgment, though, the writer blamed the conspiracy on black slaves having gotten ideas about liberty from the events in "St. Domingo." Also influencing the conspirators, the writer said, was the "indiscreet zeal in favor of universal liberty, expressed by many of our fellow-citizens" in northern states. He also suggested that the "improper indulgences" of the city's slaves and free blacks, especially "their being taught to read and write," led to the conspiracy. This brought "the powerful operation of the Press to act on their uninformed and easily deluded minds."[15] His solution was to increase the number of whites and the size of the city's militia.[16]

As some in the North questioned Charleston authorities' harsh reaction to the Vesey plot, others in Charleston justified the actions taken. Writing to his Boston friend on August 19, 1822, a "gentleman" from the city argued that "outsiders" should not judge the situation: "I wish our friends at the north should be satisfied, that severe as has been the retribution which the law has awarded, it was due to do justice, and consistent with humanity."[17]

Eleven years later Nat Turner's revolt revived talk about sectional differences over slavery. In the essay "North and South," for example, originally from the *Charleston Patriot,* the writer observed, "North and South, in particular, are words which, as the Patriot remarks, 'constitute a perpetual antithesis, on which some minds delight to dwell, and on which the sectional partisan adroitly frames his system of prejudices.'"[18] He referred to northerners as "apt to fancy that judgment and temperance, [for] industry in business, and capacity and disposition for a quiet regular enjoyment of social intercourse" while they assessed their "southern brethren" as "hot and rash, loose in their morals, and thoughtless and improvident in their general conduct." Yet, as the writer noted, those of his southern ilk were taught from the "first dawnings of reason, to believe that he [the southerner] possesses . . . those characteristics which ennoble and refine the human character." Anyone "not chivalric," according to the southerner's standard of "ideal courage," is "mean and groveling, and unworthy of an association with refined natures." Just as years earlier the "Soldier and Patriot" had made observations about the 1822 press's negative influence, this writer accused northern and southern newspaper editors and politicians of promoting sectional jealousies and differences, saying that those "unwise and exacerbating animadversions" had created "a feeling of alienation, if not of positive hostility, between many inhabitants of the southern [states] towards their brethren of the northern states." He suggested that "every honest conductor of

the press" should "do away with those disparaging and unfounded and dangerous prejudices which cause us to look on any portion of the people of this great
republic in any other light than that of equals, friends and brothers." That spirit
of unanimity would change significantly by 1859.

The dominant idea expressed in newspapers between 1800 and 1831 in the
North and the South was that slave insurrection presented a horrific calamity
that required national unity and northern aid. Such feelings encouraged amity
and cooperation, the communal glue, against the black rebel enemies. After
the 1800 conspiracy, for example, a *Philadelphia Gazette* editor assured readers
with the following words on September 24: "We have a pleasure in stating,
that should our sister states require military aid to quell the black insurgents,
the Federal corps ... will be re-organized for that duty." Thirty-one years later
most northern newspaper editors, even those with antislavery sentiments, lent
a sympathetic ear with items suggesting northerners' willingness to send help.
Comments from the *New York American* in the September 24, 1831, *National Intelligencer*, for example, said, "We detest slavery—we have striven, and ever shall
strive, against its extension in these United States." Yet the writer did not hold
southerners responsible for being "cursed" with slavery and said that the "whole
white population of the Union" would defend "Southern brethren" and "go to
the utmost length to sustain the rights and safety of those whom circumstances
have placed in the relation of the masters."

Weeks earlier a *New York Journal of Commerce* item in the September 2,
1831, *Boston Evening Transcript*, headlined "INSURRECTION IN VIRGINIA," called
the Turner insurrection "one of the most distressing occurrences which has
ever taken place in this country. Nothing can exceed the savage atrocity of
the negroes, in the execution of their purposes."[19] While acknowledging "the
slaughter" of so many blacks, the writer said that he could not understand how
Turner and his men could "even dream of success in attempting to recover their
freedom by violence and bloodshed." Arguing that the "General Government"
would put down any insurrection, he asserted that "if necessary, a million of
men could be marched, on short notice, from the non-slave holding States, to
defend their brethren in the South! For, much as we abhor slavery; much as it
is abhorred throughout the Northern and Eastern States; there is not a man
of us who would not run to the relief of our friends in the South, when surrounded by the horrors of a servile insurrection."

Similarly an Albany editor said, "The men in the North and of the West,
we repeat, if the rising were extensive or formidable and the danger real, would
come with alacrity to the aid of their fellow-citizens of the South."[20] A *Richmond Compiler* editorial in the November 10 *Charleston Courier* noted unity
among northern and southern states in times of crisis, harkening to the Revolutionary War years: "Whatever may arise in our country, the old l[e]aven of
'76 will prevail whenever it is called for." The item said that a Virginian staying
in Boston at the time of Turner's attack observed a "great deal of interest" and

"great sympathy" from the people of Boston, and many Bostonians assured him that "if ever a requisition should come from Virginia, they would march at a moment's warning," regardless of their feelings about slavery.

Despite what appeared to be a cooperative spirit concerning slave insurrections, not all comments in the newspapers expressed harmony over slavery, suggesting that a competing discourse about it was emerging in some northern newspapers even by 1831. On October 1 a *National Intelligencer* editorial warned that some southern editors were using increasing secessionist rhetoric: "It is surprising, when we find these continued and repeated incitements to a rupture of the Union."[21] The editor added that the "errors and heresies of disaffected politicians" were influencing these "fanatical and demented" editors. Earlier, on August 29, the *Boston Evening Transcript* editor put it more bluntly, saying that Turner's action was "certainly an awful warning" that another "day of tremendous retribution approaches" if one group continues to suppress another, and therefore that "slavery, in this country, cannot exist forever."[22] Still, many in the North and the South believed that the nation's citizens could work together at getting rid of slavery. The September 30, 1831, *Richmond Enquirer* published remarks from the *Boston Statesman* saying that people in the "Eastern states believe the South is as anxious to rid itself of the curse of slavery, as the East is to see the accomplishment of that event." Both sections of the country must cooperate "to devise the best means to effect this desirable result!"

By the late 1850s any conciliatory language about what to do over slavery would become intolerable in the South, as would any general antislavery talk. The cultural divide over slavery was nearing its greatest point, as Professor James W. Massie's address to the Virginia Military Institute's alumni in 1857 indicated: "American civilization is properly divisible into two; in common parlance, Northern and Southern civilizations."[23] The professor asserted to his southern audience, "We possess a common language, and in some part a common ancestry; in these we resemble each other, and I might say, in nothing else." After Harper's Ferry all pretenses of goodwill between proslavery southerners and antislavery northerners, including some antislavery southern voices, disappeared. On December 2, 1859, the day Virginia hanged Old Osawatomie, one editorial in the *New York Herald* warned of the growing division between the North and the South, asserting that southerners had a constitutional right to demand slavery's protection.[24] Another, "The Execution of Brown To-day," warned that the country was in the "midst of a crisis" that shared similarities with the fall of the Roman Republic.[25] The discourse of slavery as a threat to the nation had become reified in the press.

To southerners, Brown's attack signified northern extremism and antagonism toward slavery, and many southern elites, including politicians and newspaper editors, believed that the antislavery politics of the increasingly powerful Republican Party fueled men such as Brown. Notably, this party had gained

national prominence by asserting, among other things, that a slave power conspiracy burdened the entire nation with its demands for the expansion of slavery. This new Republican threat to slavery repelled southerners, creating an
even greater impasse over slavery.

The Harper's Ferry raid seemed to have ripped off scabs of unhealed cultural
wounds, plunging "a knife deep into the psyche of Southern whites," as Steven
Channing has observed.[26] Reaction to it, as the historian David M. Potter has
commented, "revealed a division between North and South so much deeper
than generally suspected."[27] In the slave states, as Brown's biographer Richard
Hinton keenly noted, "The Harper's Ferry raid was at once used as a means
of attack on Northern and anti-slavery opinion. More than that, however, the
attack was moulded to arouse every hostile feeling in the South."[28]

While American abolitionists viewed slavery as a moral question and as an
egregious perpetuation of human suffering, slavery's advocates had, in many
respects, the stronger argument that slavery's roots were planted firmly on U.S.
soil with the U.S. Constitution protecting it. Southern editors quickly condemned northerners for failing to demonstrate adequate empathy for the trib-
ulations that Brown caused southerners. Even worse for the nation, as William
C. Davis, biographer of *Charleston Mercury* editor Robert Barnwell Rhett, has
observed, southern politicians and editors now viewed secession as "a safer risk
than the alternative of waiting within the Union for the abolitionists and their
black minions to murder Carolinians in their beds."[29] Brown's actions released
a firestorm of secessionist talk that saturated the southern editorial responses.

In general terms, the discourse of slavery as a threat to the nation revealed
the ongoing struggle between the nation's two dominant political strands: the
conservative view of limited government and states' rights; and the liberal
view that supported a larger governmental role in the lives of Americans. In
many respects the conservative, largely Democratic position had enjoyed decades of constitutional legitimacy and political supremacy. Yet by the late 1850s
the liberal, more progressive, antislavery view became embodied in the new
northern Republican Party, which was gaining in stature and political influence.[30] Such a shift did not go unnoticed or unchallenged in the southern press,
which especially targeted northern Republican leaders and their words after
Harper's Ferry. The *Richmond Enquirer* editorial "The Harper's Ferry Riot—Its
Moral and Consequences" called it all "an iniquitous plot" and referred to William H. Seward's "irrepressible conflict." The editor suggested, "The 'irrepressible conflict' was initiated at Harper's Ferry, and though there, for the time
suppressed, yet no man is able to say when or where it will begin again or where
it will end."[31] The southern editor, now suspicious of everything northern, declared that the "whole Northern section of the Union" might be "involved in
the attempt at instigating servile insurrection in Virginia." Four days later a
more strongly worded editorial in the newspaper claimed that Harper's Ferry

"advanced the cause of Disunion, more than any other event that has happened since the formation of the Government."[32]

Harper's Ferry provided incendiary material for the editor Robert Barnwell Rhett, who spewed forth his fire-eating brand of secessionism in his *Charleston Mercury*. On October 19 he called the raid a "pregnant sign of the times" and "the progress of sectional hate."[33] Two days later a *Mercury* editorial called Harper's Ferry "a warning profoundly symptomatic of the future of the Union with our sectional enemies."[34] Rhett, who fumed over Brown, accused northern newspaper editors and politicians of failing to show sufficient outrage at what Old Osawatomie did. Fomenting his rage in the *Mercury*, he wrote on October 31, "For twenty-five years the northern people have been keeping up a continual agitation in the Union concerning the institution of slavery."[35] The next day he blustered, "The great source of the evil is, that we are under one government with these people [abolitionists and Republicans]."[36] By his reasoning, the South had endured a quarter of a century of "ignominious toleration and concession," and he warned that "there is no peace for the South in the Union. . . . The South must control her own destinies or perish." The editorial "Measures of Securing Southern Safety" went further by stating that the only "remedy sufficient" to protect southern interests was "a dissolution of the bonds that hold us in their [northerners'] power."[37]

The discourse of slavery as a threat to the nation, especially in Richmond and Charleston newspapers, turned on slavery's constitutional protection and on northerners abrogating their civic responsibilities regarding the nation's fugitive slave laws. An *Enquirer* editorial said, "Protection of slavery is demanded by the blood of slaughtered citizens."[38] About enforcing the 1850 Fugitive Slave Act, an *Examiner* editorial said that any mediation over the slave issue between the North and the South should end.[39] The writer urged northern states to be aggressive about enforcing the law and to respect slave owners' property rights: "If you make it a crime to steal money, a horse, or a cow, make it also a crime to steal a negro."

Other southern editorials pressed on about secession, relentlessly determined to make the most of John Brown and abolitionism. An October 20 *Courier* editorial put it this way: "It is not enough that this outbreak, with all its individual suffering and bereavements, will only demonstrate the impregnable safety of the South, when awakened to her own defence."[40] Also urging secession were letters to the editors, such as one in the *Richmond Enquirer* signed "Unus Populi," which said, "The Union has not 'insured domestic tranquility.' The whole South is in a state of excitement. And why is this so? Simply because the Northern legislatures, and people, have thought proper to make war upon the Southern States for holding negroes as slaves and property."[41] An inflammatory editorial appearing in the November 15, 1859, *Richmond Enquirer* read, "Every gale that sweeps from the North brings new instruments of death in our midst. . . . Better civil war than injustice and oppression."[42] The editorial, which originated from Charleston, called for a break with the North and warned what emancipation would bring about: "With five millions of negroes turned loose in the South, what would be the state of society?" The writer answered, "worse than the 'Reign of Terror.'" The December 2 *Richmond Enquirer* picked up an editorial from Bennett's *New York Herald* that warned of a "more bloody and more extensive" insurrection and asked, "Men of the South, how much longer will you sleep?"[43] This irate writer declared that abolitionists "imperil our lives, and render less secure and valuable our property."

Signed "Son of the South," a letter to the November 16 *Charleston Courier* said, "This 'irrepressible conflict' has commenced. It is very obvious that the time has come when every Southern man ought to look the signs of the times fully in the face, and prepare for the conflict which evidently awaits us."[44] The writer observed that his reading of northern newspapers convinced him that "the entire North are either *particeps criminis* in the Harper's Ferry murders or sympathize in the movement." The break from past discourses about "different States as forming . . . one great and happy nation" regardless of the presence of slavery was now evident.

To many southern newspaper editors, northerners had reneged on their promise to protect the South's peculiar institution, as an editorial headlined "1829 and 1859—The Decline and Fall of Conservatism" suggested. It reflected on this shift in northern sentiment, reminding readers of northerners' reactions after Nat Turner's revolt, a "bona fide slave insurrection," when the people in the North rushed to Virginia's aid. In referring to David Walker's *Appeal,* which the writer said "actually *aimed to excite the slaves to insurrection,*" the Boston mayor had written to Virginia's governor, "I have reason to believe that the book *is disapproved of by the decent portion of the colored people.*" According to the editorial, another mayor wrote to Savannah's mayor saying, "We regard it [Walker's Appeal] with deep disapprobation and abhorrence." The writer then observed that the northern response to Harper's Ferry was not sufficiently forceful. The decline of conservatism that favored slavery meant that "the South must stand as ONE MAN—firmly, fixed, united, presenting an undivided front, an impenetrable phalanx."[45]

On Brown's execution day, Richmond readers learned from the *Enquirer* about a proposition for a southern confederacy and how South Carolina's legislature had voted in support of it.[46] In part the proposition recommended that if the "Union endangers or seriously embarrasses that system [slavery], that the South should discard said Union at once and forever." Similarly a *New York Herald* editorial reprinted in the *Charleston Mercury* said, "For good or evil we are entering upon the most momentous political conflict in the history of the Union; nor can we imagine how this conflict, limited to the anti-slavery crusaders of the North and, the pro-slavery chivalry of the South, can end in anything but the revolutionary experiment of disunion and a southern confederation."[47] Certainly, as reflected in southern newspaper editorials, slavery had irreparably divided the nation a full year before Lincoln's election and a year and a half before Confederate forces fired on a Union garrison at Fort Sumter.

With the exception of *New York Herald* editorials, the discourse of slavery as a threat to the nation did not figure as prominently in northern antislavery newspapers after Harper's Ferry. Instead they concentrated on illustrating slave society's inherent weaknesses or expressing exasperation at the vehement southern editorial response. In sum, the northern antislavery editorials expressed disdain for slavery's deleterious effects on the nation and southern demands to keep it. An October 20, 1859, *New York Times* editorial said that the Harper's Ferry events should stop the "fanatics who have been uproariously demanding fresh supplies of Guinea negroes" and wanting to reopen the slave trade: "When our Southern friends have their quarters so easily beaten up by two or three crazy adventurers from Kansas; that it takes federal forces, led by a Colonel of the United States Army, and two or three regiments of militia, to restore their peace of mind, it may be permitted to us respectfully to inquire what the state of affairs would be if the negroes really did rise in any considerable body, and a servile war really did break out."[48] The *New York Evening Post* editor, writing two days after the raid, was of the opinion that southerners wanted too much and were making the people of the North weary of their demands: "But what a condition of society is that in which one-half the population constantly menaces the other half with civil war and murder. . . . How insane the policy which would recruit and extend this form of social existence, even while it is becoming unmanageable as it is!"[49]

A November 21 *New York Times* editorial suggested that the South should be content with northern concessions already made: "The South must realize that there is a North—that its dominant sentiment is hostile to Slavery,—and that nothing beyond toleration and acquiescence in it, as an existing local evil, can be expected at its hands."[50] A like-minded *Commercial Advertiser* item in the October 19 *Boston Evening Transcript* called acceptable the southern desire to maintain slavery but offered the opinion that "the 'institution' [should] be confined to that part of the Union, and never receive special national protection," and it should stay out of "unpolluted territories."[51] Regarding the Harper's Ferry raid, the Boston editor wrote on October 29 that he hoped "the really wise men at the South will treat the whole affair as a most foolish, impracticable and unfortunate scheme, planned and led on by a brave, simple-hearted, unselfish and modest monomaniac, whose heart has been lacerated by his own sufferings, and whose brain, touched by the hereditary taint of insanity, has at length become really affected and diseased."[52] The editor predicted that Brown's conviction and execution would bear the "most terrible fruit that slavery has ever borne."

Southern intransigence over slavery riled many northern editors and others. In a letter in the October 29 *New York Tribune,* one writer argued that southern opposition to the discussion of slavery was the real reason sectionalism had become so extreme: "The Slavery party [Democrats] insults Freedom with a still fierce intolerance, but political opposition is forbidden. The safety-valve, we say, is gone, and explosion must follow."[53] Henry Raymond, editor of the *New York Times,* seemed especially irritated by southern cries of injustice at the hands of northern politicians and abolitionists. On November 10 he wrote, "If the South really expects cordial sympathy at our hands, it must behave sensibly in this matter. It is very hard for us to participate in indignation, which appears to expend itself in nods and winks, and points of the finger, and dark insinuations and awful hints, and mysterious innuendoes."[54] Similarly, Horace Greeley labeled southerners a petulant people: "Our Southern neighbors are a very hard people to get on with. They provoked the struggle now going on between the friends of Freedom on one side, and the advocates of Slavery on the other . . . they fly into a preposterous rage. . . . They make no bones of declaring, that sooner than meet the approaching defeat [of the Democratic Party] they will break up the Government. . . . They exhibit in this not only an arrogant but a very childish temper."[55] Two days before John Brown's execution, another *New York Times* editorial accused the editors of Virginia's large-circulation newspapers the *Enquirer* and the *Whig* of fanning the fires of sectionalism: "If the people of Virginia actually regard the people of the free States as a band of marauders—reckless of their rights, hostile to their peace, and bent upon their ruin—we pity their delusion, and deprecate the evils in which it may involve them."[56]

The discourse of slavery as a threat to the nation also turned on the growing fortunes of the Republican Party and the decline of the Democratic Party. As the issue emerged in the newspapers, it mattered, especially to the southern press, if one was (conservative) pro-Democrat, proslavery, and pro-South or, especially to the antislavery northern press, pro-Republican, antislavery, and pro-North. Editors wasted little time before capitalizing on what John Brown's raid did to express those views.

After the revelation that Secretary of War John Floyd had ignored an anonymous letter warning of the incursion, Greeley's *New York Tribune* seized the opportunity to attack the Buchanan (Democratic) administration because Floyd missed an opportunity to prevent the Harper's Ferry raid. The November 2 *Tribune* contained an anonymous letter, originally from the *Albany Atlas and Argus,* implying that Floyd, a former Virginia governor, deliberately ignored the warning for political reasons: "It may be that the Administration chose to nurse the insurrection as Cromwell did the 'Papish Plot,' and that it might be turned to political account."[57] Another antislavery newspaper, William Cullen Bryant's *New York Evening Post,* carried the editorial "Impotence of the Administration" on November 8, describing the Buchanan White House as "so imbecile that it does nothing efficiently or at the right time, except it be to catch or to hold negroes."[58]

While northern Republican newspaper editors expressed shock at John Brown's actions and quickly condemned them, they countered accusations linking the Republican Party to Brown and the abolitionist movement. Headlined "Party Spirit and the Insurrection in Virginia," a *New York Times* editorial said that all northerners should consider the Harper's Ferry events reprehensible and that no Republican newspapers had "any intent or thought of foment[ing] such bloody and disastrous outbreaks as this at Harper's Ferry."[59] Soon after the raid, Bryant's *New York Evening Post* defended the party against southern claims that it helped Brown and his followers: "The Republicans have never counselled [n]or countenanced violence, either in respect to slavery or any other subject, but they have resisted and rebuked it."[60] The editor said that "southern prints" should not align abolitionism with Republicans because that may delude slaves to believe that all Republicans were abolitionists. According to an October 20 *New York Times* editorial, northern Democratic newspapers, especially the *New York Herald,* encouraged southerners to believe that the Harper's Ferry raid was "only one incident of a gigantic crusade, organized at the North, and to be waged for the emancipation of Southern slaves."[61] The *Boston Evening Transcript* editorial "The Lesson of the Day" declared, "The extraordinary course of some northern newspapers in attempting to fasten the late miserable affair at Harper's Ferry upon the leaders of the republican party [*sic*] is simply absurd and contemptible."[62] Likewise a *New York Evening Post* item made clear who was at fault: "At this moment the democratic prints and democratic politicians are the greatest disturbers of the tranquility of the South."[63]

Still, southern editorials relentlessly accused Republicans, abolitionists, and their antislavery supporters of fomenting insurrection, usually referring to Republicans as "black" Republicans. When the Georgia legislature unanimously passed a resolution that viewed "the effort to excite the slaves of the South to a servile insurrection with the most intense indignation," it was aimed at the Republicans. The resolution, published in southern newspapers, expressed a trust "that the parties to this insane and treasonable plot may meet with the most prompt and signal punishment."[64] Charleston readers learned from the *Mercury* on November 5 that a resolution by the Tennessee legislature called Harper's Ferry "the natural prints of this treasonable irrepressible conflict doctrine put forth by the great head of the black republican party [William Seward]."[65]

Of course not all northern newspapers became targets of southern editorial outrage. An October 25 *Richmond Enquirer* applauded the "tone of the conservative press of the North" for rallying "all men not fanatics against that party [Republicans] whose leaders have been implicated with this midnight murder of Virginia citizens, and the destruction of Government property."[66] Such compliments, directed to editors such as James Gordon Bennett, were not undeserved. The sympathetic *Herald* editor despised the Republicans and delighted in calling them out, especially their political leaders: "This scheme of insurrection and its terrible results may be justly charged to the bloody instructions of W. H. Seward and other anti-slavery agitators of the North."[67]

Pro-Republican editors viewed the problem as a result of southern Democrats becoming increasingly desperate to maintain their political power. As Greeley's *Tribune* noted, southern Democrats made "a bugbear of the Abolitionists for the promotion of their own political ends," and as a response to Rhett's accusation, the newspaper editorial noted that it was those in the South who had worked for the past twenty-five years for the overthrow of the Constitution.[68]

Southern political statements and editorials became embroiled in an argument demanding political loyalty to the Democratic Party regardless of region. To those in the South, a vote for Democratic candidates meant, by extension, a vote in support of their institutions. Southern editorials were adamant about this. One *Richmond Enquirer* editorial, referring to an upcoming New York election, urged northern citizens to vote Democratic because this gesture would show support for the South and national unity: "It is but just and proper that a disclaimer should be made by the Northern press; but the voice of the press is not enough, the voice of the *people* at the North, through the polls, is necessary to restore confidence and to dispel the belief that the Northern people have aided and abetted this treasonable invasion of a Southern State."[69] If the vote went Republican, the editor suggested, a "Convention of Southern States" might be called to "consider the best means of protection in the future." Readers of the *Enquirer* found Mississippi governor William McWillie's annual message in their pages on November 18. In part it said that the election of a "Black Republican" should be seen as "a declaration of hostility."[70] The governor vowed that Mississippi would "hold herself in readiness to co-operate with her sister States of the South." Comments in the November 8 *Charleston Mercury* too encouraged northerners to vote Democratic, suggesting that Brown would have been stopped in Kansas if they had done so earlier: "If the laws had been enforced in Kansas for the protection of slaveholders and their ownership of their slaves, BROWN would have been hung. He never would have lived triumphant in crime to plot its perpetration at Harper's Ferry."[71]

Such threats and cajoling prompted a November 16 *New York Tribune* editorial response that specifically criticized a *Richmond Whig* editorial advocating secession if Republicans won the 1860 election: "Now, if Virginia wants to go out of the Union, she will pretty soon effect some clearer evidence of this desire than the rather incoherent ejaculations of here and there a panic-stricken journalist or politician." Days earlier an editorial in Greeley's paper prophesized, "The year 1860 must witness a memorable conflict between these irreconcilable [slave and free] antagonists."[72] The writer asked, "Shall Human Slavery be further 'strengthened and diffused by the power and under the flag of the Federal Union'?" In a more tempered tone, an editorial in Raymond's *New York Times* said on November 23, "One thing is very clear:—the *extremists* of each section are the enemies of both."[73]

Conclusion

During the antebellum period, most Americans believed they were parties in a contract with the government and that, as part of that contract, the Constitution, in the historian Melinda Lawson's words, "guaranteed them a body of rights and bound their country to an ideal."[74] Even after John Brown's Harper's Ferry raid, many Americans likely agreed with the southern constitutional interpretation about slavery, as represented by James Gordon Bennett's words in the December 2, 1859, *New York Herald:* "The Constitution of the United States fully recognizes and amply provides for the security of the institution of slavery."[75]

Yet throughout the 1850s, as sectional animosity intensified over slavery, each side of the debate staked legitimate yet opposing claims regarding the country's future with slavery, especially as it concerned the rights guaranteed by the Declaration of Independence and the Constitution.[76] Up to that point a generally long-standing, conservative interpretation that embraced slavery had dominated political discourse; however, as the discourse indicated, a small, increasingly vocal, liberal view rejecting slavery had taken root, especially in the North. As the Civil War neared and the weight of slavery bore down on the American consciousness, including that of the nation's political leaders, newspaper editors began emphasizing competing interpretations about what these rights and ideals meant for the nation. However, this growing competition in discourse illuminated the impasse over slavery that became insurmountable, as the discourse of slavery as a threat to the nation eventually signaled. The evolution of secessionism as distinct from sectionalism became a key aspect of this discourse. From 1800 to 1831 talk about sectionalism in times of slave troubles rested on regional differences and contained an amicable tone. Up to 1831 the editorial response to the slave troubles indicated northerners' willingness to aid the South against the slave rebels and southerners appearing appreciative of that sympathy. That changed by 1859, when secessionist talk exploded in the southern newspaper discourse and replaced any conciliatory language or hope for compromise.

10 ❧ Slavery's Immorality and Destruction of Civil Liberties

"Ever since the Revolutionary War, Americans had debated whether the paradox of slavery in a society dedicated to freedom should be tolerated, and, if not, could the issue be resolved without dismembering the Republic," Lorman J. Ratner and Dwight L. Teeter Jr. have observed.[1] In that post–Revolutionary War debate, Americans hoped to preserve national unity. However, powerful secessionist talk that appeared by 1859 overwhelmed any rational discussion of compromise with southern conservatives. This discourse manifested in a direct challenge to national unity; however, other aspects of the discourse emerging during times of slave troubles signaled slavery's danger to the country as well. The first concerned slavery as an immoral institution existing in a nation founded upon Enlightenment ideals, notably the equality of men. The second was slavery's power over influential white Americans whose influence could guide the course of lawmaking and other social contracts that might destroy civil liberties for Americans, especially blacks and white enemies of slavery.

Slavery as an Immoral Institution

As early as Prosser's 1800 conspiracy, this media discourse reflected Americans' unease about slavery's immorality. "Democracy in Virginia, is like virtue in hell," noted a letter from Fredericksburg, Virginia, dated September 23, 1800, in the *New York Daily Advertiser:* "Every slave holder who has been loud in the exulte of liberty, has proved the justness of this simile, by emancipating his slaves in the hour of death, when his grim master would no longer permit him to deceive himself or others." Further employing a language familiar to many postrevolutionary Americans, he continued, "That man must be a fool, my friend, who thinks there can be any compromise between liberty and slavery." He argued further, "The love of liberty in the breast of a fierce holder is like a diminutive, a distant, and hardly visible star in the center of a black cloud in a dark night." While contending that ideas about "Liberty and Equality have brought this evil [the slave conspiracy] upon us," he reasoned that this was because those ideals "however intelligible and admirable . . . in a land of freemen" were "wholly unintelligible and inadmissible" and "dangerous and extremely wicked in this country, where every white man is a master, and every black man a slave." Unfortunately, the Fredericksburg writer spoke for his generation when he said the country had "neither the courage, nor the virtue, nor the power to surmount" to end black slavery. If it persisted, "we must restrict it . . . if we keep a ferocious monster in our country, we must keep him in chains."[2]

Throughout the early years of the Republic, it seemed, contributors to the nation's newspapers did not hold southerners responsible for slavery, despite its questionable morality. As the *Boston Recorder* essay "NORTH AND SOUTH" explained in 1822 to the "brethren at the south," "the people of Charleston have acted just as every other enlightened and humane people would have acted under similar circumstances."[3] The writer's point, which many southerners at the time would have understood, was "that the system of slavery is not a local but a national evil; that it has been handed down from one generation to another, and that the southern people, or the present generation, are not accountable for its existence." Slavery must be understood "as a common evil," and the country should stand united "in any just and honorable means to free the country of so unwelcome a burden." A united position on slavery, he reasoned, "would strengthen our union, and secure our liberties." This would never happen.

Perhaps indicative of a period when many Americans thought that slavery presented a serious moral dilemma, newspaper content in the nation's early years—both North and South—informed readers of the system's horrific nature. In the aftermath of Vesey's 1822 conspiracy, southern readers in Richmond and Charleston may have read a Portsmouth, New Hampshire, *Hampshire Telegraph* article headlined "*The Slave Trade*" in their newspapers. Giving graphic details of this "inhuman traffic," this "disgrace of Europe," the item said that the treatment of slaves on ships during the Middle Passage was almost "impossible to describe."[4] "Some were linked in shackles by the leg, in pairs; some of them were bound in cords; and many of them had their arms so lacerated, that the flesh was completely eaten through!" This witness to suffering added, "Another of the inhuman practices of their purchasers is to flog them until they dance and eat." The slaves, as "an antidote to dejection and despair . . . often throw themselves overboard in pairs!"[5] Such vivid descriptions of the slave trade's horrors provided readers exposure to slavery's inherent cruelty, perhaps giving them pause to reflect upon its baseness. However, decades later and after Harper's Ferry, only antislavery newspapers contained items suggesting the immorality of slavery. It is not surprising, then, that the *New York Tribune* would feature an "illustration of the inhumanity of slavery," only this time speaking about the slave trade existing within the United States.[6] The tract "Slavery in Missouri—Its Practical Operation" aimed at exposing southern moral hypocrisy and the claim that slavery benefited American society. It described the selling of a St. Louis slave girl (whose mother was called a "handsome mulatto woman") at the local slave market. The writer explained that the girl's father and master, "the Hon. Mr. ____, Member of Congress from this State," watched as the girl and her mother were separated after the sale.

As it became clear by 1822 that southerners and most other Americans could not devise a plan to kill slavery, southern editorials began stressing its genuine legal status in the country. Exemplifying such an emphasis were the words of a Judge Peters, who was quoted in the *Richmond Enquirer* as admitting "our abhorrence of slavery."[7] The judge, despite such sentiment, asserted a states' rights position, arguing, "Whatever may be our opinions on this point, its [slavery's] lawfulness is guaranteed by our constitution." He determined, "It should never be forgotten, that the right to hold slaves, or as it is delicately expressed, 'persons held to service or labour,' is a constitutional provision, which no law of any state can abrogate." In his view, the immorality of slavery did not outweigh its legal status or any argument against its continued existence.

Such rationalizing likely eased the southern conscience, turning the slavery argument away from its immorality to a property and states' rights issue, and, by 1831 and Nat Turner, this shift became apparent in the newspaper editorials. The editor of the *New York Daily Sentinel* raised the ire of "A Citizen of Petersburg [Virginia]," who fumed, "On more than one occasion, he [the *Sentinel* editor] contended that the negroes ought to be free—that they are as much entitled to their freedom as were our fathers."[8] While "Citizen" acknowledged that "no man is by nature, the property of another," he called the editor a "wretch" and argued that no one "has the least right, under existing circumstances to infringe, in any way, our [rights of property], by any sort of interference." Perhaps as a conciliatory measure to potential northern readers, he described "the great bulk of the people of New England" as "liberal, enlightened and philanthropic": "They are our brethren in peace, and, in war, our best and bravest friends."[9]

Eleven days later the *Enquirer* reprinted these challenging words from the *Sentinel*'s editor: "The slaves have a perfect right derived from God Almighty, to their freedom. They have done vastly wrong in the late insurrection, in killing women and children; but still it is not to be wondered at. Their struggle for freedom is the same in principle as the struggle of our fathers in '76."[10] Once *Enquirer* readers digested that excerpt, they found it coming under attack by a northern editor, whose words also appeared in the *Enquirer*. The editor of the *Albany Argus* derisively called the *Sentinel* that "African Centinel, a Journal of Liberty," believing it expressed ideas that promoted disunity. To counter it, he wrote amiable words such as those of the "Citizen of Petersburg," assuring readers that "under circumstances of real danger [slave rebellion], the men of the North would come with alacrity to the aid of their fellow-citizens of the South."[11]

By 1859 much had changed in the nation, both politically and geographically. With those changes, southern editorial apologies for slavery ceased, and it appeared that southerners no longer viewed it as a moral threat to the nation.

Brown's raid united slavery's partisans in states such as South Carolina where intense fears of slave uprisings and northern collaborators fueled citizens' white-hot hatred for slavery's critics.[12] Up north it also united antislavery editors, for example Horace Greeley and others, who stood firm against southern tirades supporting slavery despite the moral damage inflicted nationally.

Northern editors seemed determined to upbraid the southern fire-eaters, using a powerful rhetorical weapon in their editorial arsenal, namely Virginia's glorious Revolutionary War past. During the earlier slave troubles, the items recalling that past usually signaled a unified northern and southern response to slave insurrection and slavery. Afterward they became significant metaphors used to criticize slavery and the southern way of life. An October 18, 1859, *Boston Evening Transcript* editorial, for example, referring to Virginia, a state "that has nurtured so many Presidents," said, "At such times of agitation the inherent weakness of a state of society where large numbers are held in a state of servitude is revealed, and the boasted superiority of the civilization based on injustice proves to be founded on no substantial grounds. This dread which manifests itself at the slightest cause, is a natural effect of the forced relations that exist between the oppressed and the oppressing, and will continue so long as the inalienable rights of men are invaded."[13] Greeley's *Tribune* was especially harsh, accusing southerners of violating treasured American ideals. In the October 19 editorial "The Insurrection," while calling it "the work of a madman," the editor, who "deeply regret[ed] this outbreak," also criticized the slave power as "the fit hands and tongues of those who regard the fundamental axioms of the Declaration of Independence as 'glittering generalities.'"[14] The editorial expressed this future hope by recalling the state's past: "Let [Brown's and his men's] epitaphs remain unwritten until the not too distant day when no slave shall clank his chains in the shades of Monticello or by the graves of Mount Vernon." In a poignant reference, a later *Tribune* editorial of November 3 evoked Virginia's revolutionary glory as a way to indicate the sad transformation that had taken place in southern thought about slavery: "What a change has come over the spirit of Virginia since the days of her great men—her Washingtons, her Jeffersons, her Madisons, her Monroes! Then the great problem was how to get rid of Slavery. Now the problem is how to retain it."

Slavery Destroys the Civil Liberties of Black Americans

Of course it is a truism that slavery destroyed the civil liberties of black, American slaves. However, what slavery did to the civil liberties of free black Americans is worth examining for its part as forming the discourse of slavery as a threat to the nation. As the 1850s ended, ideas about slavery-as-a-positive-good convinced southerners of the institution's rightness, and this discourse was reflected in their blatant disregard for two fundamental American rights, freedom of speech and association, especially for free blacks, abolitionists, and northerners in general.

For the nation's free blacks, their lives, already challenged in racist nineteenth-century America, became more difficult whenever slave troubles appeared. By 1790 approximately sixty thousand free blacks lived in North America.[15] Considered, in Winthrop Jordan's words, "leaks in the system," they endured great disdain from all segments of white American society.[16] As a short *Montgomery Mail* item in 1859 put it, "Freedom is not the normal condition of the negro, and that blessing to the white race degrades, demoralizes and renders worthless nine negros out of every ten."[17] In both the North and the South, repressive laws against free blacks further isolated them through "legal or extra-legal means."[18] To white slave masters, their existence represented a threatening anomaly to a perverted but refined social order. Even in nonslave states free blacks were troublesome, and racial equality was hardly an issue for discussion: "In Massachusetts, a state with a very small black population . . . had abolished slavery almost without controversy. . . . In 1821, the legislature appointed a committee to look into the possibility of restricting Negro immigration [to the state], on the grounds that blacks constituted 'a species of population' that could 'become both injurious and burdensome.'"[19] Free blacks were considered especially irksome people in the South, with whites holding the view, as one 1817 writer did, that they "contribute greatly to the corruption of the slaves" and that they "aggravate the evils of their condition, by rendering them idle, discontented, and disobedient"—thus leading to direct resistance to the master's authority.[20] The master class believed that slaves, which a November 11, 1859, item in the *Charleston Mercury* described as "naturally affectionate and good-hearted people," could be "tampered" with and encouraged to do harm.[21] As a result these free black Americans contended with codes nearly as harsh as those reserved for slaves, and it became imperative for white communities to "reduce access to freedom" for slaves "and to narrow the mobility of those Negroes already free."[22]

In newspapers this remained a constant, repetitive discourse that focused on measures to restrain, control, or expel this population. In 1822, perhaps because Denmark Vesey was a free black man or because Charleston had a large black—free and slave—population, editorial attacks on free blacks became fierce. The writer signing his essay "Native Citizen" could barely contain his contempt for this "intermediate class": "*The free people of color,* intoxicated by a change from that state of order and subjection, to one of entire self control: no idea of modest medium, no demeanor corresponding to their situation is exhibited; they disregard the restraints of law; and yielding to the impulse of rude and savage feelings."[23] Referring to "many cases of their violence upon the person and lives of the citizens" in South Carolina and other states, he claimed that free blacks failed to keep their "proper place," forcing white Charlestonians to witness "the degrading spectacle of colored persons acting as clerks behind the *counters of many stores and shops; claiming respectability,* and *courting* the custom of the reputable part of the community." He implored the state legislature to begin *"commencing a rigid* system as to the conduct and morals" of all citizens, but especially free blacks.[24] Those words appeared on November 20.

Nine days later, on November 29, "Native Citizen" continued his harangue in the *Courier* by warning that the state would endure Haiti's fate unless it arrested the association of free blacks with slaves: "Banishment, is a terror painful to the ear," he wrote, 'but soft and consoling when compared with *treason, insurrection and murder."*[25] He continued, "A dismissal by law, from your State, of those who cannot have civil rights, and who have already in their liberation had more than true policy would warrant, cannot be called banished." Many years later similar sentiments appeared in southern newspapers after Harper's Ferry. An October 25 *Mercury,* for example, asked, "What are we drifting to," and below those words, "Slaveholder" suggested that northern free blacks probably were in discussion with the "black Douglas [*sic*] and the white Greeley" about liberties given northern blacks.[26] This "slaveholder" made clear what southern society should do with this population: "We would purge our community, and punish its law-breakers, and neither *talents, social position* [n]or *wealth* should screen them from public exposure and denunciation."

Although the "participation" of free blacks in slave revolts has a "cloudy history," as Eugene Genovese has suggested, southerners still feared that they influenced slaves at least to insubordination and at most to rebel.[27] After the 1822 conspiracy, one South Carolinian wrote, "We look upon the existence of our FREE BLACKS among us, as the greatest and most deplorable evil with which we are unhappily afflicted. They are, generally speaking, an idle, lazy, insolent set of vagabonds, who live by theft or gambling, or other means equally vicious and demoralising. And who, from their general carriage and insolent behaviour in the community, are a perpetual source of irritation to ourselves, and fruitful cause of dissatisfaction to our slaves."[28] The writer urged Charlestonians to expel free blacks and to discipline slaves more.

Despite some suggestions that free blacks offered help in quelling the Turner revolt, they were still viewed as dangerous. "Only *one free negro* was in arms with them, and *no white persons,"* a September 6, 1831, *Richmond Enquirer* noted about free black participation in the revolt.[29] Yet the paper still connected free blacks to the murders: "Several free negroes, however, have been taken up under strong suspicion of having been engaged in the conspiracy." These suspicions convinced many whites to urge the passage of legislation in Virginia to place restrictions on this population. "A Friend to Precaution," writing to the *Richmond Enquirer,* wanted state lawmakers to restrict the movement of black itinerant preachers and "adopt some measure to stop the increase of the free negroes and slaves, which has become an evil."[30] These transits and interminglings concerned whites, and a *Petersburg Intelligencer* item described how town citizens, appealing to the legislature for action, called free blacks "a class of persons who are neither freeman nor slaves" and observed that they were "of necessity degraded, profligate, vicious, turbulent and discontented ...; their locomotive habits fit them for a dangerous *agency* in schemes, wild and visionary."[31] "Citizens of the County of Northampton" petitioned the Virginia legislature to subdue this "anomalous population," which was naturally exposed "to distrust and suspicion" and which could never enjoy the same privileges as whites.[32] These good "Citizens" called them an "evil ... no longer endurable," warning that slaves naturally "connect[ed]" with them and their "idle and vicious habits." Because this link might lead to "dangerous intrigues with our slaves," free blacks should be expelled to Liberia.

Southern attitudes changed little by 1859, and whites' fears of free blacks' influence over their slave counterparts continued. Because southern slave owners now firmly held to the rightness of slavery, they had deluded themselves into believing that their slaves endured its ordeals willingly and would never participate in open rebellion unless an external force pressured them to do so. While a *Richmond Compiler* item described slaves as "obedient," the paper stressed that "it is the general opinion ... that the utmost security cannot be obtained without the banishment of the free people of color."[33]

Other items referred to proposed laws affecting free blacks, such as a Tennessee bill that, if enacted, would prevent or fine "free negroes travelling on the railroads in that State."[34] New York's *Tribune* readers learned of a Mississippi bill that would rid the state of free blacks, with the New York editor cynically observing that it seemed intended to "rob" free blacks and make them pay for "terror they have made [Mississippi] suffer."[35] Similarly the *New Orleans Daily Picayune* article "Monthly Passes to Negroes" urged the expulsion of free blacks and doing away with slave passes that, "for the time," leave them "virtually free" from the "restraints of masters, and bring them in contact with the worst class of society," namely free blacks.[36] The *New York Times* story "Negro Troubles in Louisiana" noted that vigilance committees had been formed to deal with "scoundrelly free negroes, white cut-throats and horse thieves, cattle stealers, horse stealers and chicken stealers."[37]

In the southern press, just as they were considered the natural allies of rebelling slaves, free blacks now became aligned with the abolitionist threat after Harper's Ferry. An editorial in the Richmond newspaper signed "Tudor" implied that free New York City blacks knew of John Brown's Harper's Ferry plans, basing the opinion on an October 17 *New York Evening Post* report that read, "Rumors, which are current among the free blacks of this city, represent that this outbreak was only a premature explosion of a more general conspiracy."[38] Keeping free blacks from associating with slaves was emphasized in a November 23 *Mercury* item that said, "The intercourse with slaves (and also with free negros) of persons whether vagrants or temporary sojourners" should be prohibited because they "in many cases, are either voluntary agents or hired emissaries of northern associations."

By the accounts, southern white authorities remained vigilant, looking for any connections between free blacks and Brown, and the stories that appeared confirmed their fears. "While searching the premises of Alfred Cox, a free negro, for a fugitive slave," a November 29 *Richmond Enquirer* item reported, "a large number of pikes were discovered. Cox had frequently been seen in consultation with a man named Brown."[39] From the *Augusta (Ga.) Dispatch*, Charleston subscribers were informed that some free blacks were involved in the raid because of "their social isolation and irresponsibility," since this caused "free negros gradually [to] become desperate and abandoned": "A free negro in a slave country is a natural incendiary. If he commits no overt act of crime or insubordination, his presence is a perpetual incentive to discontent among his brethren in bonds."[40]

Free blacks were objectified and marginalized in both northern and southern newspapers, which rarely gave insight into the thoughts of this oppressed class of Americans. Therefore, whenever a free black refused to comment on slave troubles, it was seen as another example of this population's untrustworthy nature and as a cause for concern. "The inhabitants [of Harper's Ferry] are not by any means easy in their minds as to the temper of the slaves and the *free negroes* [emphasis added] among them," a *New York Herald* item in the November 4 *Richmond Enquirer* said.[41] Readers of Charleston's two newspapers, the *Courier* and the *Mercury*, would find a *New York Express* item observing New York City's black citizens' reactions to Harper's Ferry and likely supporting the white Charlestonians' suspicions and racist ideas: "[The reporter] found them to 'keep shady' on the subject, and it was hard to draw from them any opinion whatever on the matter at issue. This [is] a characteristic of the negro race."[42]

Somewhat surprisingly one of the few enlightened comments about free blacks came from South Carolina governor Thomas Bennett after the Vesey conspiracy. He wrote in his message "No.2," which appeared in the December 11, 1822, *Courier*, "The rapid increase of the free colored population of Charleston, has been the subject of serious reflection and great anxiety," but he added that lawmakers must not be rash and send "away . . . Free Negroes and Persons of Color, who have come into this State within the last five years."[43] Free blacks posed "little danger" because "the property they hold and privileges they enjoy, afford the best guarantee for their proper demeanor," according to Bennett, whose comments likely expressed a minority opinion.

Slavery Destroys the Civil Liberties of White Americans

Because of slavery, the civil liberties of white Americans were also threatened in the South, with the natural white targets being abolitionists. However, the nation's division over slavery expanded greatly by 1859, and the discourse reflected a sentiment that called into question the civil liberties of any northerner going into the southern states. Newspaper content after Harper's Ferry, in fact, suggested that it had become unwise and unsafe for them to be there. Even one's manner of speech could bring trouble to a visitor from up north. "Arrested on Suspicion in Monroe County," read the headline of an *Enquirer* article that explained to readers how "a very suspicious looking fellow" who was "evidently a Yankee from his peculiar accent, and has the appearance of being ready for anything desperate or disreputable" had been arrested.[44]

Much southern hatred roiled from an intense fear of attempts to rescue John Brown or other abolitionist invasions, making all strangers potential enemies and putting southern authorities on guard. Item after newspaper item informed readers of the stringent measures taken to prevent any further abolitionist trouble. The *Charleston Mercury*, for example, reported calls to reinstate a local "Fire Guard"—essentially local vigilantes—in light of the Harper's Ferry incident.[45] A letter in the November 23 *Mercury* from a "SLAVE OWNER" urged South Carolinians to be prepared and to "cultivate a spirit of embittered hatred, and active and implacable hostility" toward abolitionists, whom he called a "mischievous rabble of conspirators."[46] Farther north in Virginia times were tense in Charlestown, where ten days before John Brown's execution an *Enquirer* editorial defended troop buildup as a way to monitor potential threats and "to protect life, while executing the judgment of the Court."[47] As Brown's hanging date neared, a small item in the November 25 *Richmond Enquirer*, "On the Qui Vive for Marauders," warned, "Should any suspicious-looking characters be found lurking around us, require them to give a satisfactory account of themselves, or compel to make their *exit* in *double-quick time*." While no rescue attempts occurred, authorities sealed the city on Brown's execution day, giving the military the only access to the telegraph.[48]

Challenges to freedom of speech occurred, indicating to some degree that the South was already engaged in a civil war with its enemies of slavery and resorting to all means to silence them. To express antislavery or even pro-Republican sentiment in the South was to talk sedition, a *Montgomery Mail* item in the *Charleston Courier* suggested.[49] It explained that a Bostonian now in the city could leave or pay a five-thousand-dollar fine after he "boasted of having voted Fremont, and talked of slavery in a manner that did not suit the Mobilians." The story also mentioned another man, James Murphy, who, according to the writer, had tried to "induce a free nigger woman to go with him to a free state." The *Mail* editor suggested that both Murphy and the Bostonian "should have been whipped, ducked, tarred, feathered, ridden upon a rail, and then hanged to a tree." In a story about a drunken man who remarked that slaves should be free, the November 8, 1859, *Charleston Mercury* explained what the repercussions of speaking so loosely could be: "This morning about eight o'clock, he was taken from the jail, and a number of negro men deputized to gallant him on a rail to the wharf-boat, and ship him for a Northern State." Four days later, after another careless man "indulged in abusive remarks against the institution of slavery" and then learned a difficult lesson when he was tarred and feathered and ridden out of town on a rail, the *Mercury's* editor warned, "We hope the example made of SALVO will prove a warning to all abolitionists who are travelling through the South" in disguise to promote abolition.[50] Such stories of repressive acts made their way to northern readers. An item headlined "Freedom of Speech in Georgia," appearing in the *New York Times* one day after John Brown died, described how a "shoe-dealer" was tarred and feathered for "expressing abolition sentiments."[51]

Thus in the post–Harper's Ferry frenzy, stories in southern newspapers concerned themselves less with the threat from black slave rebels and more with the threat posed by white, northern abolitionists. Just as slave rebels became objectified in newspapers during the earlier slave troubles, so too did abolitionists after Harper's Ferry. "The Way Abolition Emissaries Are Treated" described the ordeal of a suspected "agent of some Abolition Aid Society or underground railroad" who was strung up five times but not killed.[52] The man was then "kindly permitted to retrace his steps to a more congenial clime." This treatment served as an example of how the people of southwestern Virginia would deal with anyone "upon whom suspicion of tampering with negroes and peddling treason rests." According to a *Kingstree (S.C.) Star* item, "two straggling printers from the North" were ridden out of town on a rail.[53] Another *Star* account described the fate of "two Northern Abolitionists, who have been for some time teaching school" in Williamsburg, South Carolina.[54] While no proof existed that the pair had done anything wrong, "being from the North, and therefore necessarily imbued with doctrines hostile to our institutions, their presence in this section has been obnoxious, and at any rate very suspicious." The town passed a resolution to get rid of them. On November 29 a letter from a Harper's Ferry eyewitness in the *Courier* justified the community's reaction: "The atrocious outbreak at Harper's Ferry has alarmed the South to no little extent, as to the characters in her midst, and the many earnest warnings we have seen through the press, urging us to beware of Northern school-teachers, their treachery, danger, &c. have caused our citizens to join in the general vigilance."[55] The writer praised Williamsburg's citizens after the two suspected abolitionists departed: "I have never seen a more determined spirit manifested before in any public action, and, perhaps, greater excitement has never prevailed since the days of the Revolution, and more patriotism exhibited."

The panic after Harper's Ferry prompted physical as well as verbal attacks on newspaper offices, editors, and correspondents in the South. For example, a *Baltimore Sun* item in the *New York Times* reported that the publishers of the *National Era*, an African American newspaper in Washington, D.C., had asked for police protection after receiving threats.[56] In early November an item headlined "The Old Brown Panic—Mob in Kentucky" from the *Cincinnati Commercial* appeared in the *New York Evening Post*.[57] The story explained that a Newport, Kentucky, mob attacked the office of the *Free South*, an antislavery newspaper, deeming it an "incendiary" sheet unsafe for the community.

A November 5 *New York Times* editorial headlined "Mob Spirit in Kentucky" responded to the vigilantism by noting that the attack defied Kentucky law and "Kentucky Sentiment."[58] In Virginia movements of northern newspaper reporters (and others) were increasingly restricted as Brown's execution date neared. For example, an item in the November 30 *Tribune* said that reporters were told to leave and "passengers now riding on the railroads are required to procure passports from Governor Wise." On December 2 the *Boston Evening Transcript* reported that "several persons, editors of the abolition newspapers . . . were ejected from the cars for Harper's Ferry."[59]

If the level of intolerance was high in places such as Newport, Kentucky, and Mobile, Alabama, it was far worse in Charlestown, Virginia. There, as fears of abolitionist invasions peaked during the month between Brown's trial and his execution, newspaper readers learned that a "traveling daguerreotype operator" was chased out of town, according to a report in the *Tribune*.[60] A Boston sculptor who wanted an image of Brown had hired the man, but the anxious townspeople, fearing a rescue of Old Osawatomie, rushed to judgment. According to the account, "Two strange men with a camera inside of a jail was a prospect not to be calmly contemplated." In another telling of the story, the November 10 *Boston Evening Transcript* explained that the sculptor, who wanted a likeness of Brown, "has been told that he is [a] 'marked man.'"[61]

The unfortunate photographer was not the only one raising the suspicions of nervous townspeople. W. S. L. Jewett, an artist for *Frank Leslie's Illustrated Newspaper*, found himself unwelcome in Charlestown, where, according to the *Boston Evening Transcript*, the townspeople targeted him for "being the correspondent for the New York *Tribune*."[62] The November 15 *New York Times* printed Jewett's cynical comments about his abrupt and forced departure: "We were never left alone for so much as five minutes at a time; and we should have been happy to enjoy this pleasing state of society much longer, but for a sudden conviction, that hanging by a mob might injure the graceful proportion of our necks; that riding on a rail might jolt our systems seriously out of order, and that a coat of tar and feathers would be infinitely unbecoming to our complexions."[63] Even George Hoyt, one of John Brown's attorneys, was chased out of town with Jewett and was quoted as saying that he "feared most an attack on the jail."[64] An excerpt from one of Hoyt's letters appearing in the November 17 *Tribune* said, "Deeming it no valor but sheer foolhardiness to brave the populace, Mr. Jewett and I packed our bags and quitted the municipality of Charlestown." According to a *New York Tribune* correspondent a day earlier, Hoyt and Jewett did not realize their danger until the last minute. "Their last moments were, alas, not tranquil," he wrote, adding, "The painful event was witnessed by the entire population of Charlestown."[65]

If public opinion expressed in newspapers was any indication, southerners supported such actions. "Southerners! rid yourselves of everything antagonistic to your peculiar institutions," were the stirring words of "A True Virginian" in the November 22 *Richmond Enquirer*.[66] Supporting isolationism, this Virginian expressed the virulent xenophobia overwhelming the region and the attitudes that many southerners had about suspected abolitionists in their midst: "Drive it out! Purge the land of the kankering [*sic*] pest. Look around you. Abolitionism partakes of your hospitality and sits at your fireside! Get rid of it! Drive it out! Peddlars, preachers, merchants, travelers, school-teachers! Off with them, every one, old and young, male and female."

Conclusion

While the media discourse of slavery as a threat to the nation was earlier examined in terms of the growing sectionalist divide, here the discourse has reflected talk about slavery's immorality and how its preservation threatened American civil liberties, thus endangering the nation's founding ideals. Of course black American slavery had already destroyed the civil liberties of slaves. Now the discourse illustrated southern willingness to accept the destruction of American civil liberties of other Americans, most notably free blacks, white abolitionists, and, eventually, any Yankee venturing south.

Even though throughout most of the nation's early years slavery appeared as an embarrassing yet complicated economic and philosophical issue, it transitioned in the southern conservative mind, which was imbued with the powerful slavery-as-a-positive-good rationale, to a brittle, inflexible subject. Newspaper content reflected this shift and the growing discourse of slavery as a threat to the nation.

11 ❧ Slavery Destroys Freedom of the Press

The discourse of slavery as a threat to the nation had many facets and was comprised of elements that expressed extreme sectionalist talk in the form of secessionism as well as arguments over its immorality and its infringement on civil liberties. The discourse also reflected the damage that slavery did to freedom of the press, in particular the suppression of published material that America's slave oligarchy, including newspaper editors, deemed dangerous and seditious or that refuted the slavery-as-a-positive-good theory. This discourse emerged in the bitter editorial responses that northern and southern editors directed at one another whenever slave troubles erupted. The suppression of materials considered incendiary served to maintain slavery by tamping down genuine discussion over it and, importantly, by keeping suggestive material considered inflammatory from getting into slaves' hands.[1] The legal historian Amy Reynolds wrote, "Southerners who advocated suppression in the form of laws, argued that the abolitionist threatened to ignite slave rebellion and that the threat of rebellion actually threatened the survival of the union. These sentiments are clearly seen in the two words southerners used most often when denouncing abolitionist writings—'incendiary' and 'seditious.'"[2]

After Nat Turner's revolt especially, the South entered an exceptionally repressive period when state statutes, fines, or imprisonment were levied against anyone caught with abolitionist materials or trying to give them to slaves.[3] It should be remembered that not just southerners repressed abolitionists and their presses. Northern mobs silenced them with equal violence, with their attacks peaking in the mid-1830s, most notably with the murder of Elijah Lovejoy in Alton, Illinois.[4] As the political chasm widened over slavery, the definition of what southerners considered "incendiary" and "seditious" broadened to include any publication expressing even mildly antislavery sentiments. About incendiary materials, an editorial comment in William Cullen Bryant's antislavery *New York Evening Post* explained after Harper's Ferry that no matter the effort slave owners exerted to keep slaves away from words or people influencing them, those efforts would fail: "It has been impossible to keep them in entire ignorance of the blessings of freedom ... the fugitive slaves of the North have found means of communicating with their old comrades; the abolitionists have spoken to them by pictures, if not by language."[5]

Despite the reality that most abolitionists were hardly enlightened about racial equality, their publications created great consternation in the South.[6] Eight months before Nat Turner's revolt, the citizens of Hanover County sent a petition to the Virginia General Assembly to ban abolitionist literature: "It is the expectation of liberty, and by that alone," these citizens reasoned, "that they [slaves] can be rendered a dangerous population."[7] One check on the dissemination of this literature was controlling the U.S. mail at the local level. Four years after Turner, U.S. postmaster general Amos Kendell determined that local postmasters could decide how to handle such "incendiary" material in the South.[8] Decades later a *Richmond Enquirer* item, "The Post Office and Abolition Documents," referred to the "most excellent opinion" of Attorney General Tucker to make illegal the sending of abolitionist tracts and newspapers, singling out a pamphlet called "The Impending Crisis" as well as Greeley's *New York Tribune* as especially onerous.[9] Tucker's opinion determined that these "publications openly inculcate resistance to the rights of property of masters in their slaves; both advocate rebellion and insurrection, and both deserve the fire."

Of all the "incendiary" materials published before Turner's revolt, none caused greater consternation in slave country than David Walker's *Appeal* and the *Liberator.* After the 1831 rampage, many southern editors expressed in the strongest terms their anger at these publications, and their newspapers contained insistent warnings about their distribution and influence on slaves. In addition frequent notices informed readers that fines and punishment awaited anyone caught tampering with the slave population by providing them copies of such offensive materials. As a Petersburg, Virginia, writer phrased the argument, "Every society has the right to preserve public peace and order, and, therefore, has a good right to prohibit the propagation of opinions which have a dangerous tendency."[10] While it seemed unlikely that Nat Turner knew about Walker's *Appeal* or his call for slaves' resistance, some editors suggested otherwise.[11] The September 15 *National Intelligencer* item "INCENDIARY PUBLICATIONS" made the claim that copies of the *Appeal,* that "inflammatory production," had been found months before Turner's revolt. The writer accused those "misguided and deluded fanatics" for distributing the tract, which resulted in the "fruits of their diabolical projects in the Southampton massacre."[12]

In the October 18, 1831, *Richmond Enquirer,* a *Norfolk Herald* item explained that "the Vigilance Association of Columbia" had offered a fifteen-hundred-dollar reward for the "apprehension and prosecution to conviction, of any white person" distributing the "Liberator" or "Walker's Pamphlet."[13] Another item that day said that the *Liberator* contained "the most illiberal and cold-blooded allusions to the late supposed insurrection amongst our slaves."[14] Elsewhere the "Corporation of Georgetown," according to the *Enquirer,* passed a city law affecting "any free negro or mulatto person living in this town" who had or distributed abolitionist material "of a seditious and evil character, calculated to excite insurrection or insubordination among the slaves or coloured people."[15] That included the *Liberator*. The authorities considered such an agent a "disorderly person" and a "dangerous and unsafe citizen."

"Will our readers inform us," the Richmond editor asked a month after the Southampton murders, "whether Garrison's 'Boston Liberator' or (Watkins [*sic*] appeal) is circulated in any part of this State?"[16] Calling the *Liberator* "a nuisance, which ought to be arrested," the editor added, "If our fellow-citizens of Massachusetts cannot aid us in this work, we must make a vigorous effort to do it for ourselves." The editor praised a "pledge from the *Boston Statesman* that any effort to create disaffection among their slaves wou'd meet the unqualified disapprobation of almost every in [*sic*] individual in New England." The Boston writer called on fellow New Englanders to help "suppress the misguided efforts of those shortsighted and fanatical persons who would violate all the principles of justice, honor, and humanity, under the garb of philanthropy," calling the *Liberator* editor that "fanatic Garrison." For the record, Garrison called Nat Turner's revolt "the first step of the earthquake" but added that "we are horror-struck at the late tidings."[17]

A writer from Washington warned that a white man "with the avowed purpose of inciting rebellion in the South" was distributing the *Liberator* published in "Boston or Philadelphia."[18] Garrison's suspected "secret agents" he called "villains" and suggested that "you ought to barbecue them" if they are caught. Calling slavery an "evil . . . too grave to be trifled with," the writer also noted that "the real friends of humanity" could not tolerate "these incendiary undertakings"; he added that if the publications stirred any more uprisings, they would lead to the "utter extermination" of the blacks in the South, which had already been "manured with human flesh and blood." The editor of the *Intelligencer,* which contained the above stern directive, reasoned that distributing the *Liberator* would be "impossible and too dangerous for even the most desperate man to undertake"; he suggested that "intelligent" New Englanders "abhor and reprobate" such publications that could lead to insurrection and called on Boston's mayor or the Massachusetts legislature to ban them to prevent "poisoning the waters of life to a whole community."

Also in the *National Intelligencer,* "A VIRGINIAN" from Fauquier County wrote in the September 28 edition that the *Appeal* and the *Liberator* should be treated as "seditious libel."[19] The North and the South shared the "common bond of union—the Federal Constitution" and the rights granted by it, he argued, and he urged the Virginia governor or the U.S. president to demand that the Massachusetts governor turn over the "offender" for prosecution or "let the People of the South offer an adequate reward to any person who will deliver him, dead or alive, into the hands of the authorities of any State South of the Potomac." To the readers the *Intelligencer*'s editor wrote that these remarks were "written in a temper very natural under the circumstances, but which we should be sorry to be acted upon in the present case."

Days later in the Washington newspaper an item reported that someone sent to its offices and to "persons of color, slaves as well as freemen" several copies of the September 24 *Liberator*.[20] The particular issue with its bold headline "BLOOD! BLOOD!! BLOOD!!!" contained this controversial comment by Garrison about the murders: "The Avenger is abroad, scattering desolation and death in his path!" The rhetoric so offended the Washington editor that he concluded, "Our readers will know how to appreciate this madman's libels upon the National Intelligencer. For such ravings he [Garrison] is to be pitied rather than condemned," for he was a "misguided Eastern crusader."[21]

Antislavery sentiments published in other northern newspapers offended slavery's friends as much as the *Liberator* and the *Appeal* did, and newspaper contributors complained about them. "A Citizen from Petersburg" argued, "Already are our negroes stimulated to resistance and rebellion by incendiary publications from our northern brethren."[22] What upset the Petersburg man was not the *Liberator* but the *New York Sentinel*. He continued that if such publications with such an antislavery slant appeared on southern soil "to intermeddle with our property and disturb our peace," measures would be taken to confiscate them. "We know our rights, and knowing, will maintain them," he vowed. In the November 25 *Richmond Enquirer*, another commentary accused some northern newspapers of being "filled for several years past, with the most violent publications upon the subject [of slavery]."[23]

After Turner, antislavery or abolitionist ideas expressed in newspapers were not the only concerns for slave owners; they were also worried about inaccurate reporting during slave troubles. Their concern was that erroneous accounts, especially of the slave numbers involved, might give slaves false ideas about their strength during a revolt. A *Richmond Compiler* dispatch and a *Richmond Whig* item urged restraint after a number of "false, absurd and idle rumors" had been "circulated by the Press," and they blamed editors for "alarming the public mind as much as possible" and for "persuading the slaves to entertain a high opinion of their strength and consequence."[24] The *Richmond Whig* writer expressed the problem in this way: "While truth is always the best policy, and the best remedy, the exaggerations to which we have alluded, are calculated to give the slaves false conceptions of their numbers and capacity, by exhibiting the terror and confusion of the whites, and to induce them to think that practicable, which they see is so much feared by their superiors."

The discourse of slavery as a threat to the nation came to full expression in the increasingly vociferous attacks on newspaper editors by other editors and the constant accusations flying about that an offending editor was un-American or, worse, a traitor. The fiery rhetoric, always present during times of slave trouble, reached a new peak by 1859 and signaled how pronounced the political gap, found in these editor-on-editor rants, had become. Certainly during the 1800

Prosser conspiracy, occurring at the height of the contentious presidential election, the editorial content reflected the partisan-press-era mood, with editors emphasizing political affiliations in their name-calling.[25] In a lengthy column headlined "Sedition and Insurrection" in September 24, 1800, the editor of the pro-Federalist *Philadelphia Gazette* attacked the pro-Republican *Aurora* editor for a "most contemptible farrago of fury and imbecility that we ever recollect to have seen in that paper" and accused the *Aurora* of trying "to turn the blame of the late Negro insurrection [Prosser's conspiracy] upon the [Adams] government!"[26] The *Aurora* also raised the ire of the *Philadelphia Gazette's* editor by making a claim that the United States and Great Britain were at work to establish "an independent Empire of Blacks in St. Domingo!" According to the *Gazette,* the *Aurora* editor claimed that these workings were "known to the rebel *Gabriel,* to all the blacks of Virginia, and to the blacks of South Carolina, and they have been induced to rise up in consequence, to massacre and rebellion!!!"[27] The *Gazette* editor assailed his fellow editor by calling him and those like him "auxiliary Jacobins" (referring to the radicals who pushed revolutionary France into its "Reign of Terror").

After Vesey's 1822 conspiracy, the partisan tone that had rung loudly years earlier softened, with editors making generally sympathetic overtures, especially regarding how Charleston authorities handled the crisis. A comment in the August 3 *National Intelligencer* noted that the "newspapers in Charleston have been necessarily silent" about the Vesey conspiracy. In justifying the silence, the editor relied on words from the *Charleston City Gazette:* "When the investigation and labours attendant on such a state of things shall have ceased, when Justice shall be satisfied, and our city restored to its wonted tranquility. . . . It will bring to view a scheme of wildness and of wickedness."[28]

When some editors questioned the number of arrests and executions, newspaper contributors such as the writer of "The Late Plot" responded, defending Charleston authorities. Appearing in the *Maryland Gazette,* his argument supported the harsh punishments and criticized "some unprincipled editors [who] have stated they saw no justification for the severe punishment inflicted."[29] One "unprincipled" editor may have been with the *New York Daily Advertiser,* which contained these comments on July 31, 1822: "Human beings, who once breathed the air of freedom on their own mountains and in their own valleys, but who have been kidnapped by white men and dragged into endless slavery, cannot be expected to be contented with their situation. White men, too, would engender plots and escape from their imprisonment were they situated as are these miserable children of Africa."[30] "We have not been inattentive," the *Charleston Courier's* editor countered on August 12, "in this distressing period, to the notice which might be taken of our situation by the journals in our sister states."[31] While the editor thanked some for their expressions of "tenderness and sympathy, with the exception of one solitary print in New-York," he wrote, "We regard with pity the individual who could deliberately sneer at our misfortunes—we leave him to the consolations of his conscience—his nightly dreams on his pillow—and hope he may always enjoy that security, which he so much rejoices that our city has been deprived of." The editor reminded "Mr. Stone, of the N. York *Commercial Advertiser*" that in "1741, in the city of New-York, *thirteen Negroes* were BURNT ALIVE *for insurrectionary efforts*," but in Charleston the blacks received a trial. The *Advertiser* also attracted the attention of the *Charleston City Gazette* editor, who on August 14, 1822, wrote, "In the opinion of the community of Charleston . . . the *Bluelight* editor of *The New York Daily Advertiser* might invent some other way of edifying his readers than in groaning over the execution of a score of Culprits upon whose fate Justice and Humanity alike pronounced the sentence."[32]

A decade later, after Nat Turner, some southern editors found especially unnerving an Albany story about Gabriel Prosser's 1800 conspiracy.[33] The *Richmond Enquirer*'s editor deemed the *Albany Evening Journal*'s story "Gabriel's Defeat" inaccurate and informed readers of the following: "The man who penned it, sat down with the deliberate determination to dressing the Bandit Gabriel, as a Hero—and for that purpose has not hesitated to *forge* statements to suit his case.—It is a bare-faced attempt to expose upon the public—a vile tissue of fabrications."[34] Upsetting to the editor and others was that the author referred to Prosser as a hero, a sobriquet deemed inflammatory by other southern editors, including the *Courier*'s, who called the *Journal* editor that "Romancer of Albany."[35] In Richmond the *Enquirer* editor focused on fact errors. While the Albany story claimed that Prosser had been drawn and quartered and not hanged, the Richmond editor corrected the error by stating that such punishment was "utterly unknown to the criminal code of Virginia."[36] He disputed all the published details: "All romance!—Gabriel was not apprehended at *Richmond*, but at *Norfolk*—not in the Sally Ann, but the Mary—not bound to St. Domingo, but in a skipper." In addition the *Enquirer*'s correction noted that the reward for Prosser's capture was three hundred dollars and not ten thousand dollars as reported in the Albany newspaper. Branding the story as full of lies, the Richmond editor continued, "This miserable Bandit is represented as having made an eloquent speech to the Court upon his trial . . . in which he speaks of his dying 'as a Martyr to liberty'—and of his example raising up a Gabriel, like Washington to lead the Africans to freedom."[37] According to the irate editor, the slave rebel "conducted himself . . . very little like a hero," and this "libeler's [the Albany editor's]" words would produce "indignation" and were "an infamous slander upon us."

In Washington the *Intelligencer*'s editor described the story as "fabulous and very objectionable" and suggested that it would be proper "to arrest its circulation, and prevent the erroneous impressions which it is calculated to produce." He called Prosser's "atrocious plot an extensive scheme of robbery and murder" and the "prototype of the tragedy recently acted at Southampton," adding that the story was "calculated to invest [Prosser's] character and fate with a romantic interest" by putting "a dying speech into his mouth, in which he is made to compare himself to Washington, and his discovered conspiracy to the American Revolution." The editor said that the published details of Prosser's execution were purely imaginary. While acknowledging slavery as an evil British legacy of greed, the writer suggested that the Albany writer had unfairly attacked "our peculiar situation" with "unfounded representations of the manners and laws of Virginia." He added that most northerners knew that slaves were "treated with kindness" and would never call Prosser a "hero."[38]

After John Brown's raid, editors' attacks turned away from abolitionist publications such as the *Liberator* and Walker's *Appeal* and took the form of nearly daily invectives launched at one another.[39] Furious at what happened at Harper's Ferry, southern editors challenged the loyalty, political affiliations, and sympathies of, especially, New York Republican newspapers, notably Greeley's *New York Tribune*, Raymond's *New York Times*, and Bryant's *New York Evening Post*.[40] A Charleston newspaper contained this tongue-in-cheek comment about the *Tribune:* "It will be seen that the Tribune considers the act of Brown as the act of a patriot. . . . To become a hero and a martyr, in the Tribune's estimation, is to go South and excite the slaves to rise and cut the throats of their white masters. . . . Kind and considerate *Tribune*."[41] Those words seem tempered compared to others published after Harper's Ferry, such as the claim by a Richmond correspondent that the *New York Evening Post* was "cracked with abolition treason."[42] In response the tone in New York's newspapers turned from sympathy over the raid to sharp criticism of southern editors and Bennett's proslavery, pro-Democratic *New York Herald*.

Naturally the antislavery newspapers' loudest critic was the *Richmond Enquirer*. Its editor lashed out at any perceived criticisms of Virginia chivalry or military expertise and quickly corrected any errors found in the northern presses in an effort to discredit them.[43] On November 25 an *Enquirer* editorial rebutted a *New York Tribune* report that said Virginia militia had wounded Brown after his surrender and shot down his men "like dogs"; he called the *New York Evening Post* and the *Tribune* "the principal offenders against propriety and justice."[44] The Richmond editor argued that it was the paper's duty to "correct the misrepresentations and expose the falsehoods of the Black Republican papers" and to explain that federal militia, not Virginians, had wounded Brown.

When weeks earlier a *New York Times* article contained a fact error about Virginia geography, the *Enquirer* editor reproved Raymond, calling him "the little villain of the 'Times'" and a "stupid booby" for saying that Richmond was close to the Shenandoah River and the Allegheny Mountains.[45] The editorial pleaded, "Will not some humane reader of 'The Times' forthwith send that journal a map of Virginia?" If that was not a sufficient reprimand, the Richmond editor called the *Times* that "hermaphrodite journal, half Republican, half conservative, half Seward, half Douglas" that "began its existence under the aegis of Abolitionism, and for a long time vegetated in unprofitable existence under the upas shadow of the 'Tribune.' Eclipsed in enterprise and surpassed in virulence by the arch traitor of the 'Tribune' [Greeley]." Those words appeared on November 8, and two days later Raymond addressed the *Enquirer's* insulting words with the following observation: "The Enquirer's spasm of rage at our innocent mistake seems to have plunged it into a most uncomfortable frame of mind on general topics."[46] The verbal assault against the *Times* continued in a November 15 *Enquirer* editorial stating that the *New York Times's* "deep-seated malignity, mangled with the folly of geographical mistakes, alternates between contemptible abuse of Virginia, and childish whimpering, whining sympathy for John Brown."[47] Three days later an *Enquirer* editorial called Raymond's paper "the most insidious and unscrupulous of the Northern Abolitionist press" and complained that this newspaper was "inferior in editorial ability to the 'Tribune,' and reputed to be very far inferior to the same paper in circulation."[48]

When some in the northern press criticized the excessive military preparations at Charlestown and chided Virginians for their panicked state, the Richmond editor grew more defensive, arguing that northern criticism promoted disunion. A November 25 *Enquirer* editorial noted, "And what good can the press of the North accomplish by insulting a people already highly excited with indignation at the wrongs perpetrated upon them by citizens of the Confederacy?"[49] The southern editor seemed especially sensitive to the comments about the Virginia panic. "The Northern papers are serving the country to no good end by misrepresenting the excitement that exists throughout Virginia *as a panic.*" Even the *New York Herald* came under attack when it published critical content about the tense situation, with the Richmond editor claiming that the *Herald* had fallen "to the vulgar level of the 'Tribune.'"[50] In New Orleans the *Daily Picayune* editor defended Charlestown's military presence, condemning the "Abolition press" for "heaping ludicrous epithets on the Virginians and their Governor, as foolishly timid, and as unnerved and unmanly."[51]

Northern antislavery editors had a different view. Concerning the state of southern fear, an October 22 *New York Times* editorial argued that southern newspaper editors were "making the whole South ring with the most absurd and extravagant exaggerations of this affair at Harper's Ferry, and proclaiming the instant and imminent danger of being overwhelmed by the hordes of Abolition invaders from the Northern States."[52] The item "The Virginia Insurrection" in the *New York Tribune* claimed that the southern press and other southern institutions were creating a climate of irrationality:

> [Southerners] have been taught . . . from infancy—by legislation, by preaching, *by journalism* [emphasis added], by common conversation, by constant fears, by the pulpit, by apprehensions too grave almost to be whispered—that, in spite of police regulations as stringent as the ingenuity of the human

intellect could devise, daily life was lived in peril, and nightly sleep snatched in peril; and that white men and white women and white children breathed and had their being at the mercy and by the gracious permission of black men—of a race, the latent strength of which could only be prevented from breaking into open and murderous insurrection by all manner of precautions, whether savagely oppressive or simply the manifestations of timidity. The slave statutes of Virginia are but legislated, enacted, concrete fright.[53]

New York Times and *Tribune* editorials also claimed that the *Enquirer* exacerbated abolitionists' fears for political reasons, as this *Times* editorial illustrated: "The Executive and the Press of Virginia have chosen rather to wring from this matter all the waters of strife which it contained. They have fostered those insane fears and unreasoning passions of the populace."[54] Even the *Daily National Intelligencer,* which remained largely temperate editorially about Harper's Ferry, advised "some of the intemperate sheets of the South" to assume a more moderate tone: "It is by far the most effectual method of convincing Northern men of the danger of their doctrines."[55]

In a style reminiscent of the partisan press era, the pro-Republican *Tribune* took advantage of this editorial moment to harp on New York Democratic newspapers. An October 22 editorial stated that "the terror at Harper's Ferry" was subsiding and it was "time our New-York journalists may get over their panic also." The editorial added, "In the agony of their terror," newspapers such as the *New York Herald* and the *New York Express* "convert John Brown into [New York] Gov. Seward, John Brown's seventeen white men into the Republican party, and the five free negroes into all the slaves in the United States rising to cut the throats of their masters."[56]

Greeley kept lobbing rhetorical assaults at his nemesis Bennett, writing in the October 24 *Tribune* that the *Herald* had previously accused Republicans of "plotting murder and insurrection" in an "attempt . . . to hold them responsible for the civil war and murders and outrages in Kansas."[57] Greeley defended the party, making the claim that it upheld the doctrines of Virginia's Patrick Henry, Thomas Jefferson, and George Washington. Another *Tribune* editorial, headlined "Who Taught John Brown?," attacked Bennett for linking northern abolitionists to the Harper's Ferry raid and noted with irony that Virginia's motto "SIC SEMPER TYRANNIS" could be "freely translated" as "So perish every 'slaveholder,' or more freely, 'Hurrah for John Brown!'"[58] Bennett may have raised the ire of Greeley after earlier referring to his paper as that "fanatical Tribune."[59] (He did not spare his other city rivals either, calling the *New York Times* that "wishy washy" and "twaddling" *Times* and the *New York Evening Post* that "malicious" *Post.*)

William Cullen Bryant's *New York Evening Post* too scolded Democratic, proslavery newspapers. An October 21 editorial observed, "This is to be the course of all the democratic prints—a cry against Republicans as if they were rioters and insurrectionists. It will succeed tolerable well in slaveholding soil, but no where else."[60] Of particular interest for the *Evening Post* was the *Constitution*, President James Buchanan's political organ in Washington, D.C. A *Post* editorial on October 21 stated that the *Constitution* had wrongly blamed "the fanatical crusade of Brown" on Republicans. A later *Post* editorial called the *Constitution* the real "Satanic Press," adding that it (and the president) had politicized the Harper's Ferry events.[61] Two days later the newspaper's Washington correspondent predicted that John Brown's raid would become a major topic during Congress's winter session, and he urged Republicans to be "indignant" if they had to listen to a "reiteration of the malignant falsehoods which the *Constitution* has daily served up to its readers."[62]

New York newspapers were not the only ones singled out for attack in *Enquirer* editorials. Even fellow Virginians were targeted. In particular, the *Clarke (Va.) Journal*[63] and its editor Alexander Parkins appeared in the bull's-eye for the transgression of publishing a *New York Tribune* prospectus that so outraged the *Enquirer* editor, he called the *Journal* a "meager and scandalous little sheet" and Parkins a "hired disseminator of abolition treason," the kind who would "tamper with slaves to run them off" or lead an insurrection.[64] Suggesting that "the people of Clarke and the surrounding counties owe it to their own safety to suppress this incendiary sheet," the Richmond editor said they should run Parkins out of town, "but don't lynch him."

In responding editorials on November 17, editors from the *New York Times* and the *Tribune* defended the Clarke newspaper.[65] Raymond called Parkins's response to Harper's Ferry "A Sensible Virginia Protest against Unreasonable Virginia Ferocity," and in "The Virginia Tamerlanes" he claimed that the malignant spirit of Powhatan had returned to possess Virginia's newspapers.[66] "What a tinder-box the Old Dominion must be! It will be dangerous by and by for a sane man to look in that direction lest the State should instantly explode," he reasoned.[67] As for the behavior of Virginia journalists in Charlestown, he noted, "We feel that the journalists of Virginia, in spite of themselves, are worthy of a better occupation than this of dancing round a jail like naked aborigines about a stake and clamoring for a prisoner's [Brown's] head."[68] It did not take long for the *Enquirer* to respond; on November 22 the Richmond editor charged that the *New York Times* was "an Historical Smatterer," adding, "None but a drunken or cracked editor would have written an article implying that the red Indian Powhatan still rules the 'Old Dominion' in spirit."[69]

Conclusion

In identifying the discourse of slavery as a threat to the nation, the discussion recognized that slavery, whether talked about as a states' rights and property issue or as a moral concern, inflicted damage on the nation. Over time the slave power oligarchy and its allies were willing to allow civil liberties, including those of freedom of speech, association, and the press, to disintegrate so that slavery would be preserved. The nation's newspapers, which reflected nineteenth-century American public opinion, indicated how intractable things had become by 1859, with editors accusing one another of treason and southerners, in general, suspecting any northerner of being an enemy agent out to destroy slavery. "This is a sad state of things," an editorial in the November 30, 1859, *Charleston Mercury* read, as it condemned these civil rights violations.[70] It added, "In our indignation at the aggressions of the North, we are in danger of dealing with men as if they were guilty, without proof." To this writer, the problem was not slavery but those against it, and he called the suppression of civil rights the "very worst effect of Northern Abolitionism" because "it divides us amongst ourselves." As the discourse of slavery as a threat to the nation indicated, the northern antislavery press held a different view that came to dominate the northern political landscape. Inevitably these incompatible views expressed in the discourse in the nation's newspapers competed for dominance and suggested that the state of the country as it existed in 1800, 1811, 1822, and 1831 was no longer the same by 1859.

❧ Conclusion
The Press and Slavery's Legacy

"On the one side was a money-power of two thousand millions of dollars, as the prices of slaves then ranged, held by a small body of able and desperate men, who composed a political aristocracy by special constitutional provisions; with cotton, the product of slave-labor, forming the basis of our whole foreign commerce, and with the heart of the common people chilled by a bitter prejudice against the black race. On the same side was the pecuniary interests of the Northern people, who found in the Southern states the most profitable purchasers of all their products," Henry Tanner wrote.[1] As this 1881 quote suggests, slavery in America was neither strictly a southern or a northern problem. It was a national problem that eventually sectionalized the country into the *South* and the *North*. From the country's birth and up to the eve of the Civil War, America's newspaper editors and their prints reflected public opinion about slavery and its place in American society. As years passed from 1787 and the Great Compromise over slavery, the institution transformed from a regional, "peculiar" one to a labor system that ignited fierce debate on the national stage. Over time this public debate and opinion over slavery coalesced around media discourses that reflected persistent attitudes about race and slavery's connection to American culture, economics, and politics. To identify those discourses, this book examined newspaper coverage of America's important slave troubles that generated slavery discussions that could be analyzed and interpreted. These discourses about slavery and race appeared repeatedly over a seventy-year span of newspaper coverage and concerned how white Americans, especially those with strong economic and political interests in maintaining slavery, preserved a decadent labor system that marginalized slaves and other black Americans. The discourses also revealed how this culturally entrenched and powerful social system worked in ways that destroyed challenges to it and eventually destroyed the country.

Part 1 of this book laid the contextual foundation for the uncovering of discourses about slavery, and part 2 identified three of them: the discourse of slavery's enemies identified the threats to slavery and how these enemies were talked about in newspapers; the discourse of racial panic expressed whites' fears of black violence against them and described the steps taken to restore the slave system and its race-based social order; and the discourse of slavery as a threat to the nation illustrated the extreme sectionalism that slavery caused, the institution's intrinsic immorality, and its destructive influence on American ideals and civil rights. As competing discourses appeared and challenged the taken-for-granted assumptions about slavery, the discursive competition entwined around America's long-standing political ideologies that involved arguments over the powers of the central government versus those of the states. This competition led to a political stalemate that only the Civil War could break.

Because to discuss slavery was to discuss race, antebellum newspaper coverage of events up to Nat Turner's rebellion reflected a view of blacks as members of an "unfortunate" race (and slavery as an *evil*). Other than identifying the black slave rebel as a Negro or black, newspaper accounts did not contain marginalizing racist stereotypes; however, the rebels were often referred to as wretches or savages.[2] Not until John Brown's raid, as calls for an end to American slavery became louder, did the intensely racist term "nigger" appear in the newspapers. In the southern press and the conservative *New York Herald*, the word was used to label not only black Americans but also slavery's enemies, such as the Republican Party or other white, antislavery supporters. If words matter, this one certainly did.

As detailed in the book's brief narratives of slave revolts and conspiracies, newspaper discourses always constructed black slave rebels as enemies to slavery and *to the nation*, therefore objectifying them as entities that must be destroyed. The actions of black men such as Gabriel Prosser, Denmark Vesey, and Nat Turner frightened white Americans and sparked panics and intense retaliatory actions that dehumanized this enemy and rationalized the complete annihilation of him or anyone else connected to him. The black slave rebel, whose motives were largely unrevealed in newspapers, remained vilified. While Nat Turner, for example, may have confessed his motives for murder, his words were rebuked as the ravings of a lunatic who had been given a voice by a white man. Thus underlying all talk in newspapers about slavery and slave troubles were white America's fears of black vengeance against them and a belief in a normalized system that oppressed all of the nation's blacks, including those living as free people. While the black rebel and John Brown were slavery's natural enemies, so too were free blacks. To white, southern, slave-owning elites, the free black was a dangerous being who represented an anomaly in a country made for white people. Up north free blacks lived lives only marginally better, and newspapers usually depicted them as ignominious beings existing on white society's fringes.

The reactions to the actions of John Brown, a white man—as reflected in the nation's newspapers—were equally extreme. However, the nation's newspapers gave him something they denied the earlier rebels: a voice. Newspapers printed his stirring words after his capture, during his trial, and before his execution, and in the northern antislavery press Brown morphed from a madman into a martyr. Such a transformation never occurred for the black rebel, and it never occurred in the southern and conservative press for Brown. As media attention grew, Brown appeared to use the attention to spread his antislavery message, and of all the events studied, his media constructions were the most complex, coming to represent the political clash driving the nation toward destruction.

It is worth recalling a common thread connecting the discourses about Brown to those about his black rebel counterparts. Newspaper editors and their contributors highlighted religious fanaticism in account after account to describe the slave rebels and Brown. Often newspaper stories referred to these men and their followers as deluded in their misguided religious beliefs. To a religious, Christian, nineteenth-century America, such fanaticism suitably explained the actions of these men who threatened slavery or the greater social and racial order.[3]

Even though northern and southern newspapers told little about other black participants during the slave troubles, two groups of blacks did receive mention, and discourses about them were often juxtaposed. The talk about the first group formed the good Negro discourse, which emphasized the importance of slave loyalty in times of crisis and became an important element of the discourse of racial panic. These reports focused on slaves acting as informers or helping their masters fight the slave rebels or of free blacks assisting whites. Other stories concerned the lack of slave participation in the slave troubles. These accounts lent an assurance to white readers that black slavery had a natural place in America's social order. The converse of all of this formed the discourse of slavery's enemies.

The "positive good theory" also became a repeating discursive element whenever slave troubles occurred, and its use increased over time, especially in the southern and conservative press. The argument that this paternalistic system best served blacks likely made sense to many white Americans and provided a powerful justification for the continued enslavement of African Americans. In the editorial clamor following John Brown, the southern press featured the argument prominently, perhaps as a way to signal that the southern elites would not bend on the slavery question. These slaveholders intensified their rhetoric, using the theory's racist ideas about black people to counter the increasing political and moral pressure put on their economic and labor system and their way of life.

In addition to presenting discourses about slavery, this book accounted for the nation's changing newspapers. Before 1859 the northern and southern newspapers relied on sporadic correspondence and other items from affected areas for the latest information about slave revolts and conspiracies. This tended to ensure a southern (and usually proslavery) point of view at the time of slave troubles, eliciting a sympathetic editorial response in the North. In the decades between 1831 and 1859, newspapers became news gatherers, less dependent on sister newspapers for the details from an affected area. By 1859 technology had transformed nineteenth-century newspapers into a truly mass and *instant* media, so at the time of Harper's Ferry, newspapers and their subscribers received hourly updates from wire services, using the telegraph. This resulted in a change in the tenor of news coverage. In addition newspapers could quickly correct errors from earlier reports, and northern newspaper editors could send their own people to Harper's Ferry and Charlestown instead of relying on solely southern sources of information. As a result northern readers generally received news about the slave troubles from a northern point of view. Whether such editorial changes contributed to the extreme sectionalist talk remains unclear, but changes in the way news was collected and distributed coincided with stronger editorials that expressed distinct northern and southern views. What is clear is that technology created anxiety for some southern editors who feared northern control of the telegraph. So as newspaper stories became mass and instant, their content also expressed thoughts about a nation disuniting over slavery.

While the North and the South were, in general, culturally distinct throughout their antebellum union, newspaper discourses indicated that ideas about slavery as an evil were similar in 1800, 1822, and 1831. Those discourses shifted as the nation and the press transformed, with the talk about slavery signaling a change, as the discourse of slavery as a threat to the nation illustrated. The discourse that expressed extreme sectionalism in the form of secessionism was not as apparent up to 1831, when the southern editorial voice generally expressed an apologetic tone for slavery and northern editorials expressed assurances that the people of the North would rush to aid southerners in the event of slave insurrection. Such discourse disappeared in 1859, although as early as 1822 there were hints that slavery would rend the country in two. The Harper's Ferry coverage revealed a true break in the national consensus, as secessionist talk dominated southern editorials. In the North antislavery editors expressed their increasing frustration over this and what they viewed as southern intransigence over slavery.

Besides slavery's destructive influence on national unity, the discourse signaled its poisonous effect on America's ideals and civil liberties. Southern and northern editorials supported the suppression of only the most "incendiary" abolitionist materials, such as David Walker's *Appeal* and William Lloyd Garrison's *Liberator*, circulating during the earlier slave troubles. By 1859 southern editorials advocated banning and criminalizing virtually any publication with *any* antislavery thought and strongly supported the arrest of anyone possessing such material.[4] Eventually just being a Yankee down South was enough cause for alarm, and as the news items revealed, strong precautionary measures were put in place to make sure no slaves were tampered with. In addition northern and southern editors engaged in hostile attacks, with southern calls for the arrests of prominent northern politicians whom they accused of treason. The discourse of slavery as a threat to the nation after the Harper's Ferry raid indicated the extremely dangerous times ahead for the nation.

One of those men whom southern editors wanted to see arrested after Harper's Ferry was the abolitionist Wendell Phillips. His response to their calls for his arrest came in a sermon given on November 1 at the Plymouth Church in Brooklyn. Entitled "The Lesson of the Hour," it discussed the whole affair while presenting this prescient vision for America: "I think the lesson of the hour is insurrection. Insurrection of thought always precedes the insurrection of arms. The last twenty years have been insurrection of thought. We seem to be entering on a new phase of the great moral American struggle."[5] Unfortunately the moral struggle became a military one, with the southern elites convincing thousands of poor young men to die for a right they could never attain. Corey Robin has observed, "The slaveholder created a quintessentially American form of democratic feudalism, turning the white majority into a lordly class, sharing in privileges and prerogatives of governing the slave class."[6] These southern elites, through their presses, convinced all white southerners that they had the potential to become slave owners and thus members of the ruling class. To them, it became a membership worth dying for.

In a larger context, this book says something about what happens when an enemy threatens a social order and suggests that members of that structure are quite willing to diminish or even destroy their own important cultural and civic values and liberties to maintain that order. The book also says something about how media can become complicit in the destruction of those ideals. In eighteenth- and nineteenth-century America, the enemies of slavery presented a dire scenario to slave society. In contemporary times, new enemies have replaced the old, but the reactions to those threats often remain the same, following a similar course of media identification.

It must be said that while slavery's lasting effects on race in America have diminished, they have not disappeared and seem largely ignored in mainstream society. Surely the continued legacy endures, as the existing disparities of opportunities among black versus white Americans still suggest. It also remains in the strange cognitive dissonance that many Americans have over this sad chapter in their nation's history. As an example of this, in the summer of 2011 some conservative presidential candidates of a major American political party signed a controversial pledge that contained language suggesting that African American children born into slave families had a more stable home environment than those living in twenty-first-century America. Such intellectual disregard for the horrors of American slavery is stunning, but it also points out that slavery's legacy to race issues in America remains.

NOTES

Preface

1. Carroll, *Slave Insurrections*, 57.

2. "Negro Insurrections and New England Contributions," *New York Herald,* November 23, 1859.

3. The words "Negro" and "Negroes" are appropriately capitalized in text; out of respect for historical accuracy, original text is used despite its offensive tone. As W. E. B. Du Bois observed, the capital letter in the word "Negro" in the 1840s and 1850s signified another way to degrade the black race; see Du Bois, *Black Reconstruction*, 39. In addition all quoted materials appear in their original forms, including variant spellings, capitalizations, and italicizations. In instances where more clarity about spelling or capitalization is necessary, [*sic*] has been inserted.

4. A slave revolt or rebellion is defined as an armed uprising involving black slaves who may or may not have succeeded in freeing themselves from white control. A slave conspiracy (or plot) is considered a plan made by a quasi-military group of blacks, free or slave, for an armed uprising, successful or not. A raid is defined as a brief quasi-military campaign with a specific purpose that, as a complete event, may be related to subsequent events. John Brown's attempt to steal weapons from the federal arsenal and arm black slaves is an example of a raid.

5. MacDonald, *Canadian Public Opinion*, 78.

6. Stampp, *Peculiar Institution*, vii.

7. As Barbara Jeanne Fields observes in "Slavery, Race, and Ideology in the United States of America," an "American racial ideology" developed that was just "as original an invention of the Founders as is the United States itself" (101).

8. Fredrickson, *Black Image*, 53. He adds, "The danger of slave unrest and rebellion in the South was a recurring theme of colonizationist literature" (8).

9. Jordan, *White over Black*, 111, 114. Stampp too observes that slaves were hardly content, and the slave master knew they hardly "ever adapted successfully to their servitude, and few whites could defend the system without betraying the emotional stress to which slavery subjected them"; see Stampp, *Peculiar Institution*, 6. To revolt, according to Junius Rodriguez, gave slaves "one of the few methods . . . to make white society recognize their humanity"; see Rodriquez, "Ripe for Revolt," 284.

10. Fredrickson, *Black Image*, 53, notes, "In moments of candor, Southerners admitted their suspicion that duplicity, opportunism, and potential rebelliousness lurked behind the mask of Negro affability."

11. See Jordan, *White over Black*, 111.

12. Genovese, *Roll Jordan Roll*, 597–660.

13. See Rucker, *River Flows On*.

14. Halasz, *Rattling Chains*, 1–2.

15. The year was 1619; see ibid., 5.

16. Ibid. According to Halasz, this revolt, foiled by a white servant, was to take place on September 13, 1663. See also Rucker, *River Flows On*, 130–32.

17. The slave historian David Robertson has argued that the 1739 Stono River uprising was the largest slave rebellion and gave slaves encouragement that they could organize "widespread slave revolt"; see Robertson, *Denmark Vesey*, 24–25.

18. "The Negro Insurrection," *New York Times*, October 20, 1859.

19. Shaw, "News about Slavery," 483, 492. Shaw, however, notes that in southern newspapers a change in southern attitudes could be discerned around 1832. Shaw concludes that between the time of the Missouri Compromise to Nat Turner, southern newspaper coverage about slavery displayed editorial ambiguity (486–87).

20. Genovese, *Roll Jordan Roll*, 50.

21. Quoted in Stampp, *Peculiar Institution*, 136.

22. Van Dijk, "Introduction," 5.

23. Van Dijk, *Elite Discourse*, 47.

24. James Paul Gee has said that discourse freezes a moment so it can be analyzed; see Gee, *Introduction*, 21. See also McCarthy, *Knowledge as Culture*, 3.

25. Fairclough, *Language and Power*, 46. Fairclough identifies three constraints in power relationships that discourse reveals: 1) content constraints about what said and done; 2) relational constraints between those entering into discourse; and 3) subject restraints, which concern the position a person occupies (ibid., 46–55). According to Fairclough, *Discourse and Social Change*, a critical discourse analysis would show that "discourse is shaped by relations of power and ideologies" (12).

26. Wetherell and Potter, *Mapping the Language*, 85.

27. Spurr, *Rhetoric of Empire*, 11.

28. To avoid unnecessary confusion in later text, Harper's Ferry retains its apostrophe, which has been removed in contemporary spellings.

29. To identify how slave revolts, conspirators, and rebels were "talked about," all references to the events or their participants were analyzed in the selected southern and northern newspapers. To identify social constructions of a slave rebel or conspirator, what was said about the person was recorded. Prosser, Vesey, Turner, and Brown were tried, so published accounts of their trials were also studied, as were any words from others put on trial. The following outlines briefly show the method employed in the examination of Gabriel Prosser's conspiracy of 1800, Denmark Vesey's conspiracy of 1822, and Nat Turner's revolt in 1831. The research examined daily, semiweekly, and weekly newspaper coverage about Prosser, Vesey, and Turner. The research used a discourse analysis on each article about the conspiracy or revolt, participants, trials, executions, and aftermath. The list follows.

A. Gabriel Prosser's conspiracy of 1800

Four southern and four northern newspapers were selected for study of coverage of Prosser's conspiracy. The southern newspapers were *Virginia Argus* (semiweekly edition), Richmond, Va.; *City Gazette and Daily Advertiser* (daily), Charleston, S.C.;

and *Times and District of Columbia Advertiser* (daily), Alexandria, Va. The northern newspapers were *Philadelphia Gazette and Daily Advertiser* (daily), Philadelphia, Pa.; *Daily Advertiser* (daily), New York City; *Newport Mercury* (weekly), Newport, R.I.; *Massachusetts Spy; or Worcester Gazette* (weekly), Worcester, Mass. *Georgia Gazette*, a weekly southern newspaper from Savannah, Ga., was examined, but no items about Prosser's conspiracy were found. The research spanned an approximate twenty-two-week period beginning with the date of the intended insurrection, August 30, and continuing through the end of December 1800.

B. *Louisiana (German Coast) revolt of 1811*

Selected newspapers were *Louisiana Gazette and New Orleans Daily Advertiser*—later referred to as *Louisiana Gazette; Newport Mercury*, Newport, R.I.; *New York Evening Post*, New York City; *Massachusetts Spy*, Worcester, Mass.; *Charleston Courier*, Charleston, S.C.; *Virginia Argus*, Richmond, Va.; *National Intelligencer*, Washington, D.C. The research examined seventeen weeks—from January 1, 1811, through April 1811—of selected newspaper coverage, identifying all passages referring to Louisiana or the Orleans Territory, the revolt itself and its suppression, and any references to the slavery question. Two secondary sources containing newspaper items about the revolt were useful: Thomas M. Thompson's master's thesis, "National Newspaper and Legislative Reactions to Louisiana's Deslondes Slave Revolt of 1811," provides a short, essentially anecdotal, and nontheoretical examination of the revolt.

C. *Denmark Vesey's conspiracy of 1822*

For the Vesey conspiracy, the southern newspapers studied were *Charleston Courier* (daily), Charleston, S.C.; *Charleston Mercury* (daily), Charleston, S.C.; *Richmond Enquirer* (daily), Richmond, Va.; and *Maryland Gazette* (daily), Annapolis, Md. The three northern newspapers were *New York Evening Post* (daily), New York City; *Newport Mercury* (weekly), Newport, R.I.; and *National Intelligencer* (daily), Washington, D.C. The research covered an approximately twenty-seven-week period beginning with the date of the first arrest in June 1822 and ending in December of that year.

D. *Nat Turner's revolt of 1831*

For Nat Turner's revolt, the southern newspapers included *Richmond Enquirer* (daily), Richmond, Va.; *Charleston Courier* (daily), Charleston, S.C.; *Charleston Mercury* (daily), Charleston, S.C.; and *Maryland Gazette* (daily), Annapolis, Md. The four northern newspapers were *New York Evening Post* (daily), New York City; *Boston Evening Transcript* (daily), Boston, Mass.; *Newport Mercury* (weekly), Newport, R.I.; and *National Intelligencer* (weekly), Washington, D.C. The research examined an approximately nineteen-week period from the date of the first murders in the early morning hours of August 22, 1831, through the end of December 1831.

E. *John Brown's raid at Harper's Ferry, 1859*

For John Brown's raid at Harper's Ferry, the five southern newspapers examined were the *Richmond Enquirer* (semiweekly), Richmond, Va.; *Charleston Courier* (daily), Charleston, S.C.; *Charleston Mercury* (daily), Charleston, S.C.; *Baltimore Sun* (daily), Baltimore, Md.; and *New Orleans Daily Picayune* (daily), New Orleans, La. The six northern newspapers included *New York Evening Post* (daily), New York City; *New York Herald* (daily), New York City; *New York Times* (daily), New York City; *New York Tribune* (daily), New York City; *Boston Evening Transcript* (daily), Boston, Mass.; and *Daily National Intelligencer* (daily), Washington, D.C. Daily coverage between

October 17, as newspapers first reported the raid, through December 6, three days after John Brown's hanging at Charlestown, Va., was examined.

30. MacDonald, *Canadian Public Opinion,* 78.
31. Wilson, *Patriotic Gore,* xxv.
32. See Pickett et al., "Reconsidering the Relationship," 149.

Introduction

1. As Kovel, *White Racism,* 20–21, notes, "As long as [it] worked, it seemed perfectly sensible." In addition, according to Lauren, *Power and Prejudice,* 8, "Racial stereotypes . . . were clearly nourished by a long-term flow of slave labor from sub-Saharan Africa."

2. Proslavery factions managed to suppress discussion of the slavery question in Congress in the 1830s. For a full account of the House of Representatives' "gag" order, see Miller, *Arguing about Slavery.*

3. Tise, *Proslavery,* 10–14.

4. Genovese, *Roll Jordan Roll,* 68.

5. Legally the slave's recourse was about as much as that of a "brute" animal; see Stroud, *Sketch of the Laws,* 167.

6. This ideology explained why, in the historian Barbara Jeanne Fields's words, "some people could rightly be denied what others took for granted: namely, liberty"; see Fields, "Slavery, Race, and Ideology," 114.

7. Davis, *Age of Revolution,* 85.

8. Lauren, *Power and Prejudice,* 13.

9. Davis, *Slavery and Human Progress,* 1, 5: "Nature must therefore have intended to make the bodies of free men and of slaves different also; slaves' bodies strong for the services they have to do, those of free men upright and not much use for that kind of work, but instead useful for community life." Peter Garnsey adds that Aristotle divided the household into its "perfect form," which consisted of slaves and freemen; see Garnsey, *Ideas of Slavery,* 23.

10. See Garnsey, *Ideas of Slavery,* 35.

11. Davis, *Western Culture,* 35. Davis adds that slavery was long recognized as the "ultimate limit in dependence and loss of natural freedom."

12. Garnsey, *Ideas of Slavery,* 29.

13. Davis, *Slavery and Human Progress,* 56.

14. Davis, *Age of Revolution,* 57.

15. Davis, *Slavery and Human Progress,* 65. According to Davis, population estimates show that in a little more than a hundred years native populations fell from twenty-five million to one million in 1605. He adds that the combination of sugar and slaves became "keys to imperial wealth and power" (ibid., 63).

16. Fields, "Slavery, Race, and Ideology," 102. According to the historian Louis Ruchames, "Most Englishmen approved of slavery and despised the Negroes and Indians"; see Ruchames, *Racial Thought,* 5.

17. See Ruchames, *Racial Thought,* 36.

18. Davis, *Western Culture,* 10. Davis, *Slavery and Human Progress,* 76, observes, "Throughout the British New World colonies, the regions that drew the greatest total

immigration relative to their existing populations also imported the greatest proportion of black slaves," and therefore slavery became an "indispensable" commodity.

19. As Lauren, *Power and Prejudice*, 18, has observed, the economics of the slave trade encouraged the development of a racist ideology because, as Europeans increasingly met Africans in the "distorted context of slavery," they increasingly set "Africans apart from themselves, describing them as 'heathens' and 'pagans' in religion, 'bestial' and 'brutish' in behavior, and 'lewd' and 'lustful' in sex, and thus only fit for enslavement."

20. Ruchames, *Racial Thought*, 14. As a racist ideology developed, marginalizing Africans in the English colonies, it was, as Garnsey, *Ideas of Slavery*, 242–43, says, "completely consistent with the social attitudes of the intellectual, religious and political leaders of ancient societies, who were utterly committed to the institution of slavery, holding that when properly regulated, it guaranteed security for slaves, the good life for the citizenry, and the stability of the society as a whole." Adding to this, Richard Ropers and Dan Pence note, "American slavery became the first instance of a *racist ideology* used to meet the greedy economic needs of white landowners in the Atlantic and Southern States"; see Ropers and Pence, *American Prejudice*, 33.

21. Miller, *Arguing about Slavery*, 11.

22. See Davis, *Western Culture*, 8. Davis adds that the fifteen million Africans brought to the New World over three centuries created a lucrative and fierce trade in human cargo (ibid., 8–9).

23. Jordan, *White over Black*, 233.

24. Smedley, *Race in America*, 106–8.

25. Davis, *Slavery and Human Progress*, 66.

26. Smedley, *Race in America*, 106.

27. Quoted in Garnsey, *Ideas of Slavery*, 1.

28. Fields, "Slavery, Race, and Ideology," 104.

29. Davis, *Age of Revolution*, 58.

30. Davis, *Western Culture*, 447. Davis adds that early European thinkers on race even suggested that blacks may have come from hell because they were "so burnt."

31. Montesquieu, "Spirit of the Laws," 22.

32. Jordan, *White over Black*, 24.

33. Holland, *Refutation*, 86.

34. In their study of racist discourse in New Zealand, Margaret Wetherell and Jonathan Potter note that racial identity was linked to family histories: "The definition of race as a form of lineage rested on the concept of ancestry and tracing common origins back through related individuals and family lines"; see Wetherell and Potter, *Mapping the Language*, 19.

35. As the anthropologist Arthur K. Spears notes, the socially constructed notion of race-as-skin-color was "created and sustained in the minds of humans living or aware of racialized societies"; see Spears, "Race and Ideology," 17.

36. Van Dijk, *Elite Discourse*, 22–23. Smedley, *Race in America*, 7, similarly argues that race is part of a knowledge system that brings "order and understanding about complex realities" as one group (e.g., Europeans) achieves dominance over another (e.g., Africans or Native Americans). She adds, "*Race* is a shorthand term for, as well as a symbol of, a 'knowledge system'; a way of knowing and of looking at the world and rationalizing its contents in this case, other human beings in terms that are derived from previous

cultural-historical experience and reflective of contemporary social values, relationships, and conditions" (ibid., 15).

37. Smedley, *Race in America*, 171, writes that the connection between race and skin color became a "worldview evolving out of and compatible with power relationships, political goals, and economic interests of European colonizers." Lauren, *Power and Prejudice*, 16, observes that the growing economic profitability of the slave trade as it filled a desperate need for cheap labor in the Americas helped institutionalize concepts of race and racism as justifications for slavery.

38. Perlmutter, *Legacy of Hate*, 20.

39. Garnsey, *Ideas of Slavery*, 242–43.

40. Davis, *Slavery and Human Progress*, xviii. See also Jenkins, *Pro-Slavery Thought*, 13.

41. Wood, *Origins of American Slavery*, 9–11.

42. Vaughn, *Roots of American Racism*, 166.

43. "For the Mercury: Our Slaves," *Mercury*, November 15, 1859.

44. Jordan, *White over Black*, 199.

45. Mather, "Negro Christianized," 63. Even early Puritan religious reformers such as Roger Williams argued only for the humane treatment of slaves and never abolition; see Jenkins, *Pro-Slavery Thought*, 3–4.

46. Sewall, "Selling of Joseph," 51.

47. Saffin, "Brief and Candid Answer," 54, 58.

48. "Forensic Dispute," 156.

49. Takaki, *Iron Cages*, 12–13.

50. Priest, "Slavery," 321; See also Fredrickson, *Black Image*, 60–61.

51. Popkin, "Philosophical Basis," 245–46. To Popkin, many of those philosophers held four essential views of race: 1) nonwhites were intellectually inferior to whites; 2) the state of non-"whiteness" denoted "sickness or degeneracy"; 3) nonwhites were lower on the "great chain of being and represent[ed] a link between man and apes"; and 4) racial groups were separate creations with "Caucasian being the best" (ibid., 247). Jordan, *White over Black*, 218–19, notes that Africans were placed at the bottom on the "chain of being."

52. Quoted in Popkin, "Philosophical Basis," 245–46. For a separate discussion of Hume, see Lauren, *Power and Prejudice*, 21.

53. Popkin, "Philosophical Basis," 251.

54. Jefferson, *Notes on the State of Virginia*, 143. Jefferson also said that several physical and racial differences elevated whites over blacks, for example that black men had a predilection for white women and that the black race had a "very strong and disagreeable ordour." Further he argued that the African intellect had neither the artistic nor the reasoning capacity of whites. While calling their "imagination glowing and elevated," he said that they were incapable of uttering a thought "above the level of plain narration"; see ibid., 139–40.

55. Olmsted, *Cotton Kingdom*, 19.

56. Ferber, *White Man Falling*, 33.

57. Kleg, *Hate, Prejudice and Racism*, 66–67.

58. Ibid., 67–68; Ferber, *White Man Falling*, 29.

59. Blumenbach did dispute some notions about black inferiority, especially regarding character: "I am acquainted with no single distinctive bodily character," he wrote, "which is at once peculiar to the negro, and which cannot be found to exist in many

other distant nations"; see *Johann Friedreich Blumenbach,* 305.

60. Quoted in Kleg, *Hate, Prejudice and Racism,* 69.

61. Jordan, *White over Black,* 31–32.

62. This quote is from *Encyclopaedia Britannica,* 3rd ed. (Philadelphia, 1798); see Popkin, "Philosophical Basis," 249. Popkin notes that subsequent encyclopedia editions were equally racist: one entry in the 1884 edition discussed cranial differences among the races and concluded that this may be the reason for the "inherent mental inferiority of the blacks." The writer states, "No full-blood Negro has ever been distinguished as a man of science, a poet or an artist, and the fundamental equality claimed for him by ignorant philanthropists is belied by the whole history of the race throughout the historic period" (ibid., 257).

63. Fredrickson, *Black Image,* 74–75.

64. Ibid., 75.

65. *Dred Scott,* 404–7. The court ultimately decided that slaves were not citizens and lacked legal standing.

66. Fredrickson, *Black Image,* 92.

67. Rose and Rose, *America Divided,* 31–32.

68. Davis, *Western Culture,* 23.

69. Stroud, *Sketch of the Laws,* 165–66.

70. See Jordan, *White over Black,* 140.

71. Nye, *Fettered Freedom,* 26. The original text is from an article in *DeBow's Review,* March 1851.

72. Ferber, *White Man Falling,* 35.

73. Ibid.

74. Davis, *Slavery and Human Progress,* 81. Davis asserts that by the time of the Revolutionary War, the "most productive and wealthiest regions of British America . . . were the staple-producing economies dependent upon slave labor" (ibid., 77). In *The Problem of Slavery in the Age of Revolution,* Davis says that the idea of slavery was hardly repugnant; however, antislavery opinion was disdained (41–42).

75. Jordan, *White over Black,* xi.

76. Quoted in Perca et al., *Race and Races,* 98–99.

77. Franklin, "Observations," 331.

78. Franklin, "Address to the Public," 33. In *Early American Views on Negro Slavery,* Matthew T. Mellon notes that Franklin became an ardent abolitionist, joining the Pennsylvania Abolition Society and becoming its president in 1787, and he observes that this society "made Franklin really aware" of slavery's injustices (28).

79. See Mellon, *Early American Views,* 71.

80. Ellis, *American Sphinx,* 145.

81. Jefferson, "To Mr. Benjamin Banneker," 216.

82. Jefferson, *Notes on the State of Virginia,* 162.

83. Ibid., 163.

84. Ibid., 143.

85. Davis, *Age of Revolution,* 177. Davis argues, "Jefferson was attuned to the values, loyalties, sanctions, taboos, and expectations of Virginia's wealthiest families, most of whom owned more than a hundred slaves." According to Davis, Jefferson believed he had to choose between the justice of freeing slaves or preserving the status quo of Virginia's planter society, and he chose the latter; see ibid., 182–83.

86. Chernow, *Washington*, 110. Alexander Hamilton, a close aide and confidante of Washington during the war, perhaps influenced the general's views about slavery. In a letter to John Jay, Hamilton wrote in March 1779, "I hear it frequently objected to the scheme of embodying negroes that they are too stupid to make soldiers. This is so far from appearing to me a valid objection that I think their want of cultivation (for their natural faculties are probably as good as ours) joined to that habit of subordination which they acquire from a life of servitude, will make them sooner become soldiers than our white inhabitants"; see Ruchames, *Racial Thought*, 158–59.

87. Mellon, *Early American Views*, 59.

88. Ibid., 81.

89. Ibid., 76.

90. McCullough, *John Adams*, 134.

91. Finkelman, *Statutes on Slavery*, 7:1, 3.

92. "Slavery is so foreign to the human mind," Rush said, "that the moral faculties, as well as those of understanding are debased, and rendered torpid by it. All the vices which are charged upon the Negroes in the southern colonies . . . such as Idleness, Treachery, Theft, and the like are the genuine offspring of slavery"; see Rush, "Address to the Inhabitants," 141.

93. Nisbet, "Slavery Not Forbidden," 146.

94. Ibid., 148. Nisbet argues that a slave owner never deliberately overworked or abused "a parcel of new slaves" because that threatened his investment: "They are attended with the same care as if they were infants."

95. Federalist #42, 213.

96. Davis, *Slavery and Human Progress*, 163. Davis adds that slave systems throughout the Western Hemisphere, including the United States, "suffered irreparable damage from the trauma of the American Revolution, the disruption or loss of protected markets, the wars of the French Revolution, and the resulting instability and break up of the Spanish Empire" (ibid., 77–78).

97. Sixth Annual Message to Congress, December 2, 1806.

98. Federalist #54, 278.

99. The constitutional historian James Bolner Sr. has said that members to the Constitutional Convention did not openly talk about their belief in the "racial inferiority of blacks, although virtually all of the delegates evidenced a readiness to treat blacks as inferiors"; see Bolner, "Slavery and the United States Constitution," 226.

100. Ibid., 236.

101. William Lee Miller notes, "The ending of slavery in the *North* was a significant accomplishment of the idealism of the American Revolution—one that has been forgotten because Americans have no memory that it even needed to be done"; see Miller, *Arguing about Slavery*, 17.

102. Ellis, *Founding Brothers*, 90.

103. Ibid., 88–108.

104. Webster, "Effects of Slavery," 231.

105. Davis, *Age of Revolution*, 59.

106. See Miller, *Arguing about Slavery*, 10.

107. According to the 1830 U.S. Census, the U.S. population was 12,858,670. Of that 2,009,050 were slaves. See www2.census.gov/prod2/decennial/documents/1830a-01.pdf. Retrieved 12 2015.

108. Lauren, *Power and Prejudice,* 20.

109. Jordan, *White over Black,* 109.

110. See Stroud, *Sketch of the Laws,* 165.

111. Fields, "Slavery, Race, and Ideology," 107.

112. See Engerman et al., *Slavery,* 115. The Louisiana codes regulated slaves' lives, making all aspects of them subject to the masters' will.

113. Genovese, *Roll Jordan Roll,* 57. Genovese notes that the population of the original four hundred thousand Africans imported into the British American colonies and the United States had multiplied ten times by 1860. In *Black Reconstruction,* W. E. B. Du Bois observes that slavery in the South "led toward the deliberate commercial breeding and sale of human labor for profit" (11).

114. Stroud, *Sketch of the Laws,* 193–200.

115. Engerman et al., *Slavery,* 121.

116. Stroud, *Sketch of the Laws,* 193.

117. Ibid., 264–68.

118. Genovese, *Roll Jordan Roll,* 87.

119. Stroud, *Sketch of the Laws,* 253. As the slave states considered slavery a "domestic institution"—something to be controlled and maintained—within their own borders, they expected the federal government to intercede only when the institution seemed threatened by domestic violence such as a slave insurrection (or conspiracy) might cause; see Hockett, *Constitution,* 141.

120. Nye, *Fettered Freedom,* 29.

121. Ibid., 18.

122. "Presentments of the Grand Jury," *Charleston Courier,* October 16, 1822.

123. "To the Hon. Charles MacBeth and the Hon. John E. Carew, Candidates for the Mayoralty," *Charleston Courier,* October 21, 1859.

124. "Negro Costume," *Charleston Courier,* October 26, 1859. The October 29, 1859, *New York Evening Post* quoted "ANOTHER VOTER" under the headline "The Negro Uniform to Be Changed" and described the "revival of the laws of 1740 and 1788 regulating negro costume" in Charleston.

125. "'Can Such Things Be and Not Excite Our Special Wonder,'" *Charleston Mercury,* October 27, 1859. A planter's comments in the *Mercury* on November 15, 1859, noted that the white community "has long been greatly disgusted and justly outraged by their [slaves'] ridiculous display of vanity, extravagant dressing" that could only lead to trouble; see "Our Slaves," *Charleston Mercury,* November 15, 1859.

126. Genovese, *Roll Jordan Roll,* 67. Kenneth Stampp wrote that the whip was the most common instrument of punishment, with nearly every slaveholder using it; see Stampp, "Southern Negro Slavery," 53–54.

127. Du Bois, *Black Reconstruction,* 9.

128. Kovel, *White Racism,* 189. Further, Stanley Elkins observes that slaves exhibited similar personality behaviors as Nazi concentration camp survivors forced to rely on the goodwill of their oppressors to survive. In addition he maintains that the slave had to assume the role of a child to his master on the plantation. Elkins also observes that men such as Prosser, Vesey, and Turner developed their leadership skills outside the "full coercions of the plantation authority-system." See Elkins, "Slavery and Negro Personality," 235–58.

129. Fanon, *Wretched of the Earth,* 52.

Chapter 1: Haiti in 1791, Gabriel Prosser's 1800 Conspiracy, and the 1811 German Coast Slave Revolt

1. Tragle, *Southampton Slave Revolt*, 31. Carl Osthaus makes a similar observation in his book *Partisans of the Southern Press*, noting that "generalizations" about American journalism up to about 1850 were "equally valid for newspapers in any part of the country" (1).

2. Bleyer, *Main Currents*, 153.

3. These subscribers included business owners and other professionals; see Bleyer, *Main Currents*, 153.

4. Mott, *American Journalism*, 155.

5. The press historian Hazel Dicken-Garcia has observed that the press "did not identify sources, or did so rarely" and "did not specify how information was gathered"; see Dicken-Garcia, *Journalistic Standards*, 67. See also Hudson, "Fourth Epoch," 61–62.

6. Dicken-Garcia notes that most nineteenth-century journalists claimed "impartiality" in their reports but that those claims cannot be considered the same standard as objective reporting; see Dicken-Garcia, *Journalistic Standards*, 98.

7. Dicken-Garcia observes that it was not until after 1830 that news became "event oriented" (ibid., 41).

8. While similar to later published "letters to the editor," these "correspondences" cannot be considered in the same vein and must be regarded as the only available news accounts—verifiable or not—of the unfolding events. The first "Letters to the editor" did not appear in an American newspaper until 1851, which, according to Renfro, "Bias," 822, was the September 18, 1851, *New York Times*.

9. Halasz, *Rattling Chains*, 77. Similarly, David Brion Davis has said that the slave revolution in St. Dominique "terrified American and European whites"; see Davis, *Slavery and Human Progress*, 78.

10. Dillon, *Slavery Attacked*, 47.

11. Davis, *Slavery and Human Progress*, 78. Davis, *Age of Revolution*, 152, observes that American ships supplied Toussaint L'Ouverture with matériel to aid his fight against the French.

12. Halasz, *Rattling Chains*, 67.

13. "Extract of a Letter from a Gentleman at CAPE FRANCOIS. To His Friend in New-York, Dated August 26, 1791," *Pennsylvania Journal and Weekly Advertiser*, September 21, 1791.

14. "Extract from Another Letter from the Same Date," *New York Daily Advertiser*, October 13, 1791; *Boston Gazette*, October 24, 1791.

15. By the year's end, subscribers to the *Pennsylvania Journal and Weekly Advertiser* and the *Maryland Gazette* learned that no peace was to be had on the island: "The Negroes go on destroying this country, and although we are successful in our attacks, we foresee it impossible to stop the rioters without assistance from France" ("Extract of a Letter from Cape Francois, of the 16th of November, 1791," *Pennsylvania Journal and Weekly Advertiser*, December 21, 1791; *Maryland Gazette*, December 29, 1791).

16. U.S. slave owners hardly applauded the struggle for freedom on St. Dominique (Haiti). When Haiti sought diplomatic recognition, southern politicians prevented this from happening. Missouri senator Thomas Hart Benton expressed the southern view

when he said that the United States must not "permit black consuls and ambassadors to establish themselves in our cities . . . and give their fellow Blacks in the United States, proof in hand of the honors which await them, for a like successful [revolt] on their part"; see Halasz, *Rattling Chains*, 84.

17. Davis, *Age of Revolution*, 329. See also Sidbury, *Ploughshares into Swords*, 39–41.

18. "Extract of a Letter from a Gentleman in ____ Country to the Editor," *New York Daily Advertiser*, October 1, 1800; *Massachusetts Spy*, October 8, 1800. The October 7, 1800, *Virginia Argus* and the October 11, 1800 *New York Daily Advertiser* contained a *Norfolk Herald* item noting that "the firing of sky rockets is both dangerous and improper" and should be stopped: "To those who have resided in St. Domingo it is well known that the negroes at the Cape kept up their communications with the plantations by means of sky rockets."

19. Aptheker, *American Negro*, 96–97.

20. "To the Printer of the Virginia Argus," *Virginia Argus*, October 14, 1800.

21. "Harper's Ferry War," *New York Evening Post*, October 18, 1859.

22. Sidbury, *Ploughshares into Swords*, 46. Douglas Egerton has discussed the influence of the slave revolt in St. Dominique on Prosser; see Egerton, *Gabriel's Rebellion*, 46–49.

23. Egerton, *Gabriel's Rebellion*, 3; Aptheker, *American Negro*, 219n.

24. Aptheker, *American Negro*, 219; Carroll, *Slave Insurrections*, 48, 55.

25. Egerton, *Gabriel's Rebellion*, 22. Egerton and others say that Gabriel stood about 6' 2" tall, towering over most (ibid., 21; Carroll, *Slave Insurrections*, 48; Aptheker, *American Negro*, 219).

26. Egerton, *Gabriel's Rebellion*, 28–30. The historian Midori Takagi has pointed out that in 1800 Richmond it was difficult "if not impossible" to control or eliminate "illicit slave activity"; see Takagi, *Rearing Wolves*, 62–65.

27. Aptheker, *American Negro*, 220.

28. Rucker, *River Flows On*, 133.

29. Egerton, "An Upright Man," 35. According to Egerton, "Gabriel's Conspiracy," 48, Prosser's biggest mistake was failing to understand that the "Jeffersonian cry for liberty and equality was meant to apply to whites only." Sidbury, *Ploughshares into Swords*, 118, notes that Prosser's conspiracy represented an "assertion that Virginians of African descent had a rightful claim to the state's revolutionary tradition."

30. Egerton, "Gabriel's Conspiracy," 49; Egerton, *Gabriel's Rebellion*, 37; Carroll, *Slave Insurrections*, 50.

31. Carroll, *Slave Insurrections*, 49. According to Egerton, "Gabriel's Conspiracy," 42, "freedom was his [Gabriel's] only religion."

32. Egerton, *Gabriel's Rebellion*, 48. Aptheker, *American Negro*, 220, notes that the plot began earlier and was well formed by the spring of 1800.

33. Egerton, *Gabriel's Rebellion*, 25.

34. Aptheker, *American Negro*, 220. Prosser's wife Nanny possibly knew about the plot, but Gabriel chose no women to take part in the conspiracy; see Egerton, "Gabriel's Conspiracy," 44.

35. Rucker, *River Flows On*, 137–39.

36. "To the Printer of the Virginia Argus," *Virginia Argus*, October 14, 1800; "An Impartial STATEMENT of the NEGRO INSURRECTION," *Massachusetts Spy*, October 15, 1800. The writer said that Prosser and other leaders were "chiefs" operating under a military hierarchy.

37. See Egerton, "Gabriel's Conspiracy," 45.

38. Aptheker, *American Negro*, 226.

39. Egerton, *Gabriel's Rebellion*, 55–68; Carroll, *Slave Insurrections*, 49. Egerton notes that Saturday would be a good day to begin a slave rebellion because slaves worked for "half the day and then headed for the city," and therefore a large number of slaves moving toward Richmond would not alarm whites (Egerton, *Gabriel's Rebellion*, 65).

40. Egerton, *Gabriel's Rebellion*, 43–44.

41. Carroll, *Slave Insurrection*, 50–51. According to Egerton, *Gabriel's Rebellion*, 50–51, Prosser's plan called for the slave army to split into three groups, with one seizing the arms at Richmond and taking Governor Monroe hostage and the other two setting fire to parts of the city.

42. Aptheker, *American Negro*, 220–21. Aptheker also surmises that Monroe may have wanted to keep information quiet so that it "would even pass unnoticed by the community" (ibid., 157; Carroll, *Slave Insurrections*, 51).

43. Carroll, *Slave Insurrections*, 52, quotes from the journal of the Senate of the Commonwealth of Virginia, 1800–1801.

44. Aptheker, *American Negro*, 221.

45. Ibid.

46. Sidbury, *Ploughshares into Swords*, 123.

47. Later a slave by the name of Peter Smith, enticed by the reward of three hundred dollars, convinced Bowler to turn himself in, but Smith, because of his status, received only fifty dollars for his effort; see Carroll, *Slave Insurrections*, 53.

48. Ibid., 54.

49. Aptheker, *American Negro*, 222. Rucker, *River Flows On*, 62, cites October 10, 1800, as Prosser's execution date.

50. Those details of Prosser's capture came from a Richmond item dated September 30 and appearing in the *Newport (R.I.) Mercury* on October 19, 1800.

51. The writer said that authorities arrested the ship's captain "on suspicion of [his] intentionally aiding and assisting in [Prosser's] escape," and he was in jail along with "two negro men that were on board the vessel."

52. Quoted in "From Another Norfolk Paper," *New York Daily Advertiser*, October 4, 1800; "Norfolk, September 25," *Philadelphia Gazette and Daily Advertiser*, October 8, 1800. This September 25 item from a Norfolk newspaper labeled Gabriel as the "black general" who, at the time of his arrest, "speaks confidently of the important discoveries he can make." It added that Gabriel "readily avowed himself to be the person described in the governor's proclamation." The item "GABRIEL APPREHENDED" in the October 15 *Massachusetts Spy* contained the first paragraph of this excerpt with the dateline Boston, October 9, 1800.

53. Sidbury, *Ploughshares into Swords*, 125.

54. Aptheker, *American Negro*, 222.

55. The October 13 item "Richmond, October 7" in the *Philadelphia Gazette and Daily Advertiser* and the similar item "Richmond, Oct. 7" in the October 21 *Newport (R.I.) Mercury* reported, "General GABRIEL, the black fellow, who has been so instrumental in exciting an insurrection among the negroes, had his trial yesterday." The October 10, 1800, *New York Daily Advertiser* reported that "GABRIEL the Negro General . . . was to have had his trial" and that "ten of his accomplices were to be executed." Six days later it

reported that Gabriel "received his trial yesterday. He will be executed at the gallows in this city, this day."

56. A later Richmond item, "Richmond, September 30," in the October 19 *Newport (R.I.) Mercury* said that Gabriel "was determined to make no confession." Other newspapers similarly reported that Gabriel "would make no discoveries."

57. Carroll, *Slave Insurrections*, 51.

58. "Fredericksburg, Sept. 23. Extract of a letter to the editor," *Massachusetts Spy*, October 1, 1800.

59. See Nicholls, "Holy Insurrection," 37–68.

60. "At reading the following every heart must shudder with horror" (*New York Daily Advertiser*, October 1, 1800).

61. "Extract of a Letter from a Gentleman in ____ County, to the Editor," *New York Daily Advertiser*, October 1, 1800; "Extract of a Letter to the Editor," *Massachusetts Spy*, October 8, 1800.

62. "To the Printer of the Virginia Argus," *Virginia Argus*, October 14, 1800; "An Impartial Statement of the Negro Insurrection," *Massachusetts Spy*, October 15, 1800.

63. The item "Richmond, September 12" in the September 18 *Philadelphia Gazette and Daily Advertiser* said that the "public mind has been much involved in dangerous apprehensions, concerning an insurrection of the negroes." Calling the conspiracy "shallow," the writer asserted that the "plot has been entirely exploded" and that had a revolt begun, "but little resistance would have been required, to render their scheme entirely abortive." See also "RICHMOND, Sept. 12," *Newport (R.I.) Mercury*, September 23, 1800.

64. Ibid.

65. The September 12, 1800, *Virginia Argus* noted, "One of the principals in the above conspiracy, GABRIEL, the property of Mr. [illegible] Prosser, is still out."

66. "At reading the following every heart must shudder with horror" (*New York Daily Advertiser*, October 1, 1800).

67. Another small item from the October 14, 1800, *Virginia Argus* noted, "Ten of the slaves concerned in the late insurrection, were executed on Friday last. Gabriel and two of his accomplices, in this city; two near Four mile creek: and five others near the Brook. Among the latter were Smith's *George* and Young's *Gilbert*."

68. See Aptheker, *American Negro*, 223–24.

69. Thompson, "National Newspaper," 1, notes that while "other revolts, such as Nat Turner's in Virginia, resulted in greater numbers of white casualties, fewer slaves participated." See also Genovese, *Roll Jordan Roll*, 411; "Commemorate Louisiana's Heroic 1811 Slave Revolt."

70. Rodriguez, "Ripe for Revolt," 9–11.

71. Thompson, "National Newspaper," 3.

72. See Fortier, *History of Louisiana*. Louisiana joined the Union in 1812.

73. Thrasher, "*On to New Orleans*," 49.

74. Quoted in ibid., 247.

75. Gayarre, *History of Louisiana*, 266.

76. Genovese, *Roll Jordan Roll*, 592.

77. Thrasher, "*On to New Orleans*," 50. The correct spelling of Manuel André's name is unclear as newspaper accounts used the spelling "Andry," although in his official

correspondence, Gov. W. C. C. Claiborne spelled the name "André"; see Claiborne, *Official Letter Books.*

78. "INSURRECTION!," *Massachusetts Spy,* February 27, 1811. The newspaper dated the letter January 10. A version of André's letter also appeared in both French and English in a photocopy of the *Courrier de la Louisiane,* dated January 12, 1811; see Thrasher, "*On to New Orleans,*" 69.

79. The February 27 *Massachusetts Spy* published André's hurried prose under the headline "INSURRECTION!"; the February 23 *Newport (R.I.) Mercury* datelined the letter January 16, 1811, under the headline "Insurrection of Blacks," conflating André's account.

80. Gayarre, *History of Louisiana,* 266.

81. Fortier, *History of Louisiana,* 78–79, notes that four or five houses of plantations had been burnt.

82. Ibid., 267.

83. Ibid., 79.

84. Thrasher, "*On to New Orleans,*" 62.

85. Rodriguez, "Ripe for Revolt," 18. Rodriguez notes, "Apparently the press and local authorities reverted to denial as a reaction to a misunderstood phenomenon" (12).

86. See Thrasher, "*On to New Orleans,*" 56.

87. In a letter from New Orleans dated January 9, 1811, to the secretary of state, Claiborne wrote, "The Negroes in the County of German Coast in this Territory are in a state of Insurrection; their numbers are variously stated from 180 to 500. This insurrection commenced at the Plantation of Col: [*sic*] André about 36 miles above this City"; see Claiborne, *Official Letter Books,* 95.

88. "Communication," *Louisiana Gazette and New Orleans Daily Advertiser,* January 17, 1811. The same item, although unsigned, appeared in the February 27 *New York Evening Post,* and a partially quoted and paraphrased version appeared in the March 2 *Newport (R.I.) Mercury.*

89. Thompson, "National Newspaper," 13.

90. The item noted that "two citizens have fell by the hands of these brigands," yet "upwards of one hundred" of the slave insurrectionists "have been killed and hung, and more will be executed." André said that this "loss alone is immense to the planters, as the most active, prime slaves, were concerned or joined the poor deluded miscreants who first commenced the ravages."

91. "Extract of a Letter from a Gentleman in New Orleans to His Friend in Chester, Pennsylvania," *New York Evening Post,* February 20, 1811.

92. The writer estimated the number of slaves to be between two and five hundred and that about "20 Negroes had been killed." The correspondence also indicated that about five hundred militia members had been sent to quash the trouble.

93. *New York Evening Post,* February 27, 1811; *Newport (R.I.) Mercury,* March 2, 1811.

94. Also in the February 27, 1811, *New York Evening Post.*

95. A January 25 extract from New Orleans in the March 6, 1811, *Massachusetts Spy* reported, "The negroes killed and missing from Mr. Fortiers's to Mr. Andry's [*sic*] in the late insurrection, were—killed and executed 18(??); missing 17—11 have been sent to New Orleans for trial. Those reported to be missing are supposed to be dead in the woods."

96. Less than three decades after the 1791 revolt broke out, the American Colonization Society began to prevent what was, as the historian George Fredrickson notes, a "representation of the scenes of 'San Domingo'"; see Fredrickson, *Black Image,* 9.

97. Jenkins, *Pro-Slavery Thought*, 63.

98. "The Lesson of the Harper's Ferry Riot," *New York Evening Post*, October 25, 1859, repr. from a *Wheeling Intelligencer* editorial.

Chapter 2: Denmark Vesey's 1822 Conspiracy and Nat Turner's 1831 Slave Revolt

1. Jenkins, *Pro-Slavery Thought*, 65–66.

2. Jefferson wrote this in a letter to John Holmes dated April 22, 1820; see Ellis, *American Sphinx*, 265.

3. Adams, *Memoirs of John Quincy Adams*, 10.

4. The speech is taken from the *Congressional Globe*, 25th Congress, 3rd Session, February 18, 1839, p. 177; quoted in Jenkins, *Pro-Slavery Thought*, 80–81. Some southern newspaper editors, such as the *Richmond Examiner*'s editor, were as blunt: "True philanthropy to the Negro begins, like charity at home; and if Southern men would act as if the canopy of heaven were inscribed with a covenant, in letters of fire, that the Negro is here, and here forever; is our property, and ours forever ... they would accomplish more good for the race in five years than they boast the institution itself to have accomplished in two centuries. . . ."; quoted in Genovese, *Roll Jordan Roll*, 51.

5. Organized in December 1816 in Washington, D.C., the ACS hoped to colonize "Western Africa" with "freed slaves and free-born African Americans who would bring 'civilization' and Christianity to the continent of Africa," according to the historian Bruce Dorsey; see Dorsey, "Gendered History," 79. He contends that the ACS was male-dominated and "persistently tried to blend colonization with patriotism" (ibid., 81). See also Fox, "American Colonization Society," 46; Staudenraus, *Africa Colonization Movement*, 23. The thought behind the ACS was that removing free blacks would "forward the 'general good'" Staudenraus, *Africa Colonization Movement*, 20.

6. Fredrickson, *Black Image*, 6–8.

7. Ibid., 17.

8. Ibid., 34.

9. Ibid., 11.

10. Ibid.

11. "AFRICAN COLONIZATION," *National Intelligencer*, November 13, 1822. The writer said that the U.S. Navy could provide the vessels, adding that he was "delighted that our Eastern brethren have commenced to participate in the generous duty of emancipation and emigration of the race of slaves."

12. "Africa," *Charleston Courier*, August 23, 1822.

13. While many whites viewed colonization as enlightened, many free blacks opposed colonization, believing it was rooted solely in racial prejudice; see Dorsey, "Gendered History," 79. Other blacks supported it, arguing that colonizing Africa was the only solution to their predicament. Staunch abolitionists such as William Lloyd Garrison vehemently opposed the ACS, leading Henry Clay, as a procolonizationist, to say that "the roads of Colonization and Abolition lead in different directions, but they do not cross each other"; quoted in Fox, "American Colonization Society," 125. The ACS was dissolved by the late nineteenth century. See also Staudenraus, *Africa Colonization Movement*, 241–42.

14. Wade, "Vesey Plot," 143–61.

15. Johnson, "Denmark and His Co-Conspirators," 915–76.

16. Robertson, *Denmark Vesey*, 4.

17. Rosen, *History of Charleston*, 75.

18. Pearson, *Designs against Charleston*, 85.

19. Robertson, *Denmark Vesey*, 9.

20. Rucker, *River Flows On*, 161.

21. Robertson, *Denmark Vesey*, 64.

22. Starobin, *Denmark Vesey*, 1–2.

23. Robertson, *Denmark Vesey*, 35–36. Rucker, *River Flows On*, 176, maintains that because Vesey understood African cultural practices, he stood a better chance of planning and executing a slave revolt.

24. Pearson, *Designs against Charleston*, 19, 63.

25. Ibid., 20, 86. See also Starobin, *Denmark Vesey*, 2–3. However, in *An Account of the Intended Insurrection*, Hamilton claimed that, if Vesey had fled to "San Domingo," he would have left his "deluded followers" to face the swift and terrible retribution of the whites; see Hamilton, *Account*, 29.

26. Hamilton, *Account*, 2.

27. Ibid.

28. Robertson, *Denmark Vesey*, 8; Carroll, *Slave Insurrections*, 85. Carroll called Vesey the captain's pet. Rucker, *River Flows On*, 162, notes that Vesey was purchased on the then Danish-controlled island of St. Thomas, which was perhaps the origin of Vesey's first name.

29. Hamilton, *Account*, 17.

30. Ibid. Carroll, *Slave Insurrections*, 85, claims that Vesey was known to slaves "everywhere . . . as one who had a great work to do."

31. Robertson, *Denmark Vesey*, 6–8. Robertson notes that Vesey probably spoke French because of his Caribbean upbringing (32, 53).

32. Hamilton, *Account*, 17; Carroll, *Slave Insurrections*, 85.

33. Hamilton, *Account*, 29.

34. Aptheker, *American Negro*, 269.

35. Egerton, "Why They Did Not Preach," 84; Robertson, *Denmark Vesey*, 47; Pearson, *Designs against Charleston*, 18.

36. Hamilton, *Account*, 34.

37. Pearson, *Designs against Charleston*, 185. According the slave Peter Poyas, Vesey said that "we intend to see, if we can't do something for ourselves, we can't live so"; see Hamilton, *Account*, app. B, 31.

38. Hamilton, *Account*, 35.

39. Ibid., 39.

40. "Narrative of the Conspiracy and Intended Insurrection amongst a Portion of the Negroes in the State of South-Carolina, in the Year 1822," in Starobin, *Denmark Vesey*, 105.

41. Authorities released Poyas after his initial arrest. The court called him a man of "boldness and sagacity" who "spoke with great confidence of the succors which were expected from San Domingo." Later proof against another slave named Abraham came in the form of a letter found in the possession of Peter Poyas. The letter that prosecutors accused Abraham of writing said, "DEAR SIR, - With pleasure I give you an answer. I will

endeavour to do it. Hoping that God will be in the midst to help his own. Be particular and make a sure remark. Fear not, the Lord God that delivered Daniel is able to deliver us. All that I inform agreed. I am gone up to Beach Hill." Despite the incriminating letter, the court dismissed charges against Abraham. See Hamilton, *Account*, 15.

42. According to Egerton, Gullah Jack was particularly important to Vesey because other blacks believed he had "powers from some unnatural circumstance of birth"; see Egerton, "Why They Did Not Preach," 87. Egerton notes that Gullah Jack wore his hair in a "bushy" African style that dismayed Charleston authorities: "Like all charismatic leaders, Jack recognized that he possessed the gift of authority, and he labored to accentuate that gift by adopting, or perhaps maintaining, a menacing appearance" (ibid.). Hamilton's official account described Gullah Jack as a "conjurer" and "physician" in his home country of Angola who in Charleston practiced his arts for "fifteen years, without its being generally known among the whites." His account noted that Vesey enlisted Jack's help because of his "influence" among the slaves, who were "distinguished both for their credulous superstition and clannish sympathies." Accordingly, with his "charms and amulets" as protection, Gullah Jack gave the appearance of invincibility to fellow slaves. See Hamilton, *Account*, 23–24.

43. Aptheker, *American Negro*, 269; Robertson, *Denmark Vesey*, 55.

44. Robertson, *Denmark Vesey*, 70.

45. Pearson, *Designs against Charleston*, 163.

46. Hamilton, *Account*, 3. Robertson puts the date at May 25, 1822. The informer was Peter Devany, who was eventually rewarded with his freedom, and the conspirator was William (or Paul's William), who was kept in solitary confinement for nine days before revealing any new information. Starobin, *Denmark Vesey*, 7–8, notes that other conspirators were tortured to confess, while slave informers later received emancipation and monetary rewards.

47. Hamilton, *Account*, 7. Robertson, *Denmark Vesey*, 73, notes that Paul's William was probably whipped to coerce a confession.

48. Robertson, *Denmark Vesey*, 74–81. Starobin says that many slave owners were "mystified and horrified when their most trusted servants and apparently contented bondsmen were implicated in the plot," and he notes that four white men "of the lowest characters" were tried later on misdemeanor conspiracy charges; see Starobin, *Denmark Vesey*, 3–4, 57. According to Hamilton, *Account*, 6, two slaves, Mingo Harth and Peter Poyas, "behaved with so much composure and coolness, and treated the charge, alleged against them, with so much levity" that authorities discharged them.

49. Hamilton, *Account*, 11–12.

50. "From the *National Gazette*, July 9," *New York Evening Post*, July 10, 1822. The item identified "Judge Johnson" as the author and brother-in-law of Governor Bennett, who owned three slaves among the condemned.

51. Judges Lionel Kennedy and Thomas Parker published the "Official Report" months after the trial. According to the document, "The Court, on mature deliberation, determined that the public generally, or in other words those, who had no particular interest in the slaves accused, should not be present at the trials" (quoted in Starobin, *Denmark Vesey*, 15).

52. Hamilton, *Account*, 12.

53. "COMMUNICATION," *Charleston Courier*, June 21, 1822. The editorial paralleled current events with the story of a condemned slave falsely accused of wrongdoing. As

the writer explained, a "half-witted negro" was beaten "to extort a confession" and to reveal the name of the person who blew a bugle and alarmed a passing cavalry. The confessor said it was a slave named "Billy." A "Court of Magistrates and Freeholders," with men "of the first respectability," tried and convicted Billy, "a blacksmith, a fellow of uncommon worth" whose master "indulged" him "in such privileges" because of "his fidelity." The falsely accused Billy died on the gallows even though no evidence was brought forth. According to the author, "Billy was hung amidst crowds of execrating spectators;—and such appeared to be the popular demand for a victim, that it is not certain a pardon could have saved him." According to Robertson, *Denmark Vesey*, 91, the author was supposedly "William Johnson, an associate justice of the U.S. Supreme Court" and Governor Bennett's brother-in-law. It is possible that the writer criticized the city intendant James Hamilton because he aggressively opposed Governor Bennett. According to Robertson, Hamilton would later win a seat in the U.S. Congress, and Bennett would lose the governorship (ibid., 112–13). Starobin, *Denmark Vesey*, 6, notes Hamilton's aggressive handling of the conspiracy.

54. "COMMUNICATION," *Charleston Courier*, June 29, 1822. In a note titled "TO THE PUBLIC," published the same day in the *Courier*, William Johnson called criticisms of the "Melancholy" article "one of the most groundless and unprovoked attacks ever made upon the feelings [of an] individual."

55. Hamilton, *Account*, 48.

56. "Official Report," in Starobin, *Denmark Vesey*, 44.

57. Hamilton, *Account*, 16.

58. Ibid.

59. Quoted in Pearson, *Designs against Charleston*, 279. Kennedy said to Vesey, "It is difficult to imagine what infatuation could have prompted you to attempt an enterprise so wild and visionary. You were a free man; you were comparatively wealthy; and enjoyed every comfort with your situation. You had, therefore, much to risk, and little to gain. From your age and experience you ought to have known that success was impracticable." See also Robertson, *Denmark Vesey*, 98; Starobin, *Denmark Vesey*, 34.

60. Robertson, *Denmark Vesey*, 89. Starobin, *Denmark Vesey*, 112, contains a "Narrative of the Conspiracy and Intended Insurrection amongst a Portion of the Negroes in the State of South-Carolina, in the Year 1822." This document claimed that Vesey "seemed to pay great attention to the testimony given against him, but with his eyes fixed on the floor." The "Narrative" also claimed that Vesey cross-examined witnesses.

61. Hamilton, *Account*, 30. The trials ended on July 26, although a special court was called to hear the case of William Garner, who had escaped and was later arrested in Columbia.

62. Quoted in Robertson, *Denmark Vesey*, 97. Starobin, *Denmark Vesey*, 5, attributes a similar quote to Peter Poyas.

63. Hamilton, *Account*, 18–19.

64. Ibid. Aptheker, *American Negro*, 271, notes 131 arrests, 37 hangings, and 12 transported outside the state.

65. Starobin, *Denmark Vesey*, 6. The *Charleston Courier* published news items indicating that not all slaves involved received death sentences. Some sentences were "commuted to transportation beyond the limits of the United States," and others were commuted to workhouses. "We likewise understand, that the Court yesterday afternoon, altered the sentence of death which had been pronounced upon MONDAY, belonging

John Gell, CHARLES, belonging to Judge Drayton, HARRY, belonging to David Haig" (*Charleston Courier*, July 26, 1822). The notice said that the governor had "respited" the convictions of nine slaves until August 9 and listed the convictions and death sentences for twenty-two slaves. See also "From the Charleston *Courier* July 26," *New York Evening Post*, August 3, 1822. Five slaves who "served the Court as witnesses" received a "sentence of transportation" and were told never to return "under penalty of death" ("From the Charleston *Courier*, July 29, 1822," *New York Evening Post*, August 6, 1822; *National Intelligencer*, August 7, 1822; *Newport (R.I.) Mercury*, August 10, 1822). The September 17 *Charleston Courier* and the September 25 *New York Evening Post* reported that "Savy Gaillard, a free colored man," was "pardoned" but must leave the country. A November 5 *New York Evening Post* item from the October 25 *Charleston City Gazette* reported that the owners of three slaves could not comply with orders to "send the said slaves out of the United States as soon as practicable." The names of the slaves were Dublin Morris, Billy Robinson, and Seymour Kunhardt.

66. The *Charleston Courier*'s notices about the trial proceedings appeared in other newspapers and contained only brief information about the defendants involved and their sentences. In a July 19 notice, the *Courier* reported that sixteen slaves had been sentenced to die and that "the Court still continues assiduously engaged in the trial of the others apprehended for the above crime." See also "SOUTH-CAROLINA," *Newport (R.I.) Mercury*, August 3, 1822.

67. See *Charleston Courier*, July 27, 1822. Other newspapers reprinted the notices as well; see *National Intelligencer*, August 3, 1822; *Newport (R.I.) Mercury*, August 10, 1822. Similar reports appeared throughout July in the *Charleston Courier*. For example, the July 30 *Charleston Courier* reported that "Jack, the slave of Neill McNeill; Cesar, the slave of Mrs. Smith; Jacob, the slave of Mr. Lankester; and Tom, the slave of Mr. Scott, are to be executed for attempting an insurrection in this state."

68. "THE NEGRO PLOT," *Newport (R.I.) Mercury*, August 3, 1822.

69. *New York Evening Post*, August 17, 1822. Very little descriptive information was printed about the executions. Many of them were brief notices that followed the same format as the information about the trials. For example, the following notice appeared in the July 13, 1822, *Charleston Courier* about the execution of major conspirators: "Gullah Jack, the property of Mr. Paul Pritchard, and John the property of Mr. Elias Horry, were executed yesterday morning, pursuant to their sentence, between the hours of six and eight o'clock."

70. "Insurrection of Negroes," *Newport (R.I.) Mercury*, July 13, 1822. The July 8, 1822, *New York Evening Post* contained an item that called Vesey, "a Free Black Man." The July 9, 1822, *Richmond Enquirer* had a notice of Vesey's guilt and sentencing, identifying him as "a black man."

71. "Execution," *Charleston Courier*, June 29, 1822.

72. "The Negro Plot," *New York Evening Post*, July 27, 1822; "Account of the Insurrection at Charleston," *Richmond Enquirer*, July 30, 1822. The Richmond paper credited the *New York Gazette* as the source of its report.

73. "The Negro Plot," *Newport (R.I.) Mercury*, August 3, 1822.

74. "Copy of a Letter from the Governor of the State of South Carolina," *National Intelligencer*, August 24, 1822; "EXECUTIVE DEPARTMENT," *Richmond Enquirer*, August 30, 1822. The governor added this about anyone reporting false information: "And, although their authors may have no evil design, and may really be under the delusion, it is easy to

perceive what pernicious consequences may ensue from not applying the proper corrective." The Richmond newspaper credited the *Winyaw Intelligencer*.

75. "Slave Insurrections at the South," *Boston Evening Transcript*, November 14, 1859. A December 1, 1859, *New York Herald* item headlined "Servile Insurrections, Past and Present—The Projected Massacre at Charleston" referred to the "intended insurrection of the black population of Charleston, S.C., in the year 1822." The article told of the Vesey plot, saying that it resembled "several points in the Harper's Ferry rebellion," and blamed "Religious fanaticism" as well "as politics" for "its share in the conspiracy."

76. Higginson, "Denmark Vesey," *Atlantic Monthly*, June 1861.

77. Oates, *Fires of Jubilee*, 48–49.

78. Ibid., 47.

79. Hinks, *To Awaken*, 241. The appeal, according to James Turner in his introduction to the 1993 reprint, made Walker the "most controversial and most admired Black person in America"; see Turner, *David Walker's Appeal*, 17.

80. Reynolds, "Impact of Walker's Appeal," 178.

81. Walker, *Appeal* (2000), xxiii–xxiv.

82. Ibid., 30.

83. Ibid., 78.

84. Ibid., xliv. According to Hinks, Walker, *Appeal* (2000), xliv, actual circumstances surrounding Walker's death remain unclear.

85. Hinks, *To Awaken*, 240.

86. Oates, *Fires of Jubilee*, 48. According to Oates, North Carolina passed a similar law.

87. Walker, *Appeal* (2000), 45.

88. *Genius of Universal Emancipation*, April 1830; see *Liberator: Documents of Upheaval*, 4.

89. Katz, *Walker's Appeal*, ii.

90. Walker, *Appeal* (1993), 14.

91. Hinks, *To Awaken*, 113.

92. See *Liberator: Documents of Upheaval*, 6.

93. Nye, *Fettered Freedom*, 3–4. Nye identifies Arthur and Lewis Tappan's work in New York with the New York Anti-Slavery Society and similar groups in the West. According to Nye, these groups had different ideas about emancipation.

94. Ibid., 11.

95. Ibid., 17.

96. See *Liberator: Documents of Upheaval*, 28.

97. In Foner, *Nat Turner*, 59. In the letter dated November 19, 1831, Floyd recommended confining slaves to plantations, ending their religious and secular education, and banishing free blacks from Virginia; see Aptheker, *American Negro*, 305. See also Greenberg, *Confessions of Nat Turner*, 109–11.

98. Oates, *Fires of Jubilee*, 133.

99. Ibid., 105.

100. Ibid., 1–3. The 1830 census put the exact count at 9,501 blacks and 6,573 whites; see Aptheker, *American Negro*, 293. Among the blacks were 7,756 slaves and 1,745 free blacks; see Drewry, *Southampton Insurrection*, 108.

101. Turner was born on October 2, 1800; see Oates, *Fires of Jubilee*, 1–11. In his introduction to a collection of Nat Turner documents, Eric Foner wrote of Turner's mother's actions; see Foner, *Nat Turner*, 1.

102. Turner's "Confession," in Foner, *Nat Turner,* 42. See also Rucker, *River Flows On,* 180–98.

103. Oates, *Fires of Jubilee,* 51.

104. Ibid., 12–13.

105. Ibid., 21.

106. Foner, *Nat Turner,* 42. Thomas R. Gray, a slave owner and a lawyer, interviewed the prisoner Turner on November 5 and published Turner's confession in mid-November. It sold as many as fifty thousand copies.

107. Oates, *Fires of Jubilee,* 40.

108. Turner had had four masters by the time of his revolt. The first, Benjamin Turner, died, bequeathing his slaves to his son Samuel, who also died. Turner was sold to Thomas Moore. After Moore's death, Turner stayed on the plantation after his mistress married Joseph Travis. See ibid., 51.

109. See Foner, *Nat Turner,* 44.

110. Ibid., 45.

111. Oates, *Fires of Jubilee,* 52–54; Aptheker, *American Negro,* 296–97.

112. Oates, *Fires of Jubilee,* 67–68. William Sidney Drewry's racist, but important, account of the insurrection notes that August was a good period for slave insurrection because farm chores were easing, thus giving slaves more free time; see Drewry, *Southampton Insurrection,* 22.

113. Turner confessed that Travis had been a "kind master" and he had had no "cause to complain"; see Foner, *Nat Turner,* 45.

114. Oates, *Fires of Jubilee,* 70–77.

115. See Foner, *Nat Turner,* 47.

116. Ibid.

117. Oates, *Fires of Jubilee,* 91–93.

118. Ibid., 94–95. Aptheker, *American Negro,* 298, estimates that the number in Turner's group peaked at about seventy.

119. Oates, *Fires of Jubilee,* 79. Dr. Blount's story is interesting because his slaves defended the doctor and his family. According to Oates, Blount probably gave his slaves the option to fight with him or face the oncoming white militia, which would surely exact a terrible retribution (ibid., 94–95).

120. Ibid., 99–103.

121. "TRANQUILITY RESTORED," *Richmond Enquirer,* September 6, 1831.

122. Aptheker, *American Negro,* 299–300.

123. Oates, *Fires of Jubilee,* 126.

124. In his "Confession," Turner said that he knew the two blacks who discovered his hiding place and betrayed him. Eventually Benjamin Phipps discovered Turner and took him in. Turner said that he was "willing to suffer the fate that awaits me"; see Foner, *Nat Turner,* 50.

125. See ibid., 53. Court records do not provide the judge's words, so it may have been Thomas Gray who added the lines to make the circumstances at Turner's sentencing more colorful.

126. "NAT TURNER," *Richmond Enquirer,* November 22, 1831. See Oates, *Fires of Jubilee,* 125. An Associated Press story dated May 5, 2003, noted that Turner's skull turned up in Gary, Indiana. The article said that after Turner's execution, his head had been severed so doctors could more closely examine his brain. Turner's head had been sent to Chicago, where it was lost.

127. The first reports appeared on August 27, 1831, in the *New York Evening Post*. An initial account from a "Captain Degauw, of the steam boat Swan" said that between fifty-nine and two hundred whites were killed and "that the devastation and slaughter wrought by the insurgents" was "awfully extensive." It was hoped that the accounts were exaggerated. Further accounts from Virginia appeared in the August 29 *Evening Post*. The first report in the *National Intelligencer*, headlined "The Insurrection," appeared on August 31. Citing the *Richmond Whig*, the information repeated the *Enquirer* accounts but reported the number of insurgents as between 150 and 400, with their leader killed. Later reports noted, "The banditti consisted of about 25–30—no others joined in" and were led by a "fellow called Captain Nat Turner, (a black)." The *Boston Evening Transcript* printed its first reports about the Southampton events on August 31, and the *Richmond Compiler* was its main source. A letter from Greenville County noted that the insurgents had been repulsed at a bridge but not before they had massacred every white they could find. The first reports from Southampton appeared in the *Maryland Gazette* on September 1, 1831. The *Newport (R.I.) Mercury* relied on Richmond newspapers too. On September 3 stories "respecting the late atrocities in Virginia" in the newspapers noted that participants were "mostly runaway slaves, who have long lurked in the swamps of Southampton."

128. "THE BANDITTI," *Richmond Enquirer*, August 30, 1831. See also "THE INSURRECTION," *New York Evening Post*, August 29, 1831; "THE INSURRECTION," *National Intelligencer*, August 31, 1831. A descriptive passage from the *Richmond Compiler* in the October 10 *New York Evening Post* under the headline "THE BANDITTI" noted the following: "The banditti, when they were engaged upon their bloody expedition, carried destruction to every white person they found in the houses—whether the hoary head, the lovely virgin, or the sleeping infant of the cradle. They spared none." Some slaves, according to this writer, "had the impudence to return to their plantation, and to effect an ignorance of the whole transaction."

129. "News of the Day," *Richmond Enquirer*, August 26, 1831. A similar comment from the *Richmond Compiler* was in the *Boston Evening Transcript* on August 31, 1831, and was headlined "INSURRECTION IN VIRGINIA."

130. "Extract of a Letter to the Editor of the Herald, dated Winston (NC) Aug. 24," *Richmond Enquirer*, August 30, 1831.

131. "INSURRECTION IN SOUTHAMPTON COUNTY," *Richmond Enquirer*, August 30, 1831. An October 29, 1831, *Boston Evening Transcript* headline read "INSURRECTION OF THE BLACKS OF VIRGINIA." From the *New York Gazette*, reports described how "in every case, the head of the slain was severed from the body." The Boston newspaper also quoted a *New York Journal of Commerce* report saying that in all instances Turner and his men "cut of [*sic*] the heads of their victims." The report hinted at a wide-ranging conspiracy because a horse that "had been taken from a negro who was shot, was not recognized as belonging to any person in the neighborhood.... This induced the suspicion that the movement was in concert with distant negroes, and tended to increase the alarm."

132. A *Petersburg Intelligencer* report in the September 2, 1831, *Richmond Enquirer* and headlined "THE DISTURBANCE" noted, "The number of whites who have fallen victim to the ferocity of these miscreants is, about sixty-four, chiefly women and children, who were butchered in the most shocking manner." The *Enquirer* also reported from the *Norfolk Beacon*, "We saw several children whose brains were knocked out."

133. The editor of the *Richmond Whig* observed, "A bloodier and more accursed tragedy was never acted, even by the agency of the tomahawk and scalping-knife"; see "SOUTHAMPTON AFFAIR," *National Intelligencer*, September 7, 1831.

134. "INSURRECTION IN VIRGINIA," *Boston Evening Transcript*, August 31, 1831.

135. "INSURRECTION IN SOUTHAMPTON COUNTY," *Richmond Enquirer* and *New York Evening Post*, August 30, 1831.

136. "From the Compiler of Yesterday," *Richmond Enquirer*, August 30, 1831.

137. "THE BANDITTI," *New York Evening Post*, October 10, 1831.

138. "From the Compiler of Yesterday," *Richmond Enquirer*, August 30, 1831. An excerpt in the September 5 *New York Evening Post* similarly observed, "Committing the first murder, finding themselves already beyond the reach of pardon, drunk, and desperate, they proceeded in blind fury, to murder and destroy all before them." The *Richmond Whig* item "SOUTHAMPTON AFFAIR" in the September 7 *National Intelligencer* reported that when the insurgents finished their killing, "they called for drink, and food, and becoming nice, damned the brandy as Vile stuff."

139. "Extract of a Letter from Jerusalem, VA. 24th August, 3 o'clock," *Richmond Enquirer*, August 30, 1831.

140. "NEWS OF THE DAY," *Richmond Enquirer*, August 26, 1831. An account from Petersburg dated August 23 reported the number of dead. Further reports lowered the death toll and put the number in Turner's party at around thirty; see "THE BANDITTI," *Richmond Enquirer*, August 30, 1831.

141. "SOUTHAMPTON, August 25, Noon," *Newport (R.I.) Mercury*, September 3, 1831. The *Norfolk Herald* provided news about the "Insurrection in Southampton County" that appeared in the *Richmond Enquirer* and the *New York Evening Post* on August 30. The Norfolk newspaper's account said that the "number that commenced the bloody work" was "only seven." However, it included three white men as well as the four blacks. An August 29 account in the *Boston Evening Transcript* noted two white men as being involved.

142. "THE BANDITTI," *Richmond Enquirer*, August 30, 1831. The September 2, 1831, *Richmond Enquirer* item also headlined "THE BANDITTI" reported, "Everything is perfectly quiet on this side of the James River. . . . While we apprehend no danger, we ought to act as if there were a possibility of its recurrence. Vigilance is the watch-word.—The law against unlawful assemblies of the colored people should be especially put into execution. The fanatics have been at the bottom of these last movements."

143. "THE BANDITTI," *Richmond Enquirer*, August 30, 1831.

144. "BANDITTI," *Richmond Enquirer*, August 30, 1831

145. "A PROCLAMATION," *Richmond Enquirer*, October 4, 1831; *National Intelligencer*, September 24, 1831.

146. "From the Compiler of Yesterday," *Richmond Enquirer*, August 30, 1831.

147. "SOUTHAMPTON AFFAIR," *National Intelligencer*, September 7, 1831. According to a Negro boy's trial testimony, Turner's followers, "animated by the example and exhortations of their leader[,] . . . became as ferocious as their leader wished them."

148. The circumstances eventually exasperated the *Richmond Enquirer*'s editor, who wrote, "Cannot one of the Editors in Baltimore favor us with a particular description of the fugitive?" (see *Richmond Enquirer*, September 16, 1831). The September 17 *National Intelligencer* reported, "We understand that the negro man confined in gaol as a runaway, who was suspected to be concerned in the Southampton insurrection, has been demanded by, and delivered to, the Executive of Virginia."

149. "LATEST," *Richmond Enquirer,* September 20, 1831.

150. The October 8 *Charleston Mercury,* under the headline "Capture of Gen. Nat," provided readers with the information but did not provide the caveat.

151. "THE BANDIT NAT. TURNER," *Richmond Enquirer,* October 18, 1831. See also *Charleston Mercury,* October 25, 1831. The October 21 *New York Evening Post* carried a *Richmond Compiler* item that doubted the person was Turner.

152. Benjamin Phipps was credited with the arrest. A *Petersburg Intelligencer* item in the November 8, 1831, *Richmond Enquirer* and headlined "Capture of Nat Turner" indicated that "the murderer Nat Turner has been taken and safely lodged in prison."

153. "Capture of Nat Turner," *Richmond Enquirer,* November 8, 1831; "General Nat," *National Intelligencer,* November 9, 1831; "Capture of Nat Turner," *Maryland Gazette,* November 10, 1831.

154. *New York Evening Post,* November 8, 1831; *National Intelligencer,* November 9, 1831; *Maryland Gazette,* November 10, 1831.

155. "Item of News," *Newport (R.I.) Mercury,* November 12, 1831.

156. "NAT TURNER CERTAINLY TAKEN," *Richmond Enquirer,* November 8, 1831.

157. Ibid. See also *New York Evening Post,* November 8, 1831.

158. "Post Office Jerusalem," *Richmond Enquirer,* November 8, 1831.

159. A November 14 *Norfolk Herald* item headlined "NAT TURNER" in the November 21 *Charleston Courier* said that Turner had "expiated his crimes (crimes at the bare mention of which the blood runs cold) on Friday last."

160. The November 8 *Richmond Enquirer* item "THE BANDIT TAKEN" informed readers that the "confession will be published in pamphlet form (by Thomas R. Gray)."

161. Oates, *Fires of Jubilee,* 145.

162. Carroll, *Slave Insurrections,* 190; Aptheker, *American Negro,* 346.

163. Carroll, *Slave Insurrections,* 191.

164. Nye, *Fettered Freedom,* 30–31.

165. "THE NEGRO INSURRECTION OF 1856," *New York Herald,* October 19, 1859. This report appeared as part of the coverage following John Brown's Harper's Ferry raid. The report continued, "A newspaper correspondent who was present at the execution saw a list of the negroes that had been whipped, and was told what they all had stated; and then he witnessed the examination of the rest, some taking five or six hundred lashes before they would tell the tale. One of the negroes died from the whipping."

Chapter 3: Slavery, the Press, and America's Transformation, 1831–59

1. Nye, *Fettered Freedom,* 1. Nye said that antislavery societies grew dramatically with just sixty in 1835 to thirteen hundred in 1838 (6).

2. Potter, *Impending Crisis,* 29.

3. Jordan, *White over Black,* 359.

4. Donnarae MacCann concludes in her examination of nineteenth-century children's literature that "abolitionists seldom opposed the idea of white superiority, even when presenting strong challenges to the proslavery forces in the South"; see MacCann, *White Supremacy,* 3.

5. Davis, *Age of Revolution,* 165. See also Nye, *Fettered Freedom,* 1; Jordan, *White over Black,* 264, 272.

6. Nye, *Fettered Freedom,* 35.

7. "MONDAY EVENING, AUG. 29, 1831," *Boston Evening Transcript,* August 29, 1831.

8. Nye, *Fettered Freedom,* 6–8.

9. "THE NEGRO INSURRECTION," *Boston Evening Transcript,* October 13, 1831. Among those endorsing colonization of free blacks as a solution, one Boston editor said that it "shews [*sic*] the opinion of VIRGINIA, relative to her coloured population" that the state would allow free blacks to emigrate to Liberia where "real freedom" would exist (*Boston Evening Transcript,* October 11, 1831).

10. "FOR THE ENQUIRER. FREE PEOPLE OF COLOR," *Richmond Enquirer,* October 21, 1831. "Appomattox" added, "It perhaps deserves notice, that immediately after the suppression of Gabriel's Insurrection, our Legislature felt, as our people now feel, the importance of removing the free negroes."

11. Originally published in the *Norfolk Herald* and quoted in the *Richmond Enquirer,* October 18, 1831.

12. *Newport (R.I.) Mercury,* November 19, 1831.

13. See "Virginia Legislature. HOUSE OF DELEGATES. *Wednesday Dec. 11* SLAVES AND FREE NEGROES," in the *Richmond Enquirer* of December 15 and 17, 1831. On December 17 one delegate discussed getting rid of the greater "nuisance," that of slavery.

14. "Extract of a Letter from Wilmington, N. Carolina, Dated 19th September," *Richmond Enquirer,* September 30, 1831.

15. *Richmond Enquirer,* November 25, 1831.

16. The governor's word appeared in the item "Louisiana. Extracts from Governor Roman's Message," *Richmond Enquirer,* December 4, 1831. Roman criticized Virginia for expelling those who took part in the insurrection because they could possibly "carry into neighboring states the contagion of their crimes."

17. "For the Mercury," *Charleston Mercury,* August 30, 1831. Under the headline "SLAVERY ABOLITIONISTS" in the October 12, 1831, *National Intelligencer,* another writer warned that abolitionists did not account for the dire consequences of emancipation.

18. Ambler, *Diary of John Floyd,* 170.

19. Quoted in *Liberator: Documents of Upheaval,* 48–49.

20. The nullification crisis of 1832–33, for example, diverted southern attention from emancipation proposals to states' rights issues.

21. "SLAVERY ABOLITIONISTS," *National Intelligencer,* October 12, 1831. Other comments such as those in the October 29, 1831, *National Intelligencer* said that the federal government had no power over slavery "except in case of such an outbreak as lately occurred, and which fanatics are endeavoring to fan into one wide devouring flame."

22. Jenkins, *Pro-Slavery Thought,* 65–66.

23. Potter, *Impending Crisis,* 39.

24. Amy Reynolds, "Impact of Walker's Appeal," 77, says, "Southerners who advocated suppression in the form of laws, argued that the abolitionists threatened to ignite slave rebellion and that the threat of rebellion actually threatened the survival of the union." Dicken-Garcia and Dell'Orto, *Hated Ideas,* 9, notes that the decade of the 1830s in the South was the "most repressive period in American peacetime history because of efforts to prevent the printing, circulation and reading of abolition materials."

25. Genovese, *Roll Jordan Roll,* 51.

26. Hockett, *Constitution,* 178.

27. Richards, *"Gentlemen of Property,"* 15.

28. Dillon, *Elijah P. Lovejoy,* 177.

29. Remini, *John Quincy Adams*, 137.

30. Quoted in McPherson, "Fight against the Gag Rule," 235.

31. Sewall, *House Divided*, 20; Borden and Graham, *Portrait of a Nation*, 209.

32. Sewall, *House Divided*, 20.

33. Richards, *Slave Power*, 1, argues that the United States up to the Civil War had always been controlled by a "slaveholding oligarchy" that "ran the country—and ran it to their own advantage."

34. Fredrickson, *Black Image*, 56. MacCann, *White Supremacy*, 40, observes that the popularity of the minstrel shows also promoted a negative stereotype of blacks while advocating and justifying the slave system: blacks were seen as people who "loved 'massa' and dreaded freedom. They could not imagine a more benign [slave] environment, for they were neither self-possessed nor capable of normal human emotions."

35. Fredrickson, *Black Image*, 53–54. Fredrickson notes that the slaveholder argued that slavery kept the black man docile but freedom would make him a monster.

36. Genovese, *Roll Jordan Roll*, 76.

37. Reverend Dr. Thornwell, a professor of theology at Presbyterian Seminary of Charleston, S.C.; quoted in Genovese, *Roll Jordan Roll*, 76.

38. Jenkins, *Pro-Slavery Thought*, 76. The message appeared in the *Charleston Courier* on November 28, 1829, and in it the governor added, "In a political point of view, involuntary slavery has the advantage, since all who enjoy liberty are then in fact free. Wealth gives no influence at the polls; it does where white men perform the menial services which slaves do here."

39. Quoted in Fredrickson, *Black Image*, 46.

40. Ibid., 44–45.

41. Foner, *Nat Turner*, 120–25. See also Oates, *Fires of Jubilee*, 41.

42. "THE LATE PLOT. Extract of a letter to a Gentleman in Boston ___ dated Charleston, August 19," *Maryland Gazette*, October 3, 1822. The Charlestonian added, "A negro cannot by marriage mingle with the whites, he cannot as a soldier or a magistrate command a white man in a word the pride and ambition of a negro has no room to act." He said that because of their low status, they are "incited to vent in crime those feelings which lead the whites to the pursuits of worldly ambition."

43. Fredrickson, *Black Image*, 49.

44. Jenkins, *Pro-Slavery Thought*, 77. The article appeared originally in the *Charleston Courier* on July 25, 1833. The editor of the *Charleston Mercury* on November 13, 1833, disputed a northern editor's belief that many southerners believed slavery to be an evil: "'The great mass of the South' now sanction no such admission, as that Southern slavery is an evil to be deprecated" (ibid., 78).

45. Nye, *Fettered Freedom*, 39. The passages are from the *Richmond Examiner* and appeared in the July 26, 1855, *National Era*.

46. Elliott, *Cotton Is King*, vii. Elliott says that the "Negro is *now* an inferior race" and that liberty, which is a blessing to whites, is "a curse" to slaves (ibid., ix, xiii). Genovese, *Roll Jordan Roll*, 76, quotes Elliott, who defined the slave system: "The master, as head of the system, has a right to the obedience of and labor of the slave, but the slave has also his mutual rights in the master; the right of protection, the right of counsel and guidance, the right of subsistence, the right of care and attention in sickness and old age. He has also a right in his master as the sole arbiter in all his wrongs and difficulties, and as a merciful judge and dispenser of law to award the penalty of his misdeeds."

47. "Communicated," *Charleston Mercury*, November 22, 1831. The newspaper cited the following figures: "Yet of the 249 criminals in the State Prison, 84 are negroes, (upwards of one-third); and of 774 in the Penitentiary, 313 (nearly one half) are negroes."

48. "MASSACHUSETTS HUMANITARIANS," *New Orleans Daily Picayune*, October 21, 1859.

49. Potter, *Impending Crisis*, 39.

50. Ibid.

51. Oates, *Fires of Jubilee*, 137, 143.

52. "The Negro Insurrection," *New York Times*, October 20, 1859.

53. Another editorial, which appeared in the October 26, 1859, *Charleston Courier*, claimed that slaves "themselves were terrified and panic stricken by the audacious invasion of these Abolition conspirators."

54. "Trial of John Brown and Others," *Richmond Enquirer*, October 28, 1859. Associated Press coverage of John Brown's trial too alluded to blacks' inferiority, illustrated by John Alstadt's testimony, which used the common stereotype of blacks as stupid and lazy: "The slaves were placed in the watchhouse with spears in their hands, but the slaves showed no disposition to use them." Alstadt continued, "The other negroes were doing nothing, and had dropped their spears. Some of them were asleep nearly all the time [Laughter.]" The *Richmond Enquirer* editor added the bracketed remark, indicating subtle racism; see "Trial of the Harper's Ferry Insurgents in Jefferson County Circuit Court," *Richmond Enquirer*, November 1, 1859.

55. Nye, *Fettered Freedom*, 27. A *Richmond Enquirer* writer said that the campaign slogan for the Republican Party in 1856 should be "free niggers, free women, free land, free love, and Fremont" (ibid., 24).

56. Ibid., 22.

57. Robin, "Conservatism and Counterrevolution," 14. A November 23, 1859, *Charleston Mercury* editorial headlined "TO THE GENERAL ASSEMBLY OF VIRGINIA" said that the "subordination of the inferior black to the dominant white class" was necessary. The November 22, 1859, *New York Tribune* contained an excerpt from Kentucky senator Cassius Clay's speech that said some people speak about Republicans as a "nigger party."

58. For example, see ibid.

59. "Pink," *Charleston Courier*, October 31, November 1, 1859.

60. *Charleston Mercury*, October 27, 1859.

61. "CITY AND STATE NEWS," *Richmond Enquirer*, November 22, 1859.

62. The word "nigger" also appeared in a November 26, 1859, *New York Evening Post* article under the headline "The 'Irrepressible Conflict' at Paris." From a London paper, the report told of white Americans refusing to sit in a Paris restaurant with two American black men until the maître d' evicted the "'niggers' out of the hotel." The report noted that no French customers "had the courage to take the 'niggers'' part!"

63. "Political Excitement on the Rise," *Charleston Mercury*, November 3, 1859.

64. "Historical Curiosity," *Charleston Mercury*, November 18, 1859.

65. "A Calm Southern Appeal," *Richmond Enquirer*, November 1, 1859.

66. Sewall, *House Divided*, 22–39; Borden and Graham, *Portrait of a Nation*, 206–30; O'Connor, *Disunited States*, 2–14.

67. Richards, *Slave Power*, 1, 4.

68. Grant, *North over South*, 9.

69. Emery and Emery, *Press and America*, 159. The Emerys identify three factors controlling the development of newspapers: 1) readers; 2) system of communication; and 3) improvements in production (ibid., 109).

70. Dicken-Garcia, *Journalistic Standards*, 48.

71. Reynolds, *Editors Make War*, vii. There is much debate about when "professional" journalism emerged, despite claims by some that it existed by the Civil War; see Osthaus, *Partisans*, 6.

72. Dicken-Garcia, *Journalistic Standards*, 51.

73. The press historian Luther Mott saw the period as one of great newspaper expansion as well. He quotes Alexis de Tocqueville's observation about Americans' love for newspapers: "The influence and circulation of the newspapers is great beyond anything ever known in Europe. In truth 9/10's of the population read nothing else. . . . Every village, nay almost every hamlet has its press. . . . Newspapers penetrate to every crevice of the nation." He observes that newspapers in the young United States focused on European events and relied on information from abroad, primarily England. During the 1790s the most important news of the day was the French Revolution. See Mott, *American Journalism*, 168, 113–14, 167. Leonard, *News for All*, xi–xii, makes the point that Americans were determined "to bring the newspaper everywhere they went, and to use it for every social enjoyment." See also James L. Crouthamel's study of New York newspapers that found, despite the expense, that newspaper production and consumption were a community focal point, intertwined in the nation's cultural traditions (Crouthamel, "Newspaper Revolution," 91).

74. Emery and Emery, *Press and America*, 134–39; Crouthamel, "Newspaper Revolution," 105; Mott, *American Journalism*, 215; Shaw, "News about Slavery," 485.

75. Emery and Emery, *Press and America*, 165.

76. Dicken-Garcia, *Journalistic Standards*, 41.

77. Crouthamel, "Newspaper Revolution," 106. Within twenty years the *Baltimore Sun*, Horace Greeley's *Tribune*, and Henry Raymond's *New York Times* were in circulation; see Reynolds, *Editors Make War*, 4. By 1860 Bennett's *Herald* had become the world's largest daily, with a circulation of seventy-seven thousand; see Emery and Emery, *Press and America*, 144.

78. Mott, *American Journalism*, 243–44, says, "Thus, news to the colonial editor was chiefly a compilation of clippings from London newspapers some months old; thus, news had continued to be a composite of matters understood to be deemed 'important' by the 'respectable public.'"

79. According to Dicken-Garcia, *Journalistic Standards*, 42, newspapers' jobs became more differentiated with reporters, editors, typesetters, etc., performing specific tasks at full-time jobs, and newswriting style became more readable and less dense.

80. Osthaus, *Partisans*, 6.

81. Ibid., 8.

82. Reynolds, *Editors Make War*, 3–4. Reynolds calculates that southern newspaper circulation was 103,041,436 compared to the rest of the country's 824,910,112. New York alone had three times the newspaper circulation as that in the South, and by 1860 the South had merely 847 newspapers and periodicals.

83. Osthaus, *Partisans*, 9.

84. Reynolds, *Editors Make War*, 16, 23.

85. Emery and Emery, *Press and America*, 175–85.

86. Reynolds, "Impact of Walker's Appeal," 77.

87. Potter, *Impending Crisis,* 48.

88. Ibid., 30–31.

Chapter 4: John Brown's "Greatest or Principal Object"

1. Anderson, *Voice from Harper's Ferry,* 2.

2. Finkelman, "John Brown and His Raid," 4.

3. Stoneham, *John Brown,* 6.

4. Wyatt-Brown, "John Brown's Antinomian War," 103.

5. Du Bois, *John Brown,* 22.

6. Douglass et al., *Life and Times of Frederick Douglass,* 236–53. See also Du Bois, *John Brown,* 5; Sanborn, *Life and Letters of John Brown,* 418–19.

7. Chowder, "Father of American Terrorism," 81. Similarly, Wyatt-Brown, "Volcano Beneath," 10–11, notes that Brown was a man of "highest of ideals with ruthless deeds," a man who ran a terrorist campaign.

8. See Wyatt Brown, "Volcano Beneath," 21.

9. Du Bois, *John Brown,* 53.

10. Villard, *John Brown,* 43. See also Sanborn, *Life and Letters of John Brown,* 41.

11. Finkelman, "John Brown and His Raid," 5.

12. Littlefield, "Blacks, John Brown, and a Theory of Manhood," 68. See also Wyatt-Brown, "John Brown's Antinomian War," 124.

13. Finkelman, "John Brown and His Raid," 3.

14. See Joyner, "Guilty of the Holiest Crime," 301. Joyner calls Harper's Ferry a "John Brown" drama in four acts: the Breach, the Crisis, the Trial, the Outcome (ibid., 296–334).

15. Du Bois, *John Brown,* 40–45. Du Bois observes that the only thing that saved the United States from massive slave revolts like that in Haiti was the potential for slaves to escape to freedom in the North. Du Bois also asserts that Brown studied the plans of Prosser, Vesey, and Turner.

16. See Hinton, *John Brown and His Men;* Du Bois, *John Brown,* 41.

17. Wyatt-Brown, "John Brown's Antinomian War," 104–15. See also Hinton, *John Brown and His Men,* 13. Brown then married Mary Anne Day.

18. Hinton, *John Brown and His Men,* 415–16.

19. Du Bois, *John Brown,* 49.

20. Hinton, *John Brown and His Men,* 16.

21. Anderson, *Voice from Harper's Ferry,* 23–24.

22. Ibid., 4–15. In testimony before the Senate committee, Richard Realf, a Brown supporter, told senators of one instance during a trip by train to Canada when Brown demanded that a black man in his party be served at a Chicago hotel. When told that was not possible, Brown left and found a hotel that would serve the man. See Mason and Collamer, *Report,* 95.

23. Wyatt-Brown, "John Brown's Antinomian War," 118.

24. Ibid.

25. Du Bois, *John Brown,* 90; Hinton, *John Brown and His Men,* 63–64.

26. Wyatt-Brown, "John Brown's Antinomian War," 118. According to Hinton, *John Brown and His Men,* 92, Brown accepted violent means to overthrow the social evil of

slavery and believed "that the people of Kansas would surely sustain and justify the deed done on the 24th of May, 1856."

27. Villard, *John Brown*, 7; Sanborn, *Life and Letters of John Brown*, 17.

28. Hinton, *John Brown and His Men*, 235.

29. Du Bois, *John Brown*, 112–14; Hinton, *John Brown and His Men*, 32, 199–228.

30. Finkelman, "John Brown and His Raid," 7.

31. For a complete assessment of Brown's connection to these men, see Renehan, *Secret Six*.

32. Ibid., 147.

33. See "Report [of] the Select Committee," 242.

34. Ibid., 7–8, 22. John Brown's men included five African Americans: Osborne Perry Anderson (escaped); Shields Green (arrested); Dangerfield Newby (killed); John Copeland (arrested); Lewis Sherrard Leary (killed); John Anderson (killed). The white men in his group included the following: William Thompson (killed); Jeremiah Anderson (killed); Dauphin Thompson (killed); Owen Brown (escaped); Watson Brown (killed); John Henry Kagi (killed); Aaron Stephens (arrested); John Edwin Cook (escaped and later arrested); Francis Jackson Merriam (escaped); Edwin Coppoc (arrested); Barclay Coppoc (escaped); Charles Tidd (escaped); William Leeman (killed); Steward Taylor (killed); Albert Hazlett (escaped and later arrested); Oliver Brown (killed).

35. In the spring of 1858, Brown and his supporters gathered in Chatham, Ontario, where Brown wrote "Provisional Constitution and Ordinances for the People of the United States." In the preamble he wrote, "Slavery . . . is none other than a most barbarous, unprovoked, unjustifiable War of one portion of its citizens upon another portion" (Oates, *To Purge This Land*, 243–47). See also Villard, *John Brown*, 330–38; Du Bois, *John Brown*, 156.

36. Anderson, *Voice from Harper's Ferry*, 17–18. Anderson called Forbes a Judas because the only thing that mattered to Forbes, according to Anderson, was money.

37. "COLONEL HUGE FORBES AND HIS CONNECTION WITH OSSAWATOMIE BROWN—A CHANCE OF FURTHER DISCLOSURES," *New York Herald*, October 26, 1859.

38. "Well-Matured Plan," *New York Herald*, October 27, 1859.

39. Anderson, *Voice from Harper's Ferry*, 24–25; Hinton, *John Brown and His Men*, 272.

40. Anderson, *Voice from Harper's Ferry*, 28.

41. "Report [of] the Select Committee," 4. The Senate began hearings in December 1859 and issued its report in June.

42. Hinton, *John Brown and His Men*, 32.

43. Sanborn, *Life and Letters of John Brown*, 561.

44. Tragle, *Southampton Slave Revolt*, 251.

45. Cited in Villard, *John Brown*, 410–11; Sanborn, *Life and Letters of John Brown*, 543; Hinton, *John Brown and His Men*, 255.

46. *New York Evening Post*, October 20, 1859.

47. "News from Virginia," *Charleston Courier*, October 20, 1859.

48. "Report [of] the Select Committee," 251.

49. *Richmond Enquirer*, October 18, 1859.

50. "Report [of] the Select Committee," 5.

51. According to Anderson, *Voice from Harper's Ferry*, 38, "It was no part of the original plan to hold on to the Ferry, or to parley with prisoners; but by so doing, time was

afforded to carry the news of its capture to several points, and forces were thrown into the place, which surrounded us."

52. Ibid., 35. See also Hinton, *John Brown and His Men*, 288–89.

53. See Villard, *John Brown*, 436–66. Osborne Anderson remarked that Brown ordered that Anderson should keep charge of the prisoners, and he also wrote that Lewis Washington "cried heartily" when taken; see Anderson, *Voice from Harper's Ferry*, 31, 35.

54. Sanborn, *Life and Letters of John Brown*, 558.

55. Ibid., 557–59.

56. "Official Reports," *Richmond Enquirer*, October 28, 1859.

57. Anderson, *Voice from Harper's Ferry*, 39.

58. Hinton, *John Brown and His Men*, 303–4.

59. "Report [of] the Select Committee," 17.

60. Hinton, *John Brown and His Men*, 317.

61. Villard, *John Brown*, 439.

62. "Too Much of a Good Thing Done Brown," *New York Herald*, November 6, 1859.

63. "A Questionable Service," *New York Times*, November 11, 1859.

64. "Special Dispatches to the Herald," *New York Herald*, October 18, 1859.

65. "Riot at Harper's Ferry—Military Called Out, &c.," *Richmond Enquirer*, October 18, 1859.

66. "Latest by Telegraph," *Charleston Mercury*, October 18, 1859.

67. "Riot at Harper's Ferry—Military Called Out, &c.," *Richmond Enquirer*, October 18, 1859.

68. Ibid.

69. Anderson, *Voice from Harper's Ferry*, 60–61.

70. Ibid., 41. Anderson claimed that the true number of slaves helping Brown and the actual number of Virginia whites killed will never be known.

71. Villard, *John Brown*, 468.

72. "The Conspiracy at Harper's Ferry," *National Intelligencer*, October 20, 1859. The *Richmond Enquirer*, the *Charleston Courier*, the *New York Times*, and the *New York Tribune* contained the *Baltimore American's* reports about the raid.

73. "The Insurrection at Harper's Ferry," *Baltimore Sun*, October 19, 1859.

74. "The Harper's Ferry Insurrection," *Charleston Mercury*, October 19, 1859.

75. "News from Virginia," *Charleston Courier*, October 20, 1859.

76. "The Conspiracy at Harper's Ferry," *National Intelligencer*, October 19, 1859.

77. "The Tragedy and Its Moral," *National Intelligencer*, October 21, 1859.

78. "Startling News from Virginia and Maryland—Negro Insurrection at Harper's Ferry and EXCITING INTELLIGENCE," *New York Herald*, October 18, 1859. Gerrit Smith wrote a letter dated August 27, 1859, to the New York "Jerry Rescue" Anniversary Committee, in which he said, "No wonder they ['intelligent black men'] are brought to the conclusion that no resource is left to them but in God and insurrections. For insurrections then we may look any year, any month, any day"; see Oates, *To Purge This Land*, 285.

79. "The Virginia Insurrection—Its Causes and Probable Consequences," *New York Herald*, October 19, 1859.

80. "William H. Seward's Irrepressible Conflict at Harper's Ferry—A Warning to the Men of New York," *New York Herald*, October 19, 1859.

81. In addition the October 25, 1859, *Richmond Enquirer* item headlined "Insurrection at Harper's Ferry" reported that "Old Brown" and his men engaged in "their ravings

... giving vent to the overcharged brains." According to the report, Brown remarked that if Harper's Ferry had been successful, he and his men would have marched to Washington, D.C., to seize the federal government and imprison the president and his cabinet.

82. "THE INSURRECTION IN VIRGINIA," *Boston Evening Transcript,* October 19, 1859. The editor noted, "This affair will create a deep feeling throughout the North. The people of the free States will frown upon every indication from whatever quarter it may come, looking to an invasion of the rights of the South."

83. "THE HARPER'S FERRY WAR," *New York Evening Post,* October 18, 1859.

84. "THE MILITARY ATTACK ON HARPER'S FERRY," *Richmond Enquirer,* October 25, 1859.

85. The October 21, 1859, *Richmond Enquirer* item headlined "Federal and State Jurisdiction at Harper's Ferry" reported that "the affair of Harper's Ferry is the first case of the kind which has ever occurred in this country, involving at the same time both State and Federal jurisdiction." The October 19 *New York Times* noted the problem of jurisdiction. An editorial in the October 20 *New York Evening Post* headlined "WRANGLE ABOUT 'OLD BROWN'" said that Gov. Henry Wise and President James Buchanan, both Democrats, who represented the state and federal legal positions respectively, may have to fight for the "honor of killing Brown and saving the Union from his twenty-two crazy disciples."

86. "Trial of the Harper's Ferry Conspirators," *New York Herald,* October 24, 1859.

Chapter 5: From Madman to Martyr

1. Wyatt-Brown, "John Brown's Antinomian War," 122.

2. "Osawatomie Brown," *Chicago Press and Tribune,* October 20, 1859. The *New York Tribune* published the story four days later. The story contained this description: "Brown is about five feet eight inches in hight [*sic*]. He has short, gray hair, and diversides [?] his appearance with iron gray whiskers and mustache, to suit the dangerous exigencies of his situation. His appearance is that of intense peacefulness, combined with hopeless verdancy."

3. According to Finkelman, "Manufacturing Martyrdom," 43, "Brown played his role as the soon to be martyred philanthropist self-consciously, and with consummate skill."

4. "From our SPECIAL REPORTER, Harper's Ferry. Oct. 19, 1859," *New York Herald,* October 21, 1859. The *Richmond Enquirer,* which did not print the full interview, described Brown as having a "rather peculiar shaped head, long gray hair, which at this time was matted, the sabre cut in his head having caused blood to flow freely, to the complete disfigurement of his face" ("A Conversation with 'Old Brown,'" *Richmond Enquirer,* October 25, 1859). A reporter for *Harper's Weekly* described Brown's physical bearing: "His hair was a mass of clotted gore ... his eye a pale blue or gray, nose Roman, and beard (originally sandy) white and blood-stained" (Sanborn, *Life and Letters of John Brown,* 570).

5. "Conversation with Brown," *Charleston Mercury,* October 24, 1859.

6. Brown confessed nothing, and the *Richmond Enquirer* printed a retraction on October 28, 1859: "Old Brown has made no confession, as reported."

7. Sanborn, *Life and Letters of John Brown,* 559.

8. "Correspondence of the *Mercury,*" *Charleston Mercury,* October 26, 1859.

9. "Old Brown a Common Thief—Statement of a Virginia Senator," *Richmond Enquirer*, November 22, 1859.

10. "Torturing the Dying for Political Capital," *New York Evening Post*, October 24, 1859.

11. "The Virginia Abolition Insurrection—Its Causes and Probable Consequences," *New York Herald*, October 19, 20, 1859.

12. "Letters from New York," *Richmond Enquirer*, November 8, 1859. On the same date the *Charleston Mercury* reported an item from the *Lawrence (Kans.) Herald of Freedom* that called Brown a "monomaniac" on the subject of slavery. The *Enquirer* also published a letter under the headline "Character of John Brown, the Murderer and Negro Stealer." The letter, from Kansas City, Missouri, called Brown a liar and an "unexampled villain" (*Richmond Enquirer*, November 18, 1859).

13. "Ossawatomie Brown," *Richmond Enquirer*, October 28, 1859.

14. *New Orleans Picayune* coverage referred to Brown's past: "The insurgent leader—Brown—appears to have been a desperado in Kansas; one who had learned in the conflicts, stimulated by Northern rapacity for power in that distracted territory, an intense hatred of Southern men and Southern institutions" ("Where Is the Responsibility?," *New Orleans Picayune*, October 25, 1859).

15. "Important from Harper's Ferry Confession of Brown," *Richmond Enquirer*, October 21, 1859. The newspaper reported that despite Brown's condition, he received Wise with "the utmost composure."

16. "Speech of Governor Wise," *Richmond Enquirer*, October 25, 1859. Northern and southern newspapers printed all or part of Wise's speech.

17. The quote also appeared in the October 22, 1859, *New York Tribune* item headlined "Brown's Appearance—Gov. Wise's Opinion."

18. "News from Virginia," *Charleston Courier*, October 20, 1859. Similarly a letter appearing in the October 28 *Richmond Enquirer* called Wise "the man for the times," suggesting that delegates to the upcoming Democratic Convention in Charleston should nominate him for president. According to the writer, the actions of our "noble Governor" stopped these "miserable fanatics, who so signally failed in attracting to their standard, any portion of the black population of the surrounding country."

19. Hinton, *John Brown and His Men*, 321.

20. "Threatening and Appalling Letters to Gov. Wise," *Richmond Enquirer*, November 4, 1859. A week later the November 11, 1859, *Richmond Enquirer* contained *Richmond Dispatch* reports saying that Wise was still getting "vile and threatening letters from abolitionists." The *Philadelphia Press* item "Honor for Governor Wise" in the November 4, 1859, *Richmond Enquirer* warned that "political demagogues" would want to increase the "excitement" of a white population surrounded by slaves. It said that Wise displayed "sagacity and a liberality" that should receive praise and thanks from all corners of the Union.

21. Reynolds, *John Brown*, 378.

22. *New York Tribune*, November 23, 1859.

23. "Brown and Wise," *New York Evening Post*, November 25, 1859. Compare those comments with words in the November 24, 1859, *Charleston Mercury:* "Governor Wise exhibits no sort of fear of a rescue [of Brown] being attempted." The November 21 *Boston Evening Transcript* editorial "Virginia" suggested that the governor was making much of the various alarms and panics occurring as the December 2 execution date

neared because of his presidential aspirations: "One cause for the groundless alarms proceeds from the efforts of Virginia politicians to make themselves conspicuous." Two days later the Boston paper quoted an editorial from the *Albany Argus* that asserted, "We regret that Virginia has not the cool head and firm hand of its Governor elect, Letcher, to guide it in this crisis" ("Governor Wise Criticised by a Fellow DEMOCRAT," *Boston Evening Transcript*, November 23, 1859).

24. Finkelman, "John Brown and His Raid," 8.

25. "The Harper's Ferry Trials," *New York Tribune*, October 25, 1859.

26. "Federal Jurisdiction," *Boston Evening Transcript*, November 1, 1859.

27. Hinton, *John Brown and His Men*, 343.

28. Ibid., 351.

29. Oates, *To Purge This Land*, 308–9, says that newspapers recounted the speech to "thousands of readers during the next few days," adding that Brown "was determined to use the Charlestown court as a forum to rally Northern sentiment to his cause."

30. The speech appeared in the daily wire reports: *New York Herald, New York Tribune, New York Times, New York Evening Post,* October 26, 1859; *National Intelligencer,* October 27, 1859; *Richmond Enquirer,* October 28, 1859; *Charleston Courier,* October 29, 1859; *Charleston Mercury,* November 1, 1859. See also Hinton, *John Brown and His Men,* 572–73.

31. "Trial of Captain Brown," *New York Evening Post*, October 27, 1859.

32. "The Third Day's Proceedings," *New York Herald*, October 29, 1859.

33. This transcript of Brown's address to the court appeared under the headline "John Brown Sentenced to Death" in the *New York Times* on November 3, 1859.

34. "Sentence of Brown," *Boston Evening Transcript*, November 3, 1859. The newspaper reported that Brown's junior counsel said, "He [Brown] convinces all who approach him that he possesses an original nobility of soul which is to be found in very few individuals" ("The Harper's Ferry Prisoners," *Boston Evening Transcript*, November 3, 1859). The next day the Boston newspaper editor suggested the release of Brown and his men "if they promised to devote the remainder of their lives to keeping the peace of the city of Baltimore. No others can do it" ("A Hint to Governor Wise," *Boston Evening Transcript*, November 4, 1859).

35. "The Riot at Harper's Ferry," *Richmond Enquirer*, November 8, 1859.

36. "John Brown's Speech," *New York Times*, November 3, 1859. Eleven days later another editorial in the newspaper remarked, "The Executive and the Press of Virginia have chosen to wring from the matter all the waters of strife it contained"; the writer warned, "They have fostered those insane fears and unreasoning passions of the populace in their own state" ("Virginia and Her Conspiracy," *New York Times*, November 14, 1859).

37. "Pardon for John Brown," *New Orleans Daily Picayune*, November 16, 1859.

38. "The Virginia Trials," *New York Times*, October 24, 1859.

39. "The Virginia Trials," *New York Times*, October 25, 1859.

40. "Judicial Assiduity in Virginia," *New York Tribune*, October 28, 1859. The October 31, 1859, editorial "Brown's Trial" in the *New York Tribune* said that Brown needed more time to prepare.

41. "The Trial of John Brown," *New York Times*, November 1, 1859. The editorial criticized the court for not giving Brown more time to prepare, asserting that a motion for a delay was denied because "jurors wanted to go home to their families and that every

female in Virginia 'was trembling with anxiety and apprehension.'" The *Times* editorial "John Brown and Virginia" on October 29 criticized the Virginia court for refusing a delay, saying, "It is time now for the calmness and forbearance of conscious power to show themselves in [the South's] bearing," and predicted that a speedy trial would turn Brown into a martyr.

42. In addition a November 3 *Evening Post* editorial urged clemency for Brown because "his real offense, therefore, has been enticing of slaves away, and not treason, conspiracy or murder."

43. "A Standing Army Needed," *New York Evening Post*, November 1, 1859. The writer chided Virginians for troop buildup at Charlestown and southern fears of abolitionist attacks or slave insurrection: "It is impossible to say on what point the abolitionists may make their attack, in what force they may appear, or to what extent the negroes may join them."

44. "The Lesson of the Day," *Boston Evening Transcript*, October 29, 1859. A later Boston editorial on November 10 noted that even southern lawyers agreed that the "allegations are so loosely drawn, and contain so many inaccuracies, that no judicial tribunal, acting upon legal principles, would have proceeded to the extremity of sentencing the prisoners to death."

45. The October 27 *New York Herald* reported that its correspondent had talked to Brown, quoting Brown as saying, "I will give the *Herald* credit for one thing—although I do not agree with its sentiments of course—it is very fair in its reports towards all sides."

46. "From Charlestown," *New York Tribune*, November 30, 1859. That day the *Tribune* reported that the rope to hang John Brown, displayed in Charlestown, created "the horrible, bloodthirsty discourses for which it afforded the text, [which] were almost startling, even in this region of barbarous freedom of speech."

47. Oates, *To Purge This Land*, 337.

48. Ibid., 349.

49. "The News," *New York Herald*, December 3, 1859.

50. "The Execution," *New York Herald*, December 3, 1859.

51. See Oates, *To Purge This Land*, 351.

52. "The Execution on Friday Last," *New York Tribune*, December 5, 1859.

53. See Reynolds, *John Brown*, 395.

54. "The Execution," *New York Herald*, December 3, 1859.

55. "The Great Events of the Today," *Boston Evening Transcript*, December 2, 1859.

56. "The Fate of Brown," *New York Evening Post*, December 1, 1859.

57. "The Execution and Its Effects," *New York Evening Post*, December 3, 1859.

58. "John Brown's Execution," *New York Times*, December 2, 1859.

59. However, the December 2 *National Intelligencer* editorial "The Execution of Brown" did express a hope that the excitement surrounding the death of this "misguided and unfortunate man" would "rapidly die out, and the minds of the community be restored to the usual calmness and tranquillity."

60. "The Execution of Brown," *Charleston Courier*, December 3, 1859. The editorial appeared originally in the *Charlotte (N.C.) Bulletin*.

61. "The Execution of John Brown," *New Orleans Daily Picayune*, December 1, 1859.

62. See Oates, *To Purge This Land*, 351.

Chapter 6: Dealing with Slavery's Enemies

1. Volkan, *Need to Have Enemies*, ix.

2. Rieber and Kelly, "Substance and Shadow," 11–12.

3. Broughton, "Babes in Arms," 109. Paradoxically, as the sociologist James Aho argues, enemies create social chaos while creating social balance and "social solidarity" among group members; see Aho, *Thing of Darkness*, 15.

4. Aho, *Thing of Darkness*, 15, cites as an example the U.S. government's contemporaneous creation of a new enemy in Iraq's Saddam Hussein as its old enemy the Soviet Union collapsed. Likewise, Spillman and Spillman, "Sociological and Psychological Aspects," 50, argues that enemies exist for social groups as part of the "evolutionary fight for survival."

5. Rieber and Kelly, "Substance and Shadow," 15.

6. Aho, *Thing of Darkness*, 109. This is, as Aho notes, because an "enemies' visitation" near the "borders is tantamount to impending pestilence."

7. The enemy's social constructions, as Ragnhild Fiebig-von Hase argues, become symbolic weapons in the "fight for political power and material advantage"; see Fiebig-von Hase, "Introduction," 31. Spillman and Spillman, "Sociological and Psychological Aspects," 50, identifies six stages of enemy creation: 1) negative anticipation; 2) blame-placing; 3) identification with evil; 4) zero-sum thinking; 5) stereotyping/deindividualization; and, 6) lack of empathy for the enemy.

8. Rucker, *River Flows On*, 7.

9. Ibid., 133–39.

10. "Extract of a Letter from a Gentleman in ___ County to the Editor," *New York Daily Advertiser*, October 1, 1859.

11. "Extract of a Letter from a Gentleman in This City to His Friend in New York, Dated September 20, 1800," *Virginia Argus*, October 14, 1800; "An Impartial Statement of the Negro Insurrection," *Massachusetts Spy*, October 15, 1800.

12. Rucker, *River Flows On*, 176.

13. Pearson, *Designs against Charleston*, 49–50; Starobin, *Denmark Vesey*, 2.

14. This is from "An Account . . .," reprinted in Starobin, *Denmark Vesey*, 97–98. The Charleston city intendant James Hamilton said that the black Methodist Church congregations "formed a hot-bed" of dissent and rebellion.

15. "The Late Plot," *Maryland Gazette*, October 3, 1822.

16. "THE NEGRO PLOT," *Newport (R.I.) Mercury*, August 3, 1822.

17. "The Projected Servile Insurrection at Charleston, S.C.," *New York Herald*, December 1, 1859. According to Rucker, *River Flows On*, 161, Vesey used his knowledge of "pan-African cultural phenomena and intercultural connections to his advantage."

18. "Southampton Affair," *National Intelligencer*, September 7, 1831.

19. "From Southampton," *National Intelligencer*, October 5, 1831.

20. "Jerusalem, Saturday 27," *New York Evening Post*, September 5, 1831. The writer said that the "more intelligent opinion" was that Turner and his followers might have wanted "to get to Norfolk, seize a ship, and go to Africa."

21. Originally from the *Richmond Compiler*, the item, headlined "The Tragedy of Southampton," appeared in the *Richmond Enquirer* on September 6, 1831.

22. "Letter from Southampton," *New York Evening Post*, September 12, 1831.

23. "The Southampton Tragedy," *Richmond Enquirer,* September 30, 1831. "A True Prophecy," *Richmond Enquirer,* October 18, 1859, reported that blacks preaching to other blacks could lead to civil problems. The report cited an 1825 article claiming that those "ignorant preachers" were teaching slaves to be impertinent. According to the writer, slaves were not learning the "true character of christianity [*sic*]." In addition black preachers insisted "on holding meetings in their own way, and having preachers of their own color." The writer insisted that black preachers could not properly read the Bible, if even read at all, and that some were likely going to take advantage of "their brethren . . . assume the part of men of great consequence." The writer feared that "some [crisp-haired] prophet, some pretender to inspiration . . . will rouse the fanaticism of his brethren."

24. "From the *Compiler,*" *New York Evening Post,* October 10, 1831.

25. "Extracts of Letters," *Richmond Enquirer,* November 8, 1831. According to the writer, Turner said that "indiscriminate massacre was not their intentions," but rather their purpose was to "strike terror and alarm." Another letter stated that Turner admitted there was not "concert of an insurrection."

26. "A True Prophecy," *Richmond Enquirer,* October 18, 1831.

27. "To the Editors of the *Enquirer,*" *Richmond Enquirer,* November 25, 1831.

28. "The Banditti," *Richmond Enquirer,* August 30, 1831.

29. "The Trial of Capt. Brown and Others," *New York Tribune,* October 27, 1859.

30. "Trial of the Harper's Ferry Insurgents," *Richmond Enquirer,* November 1, 1859.

31. "A Suggestion for Governor Wise," *Richmond Enquirer,* November 4, 1859.

32. "Latest from Charlestown—Correspondence from the *Baltimore American,*" *Richmond Enquirer,* November 25, 1859.

33. Ibid.

34. See the following: "A Hope Still for John Brown," *New York Evening Post,* November 8, 1859; "A Hope for John Brown," *Boston Evening Transcript,* November 9, 1859; "Too Much Zeal," *New York Times,* November 11, 1859. "John Brown's Insanity," *New York Tribune,* November 19, 1859, quoting the *Richmond Enquirer,* said that Virginia could not hang an insane man. Another "John Brown's Insanity," *New York Tribune,* November 25, 1859, claimed that insanity ran in Brown's family. See also McGlone, "Politics of Insanity," 215–16.

35. McGlone, "Politics of Insanity," 214–18. By nineteenth-century standards, forms of insanity ranged from manic-depressive behavior to dementia or mental retardation.

36. They did not want to lose, and "members of the anti slavery community soon realized that John Brown was potentially the most significant martyr to the cause since Elijah P. Lovejoy" (Finkelman, "Manufacturing Martyrdom," 42–43).

37. Sanborn, *Life and Letters of John Brown,* 575; Hinton, *John Brown and His Men,* 353.

38. Channing, *Crisis of Fear,* 39.

39. Aptheker, *American Negro,* 101.

40. For a full discussion, see Nicholls, "Holy Insurrection," 37–68.

41. A Virginian wrote to the *Virginia Herald,* "This doctrine of equality cannot fail in producing either a general Insurrection or a general emancipation." The Virginian also wrote, "Slavery is a monster, —most horrible of all monsters, —tyranny, excepted. Democracy in Virginia is like virtue in Hell" (quoted in Carroll, *Slave Insurrections,* 55–56).

42. "Sedition and Insurrection," *Philadelphia Gazette and Daily Advertiser;* "Sedition and Insurrection," *New York Daily Advertiser,* September 24, 1800; "From the Richmond *Gazette*," *Massachusetts Spy,* October 1, 1800. The Philadelphia editor said that blaming the French for the plot was a ruse to convince electors to vote against the pro-French Jefferson and to vote for Adams and Pinckney in the presidential election.

43. "Fredericksburg. (Vir.) Sept. 23," *New York Daily Advertiser,* October 1, 1800.

44. "Sedition and Insurrection," *Philadelphia Gazette and Daily Advertiser,* September 24, 1800; "Sedition and Insurrection," *New York Daily Advertiser,* September 27, 1800; "From the Richmond *Gazette*," *Massachusetts Spy,* October 1, 1800. The October 1, 1800, *Times and District of Columbia Advertiser* editor paraphrased the Richmond article.

45. "SEDITION AND INSURRECTION," *Philadelphia Gazette and Daily Advertiser,* September 24, 1800.

46. Callender used the *Richmond Examiner* to praise Jefferson, who informed James Madison about the campaign and said, "Do not let my name be connected with the business"; see McCullough, *John Adams,* 536–37.

47. According to McCullough, *John Adams,* 505, "There was rampant fear of the enemy within. French emigres in America, according to the French consul in Philadelphia, by now numbered 25,000 or more. Many were aristocrats who had fled the Terror; but the majority were refugees from the slave uprisings on the Caribbean island of San Domingo." McCullough noted the influx of Irish as well.

48. For the Virginia *Argus, Times and District of Columbia Advertiser,* October 8, 1800. Callender further said, "The faction, since I came into my present lodgings, have been extremely busy in circulating all sorts of falsehoods respecting me." Ibid.

49. A separate letter attributed to Callender in the October 11, 1800, *Times and District of Columbia Advertiser* sarcastically noted that the editor of the *Philadelphia Gazette* deserved the three-hundred-dollar reward for "General Gabriel" because he identified Callender as the "Field Marshall" in charge. The writer said, "Callender has been examined by the magistrates and has confessed that his object in the conspiracy was to promote the election of Mr. Jefferson."

50. Reprinted as "INSURRECTION OF THE BLACKS IN VIRGINIA," *Boston Evening Transcript,* August 29, 1831.

51. "State Insurrection in Virginia," *New York Evening Post,* August 29, 1831.

52. Following the Vesey conspiracy, a letter in the *New York Evening Post* and the *Richmond Enquirer* suggested that an "old pirate," likely Vesey, whom the writer referred to as a "monster," incited "some blacks to an insurrection"; see "The Negro Plot," *New York Evening Post,* July 27, 1822; "Account of the Insurrection at Charleston," *Richmond Enquirer,* July 30, 1822.

53. "THE LATE PLOT," *Maryland Gazette,* October 3, 1822.

54. "Confession of an Abolitionist," *Charleston Mercury,* October 27, 1859.

55. Ellis and Wildavsky, "Cultural Analysis," 111, 116, notes that the "abolitionists' role in the coming Civil War was that of a spark and bellows."

56. "Correspondence of the Courier," *Charleston Courier,* October 25, 1859.

57. "Correspondence of the Courier," *Charleston Courier,* November 11, 1859.

58. "No False Issue," *New Orleans Daily Picayune,* November 3, 1859.

59. "NEGROPHILLISM—ITS EFFECTS," *Richmond Enquirer,* November 15, 1859.

60. "The Harper's Ferry Outbreak," *New Orleans Daily Picayune,* October 22, 1859.

61. "Where Is the Responsibility," *New Orleans Daily Picayune,* October 25, 1859.

62. "The Irrepressible Conflict," *New York Herald,* October 19, 1859.

63. See "Seward's Speech at Rochester," *New York World Herald,* October 19, 1859; "Freedom and Slavery Cannot Exist under One Government," *Charleston Mercury,* October 22, 1859.

64. "The Harper's Ferry Affair—Who Are the Responsible Parties?," *New York Herald,* November 3, 1859.

65. "The Harper's Ferry Riot—Its Moral and Consequences," *Richmond Enquirer,* October 21, 1859.

66. "The End of the Black Republicans," *Charleston Mercury,* October 22, 1859. In "Correspondence of the *Mercury,*" *Charleston Mercury,* November 14, 1859, the editor wrote that Brown was a "concrete and practical manifestation of the 'irrepressible conflict.'"

67. The *Washington Constitution* item headlined "Administration View a Shot at Mr. Seward from the Harper's Ferry Arsenal" appeared in the October 21, 1859, *New York Times.*

68. "An Opposition View. Who Encourages Insurrection?," *New York Times,* October 21, 1859.

69. "The Outbreak at Harper's Ferry—Complicity of Leading Abolitionists and Black Republicans," *New York Herald,* October 20, 1859.

70. "The Harper's Ferry Invasion—The Duty of the Government at Washington," *New York Herald,* October 30, 1859.

71. See "Brown's Correspondence," *New York Tribune,* October 31, 1859; "The Harper's Ferry Invasion," *Charleston Courier,* October 31, 1859; "A Confession," *Richmond Enquirer,* November 1, 1859.

72. *New York Tribune,* October 27, 1859.

73. "Whose Ox Is Gored?," *New York Tribune,* November 12, 1859.

74. "The True Lesson," *New Orleans Daily Picayune,* October 30, 1859.

75. A notice in the *Richmond Enquirer,* for example, offered a ten-thousand-dollar reward for delivering the abolitionist Joshua Giddings alive to Richmond to stand trial for complicity with Brown at Harper's Ferry. Ohio representative Joshua Giddings wrote, in a letter published in several newspapers, including the October 25, 1859, *Baltimore Sun,* that "To the public I will say that Brown never consulted me in regard to his Virginia expedition or any other expedition or matter whatever."

76. Details of Col. Hugh Forbes's "Well-Matured Plan" first appeared in the *New York Herald* on October 18, 1859. Southern and northern newspapers reprinted the story. A November 4 *Richmond Enquirer* headline called it "Startling Revelations." The Forbes document implicated leading abolitionists, and the *Enquirer* noted, "The main thing proved by this correspondence is, that for the last year and a half . . . the project of the Harper's Ferry outbreak was well-known to Seward, Sumner, Hale and others. . . . They—not the crazy fanatic John Brown—are the real culprits; and it is they not he, who, if justice were fairly meted out, would have to grace the gallows."

77. "Wind-Blowing and Whirlwind-Reaping," *New Orleans Daily Picayune,* October 26, 1859.

78. "Surrender of Fugitives from Justice," *New Orleans Daily Picayune,* November 4, 1859.

79. *Charleston Courier,* October 22, 1859. The November 11, 1859, *Richmond Enquirer* item "A Sound Northern View of the Plea of Insanity" from a Belleville, Ill., newspaper

asked, "Will the Governor of New York hand over those distinguished agitators to be dealt with by the chivalric Virginians?"

80. The October 29, 1859, *New Orleans Daily Picayune* contained the headline "What Is 'Kansas Work'?" and published a Gerrit Smith letter supporting Brown. The November 1, 1859, *Richmond Enquirer* item "A Confession" contained Brown's trial transcripts and his letter implicating Smith and indicating that he had given Brown $180.

81. "In Commenting on the Harper's Ferry Outbreak, the NY *Herald* Says," *Charleston Mercury*, October 22, 1859. The October 26, 1859, *Charleston Courier* carried the text of Smith's August letter.

82. "Gerrit Smith and the Harper's Ferry Conspiracy," *New York Herald*, November 2, 1859.

83. "Gerrit Smith's Insanity," *New Orleans Daily Picayune*, November 14, 1859. Similarly a *New York Journal of Commerce* article headlined "The Insanity of Gerrit Smith" in the November 15, 1859, *Richmond Enquirer* said that Smith should "not have attempted to trifle with the rights of existing authority."

84. "Correspondence of the Courier," *Charleston Courier*, October 25, 1859.

85. *New York Tribune*, October 21, 1859. The *New York Tribune* editor said again that Gerrit Smith was not a member of the Republican Party and his name should not be associated with it; see "Mistaken Souls," *New York Tribune*, November 1, 1859.

86. "The Herald on Republicanism," *New York Tribune*, October 24, 1859.

87. Quoted in Reynolds, *John Brown*, 359.

88. Renehan, *Secret Six*, 223–24.

89. The November 11, 1859, *Richmond Enquirer* item "Gerrit Smith in a Lunatic Asylum" reported that Smith was in a "lunatic asylum" and called him one of Brown's "counsellors and confidants." The November 14, 1859, *Charleston Courier* reported Smith's insanity in the item "Condition of Gerrit Smith."

90. "Gerrit Smith at Home," *Charleston Courier*, November 8, 1859.

91. "Supposed Search for Fred. Douglass," *New York Times*, October 27, 1859; "Frederick Douglass," *Boston Evening Transcript*, October 27, 1859.

92. See, for example, "Letter from Frederick Douglass," *New York Tribune*, November 4, 1859.

93. "Fred. Douglass Fled," *Charleston Courier*, October 29, 1859.

94. "Fred Douglas Has an Aversion to Being Bagged," *Richmond Enquirer*, November 8, 1859.

95. "Too Much Zeal," *New York Times*, November 11, 1859.

96. "Virginia's Bounty on Assassination," *New York Evening Post*, November 10, 1859. The newspaper editor criticized the bounty offer "for the production of his [Giddings's] head."

97. "Virginia Fanaticism," *Boston Evening Transcript*, November 7, 1859.

98. "ARRAIGN THEM!," *New York Tribune*, November 2, 1859.

99. "The Irrepressible Terror," *Boston Evening Transcript*, November 28, 1859.

100. Litwack, *North of Slavery*, viii.

101. Holland, *Refutation*, 83.

102. "To the Members of the Legislature," *Charleston Courier*, November 29, 1822.

103. According to Oates, *Fires of Jubilee*, 107, even when no "slave army" appeared, "whites turned on the local Negro population." As a result, six innocent blacks were

hanged and four others were lynched. The newspapers failed to acknowledge the innocence of slaves wrongly accused. Instead newspaper accounts indicated that regardless
of guilt or innocence, it was best to eliminate any potential Turner imitators.

Chapter 7: A Racial Panic

1. "Negro Insurrection and New England Contributions," *New York Herald*, November 23, 1859.

2. Fredrickson, *Black Image*, 53. Fredrickson also observed, "The danger of slave
unrest and rebellion in the South was a recurring theme of colonizationist literature"
(ibid., 8).

3. See Gabrial, "From Haiti to Nat Turner."

4. Coining the term "moral panic" in 1973, the sociologist Stanley Cohen observed
that "societies go through periodic moral panics where persons or groups are presented
in 'stylized or stereotypical' fashion by the mass media," where "moral barricades are
manned by editors, bishops, politicians and other right-thinking people" (quoted in
Thompson, *Moral Panics*, 7–8).

5. Nicholas and O'Malley, "Introduction," 2.

6. Thompson, *Moral Panics*, 8.

7. Critcher, *Moral Panics*, 5, identifies moral panics as having three dimensions involving 1) "a process of definition and action"; 2) the demarcation of a society's "moral
boundaries"; and 3) "a set of discourses of various kinds and levels."

8. See Levin, *Political Hysteria;* Goode and Ben-Yehuda, *Moral Panics.*

9. Nicholas and O'Malley, "Introduction," 3–4.

10. *New York Daily Advertiser*, October 1, 1800. An item from Richmond dated September 12 noted, "The public mind has been much involved in dangerous apprehensions,
concerning an insurrection of the negroes"; see "Richmond, September 12," *Philadelphia
Gazette and Daily Advertiser*, September 18, 1800; "Richmond, September 12," *Newport
(R.I.) Mercury*, September 23, 1800.

11. "NEW YORK, September 23, *from the Richmond Gazette of Sept. 16*," *Massachusetts
Spy*, October 1, 1800. The item also appeared in the *New York Daily Advertiser*, September 24, 1800.

12. "To the Printer of the Virginia *Argus*," *Virginia Argus*, October 14, 1800; "An
Impartial Statement of the Negro Insurrection," *Massachusetts Spy*, October 15, 1800.

13. "New-York Sept. 22," *New York Daily Advertiser*, September 22, 1800.

14. "New-York, Sept. 26," *New York Daily Advertiser*, September 26, 1800.

15. "An Extract of a Letter from a Gentleman at New Orleans, to a Member of
Congress, Dated January 1811," *New York Evening Post*, February 19, 1811.

16. "Communication," *Louisiana Gazette*, January 17, 1811. Perhaps reluctantly Claiborne admitted that a serious revolt involving the territory's black slaves had occurred.
Writing in the January 10, 1811, *Louisiana Gazette*, he said that "there is, however, reason
to apprehend that several of our fellow citizens have been massacred, some dwelling
houses burnt and others pillaged." He urged the citizens of New Orleans to "continue
their vigilance."

17. Thrasher, "*On to New Orleans*," 48, notes that the 1811 population of New Orleans was "about 25,000; nearly 11,000 were slaves, some 8,000 whites and about 6,000
free people of color." According to the February 23, 1811, *Newport (R.I.) Mercury* item

"Insurrection of Blacks," "*The population of* New-Orleans *is 24,554, of which 16,654 are blacks and mulattoes!*"

18. "Insurrection! *Mr. Andry to Governour Claiborne,*" *Massachusetts Spy,* February 27, 1811, dated the letter January 10. A version of André's letter appeared in both French and English in a photocopy of the *Courrier de la Louisiane,* dated January 12, 1811; quoted in Thrasher, "*On to New Orleans,*" 69. The February 27 *Massachusetts Spy* published André's hurried prose under the headline "INSURRECTION"; the February 23 *Newport (R.I.) Mercury* dated the letter January 16, 1811, under the headline "INSURRECTION OF BLACKS." Another André account, "Communication," *Louisiana Gazette* and *New Orleans Daily Advertiser,* January 17, 1811, noted that "the most active, prime slaves, were concerned or joined the poor deluded miscreants."

19. "THE NEGRO PLOT," *Newport (R.I.) Mercury,* August 3, 1822.

20. *National Intelligencer,* August 3, 1822.

21. Starobin, *Denmark Vesey,* 6.

22. "Later," *Richmond Enquirer,* August 26, 1831. A similar comment from the *Richmond Compiler* was in the *Boston Evening Transcript* on August 31, 1831.

23. "The Banditti," *Richmond Enquirer,* August 30, 1831. See also "Insurrection," *New York Evening Post,* August 29, 1831; "The Insurrection," *National Intelligencer,* August 31, 1831.

24. A descriptive passage from the *Richmond Compiler* in an October 10 *New York Evening Post* item headlined "The Banditti" noted, "The banditti, when they were engaged upon their bloody expedition, carried destruction to every white person they found in the houses—whether the hoary head, the lovely virgin, or the sleeping infant of the cradle. They spared none." Some slaves, according to this writer, "had the impudence to return to their plantation, and to effect an ignorance of the whole transaction."

25. See "Extract of a Letter from Jerusalem" in "The Banditti," *Richmond Enquirer,* August 30, 1831. Under the column headline "News of the Day," the editor noted that the newspaper had not received "*authentic*" accounts but warned that if reports proved true, "these wretches will rue the day on which they broke loose upon the neighboring population.—Dearly will they pay for their madness and their misdeeds." The August 31, 1831, *Boston Evening Transcript* item "Insurrection in Virginia," originally from the *Richmond Compiler,* said that the "wretches who have contrived this thing" were "mad—infuriated—deceived by some artful knaves, or stimulated by their miscalculating passions."

26. An August 29, 1831, account, "Slave Insurrection in Virginia," in the *Boston Evening Transcript* discussed two white men as being involved.

27. Hamilton, *Account,* 13.

28. Anna Hayes Johnson to her cousin, in Starobin, *Denmark Vesey,* 72.

29. John Potter to Langdon Cheves, in Starobin, *Denmark Vesey,* 75.

30. *New York Evening Post,* September 1, 1831.

31. "Southampton Affair," *National Intelligencer,* September 7, 1831.

32. *Charleston Courier,* November 21, 1859.

33. Because the initial stories about the raid magnified the crisis and slave participation, they would be sure to raise alarm among the white population. The early headlines used words such as "Riot," "Insurrection," "Stampeded of Slaves," and even "Negro Insurrection" to catch the readers' attention. The October 17, 1859, *Charleston Courier*

headline, for example, read "Insurrection in Virginia," and an October 18 *New Orleans Daily Picayune* said, "Riot at Harper's Ferry." In Richmond an October 18 *Enquirer* headline announced "A Desperate Riot at Harper's Ferry." A *National Intelligencer* headline similarly was "Serious Disturbance at Harper's Ferry." In New York readers of the October 18 *New York Times* learned of "Servile Insurrection" with a "General Stampede of Slaves."The next day the *New York Times* referred to Harper's Ferry as "The Negro Insurrection." See also Gabrial, "Haystack Excitement."

34. "Riot at Harper's Ferry—Military Called Out, &c.," *Richmond Enquirer,* October 18, 1859.

35. The governor's proclamation appeared in the *New York Herald* and *Boston Evening Transcript* on November 30, 1859.

36. "Gov. Willard's Visit to Cook—A Written Confession Expected from the Latter," *Richmond Enquirer,* November 1, 1859. On November 18, just weeks before John Brown's execution, the *Boston Evening Transcript* reported Charlestown's crackdown on strangers under the headline "Virginia Chivalry."

37. "Letters to Governor Wise," *Richmond Enquirer,* November 22, 1859. On November 22 the *Richmond Enquirer* and the *New Orleans Daily Picayune* reported that Ohio governor Chase had sent a dispatch to Governor Wise that a hundred to a thousand men were heading to Charlestown.

38. "The Anti-Pedler Panic in Virginia," *New York Evening Post,* November 18, 1859.

39. "Apples and Hay Stacks," *New York Evening Post,* November 19, 1859.

40. "Brown and the Virginians," *New York Tribune,* November 19, 1859.

41. "The Panic in Virginia," *New York Herald,* November 22, 1859. Some antislavery northern editors claimed that southern politicians created fears of slave uprisings and abolitionist invasions for political reasons. The editorial "A Cry for Help," *New York Evening Post,* November 26, 1859, said, "By exciting the fears and inflaming the passions of the South, and through the South operating upon the timidity of the North, they hope to continue their ascendancy, yet for a while."

Chapter 8: Maintaining Slavery

1. According to Rieber and Kelly, "Substance and Shadow," 15, by recalling the enemies' negative attributes that include racial, linguistic, religious, cultural, ethnic, and physical qualities, they became repellent. This abetted the objectification of the enemies so that they were no longer human but rather "noxious" and even dangerous beings worthy of destruction. As Aho, *Thing of Darkness,* 109, notes, "enemies' visitation" near the "borders [was] tantamount to impending pestilence."

2. Sidbury, *Ploughshares into Swords,* 123.

3. "Communication," *Louisiana Gazette,* January 17, 1811. The same item, although unsigned, appeared in the February 27 *New York Evening Post,* and a partially quoted and paraphrased version appeared in the March 2 *Newport (R.I.) Mercury.* While the exact number of slaves killed during the revolt is not clear, it is possible that sixty-six died in battle and that "numerous uncounted bodies remained scattered through the woods, victims of a shooting spree that continued until no other suspected blacks could be found in the vicinity," according to Thompson, "National Newspaper," 4.

4. See "February 25," *Newport (R.I.) Mercury,* March 2, 1811.

5. From the *Louisiana Gazette,* January 11, 1811, in the *New York Evening Post,*

February 19, 1811. Further reports describing troop movements appeared in the *Louisiana Gazette* on January 14 and 15.

6. From the *Louisiana Gazette,* January 11, 1811, in the *New York Evening Post,* February 19, 1811.

7. "Account of the Insurrection at Charleston," *Richmond Enquirer,* July 30, 1822; "The Negro Plot," *New York Evening Post,* July 27, 1822. The Richmond paper credited the *New York Gazette* as its source.

8. "Latest Accounts," *Richmond Enquirer,* August 26, 1831.

9. The Richmond newspaper accounts appeared in the *New York Evening Post,* August 31, 1831.

10. "Official, Sunday night 28th," *New York Evening Post,* September 5, 1831.

11. "The Southampton Tragedy," *Richmond Enquirer,* September 30, 1831. In the September 2 *New York Evening Post,* the item "Insurrection in Virginia" contained a worried observer's concern that slaves could be affected as reports "may spread among the slaves in other parts of the State" and "excite those to insurrection that never thought of such a thing before." The writer added that "we are not without fears that more damage will arise before the slaves are learnt what their best interest is."

12. "Natchez January 12," *National Intelligencer,* February 23, 1811.

13. See "The Latest," *Richmond Enquirer,* September 20, 1831.

14. The report said that information about the "insurrection" was obtained from the confessions of two young slave boys who were beaten and coerced.

15. "Summary Justice," *Richmond Enquirer,* October 4, 1831.

16. "Extract of a Letter from a Gentleman in New Orleans to His Friend in Chester County, Pennsylvania," *New York Evening Post,* February 20, 1811.

17. Thompson, "National Newspaper," 4.

18. "Insurrection! Mr. Andry [*sic*] to Governor Claiborne," *Massachusetts Spy,* February 27, 1811.

19. Gayarre, *History of Louisiana,* 267. See also Fortier, *History of Louisiana,* 78–79. A January 21, 1811, *Louisiana Gazette* item noted, "An accurate enumeration was taken . . . of the negroes killed and missing" that indicated sixty-six slaves killed or executed, seventeen still missing, and sixteen others sent to New Orleans for trial. "Those reported missing," the writer said, "are generally [thought] to be in the woods, as many bodies have been seen by the patrols." A March 2 *Newport (R.I.) Mercury* item said, "About 100 brigands have been killed and hung, and several more would be executed." A January 25 extract from New Orleans in the March 6 *Massachusetts Spy* reported, "The negroes killed and missing from Mr. Fortiers's to Mr. André's in the late insurrection were— killed and executed 18(??); missing 17—11 have been sent to New Orleans for trial. Those reported to be missing are supposed to be dead in the woods."

20. See Thompson, "National Newspaper," 12.

21. "*To John N. Detrehan Esqr. N. Orleans January 16, 1811*" (Claiborne, *Official Letter Books,* 101).

22. Oates, *Fires of Jubilee,* 99–103.

23. "Conspiracy at Harper's Ferry," *National Intelligencer,* October 20, 1859.

24. "Insurrection at Harper's Ferry," *National Intelligencer,* October 19, 1859.

25. The letter from the January 21 *Louisiana Gazette* appeared in the February 27, 1811, *New York Evening Post.*

26. "Tranquility Restored," *Richmond Enquirer,* September 6, 1831.

27. The item, datelined Richmond, August 28, originated with the *Journal of Commerce*. Other reports identified "Nathaniel" Turner's men as a group of runaway slaves who lived in the swamps; see, for example, "New-York," *Newport (R.I.) Mercury*, September 3, 1831. A similar *Richmond Compiler* report, "The Insurrection," appeared in the *New York Evening Post* on August 29, 1831. A *Richmond Whig* report, "The Insurrection," appeared in the *Maryland Gazette* on September 1, 1831. Under the headline "Southampton, August 25," the September 3 *Newport (R.I.) Mercury* had an August 25 report from Southampton that said "the insurrection was urged and headed by a black preacher, who is not yet taken." The article noted that the insurgents believed they did not need a large core group because other slaves would join "if their masters were murdered." One troop volunteer noted that the whites had taken a woman from among Turner's men as well as the "head of the celebrated Nelson," a man first thought to be leading the insurrectionists.

28. "Latest Account," *Richmond Enquirer*, August 26, 1831. Several other newspapers, including the August 31 *New York Evening Post* and the August 3 *Newport (R.I.) Mercury*, noted that slave collusion did not exist. A September 7 headline in the *National Intelligencer* read, "THE DISTURBANCES IN VIRGINIA." The report from the *Richmond Compiler* discussed the "rumors enough afloat to keep the people on the alert" and noted that there was no "concert" among the slaves but urged a "duty to be vigilant."

29. "The Insurrection," *New York Evening Post*, August 29, 1831.

30. "The Banditti," *Richmond Enquirer*, August 30, 1831.

31. "Incendiary Publications," *Richmond Enquirer*, October 18, 1831.

32. "Riot at Harper's Ferry—Military Called Out, &c.," *Richmond Enquirer*, October 18, 1859.

33. "Insurrection at Harper's Ferry," *Richmond Enquirer*, October 21, 1859.

34. "The Harper's Ferry Riot—Its Moral and Consequences," *Richmond Enquirer*, October 21, 1859. An October 25 *New Orleans Daily Picayune* item noted this "important fact" from the *Baltimore Sun* about "The Harper's Ferry Affair": "Several slaves were found in the room with the insurrectionists, but it is believed that they were there unwillingly."

35. "Harper's Ferry Outbreak," *New Orleans Daily Picayune*, October 22, 1859.

36. "Not an Insurrection," *Charleston Courier*, October 26, 1859.

37. "The True Lesson," *New Orleans Daily Picayune*, October 30, 1859.

38. "A Nut to Be Cracked," *Charleston Courier*, November 1, 1859; *Charleston Mercury*, November 4, 1859.

39. "Letter from Senator Mason," *Richmond Enquirer*, October 28, 1859. Several other newspapers reprinted the letter. The *New York Evening Post* paraphrased Mason's letter on October 25, 1859. The *Daily National Intelligencer* and the *New York Tribune* had versions of the letter on October 26, and the *Charleston Mercury* contained his comments on October 29, 1859.

40. The text of Wise's speech appeared in the October 25, 1859, *Richmond Enquirer*.

41. The October 24, 1859, *Boston Evening Transcript* item "Gov. Wise's Richmond Speech" paraphrased him as saying, "This Kansas border ruffian made a great mistake as to the disposition of the slaves to fly to his standard. The abolitionists cannot comprehend that they are held among us by a patriarchal tenure."

42. "An Impartial Statement of the Negro Insurrection," *Massachusetts Spy*, October 15, 1800; "Extract of a Letter from a Gentleman in This City, to His Friend in New

York, Dated September 20th, 1800," *Virginia Argus,* October 14, 1800. According to the *Virginia Argus* item, "A mulatto named Ben Woolfolk, after receiving sentence of condemnation on Monday declared to the court, that, though he deserved to die as much as any of those who had preceded him, yet he would make some important discoveries on condition of having mercy extended to him."

43. "Richmond, September 3d," *Newport (R.I.) Mercury,* October 19, 1800.

44. "From Another Norfolk Paper," *New York Daily Advertiser,* October 4, 1800; "Norfolk, September 25," *Philadelphia Gazette and Daily Advertiser,* October 8, 1800.

45. "Account of the Insurrection at Charleston," *Richmond Enquirer,* July 30, 1822; "The Negro Plot," *New York Evening Post,* July 27, 1822. Much later, in the December 11, 1822, *Charleston Courier,* the item "Private Correspondence at Columbia" noted that a delegation from Charleston introduced in the legislature a bill to reward these "three of the Negroes who gave information of the late intended insurrection." About other "faithful blacks," the September 11 *Charleston Mercury* reported, "Two negro fellows" wanted to rob a store. Their designs came to an end when "a negro boy" reported the pair to "two peace officers, who proceeded to the spot, and caught the villains in the act of carrying off several boxes of Spanish segars." The two men received eight days and "fifty lashes."

46. "Servile Conspiracy in South Carolina," *National Intelligencer,* August 24, 1822; "Executive Department. Charleston, August 10, 1822," *Richmond Enquirer,* August 30, 1822.

47. "The Banditti," *New York Evening Post,* October 10, 1831.

48. "The Banditti," *Richmond Enquirer,* August 30, 1831; "Insurrection in Southampton County," *New York Evening Post,* August 30, 1831. The Blount story is told again in "The Tragedy of Southampton," *Richmond Enquirer,* September 6, 1831.

49. "The Banditti," *Richmond Enquirer,* August 30, 1831.

50. This story appeared three days later in the *Charleston Courier* and the *Richmond Enquirer.*

51. "Ardor of a Virginia Black Smith," *New York Times,* November 24, 1859.

52. "Not an Insurrection," *Charleston Courier,* October 26, 1859.

53. "From the Baltimore Sun," *New York Tribune,* November 28, 1859.

54. "Abolition Philanthropy," *Charleston Mercury,* November 12, 1859.

55. "The Riot at Harper's Ferry," *Richmond Enquirer,* November 8, 1859. In reference to Nat Turner's revolt, this author blamed a "corrupt leader and bad counsels" as its causes.

56. "Brown's Foray," *New Orleans Daily Picayune,* November 8, 1859.

57. "The Abolition Invasion of Harper's Ferry—A Lesson from the Slaves," *New York Herald,* October 27, 1859.

58. "Not an Insurrection," *Charleston Courier,* October 26, 1859. The *New York Times* printed a shorter version of the same *Whig* editorial on October 27.

59. "The Harper's Ferry War," *New York Evening Post,* October 18, 1859.

60. "John Brown's Work," *New York Times,* October 27, 1859.

61. "Insurrection to Be Anticipated," *New York Times,* November 3, 1859.

62. Martin's sermon appeared in the *Liberator* on December 9, 1859, as cited in Littlefield, "Blacks, John Brown, and a Theory of Manhood," 75.

63. Carroll, *Slave Insurrections,* 57.

64. "From Norfolk, October 2," *Virginia Argus,* October 7, 1800; *New York Daily Advertiser,* October 11, 1800.

65. See *Louisiana Gazette*, January 10, 1811; *New York Evening Post*, February 19, 1811.

66. "Alexandria, Feb. 12," *Virginia Argus*, February 22, 1811; *National Intelligencer*, February 23, 1811.

67. "Insurrection of Blacks," *Newport (R.I.) Mercury*, February 23, 1811.

68. "Latest from Harper's Ferry," *National Intelligencer*, December 1, 1859.

69. "Indicted for Sedition," *Richmond Enquirer*, November 22, 1859.

70. "John Brown's Invasion," *New York Tribune*, November 9, 1859.

71. "A Fulmination from Virginia," *New York Times*, November 17, 1859.

72. "Excitement at Charlestown," *Richmond Enquirer*, November 18, 1859.

73. "John Brown and Southern Politics," *New York Times*, November 21, 1859.

74. "The South and the Insurrection," *New York Times*, October 22, 1859.

Chapter 9: Slavery Divides the Nation

1. Lawson, *Patriot Fires*, 6.

2. Zelensky, *Nation into State*, 231.

3. Channing, *Crisis of Fear*, 288–93.

4. See McCurry, *Masters of Small Worlds*, 209–15.

5. Ford, "Social Origins," 538. Ford refers to South Carolina slaveholders and non-slaveholders, but the observation applies to all slave owners. Ford observes that South Carolina radicals believed that a republican form of government could exist only in a slave society (ibid., 543).

6. Curti, *Roots of American Loyalty*, viii. Curti cites examples of Americanism as represented by individualism, Protestantism, and laissez-faire capitalism.

7. Dangerfield, *Era of Good Feelings*, 244. He adds about the period that "political conflicts on a national scale were apt to be conflicts between personalities and not between principles or programs" (ibid., xiii).

8. "From a Correspondent at Columbia," *Charleston Courier*, December 11, 1822. Bennett would add that "we should frown indignantly on every project of partial and general emancipation, as destructive of their happiness and subversive of our own."

9. Carroll, *Slave Insurrections*, 84. Dangerfield, *Era of Good Feelings*, 244, says that "the Denmark Vesey insurrection must be regarded as having spoken, directly with a dreadful eloquence, concerning the impact of the Missouri debate upon one fragment of this silent and isolated group."

10. "Joel R. Poinsett to James Monroe," in Starobin, *Denmark Vesey*, 84.

11. "Servile Conspiracy in South Carolina," *National Intelligencer*, August 24, 1822; "Executive Department," *Richmond Enquirer*, August 30, 1822.

12. "NORTH AND SOUTH," *Charleston Courier*, November 15, 1822.

13. Pinckney, "Reflections," 5.

14. Ibid., 24.

15. Ibid., 6–7. The writer added that the ease with which slaves and free blacks could obtain money through their occupations and the growing population "disparity" between Charleston's white and black populations encouraged Vesey.

16. Ibid., 28. It was noted that there were 22,432 blacks in Charleston at the time of Vesey's conspiracy (ibid., 23).

17. "The Late Plot," *Maryland Gazette*, October 3, 1822.

18. "North and South," *New York Evening Post*, November 14, 1831.

19. The writer continued, "The mind shrinks with horror from the spectacle, when it contemplates whole families murdered, without regard to age or sex, and weltering in their gore."

20. The reprinted item was headlined "Incendiary Publications" in the October 18, 1831, *Richmond Enquirer.*

21. "Incendiary Publications," *National Intelligencer,* October 1, 1831.

22. "Monday Evening, August 29, 1831," *Boston Evening Transcript,* August 29, 1831.

23. Quoted in Curti, *Roots of American Loyalty,* 47.

24. "The Crisis of the Slavery Question. Startling Southern Programme of Protection or Dissolution," *New York Herald,* December 2, 1859.

25. "The Execution of Brown To-day," *New York Herald,* December 2, 1859.

26. Channing, *Crisis of Fear,* 23. According to Curti, *Roots of American Loyalty,* 46, the antebellum South's "growing political and economic antagonism to the North called for its declaration of cultural, economic, and political independence."

27. Potter, *Impending Crisis,* 384.

28. Hinton, *John Brown and His Men,* 327.

29. Davis, *Rhett,* 381.

30. As Wyatt-Brown, "John Brown's Antinomian War," 126, observes, "The issue of black emancipation mattered less to most people in both the North and the South than what the slavery question meant in terms of regional self-regard."

31. "The Harper's Ferry Riot—Its Moral and Consequences," *Richmond Enquirer,* October 21, 1859.

32. "The Harper's Ferry Invasion as Party Capital," *Richmond Enquirer,* October 25, 1859.

33. "The Harper's Ferry Insurrection," *Charleston Mercury,* October 19, 1859.

34. "The Insurrection," *Charleston Mercury,* October 21, 1859.

35. "The Insurrection," *Charleston Mercury,* October 31, 1859.

36. "The Plan of Insurrection," *Charleston Mercury,* November 1, 1859.

37. "Measures of Securing Southern Safety," *Charleston Mercury,* November 23, 1859. Items in the *Courier* and the *Mercury* suggested that the South must arm itself in light of John Brown's actions; see "The Harper's Ferry Affair," *Charleston Courier,* November 3, 1859; "Let the South Arm," *Charleston Mercury,* November 4, 1859.

38. "Non-Intervention and How It Works," *Richmond Enquirer,* October 28, 1859.

39. "The End of the Chapter of Compromise, Concessions, and Adjustments," *Charleston Mercury,* November 22, 1859.

40. "News from Virginia," *Charleston Courier,* October 20, 1859.

41. "The Impending Crisis," *Richmond Enquirer,* November 18, 1859.

42. "A Southern Confederacy," *Richmond Enquirer,* November 15, 1859.

43. The *New York Herald* editorial appeared in that paper on December 2, 1859.

44. "The Signs of the Times," *Charleston Courier,* November 16, 1859.

45. "1829 and 1859—the Decline and Fall of Conservatism," *Richmond Enquirer,* November 29, 1859.

46. "Proposition for a Southern Confederacy," *Richmond Enquirer,* December 2, 1859. The *New York Times* and the *New York Tribune* reported the story on December 2. Charleston readers learned about the resolution in their December 5 *Mercury.*

47. "The Presidential Campaign—the Opening of the Great Contest," *Charleston Mercury,* November 12, 1859.

48. "The Insurrection and Its Lessons to Southern Advocates of the Slave-Trade," *New York Times*, October 20, 1859.

49. "The Harper's Ferry War," *New York Evening Post*, October 18, 1859.

50. "John Brown and Southern Politics," *New York Times*, November 21, 1859.

51. "The Insurrection in Virginia," *Boston Evening Transcript*, October 19, 1859.

52. "The Lesson of the Day," *Boston Evening Transcript*, October 29, 1859.

53. "Thoughts Suggested by the Harper's Ferry Affair," *New York Tribune*, October 29, 1859.

54. "A Little Light Wanted," *New York Times*, November 10, 1859.

55. "Where Is the Blame," *New York Tribune*, November 25, 1859.

56. "The North and South," *New York Times*, November 30, 1859.

57. "The Warning to Secretary Floyd," *New York Tribune*, November 2, 1859.

58. In addition a November 11 *New York Tribune* item called the Harper's Ferry raid "Kansas Fruit" and blamed Democrats for Brown's action. The November 25 *New York Evening Post* reported "Western Virginia Growling at Governor Wise" and said that according to a Wheeling letter, the western Virginians were not happy about paying for the Harper's Ferry costs or for increased security at Charlestown.

59. "Party Spirit and the Insurrection in Virginia," *New York Times*, October 21, 1859.

60. "Brown's Slave Stampede," *New York Evening Post*, October 19, 1859.

61. "The Negro Insurrection," *New York Times*, October 20, 1859.

62. "The Lesson of the Day," *Boston Evening Transcript*, October 29, 1859.

63. "Who Are the Agitators," *New York Evening Post*, November 18, 1859.

64. "Harper's Ferry Resolutions," *Charleston Mercury*, November 7, 1859; "Cardinal Democratic Principles on the Slavery Question," *Richmond Enquirer*, November 8, 1859; "*Harper's Ferry Resolutions*," *Charleston Courier*, November 9, 1859.

65. "The Legislature of Tennessee on the Harper's Ferry Affair," *Charleston Mercury*, November 5, 1859.

66. "The Harper's Ferry Invasion as Party Capital," *Richmond Enquirer*, October 25, 1859.

67. "The Harper's Ferry Outbreak and the Republican Party," *New York Herald*, October 21, 1859. James Gordon Bennett wrote, "These agitating leaders have furnished the ideas upon which the minds of such inflammable and reckless fanatics as Brown and his associates take fire. Seward, and all such slavery agitating demagogues, therefore, are the guilty instigators of these outbreaks of treason and insurrection, and their bloody consequences; and these guilty men should be held to a prompt responsibility at the bar of public opinion."

68. "Peace and Harmony," *New York Tribune*, November 8, 1859.

69. "The Harper's Ferry Invasion as Party Capital," *Richmond Enquirer*, October 25, 1859.

70. "The Governor of Mississippi on the Position of the South," *Richmond Enquirer*, November 18, 1859.

71. "The Democratic Party and Old Brown," *Charleston Mercury*, November 8, 1859.

72. "The Tribune for 1860," *New York Tribune*, November 11, 1859.

73. "The State of Virginia," *New York Times*, November 23, 1859. Things had gotten so heated by 1859 that some southern newspaper editorials suggested a boycott of northern goods and other economic retributions. "Thousands and thousands of dollars are paid out by Abolitionists every year," a *Richmond Enquirer* editorial read, "to promulgate

their poisonous theories." Would New Englanders like it if "a man in Richmond . . . would send a thousand dollars to a band of negro thieves in New York or Boston . . . and steal the negroes of his neighbors?" Another writer said, "Let Virginia citizens work for Virginia, is our motto at present" and advised, "Knock off all the possible trade with abolitionists, and, by touching their pockets you touch their principles, and thus make them eschew all assistance to such fanatic fools as old Brown & Company"; see *Richmond Enquirer,* November 4, 25, 1859; *Charleston Courier,* November 26, 1859. The *Richmond Dispatch* item "Do Not Buy of Them" in the November 28, 1859, *Charleston Courier* said, "Men and women, old and young, the most moderate and conservative, as well as the most fiery and determined are in favor of this peaceful remedy [a boycott]." On December 2 the *Richmond Enquirer* published under the headline "Uniforms for Volunteers—Virginnia [*sic*] Cloth vs. Yankee Cloth" the words "resolve and *will* wear *Virginny cloth!*" and not "Yankee cloth."

74. Lawson, *Patriot Fires,* 5, observed that after the Revolutionary War the new nation would be "dedicated to the protection of individual freedom and equality."

75. "The Crisis on the Slavery Question—Startling Southern Programme of Protection or Dissolution," *New York Herald,* December 2, 1859.

76. According to Ratner and Teeter, *Fanatics and Fire-eaters,* x, "Americans of both the North and the South believed themselves to be custodians of the legacy of 1776."

Chapter 10: Slavery's Immorality and Destruction of Civil Liberties

1. Ratner and Teeter, *Fanatics and Fire-eaters,* x.

2. "Extract of a Letter from a Gentleman in ___ County, to the Editor," *New York Daily Advertiser,* October 1, 1800. The writer added, "The slave holder can never be a democrat, and is, at the same time, an owner of slaves." The slaveholder "is a devil incarnate . . . [and] tells a damnable and diabolical lie in the face of day." The writer applauded Gov. James Monroe's efforts in handling the conspiracy. A shorter version of this letter appeared in the October 8, 1800, *Massachusetts Spy.*

3. Published as "NORTH AND SOUTH" in the *Charleston Courier,* November 15, 1822.

4. "THE SLAVE TRADE," *Richmond Enquirer,* October 1, 1822, and *Charleston Courier,* October 5, 1822.

5. The *Boston Patriot* item "Sierra Leone, June 15" in the December 7, 1822, *Richmond Enquirer* discussed saving slaves from Spanish, Portuguese, and French "renegades" and taking them to Sierra Leone. The writer accused the French of carrying on slave trade.

6. "Slavery in Missouri—Its Practical Operation," *New York Tribune,* November 5, 1859.

7. "Charge to the Jury," *Richmond Enquirer,* August 9, 1822.

8. "New York Daily Sentinel," *Richmond Enquirer,* October 7, 1831.

9. *Richmond Enquirer,* October 7, 1831.

10. "Incendiary Publications," *Richmond Enquirer,* October 18, 1831.

11. Ibid.

12. Davis, *Rhett,* 381.

13. "Exciting Intelligence," *Boston Evening Transcript,* October 18, 1859.

14. The editorial said that Brown and his men "died for what they felt to be the right, though in a manner which seems to us fatally wrong."

15. Genovese, *Roll Jordan Roll,* 400.

16. Jordan, *White over Black*, 108. As Litwick, *North of Slavery*, 15, observes, "Until the post–Civil War era, in fact, most northern whites would maintain a careful distinction between granting Negroes legal protection—a theoretical right to life, liberty, and property—and social equality. No statute or court decision could immediately erase from the public mind, North or South, that long and firmly held conviction that the African race was inferior and therefore incapable of being assimilated politically, socially, and most certainly physically with the dominant and superior white society." Racial prejudice also fueled sentiments against free blacks and would "make them a dangerous and degraded pariah class" (Fredrickson, *Black Image*, 3).

17. "Free Negro Expulsion—Slaves Living as Free Negros—Revision of the Law as to Slaves," *Charleston Courier*, November 12, 1859.

18. Jordan, *White over Black*, 414. Ruchames, *Racial Thought*, 238, says that restricting free blacks helped preserve the slave system.

19. Fredrickson, *Black Image*, 4–5.

20. Ibid., 8. Genovese agrees, adding that free Negroes inspired fear and apprehension among whites in the Old South; see Genovese, *Roll Jordan Roll*, 398. W. E. B. Du Bois believed that white society considered the "free Negro" "a contradiction, a threat and a menace"; see Du Bois, *Black Reconstruction*, 7.

21. "For the *Mercury*," *Charleston Mercury*, November 11, 1859.

22. Genovese, *Roll Jordan Roll*, 398. See also Jordan, *White over Black*, 406–14. Free blacks had the right to vote in North Carolina and Tennessee until 1835 (Genovese, *Roll Jordan Roll*, 401).

23. "To the Members of the Legislature, *No. 2*," *Charleston Courier*, November 20, 1822.

24. A *Raleigh Register* item in the July 23, 1822, *Charleston Courier* reported a "melancholy occurrence" at "one of those pests of the City, the habitation of a free negro in the suburbs, where slaves and negroes of every description are permitted to dance and frolic." The report said that a fight broke out and "one negro struck another with the standard of a spinning-wheel in which was an iron axle which was forced into his skull." A July 9, 1822, *New York Evening Post* item from Georgia reported that a free black, "a colored man" named "Joseph Lawrence," was sentenced to prison for a year and then to slavery thereafter for "inveigling away from his master . . . a negro slave, with an intention to bring him to New-York."

25. "To the Men of the Legislature, No. 3," *Charleston Courier*, November 29, 1859.

26. "What Are We Drifting To?," *Charleston Mercury*, October 25, 1859.

27. Genovese, *Roll Jordan Roll*, 411.

28. Holland, *Refutation*, 83.

29. "The Tragedy of Southampton," *Richmond Enquirer*, September 6, 1831.

30. "Precautions," *Richmond Enquirer*, September 13, 1831. The writer warned the legislature, "We certainly have, for many years back been carefully rearing those 'wolves' to our own destruction." As a solution, the writer said that free Negroes and slaves should be taxed so as to "drive the former out of the country . . . and upon slaves, in such proportions as no longer to make it possible to breed young negroes as a crop." A later editorial, "To the Editors of the *Enquirer*," signed "OLD VIRGINIA," appearing in the November 25, 1831, *Richmond Enquirer* said that getting rid of slaves would be ruinous because "the principal part of the taxable property of the State consists in its slave population." The writer said that if slave laborers left, "we shall have no necessity for our horses, mules

and oxen to plough." As for white, foreign immigrant workers coming to the South, the author noted that that would not occur, and as to free blacks, each could remain if he "can give bond with efficient security for his good behaviour."

31. The item appeared in the *Richmond Enquirer,* October 18, 1831, under the headline "Free Negroes."

32. "To the Legislature of Virginia," *Richmond Enquirer,* November 11, 1831.

33. Reprinted in the October 10, 1831, *New York Evening Post.*

34. According to the report, "One of the results of the Brown foray at the South may be observed in the increased restrictions upon free colored people"; see "Free Negroes on Railroads," *Boston Evening Transcript,* October 29, 1895; *National Intelligencer,* October 29, 1859; *New York Evening Post,* October 28, 1859.

35. "The Irrepressible Terror," *New York Tribune,* November 22, 1859.

36. "Monthly Passes to Negroes," *New Orleans Daily Picayune,* October 22, 1859.

37. "Negro Troubles in Louisiana," *New York Times,* October 21, 1859.

38. "The Broderick and Terry Duel," *Richmond Enquirer,* October 25, 1859. The October 25 *Charleston Mercury* item "Where Are We Drifting To?" contained the comments of "ANOTHER SLAVEHOLDER," who said, "Let us ask ourselves, are the free negros who are among us desirable as *citizens?*"

39. "Discovery of Insurrectionary Weapons," *Richmond Enquirer,* November 29, 1859. Shortly following the raid, northern and southern newspapers reported that a Philadelphia volunteer troop of blacks had been disarmed on October 22: "The arms recently furnished to a colored volunteer company of this city have been taken away by the Adjutant General, in consequence of the Harper's Ferry affair"; see "Arms Taken from a Colored Company," *New York Evening Post,* October 22, 1859; "Arms Taken from a Colored Company," *New York Tribune;* "Arms Taken Away from Negro Company," *New York Times,* October 24, 1859; "Negro Company Disarmed," *Richmond Enquirer,* October 25, 1859.

40. "For the *Mercury,*" *Charleston Mercury,* November 2, 1859.

41. "News, Rumors and Gossip from Harper's Ferry," *Richmond Enquirer,* November 4, 1859.

42. "City Rumors—Strange Stories," *Charleston Courier,* October 22, 1859, and *Charleston Mercury,* October 24, 1859. The *Charleston Mercury* editor may have taken out of context the words of Henry Ward Beecher to disparage free blacks: "They are almost without education, with but little sympathy for ignorance. They are refused the common rights of citizenship, which the whites enjoy. We heap upon them moral obloquy more atrocious than that which the master heaps upon the slave" ("Beecher on Free Negros," *Charleston Mercury,* November 26, 1859).

43. "From a Correspondent at Columbia," *Charleston Courier,* December 11, 1822. Notice of this bill immediately preceded the message from Bennett. The governor blamed other states for their repressive laws forcing free blacks to leave and come into South Carolina, and he wisely said, "The natives of that description and those who have accepted their freedom under the guarantee of our own laws" should enjoy protection of person "and property."

44. "Arrested on Suspicion in Monroe County," *Richmond Enquirer,* November 25, 1859. Four days after John Brown's execution, the *Charleston Mercury* reported the "Arrest of Suspicious Characters" and "sympathizers with old Brown" who were "suspected of tampering with slaves" in Glennville, N.C.

45. "The Fire Guard," *Charleston Mercury,* November 10, 1859.

46. "A Southern Vigilance Association," *Charleston Mercury,* November 23, 1859.

47. "The Charlestown Reports, *Richmond Enquirer,* November 22, 1859.

48. A December 1, 1859, article from "New York, 1st" in the *Boston Evening Transcript* reported, "No strangers are admitted here." The December 1 *New York Tribune* item "Other Matters" noted, "The town is densely crowded" and "Communication with the North is not easy. The telegraph is in the hands of the authorities."

49. "Abolitionists in Mobile," *Charleston Courier,* November 1, 1859.

50. "Tar and Feathers," *Charleston Mercury,* November 12, 1859.

51. "Freedom of Speech in Georgia," *New York Times,* December 3, 1859.

52. "The Way Abolition Emissaries Are Treated," *Charleston Courier,* November 21, 1859, and *Richmond Enquirer,* November 22, 1859.

53. "Rode on a Rail," *Charleston Courier,* November 26, 1859.

54. "Public Meeting in Williamsburg," *Charleston Courier,* November 26, 1859.

55. "Great Excitement in Williamsburg," *Charleston Courier,* November 29, 1859.

56. "Excitement in Washington—the Office of the 'National Era' I Danger," *New York Times,* October 21, 1859, and *Charleston Mercury,* October 22, 1859.

57. "The Old Brown Panic—Mob in Kentucky," *New York Evening Post,* November 1, 1859.

58. "Mob Spirit in Kentucky," *New York Times,* November 5, 1859.

59. "Northern Reporters Expelled—More Arrests," *Boston Evening Transcript,* December 2, 1859.

60. "A Revival of Wrath," *New York Tribune,* November 7, 1859, and *New York Times,* November 11, 1859.

61. "The Terrors of a Camera," *Boston Evening Transcript,* November 10, 1859.

62. "Affairs at Charleston," *New York Tribune,* November 14, 1859; "Excitement at Charlestown," *New York Evening Post,* November 14, 1859; "Virginia Still Afraid," *Boston Evening Transcript,* November 14, 1859.

63. "Art in Virginia," *New York Times,* November 15, 1859. See also "Art in Virginia," *Boston Evening Transcript,* November 16, 1859.

64. "The Expulsion of Mr. Hoyt from Charlestown," *New York Tribune,* November 16, 1859. Under the headline "Excitement at Charlestown, VA," the November 18 *Richmond Enquirer* reported Jewett's and Hoyt's expulsions but not Jewett's observation that he had been unjustly suspected of being a correspondent for the *Tribune,* which the Richmond newspaper said had "recently published some letters from Charlestown of an irritating character."

65. "Expulsion of Strangers," *New York Tribune,* November 16, 1859.

66. "The Next Presidency—the Duty of the South—Energy and Vigilance—the Man for the Crisis," *Richmond Enquirer,* November 22, 1859.

Chapter 11: Slavery Destroys Freedom of the Press

1. In general after slave troubles southern states passed laws designed to prevent slaves' literacy, hoping to keep them ignorant of any news of trouble and abolitionist literature that might influence them. According to Richards, *"Gentlemen of Property,"* America's slaveholding elites held political sway before and after the Civil War in the country.

2. Reynolds, "Impact of Walker's Appeal," 77.

3. Ibid. According to Dicken-Garcia and Dell'Orto, *Hated Ideas,* 9, the decade of the 1830s in the South was the "most repressive period in American peacetime history because of efforts to prevent the printing, circulations and reading of abolition materials."

4. Richards, *"Gentlemen of Property,"* 15.

5. "The Harper's Ferry War," *New York Evening Post,* October 18, 1859. On November 3, 1859, the *New York Times* published a *National Era* editorial headlined "Insurrection to be Anticipated," which said, "Southern men know that it is impossible to publish anything in their newspapers relating to the freedom of the negroes, without the glad tidings reaching their ears. Many of the negroes can read."

6. MacCann, *White Supremacy,* 3. MacCann asserts that no great differences existed between whites in the North and whites in the South in the nineteenth century with regard to their negatives attitudes toward blacks, and that included abolitionists and other whites against slavery. In the nineteenth-century United States, racist white supremacist discourse was normative in children's literature: "Children's books generally treated black characters stereotypically" or excluded them completely (ibid., xvi).

7. Genovese, *Roll Jordan Roll,* 51.

8. Hockett, *Constitution,* 178.

9. "The Post Office and Abolition Documents," *Richmond Enquirer,* December 2, 1859. On John Brown's execution day, *New York Times* readers learned from the story "Post-Office Espionage Established in Virginia" about a Virginia law making it illegal to bring abolitionist documents into that state.

10. "From the Petersburg *Intelligencer,*" *Richmond Enquirer,* October 7, 1831.

11. See Oates, *Fires of Jubilee,* 51.

12. "INCENDIARY PUBLICATIONS," *National Intelligencer,* September 15, 1831. He added that any slave insurrection would "overwhelm the actors in ruin, and curtail the privileges of others."

13. "Incendiary Publications," *Richmond Enquirer,* October 18, 1831. In December the *Enquirer* described a Georgia state senator's resolution that proposed a one-thousand-dollar reward for anyone who "shall arrest and bring to trial" Garrison or "any other persons who shall utter, publish, or circulate" the *Liberator* or any publication of "a seditious character" (*Richmond Enquirer,* December 10, 1831).

14. *Richmond Enquirer,* October 18, 1831. The original item from the *Raleigh Star* referred to slave troubles in North Carolina. The *Enquirer* reported four days earlier a *Baltimore Republican* notice crediting the "Vigilance Association of Columbia (SC)" for offering the fifteen hundred dollars. See *National Intelligencer,* October 15, 1831; *Boston Evening Transcript,* October 17, 1831; *Newport (R.I.) Mercury,* October 22, 1831.

15. If caught, they would have to pay a twenty-dollar fine and spend a month in jail. In addition the free black population had to "exhibit as satisfactory evidence of their title to freedom" and "execute a bond." See *Richmond Enquirer,* October 18, 1831.

16. *Richmond Enquirer,* September 30, 1831.

17. The *Liberator,* September 3, 1831. Garrison said, "The blood of millions of her sons cries aloud for redress! IMMEDIATE EMANCIPATION can alone save her from the vengeance of Heaven, and cancel the debt of ages."

18. "Incendiary Publications," *National Intelligencer,* September 15, 1831.

19. "Communications," *National Intelligencer*, September 28, 1831.

20. The *Liberator* item headlined "BLOOD! BLOOD!! BLOOD!!!" appeared in the October 1, 1831, *National Intelligencer* under the headline "Incendiary Publications." The *Intelligencer* reported that Garrison claimed to have "no traveling agent or agents" and that the *Liberator*'s goal was not to "stir up insurrections," saying that the remarks of the *Intelligencer*'s publishers "Messrs. Gales & Seaton are libelous and silly."

21. Similarly the *Richmond Enquirer* editor branded as "odious libels" Garrison's clams that Turner acted out of revenge for brutal treatment by the "'Slavists' as they are now courteously called by the New York Sentinel"; see "Gabriel's Defeat," *Richmond Enquirer*, October 21, 1831.

22. "New York Daily Sentinel," *Richmond Enquirer*, October 7, 1831. Such actions to maintain their rights would include the suppression of "the propagation of opinion, which have a dangerous tendency."

23. "To the Editors of the *Enquirer*," *Richmond Enquirer*, November 25, 1831. According to the Richmond writer, antislavery comments were frequently and "imprudently expressed" by "representatives" carrying them into "public councils of the nation" and shaking "the foundation of our government."

24. Both items appeared in the *National Intelligencer*, September 7, 1831, under the headline "The Disturbances in Virginia." The general who put down the revolt sent notice to Virginia's governor complaining that newspapers had circulated "Extravagant reports" that were not "correct."

25. Although unrelated to Gabriel Prosser's conspiracy, a remark by the *Virginia Argus* editor on October 14, 1800, said that Charleston, S.C., newspapers were not reporting a suspected slave insurrection in that state: "*We have received the Charleston papers regularly up to the most instant and they are totally silent on the subject.*"

26. The editor added this cautionary parenthetical comment: "(Aye, reader, do not stare—upon the government!)"; the *New York Daily Advertiser*'s editor printed the comments three days later. McCullough, *John Adams*, 457, observes that the *Aurora*'s editor Benjamin Franklin Bache, grandson of Benjamin Franklin, "assailed [Adams] as never before." Bache, who was pro-Jefferson and vehemently anti-Federalist, also assailed the passage of the Alien and Sedition Acts.

27. The Philadelphia newspaper editor dismissed the claim, saying that readers knew that "negotiations between our government and Toussaint have been wholly of a commercial nature."

28. *National Intelligencer*, August 3, 1822.

29. "The Late Plot," *Maryland Gazette*, October 3, 1822.

30. Starobin, *Denmark Vesey*, 87.

31. "To Correspondents," *Charleston Courier*, August 12, 1822.

32. Starobin, *Denmark Vesey*, 89.

33. See *Albany Evening Journal*, September 7, 1831.

34. "Gabriel's Defeat," *Richmond Enquirer*, October 21, 1831. Later, after Nat Turner's capture, the Richmond editor added this caveat in the item announcing the arrest: "We shall attempt to obtain as accurate an account as possible, of the conduct of this murderous Bandit. We shall place it upon record—in order, that if any future historian should hereafter paint him incorrectly as the *Albany Fabulist has done the Insurgent Gabriel* [emphasis added], the facts may be ready to refute his falsehoods" ("Gen. Nat Turner Apprehended," *Richmond Enquirer*, November 4, 1831).

35. *Charleston Courier,* November 14, 1831.

36. The same October 21 *Richmond Enquirer* reprinted a *Norfolk Herald* item dated September 21, 1800, about Prosser's capture: "His person was immediately recognized, and he was committed to prison in irons. It appeared on his examination, that he went on board the above vessel on the 14th inst. four miles below Richmond, and remain[ed] on board eleven days; that when he went on board he was armed with a bayonet and a bludgeon, both of which he threw into the river." The *Enquirer* editor also reprinted details from the *Norfolk Epitome:* "On Tuesday the black General Gabriel, was discovered in a small vessel, in which he came from Richmond. . . . He sometimes affects to have learnt more respecting the late conspiracy among the negroes since he effected his escape to this place [. . . Gabriel] speaks confidently of the important discoveries he can make."

37. The Richmond editor also defended the legal process, remarking, "All slaves tried in 1800, were submitted to the regular tribunal, not less than five magistrates constituting the court."

38. *"Gabriel's Defeat," National Intelligencer,* September 24, 1831. The *National Intelligencer* of September 7, 1831, made a small mention of this Albany story.

39. See also Gabrial, "Crisis of Americanism."

40. The *Enquirer* editorial "The Abolitionists at the Insurrection at Harper's Ferry," appearing shortly after the raid, remarked that the "New York papers are puzzled to know what to make of the insurrection at Harper's Ferry"; see *Richmond Enquirer,* October 21, 1859.

41. "Murder and Treason vs. Patriotism," *Charleston Mercury,* November 4, 1859.

42. "Letter from New York," *Richmond Enquirer,* November 15, 1859.

43. A November 16 *Charleston Mercury* editorial accused the *New York Courier* and *Enquirer* editors of hating the South because the New York newspaper published an article saying that Brown and his men were able to take an entire Virginia town.

44. "More Black Republican Misrepresentations," *Richmond Enquirer,* November 25, 1859. The *Enquirer* editorial continued, "These misrepresentations of the 'Enquirer' are designed to prejudice Gov. Wise in the estimation of the Northern people, and by operating on the Northern Democracy, prevent his nomination at Charleston."

45. "The New York Times' Geography—Solferino and Harper's Ferry," *Richmond Enquirer,* November 8, 1859.

46. "A Geographical Spasm," *New York Times,* November 10, 1859.

47. "Negrophillism—Its Effects," *Richmond Enquirer,* November 15, 1859.

48. "An Incendiary Sheet," *Richmond Enquirer,* November 18, 1859. The *Richmond Enquirer*'s editor observed that "Mr. Henry J. Raymond (we believe that is his name) was one of the first among the Northern journalists to give in his adhesion to the system of anti-slavery tactics." On John Brown's execution day, a *Richmond Enquirer* editorial criticized the *New York Times* editor for insinuating that Henry Wise used Harper's Ferry events for political gain: "We earnestly tell the 'Times' to abandon the idea that Harper's Ferry is a mere party trick, and we invoke our contemporary not to misinterpret the silent but settled purpose of the Southern people, for the deceitful calm of indifference, or the contemptible subterfuge of political parties" ("Non-Intercourse the First Remedy," *Richmond Enquirer,* December 2, 1859).

49. "The Northern Press and Executive," *Richmond Enquirer,* November 25, 1859.

50. "More Black Republican Misrepresentations," *Richmond Enquirer*, November 25, 1859.

51. "The Laughers," *New Orleans Daily Picayune*, November 30, 1859.

52. "The South and the Insurrection," *New York Times*, October 22, 1859.

53. "The Virginia Insurrection," *New York Tribune*, October 27, 1859.

54. "Virginia and Her Conspiracy," *New York Times*, November 14, 1859. The November 24 *New York Tribune* editorial "The Virginia Fright" noted that the *Richmond Enquirer* "hastens to shield its protege [Governor Wise] from the storm of ridicule and anger which will follow upon his senseless réveille of all the militia in Virginia." Not all southern newspapers expressed sympathy. A *Mobile Register* editorial in the *New York Tribune*, for example, criticized the *Enquirer*, labeling as insulting its call for federal protection for slavery: "*We are heartily sick of this unmanly whining*," the Mobile editor said, "*this crying like a spanked baby over imaginary grievances*" ("Southern Protest against the Virginia View of Harper's Ferry," *New York Tribune*, November 16, 1859). The *Register's* editor said that the South could take care of itself.

55. "Zeal without Discretion," *National Intelligencer*, November 12, 1859.

56. "Panic," *New York Tribune*, October 22, 1859. "A Terrific Visitation" in the November 30 *New York Tribune* announced, "A heavy affliction has befallen us," noting, "The town [Charlestown] is deluged with *Richmond Enquirers*." Sarcastically the writer added that he was sure there was "no malicious intent about this."

57. "The Herald on Republicanism," *New York Tribune*, October 24, 1859.

58. "Who Taught John Brown?," *New York Tribune*, November 12, 1859.

59. "The Honest Republicans and Seward's Traitor Idea—Issue before the People of New York," *New York Herald*, October 23, 1859.

60. "What They Think in Washington," *New York Evening Post*, October 21, 1859. The editor of the *New York Evening Post* criticized the *New York Journal of Commerce* for the same reason.

61. "The Real Satanic Press Discovered," *New York Evening Post*, November 7, 1859.

62. "A Lull in Political Affairs—Brown's Execution—Quarrels over Brown in Congress—Organization of the House, &c., &c.," *New York Evening Post*, November 9, 1859.

63. The *Clarke Journal*, published in Berryville, Va., was near Charlestown and Harper's Ferry.

64. See "A Suggestion" and "A Hired Traitor in Our Midst—Pass Him Round," *Richmond Enquirer*, November 15, 1859. Coincidentally, an article following the *Enquirer* editorial mentioned that "two men were ordered from Buckingham county, Va., last week for expressing incendiary opinions."

65. A *New York Tribune* editorial contained this commentary: "The Richmond Enquirer is getting decidedly crazy on the subject of John Brown and his sympathizers and supposed aiders and abettors."

66. See "A Sensible Virginia Protest against Unreasonable Virginia Ferocity" and "The Virginia Tamerlanes," *New York Times*, November 17, 1859.

67. "Fresh Panic," *New York Times*, November 17, 1859.

68. "The Virginia Tamerlanes," *New York Times*, November 17, 1859.

69. "The New York 'Times,' an Historical Smatter," *Richmond Enquirer*, November 22, 1859.

70. "The Excitement in Williamsburg," *Charleston Mercury*, November 30, 1859.

Conclusion

1. Tanner, *Martyrdom of Lovejoy*, 2.

2. It is worth noting that the term "Negro" was generally not capitalized in southern newspapers and may indicate subtle marginalization of African Americans.

3. Turner and Brown shared another characteristic: insanity. Newspaper reports also gave Gabriel Prosser, Nat Turner, and John Brown military titles such as "general" or "captain." Constructions of other important characteristics—courage, integrity, and intelligence—were found, but these were rare. From newspaper coverage it appears that the men demonstrated their resolve to reveal nothing about their fellow conspirators or supporters to authorities. According to published accounts, the men died bravely on the gallows. In addition even southern newspaper editors begrudgingly praised Brown for his "manly" bearing.

4. While some editorial attacks appeared at the time of Gabriel Prosser's 1800 conspiracy and Nat Turner's 1831 revolt, they were focused on attacking political affiliations or antislavery tracts.

5. "The Lesson of the Hour?," *New York Times*, November 2, 1859.

6. Robin, "Conservatism and Counterrevolution," 13.

BIBLIOGRAPHY

Adams, John Q. *Memoirs of John Quincy Adams, Comprising Portions of His Diary from 1795 to 1848.* Vol. 5, ed. Charles Francis Adams. Philadelphia: Lippincott, 1874.

Aho, James. *This Thing of Darkness: A Sociology of the Enemy.* Seattle: University of Washington Press, 1994.

Ambler, Charles H. *The Life and Diary of John Floyd Governor of Virginia, an Apostle of Secession, and the Father of Oregon Country.* Richmond, Va.: Richmond Press, 1918.

Anderson, Osborne P. *A Voice from Harper's Ferry: A Narrative of Events at Harper's Ferry with Incidents Prior and Subsequent to Its Capture by Captain Brown and His Men.* Boston, 1861.

Aptheker, Herbert. *American Negro Slave Revolts.* New York: International Publishers, 1993.

Bleyer, Willard G. *Main Currents in the History of American Journalism.* New York: Da Capo, 1973.

Blumenbach, Johann Friedrich. *On the National Varieties of Mankind: De Generis Humani Varietate Nativa.* 1776. Reprinted, New York: Bergman, 1969.

Bolner, James, Sr. "Slavery and the United States Constitution." In *Slavery in the Americas,* ed. Wolfgang Binder. 225–40. Wurzburg: Konigshausen and Neumann, 1993.

Borden, Morton, and Otis Graham Jr. *Portrait of a Nation: A History of the United States, Vol. 1.* Lexington, Mass.: D. C. Heath and Co., 1973.

Broughton, John M. "Babes in Arms Object Relations and Fantasies of Annihilation." In *The Psychology of War and Peace: The Image of the Enemy,* ed. Robert W. Rieber. 85–127. New York: Plenum, 1991.

Carroll, Joseph Cephas. *Slave Insurrections in the United States 1800–1865.* New York: Negro Universities Press, 1938.

Channing, Steven A. *Crisis of Fear: Secession in South Carolina.* New York: Simon and Schuster, 1970.

Chernow, Ron. *Washington: A Life.* New York: Penguin, 2010.

Chowder, Ken. "The Father of American Terrorism." *American Heritage* 51, no. 1 (2000): 81–91.

Claiborne, W. C. C. *Official Letter Books of W. C. C. Claiborne 1801–1816 , Vol. V.* Ed. Dunbar Rowland. Jackson, Miss.: State Department of Archives and History, 1917.

Commemorate Louisiana's Heroic 1811 Slave Revolt. New Orleans: African American History Alliance of Louisiana, 1997.

Critcher, Chas. *Moral Panics and the Media.* Philadelphia: Open University Press, 2003.

Crouthamel, James L. "The Newspaper Revolution in New York 1830–1860." *New York History* 45 (April 1964): 91–113.

Curti, Merle. *The Roots of American Loyalty*. New York: Columbia University Press, 1946.

Dangerfield, George. *The Era of Good Feelings*. New York: Harcourt, Brace, 1952.

Davis, David Brion. *The Problem of Slavery in the Age of Revolution: 1770–1823*. New York: Oxford, 1999.

———. *The Problem of Slavery in Western Culture*. Ithaca, N.Y.: Cornell University Press, 1966.

———. *Slavery and Human Progress*. Oxford: Oxford University Press, 1984.

Davis, Howard, and Paul Walton. *Language, Image, Media*. Oxford: Blackwell, 1983.

Davis, William C. *Rhett: The Turbulent Life and Times of a Fire-eater*. Columbia: University of South Carolina Press, 2001.

Dicken-Garcia, Hazel. *Journalistic Standards in Nineteenth-Century America*. Madison: University of Wisconsin Press, 1988.

Dicken-Garcia, Hazel, and Giovanna Dell'Orto. *Hated Ideas and the American Civil War Press*. Spokane, Wash.: Marquette Books, 2008.

Dillon, Merton L. *Elijah P. Lovejoy: Abolitionist Editor*. Urbana: University of Illinois Press, 1964.

———. *Slavery Attacked: Southern Slaves and Their Allies, 1619–1865*. Baton Rouge: Louisiana State University Press, 1990.

Dorsey, Bruce. "A Gendered History of African Colonization in the Antebellum United States." *Journal of Social History* 34(1) (2000): 77–103.

Douglass, Frederick, John Lobb, and John Bright, eds. *Life and Times of Frederick Douglass*, pt. 2, chap. 8. London: Christian Age Office, 1882.

Dred Scott v. Sanford. 19 Howard 393.

Drewry, William Sidney. *The Southampton Insurrection*. Washington, D.C.: Neale Company, 1900.

Du Bois, W. E. B. *Black Reconstruction: An Essay toward a History of the Part Which Black Folk Played in the Attempt to Reconstruct Democracy in America, 1860–1880*. New York: Russell and Russell, 1935.

———. *John Brown*. New York: Modern Library, 2001.

Egerton, Douglas R. "Gabriel's Conspiracy and the Election of 1800." In *Rebels, Reformers and Revolutionaries: Collected Essays and Second Thoughts*, ed. Douglas R. Egerton. 39–56. New York: Routledge, 2002.

———. *Gabriel's Rebellion: The Virginia Slave Conspiracies of 1800 and 1802*. Chapel Hill: University of North Carolina Press, 1993.

———. "An Upright Man." In *Rebels, Reformers, and Revolutionaries: Collected Essays and Second Thoughts*, ed. Douglas R. Egerton. 21–38. New York: Routledge, 2002.

———. "'Why They Did Not Preach Up This Thing': Denmark Vesey and Revolutionary Theology." In *Rebels, Reformers, and Revolutionaries: Collected Essays and Second Thoughts*, ed. Douglas R. Egerton. 75–90. New York: Routledge, 2002.

Elkins, Stanley. "Slavery and Negro Personality." In *American Negro Slavery: A Modern Reader*, ed. Allen Weinstein and Frank Otto Gatell. 234–58. Oxford: Oxford University Press, 1968.

Elliott, E. N. *Cotton Is King and Pro-Slavery Arguments*. Augusta, Ga.: Pritchard and Loomis, 1860.

Ellis, Joseph. *American Sphinx: The Character of Thomas Jefferson*. New York: Knopf, 1997.

————. *Founding Brothers: The Revolutionary Generation*. New York: Knopf, 2001.

Ellis, Richard, and Aaron Wildavsky. "A Cultural Analysis of Abolitionists in the Coming Civil War." In *Comparative Studies in Society and History* 32 (January 1990): 89–116.

Emery, Edwin, and Michael Emery. *The Press and America*, 5th ed. Englewood Cliffs, N.J.: Prentice-Hall, 1984.

Engerman, Stanley, Seymour Drescher, and Robert Paquette, eds. *Slavery*. Oxford: Oxford University Press, 2001.

Fairclough, Norman. *Discourse and Social Change*. Cambridge: Polity Press, 1992.

————. *Language and Power*. London: Longman Group, 1989.

————. *Media Discourse*. London: Edward Arnold, 1995.

Fanon, Frantz. *The Wretched of the Earth*. Trans. Constance Farrington. New York: Grove Press, 1963.

"Federalist #42" and "Federalist #54." In *The Federalist Papers: 1787–1788*. New York: Bantam, 1982.

Ferber, Abby L. *White Man Falling: Race, Gender, and White Supremacy*. New York: Rowman and Littlefield, 1998.

Fiebig-von Hase, Ragnhild. "Introduction." In *Enemy Images in American History*, ed. Ragnhild Fiebig-von Hase and Ursula Lehmkuhl. 1–40. Providence, R.I.: Berghahn Books, 1997.

Fields, Barbara Jeanne. "Slavery, Race, and Ideology in the United States of America." *New Left Review* 181 (May/June 1990): 95–118.

Finkelman, Paul. "John Brown and His Raid." In *His Soul Goes Marching On: Responses to John Brown and the Harper's Ferry Raid*, ed. Paul Finkelman. 3–9. Charlottesville: University Press of Virginia, 1995.

————. "Manufacturing Martyrdom: The Antislavery Response to John Brown." In *His Soul Goes Marching On: Responses to John Brown and the Harper's Ferry Raid*, ed. Paul Finkelman. 41–66. Charlottesville: University Press of Virginia, 1995.

————, ed. *Statutes on Slavery*. New York: Garland, 1988.

Foner, Eric, ed. *Nat Turner*. Englewood Cliffs, N.J.: Prentice-Hall, 1971.

Ford, Lacy K. "Social Origins of a New South Carolina: The Upcountry in the Nineteenth Century." Ph.D. diss., University of South Carolina, 1983.

"A Forensic Dispute on the Legality of Enslaving the Africans Held at the Public Commencement in Cambridge, New England, July 21st, 1773. . . ." In *Racial Thought in America: From the Puritans to Abraham Lincoln, a Documentary History*, ed. Louis Ruchames. 152–56. Amherst: University of Massachusetts Press, 1969.

Fortier, Alcee. *A History of Louisiana*. Vol. 3. New York: Manzi, Joyant, 1903.

Fox, Early Lee. "The American Colonization Society 1817–1840." Ph.D. diss., Johns Hopkins University, 1919.

Franklin, Benjamin. "An Address to the Public, from the Pennsylvania Society for Promoting the Abolition of Slavery, and the Relief of Free Negroes Unlawfully hld in Bondage." In *A Benjamin Franklin Reader*, ed. Nathan G. Goodman. 32–33. New York: Thomas Y. Crowell, 1945.

————. "Observations Concerning the Increase of Mankind, People of Other Countries: Written in Pennsylvania, 1751." In *A Benjamin Franklin Reader*, ed. Nathan G. Goodman. 329–36. New York: Thomas Y. Crowell, 1945.

Fredrickson, George M. *The Black Image in the White Mind: The Debate on Afro-American Character and Destiny, 1817–1914*. New York: Harper and Row, 1971.

Gabrial, Brian. "A Crisis of Americanism: Newspaper Coverage of John Brown's 1859 Raid at Harper's Ferry and a Question of Loyalty." *Journalism History* 34, no. 2 (2008): 98–106.

———. "From Haiti to Nat Turner: Racial Panic Discourse during the Nineteenth Century Partisan Press Era." *American Journalism* 30, no. 3 (2013): 336–64.

———. "'The Hay Stack Excitement': Moral Panic and Hysterical Press after John Brown's Raid at Harper's Ferry." In *Words at War: The Civil War and American Journalism,* ed. David Sachsman, S. Kittrell Rushing, and Roy Morris. 109–24. Purdue, Ill.: Purdue University Press, 2008.

Garnsey, Peter. *Ideas of Slavery from Aristotle to Augustine.* Cambridge: Cambridge University Press, 1996.

Gayarre, Charles. *History of Louisiana: The American Domination.* New Orleans: F. F. Hansell and Bros., 1903.

Gee, James Paul. *An Introduction to Discourse Analysis: Theory and Method.* London: Routledge, 1999.

Genovese, Eugene D. *From Rebellion to Revolution: Afro American Slave Revolts in the Making of the Modern World.* Baton Rouge: Louisiana State University Press, 1979.

———. *Roll, Jordan, Roll: The World the Slaves Made.* New York: Vintage Books, 1976.

Goode, Erich, and Nachman Ben-Yehuda. *Moral Panics: The Social Construction of Deviance.* Oxford: Blackwell, 1994.

Grant, Susan-Mary. *North over South: Northern Nationalism and American Identity in the Antebellum Era.* Lawrence: University Press of Kansas, 2000.

Greenberg, Kenneth S., ed. *The Confessions of Nat Turner and Related Documents.* Boston: St. Martin's Press, 1996.

Halasz, Nicholas. *The Rattling Chains: Slave Unrest and the Antebellum South.* New York: David Mackay Company, 1966.

Hamilton, James. *An Account of the Late Intended Insurrection among a Portion of the Blacks in This City* (Corporation of Charleston, 1822). In *Slave Insurrections: Selected Documents.* 1–47. Westport, Conn.: Negro Universities Press, 1970.

Higginson, Thomas Wentworth. "Denmark Vesey," *Atlantic Monthly* (June 1861). www.theatlantic.com/past/issues/1861jun/higgin.htm, accessed July 21, 2014.

Hill, Truman Nelson, ed. *Liberator: Documents of Upheaval.* New York: Wang, 1966.

Hinks, Peter P. *To Awaken My Afflicted Brethren: David Walker's Appeal and the Problem of Antebellum Slave Resistance.* University Park: Penn State Press, 1997.

Hinton, Richard J. *John Brown and His Men.* New York: Funk and Wagnalls, 1894.

Hockett, Homer Carey. *The Constitution of the United States 1826–1876: A More Perfect Union.* New York: Macmillan, 1939.

Holland, Edwin C. *A Refutation of the Calumnies Circulated against the Southern and Western States, Respecting the Institution and Existence of Slavery among Them, to Which Is Added, a Minute and Particular Account of the Actual State and Condition of Their Negro Population: Together with Historical Notices of All the Insurrections That Have Taken Place since the Settlement of the Country.* Charleston, S.C.: A. E. Miller, 1822. Reprinted, New York: Negro Universities Press, 1969.

Hudson, Frederic. "The Fourth Epoch 1783–1832." In *The American Journalism History Reader: Critical and Primary Texts,* ed. Bonnie Brennen and Hanno Hardt. 61–75. New York: Routledge, 2011.

Jefferson, Thomas. *Notes on the State of Virginia.* New York: W. W. Norton, 1954.

———. "To Mr. Benjamin Banneker, Philadelphia, August 30, 1791." In *Racial Thought in America: From the Puritans to Abraham Lincoln, a Documentary History,* ed. Louis Ruchames. 216. Amherst: University of Massachusetts Press, 1969.

Jenkins, Williams Sumner. *Pro-Slavery Thought in the Old South.* Gloucester, Mass.: Peter Smith, 1960.

Johnson, Michael P. "Denmark and His Co-Conspirators." *William and Mary Quarterly* 58, no. 4 (2001): 915–76.

Jordan, Winthrop D. *White over Black: American Attitudes toward the Negro, 1550–1812.* New York: W. W. Norton, 1968.

Joyner, Charles. "'Guilty of the Holiest Crime': The Passion of John Brown." In *His Soul Goes Marching On: Responses to John Brown and the Harper's Ferry Raid,* ed. Paul Finkelman. 269–334. Charlottesville: University Press of Virginia, 1995.

Kleg, Milton. *Hate, Prejudice and Racism.* Albany: State University of New York Press, 1993.

Kovel, Joel. *White Racism: A Psychohistory.* New York: Columbia University Press, 1984.

Lauren, Paul Gordon. *Power and Prejudice: The Politics and Diplomacy of Racial Discrimination.* Boulder, Colo.: Westview Press, 1988.

Lawson, Melinda. *Patriot Fires: Forging a New American Nationalism in the Civil War North.* Lawrence: University Press of Kansas, 2002.

Leonard, Thomas C. *News for All: America's Coming-of-Age with the Press.* New York: Oxford University Press, 1995.

Levin, Murray B. *Political Hysteria in America: The Democratic Capacity for Repression.* New York: Basic Books, 1971.

Littlefield, Daniel C. "Blacks, John Brown, and a Theory of Manhood." In *His Soul Goes Marching On: Responses to John Brown and the Harper's Ferry Raid,* ed. Paul Finkelman. 67–97. Charlottesville: University Press of Virginia, 1995.

Litwack, Leon. *North of Slavery: The Negro in the Free States.* Chicago: University of Chicago Press, 1961.

MacCann, Donnarae. *White Supremacy in Children's Literature: Characterizations of African Americans, 1830–1900.* New York: Garland, 1998.

MacDonald, Helen G. *Canadian Public Opinion on the American Civil War.* New York: Columbia University Press, 1926.

Mason, James M., and Jacob Collamer, eds. *Report [of] the Select Committee of the Senate Appointed to Inquire into the Late Invasion and Seizure of the Public Property at Harper's Ferry 1860.* Washington, D.C., 1860.

Mather, Cotton. "The Negro Christianized." In *Racial Thought in America: From the Puritans to Abraham Lincoln, a Documentary History,* ed. Louis Ruchames. 59–70. Amherst: University of Massachusetts Press, 1969.

McCarthy, E. Doyle. *Knowledge as Culture: The New Sociology of Knowledge.* London: Routledge, 1996.

McCluhan, Marshall. *Understanding Media: The Extensions of Man.* New York: McGraw-Hill, 1964.

McCullough, David. *John Adams.* New York: Simon and Schuster, 2001.

McCurry, Stephanie. *Masters of Small Worlds: Yeomen Households, Gender Relations, and the Political Culture of the Antebellum South Carolina Low Country.* New York: Oxford, 1995.

McGlone, Robert. "John Brown, Henry Wise, and the Politics of Insanity." In *His Soul Goes Marching On: Responses to John Brown and the Harper's Ferry Raid*, ed. Paul Finkelman. 213–52. Charlottesville: University Press of Virginia, 1995.

McPherson, James M. "The Fight against the Gag Rule: Joshua Leavitt and Antislavery Insurgency in the Whig Party, 1839–1842." In *Abolitionism and American Politics and Government*, ed. John R. McKivigan. 235–54.New York: Garland, 1999.

Mellon, Matthew T. *Early American Views on Negro Slavery: From the Letters and the Papers of the Founders of the Republic*. New York: Bergman, 1969.

Miller, William L. *Arguing about Slavery: The Great Battle in the United States Congress*. New York: Knopf, 1996.

Montesquieu, Baron de. "The Spirit of the Laws, 1748." In *Slavery*, ed. Stanley Engerman, Seymour Drescher, and Robert Paquette. 20–23. Oxford: Oxford University Press, 2001.

Mott, Frank Luther. *American Journalism: A History 1690–1960*. 3rd. ed. New York: Macmillan, 1962.

Nisbet, Richard, "Slavery Not Forbidden by Scripture; Or a Defence of the West-India Planters, from the Aspersions Thrown out against Them, by the Author of a Pamphlet Entitled, 'An Address to the Inhabitants of the British Settlements in America, upon Slave-Keeping,' 1773." In *Racial Thought in America: From the Puritans to Abraham Lincoln, a Documentary History*, ed. Louis Ruchames. 144–49. Amherst: University of Massachusetts Press.

Nicholas, Siân, and Tom O'Malley. "Introduction." In *Moral Panics, Social Fears, and the Media: Historical Perspectives*, ed. Siân Nicholas and Tom O'Malley. 1–9. New York: Routledge, 2013.

Nicholls, Michael L. "Holy Insurrection: Spinning the News of Gabriel's Conspiracy." *Journal of Southern History* 78, no. 1 (2012): 37–68.

Nye, Russell Blaine. *Fettered Freedom*. Lansing: Michigan State University Press, 1963.

Oates, Stephen B. *The Fires of Jubilee: Nat Turner's Fierce Rebellion*. New York: Harper and Row, 1975.

———. *To Purge This Land with Blood*. Amherst: University of Massachusetts Press, 1984.

O'Connor, Thomas. *The Disunited States: The Era of Civil War and Reconstruction*. New York: Dodd, Mead, 1974.

Olmsted, Frederick Law. *The Cotton Kingdom: A Traveler's Observations on Cotton and Slavery in the American Slave States*. New York: Knopf, 1966.

Osthaus, Carl. *Partisans of the Southern Press: Editorial Spokesmen of the Nineteenth Century*. Lexington: University Press of Kentucky, 1994.

Pearson, Edward A., ed. *Designs against Charleston: The Trial Record of the Denmark Vesey Slave Conspiracy of 1822*. Chapel Hill: University of North Carolina Press, 1999.

Perca, Juan, Richard Delgado, Angela P. Harris, and Stephanie Wildman, eds. *Race and Races: Cases and Resources for a Multicultural America*. St. Paul, Minn.: West, 2000.

Perlmutter, Philip. *Legacy of Hate: A Short History of Ethnic, Religious, and Racial Prejudice in America*. New York: M. E. Sharpe, 1998.

Pickett, Justin T., Ted Chiricos, Kristin M. Golden, and Marc Gertz. "Reconsidering the Relationship between Perceived Neighborhood Racial Composition and Whites' Perceptions of Victimization Risk: Do Racial Stereotypes Matter?" *Criminology* 50, no. 1 (2012): 145–86.

Pinckney, Thomas. "Reflections, Occasioned by the Late Disturbances in Charleston by Achates" (Charleston: A. E. Miller, 1822). Reprinted in *Slave Insurrections: Selected Documents.* 1–30. Westport, Conn.: Negro Universities Press, 1970.

Popkin, Richard H. "The Philosophical Basis of Eighteenth-Century Racism." In *Racism in the Eighteenth Century,* ed. Harold Pagliaro. 245–62. Cleveland: Case Western Reserve Press, 1973.

Potter, David M. *The Impending Crisis: 1848–1861.* New York: Harper and Row, 1976.

Priest, Josiah. *Slavery, as It Relates to the NEGRO, Oreg. AFRICAN RACE, Examined in the Light of Circumstances, History and the HOLY SCRIPTURES; with an Account of the ORIGIN OF THE BLACK MAN'S COLOR, Causes of His State of Servitude and Traces of His Character as Well in Ancient as in Modern Times: WITH STRICTURES ON ABOLITIONISM.* Albany, N.Y.: C. Van Benthuysen, 1843.

Ratner, Lorman A., and Dwight L. Teeter Jr. *Fanatics and Fire-eaters: Newspapers and the Coming of the Civil War.* Urbana and Chicago: University of Illinois Press, 2003.

Remini, Robert V. *John Quincy Adams.* New York: Henry Holt, 2002.

Renehan, Edward J., Jr. *The Secret Six: The True Tale of the Men Who Conspired with John Brown.* New York: Crown, 1995.

Renfro, Paula C. "Bias in Selection of Letters to the Editor." *Journalism Quarterly* 56, no. 4 (1979): 822–26.

Reynolds, Amy. "The Impact of Walker's Appeal on Northern and Southern Conceptions of Free Speech in the Nineteenth Century." *Communication Law and Policy* 9, no. 1 (2004): 73–100.

Reynolds, David S. *John Brown, Abolitionist: The Man Who Killed Slavery, Sparked the Civil War, and Seeded Civil Rights.* New York: Knopf, 2005.

Reynolds, Donald E. *Editors Make War.* Nashville, Tenn.: Vanderbilt Press, 1970.

Richards, Leonard L. *"Gentlemen of Property and Standing": Anti-Abolition Mobs in Jacksonian America.* New York: Oxford, 1970.

———. *The Slave Power: The Free North and the Southern Domination 1780–1860.* Baton Rouge: Louisiana State University Press, 2000.

Rieber, Robert W., and Robert J. Kelly. "Substance and Shadow: Images of the Enemy." In *The Psychology of War and Peace: The Image of the Enemy,* ed. Robert W. Rieber. 3–38. New York: Plenum Press, 1991.

Robertson, David. *Denmark Vesey: The Buried Story of America's Largest Slave Rebellion and the Man Who Led It.* New York: Knopf, 2000.

Robin, Corey. "Conservatism and Counterrevolution." *Raritan: A Quarterly Review* 30, no.1 (2010): 1–17.

Rodriguez, Junius P. "Ripe for Revolt: Louisiana and the Tradition of Slave Insurrection, 1803–1865." Ph.D. diss., Auburn University, 1992.

Ropers, Richard H., and Dan J. Pence. *American Prejudice: With Liberty and Justice for Some.* New York: Plenum Press, 1995.

Rose, Arnold, and Caroline Rose. *America Divided: Minority Group Relations in the United States.* New York: Knopf, 1948.

Rosen, Robert N. *A Short History of Charleston.* Charleston, S.C.: Peninsula Press, 1982.

Ruchames, Louis, ed. *Racial Thought in America: From the Puritans to Abraham Lincoln, a Documentary History.* Amherst: University of Massachusetts Press, 1969.

Rucker, Walter C. *The River Flows On: Black Resistance, Culture, and Identity Formation in Early America.* Baton Rouge: Louisiana State University Press, 2006.

Rush, Benjamin, "An Address to the Inhabitants of the British Settlements in America, upon Slave-Keeping." In *Racial Thought in America: From the Puritans to Abraham Lincoln, a Documentary History*, ed. Louis Ruchames. 140–43. Amherst: University of Massachusetts Press, 1969.

Saffin, John. "A Brief and Candid Answer to the Late Printed Sheet Entituled, 'The Selling of Joseph.'" In *Racial Thought in America: From the Puritans to Abraham Lincoln, a Documentary History*, ed. Louis Ruchames, 53–58. Amherst: University of Massachusetts Press, 1969.

Sanborn, Franklin B. *The Life and Letters of John Brown*. New York: Negro Universities Press, 1969.

Sewall, Richard H. *A House Divided: Sectionalism and Civil War, 1848–1865*. Baltimore, Md.: Johns Hopkins University Press, 1988.

Sewall, Samuel. "The Selling of Joseph." In *Racial Thought in America: From the Puritans to Abraham Lincoln, a Documentary History*, ed. Louis Ruchames, 47–52. Amherst: University of Massachusetts Press, 1969.

Shaw, Donald Lewis. "News about Slavery from 1820–1860 in Newspapers of the South, North and West." *Journalism Quarterly* 61, no. 3 (1984): 483–92.

Sidbury, James. *From Ploughshares into Swords: Race, Rebellion, and Identity in Gabriel's Virginia, 1730–1810*. New York: Cambridge University Press, 1987.

Smedley, Audrey. *Race in America: Origin and Evolution of a Worldview*. Boulder, Colo.: Westview Press, 1993.

Spears, Arthur K. "Race and Ideology: An Introduction." In *Race and Ideology: Language, Symbolism, and Popular Culture*, ed. Arthur K. Spears. 11–60. Detroit: Wayne State University Press, 1999.

Spillman, Kurt R., and Kate Spillman. "Some Sociological and Psychological Aspects of Images of the Enemy." In *Enemy Images in American History*, ed. Ragnhild Fiebig-von Hase and Ursula Lehmkuhl. Providence, R.I.: Berghahn Books, 1997.

Spurr, David. *The Rhetoric of Empire: Colonial Discourse in Journalism, Travel Writing, and Imperial Administration*. Durham, N.C.: Duke University Press, 1993.

Stampp, Kenneth M. *The Peculiar Institution*. New York: Knopf, 1965.

———. "Southern Negro Slavery: 'To Make Them Stand in Fear.'" In *American Negro Slavery: A Modern Reader*, ed. Allen Weinsten and Frank Ott Gatell. 51–73. Oxford: Oxford University Press, 1968.

Starobin, Robert S., ed. *Denmark Vesey: The Slave Conspiracy of 1822*. Englewood Cliffs, N.J.: Prentice-Hall, 1970.

Staudenraus, P. J. *The Africa Colonization Movement 1816–1865*. New York: Columbia University Press, 1961.

Stoneham, Michael. *John Brown and the Era of Literary Confrontation*. New York: Routledge, 2009.

Stroud, George M. *Sketch of the Laws Relating to Slavery in the Several States of the United States of America*. Philadelphia: Kimber and Sharpless, 1827.

Takagi, Midori. *Rearing Wolves to Our Own Destruction: Slavery in Richmond, Virginia, 1782–1865*. Charlottesville: University Press of Virginia, 1999.

Takaki, Ronald T. *Iron Cages: Race and Culture in Nineteenth Century America*. New York: Knopf, 1979.

Tanner, Henry. *The Martyrdom of Lovejoy. An Account of the Life, Trials, and Perils of Rev. Elijah P. Lovejoy Who Was Killed by a Pro-Slavery Mob, at Altpon, Ill., on the Night of November 7, 1837*. Chicago: Fergus Printing Co., 1881.

Teymour, Mary Ann. "Political Conflict and Media Legitimation of the Anti-nuclear Weapons Movement." M.A. thesis,. University of Minnesota, 1992.

Thompson, Kenneth. *Moral Panics.* New York: Routledge, 1998.

Thompson, Thomas M. "National Newspaper and Legislative Reactions to Louisiana's Deslondes Slave Revolt of 1811." M.A. thesis, University of New Orleans, 1990.

Thrasher, Albert. *"On to New Orleans": Louisiana's Heroic 1811 Slave Revolt.* New Orleans, La.: Cypress Press, 1995.

Tise, Larry E. *Proslavery: A History of the Defence of Slavery in America, 1701–1840.* Athens: University of Georgia Press, 1987.

Tragle, Henry Irving, ed. *The Southampton Slave Revolt of 1831.* New York: Vintage Books, 1973.

United States. Cong. Senate. "Report of the Select Committee of the Senate Appointed to Inquire in the Late Invasion and Seizure of Public Property at Harper's Ferry." Washington, D.C., 1860.

Van Dijk, Teun A. "Discourse and Racism." *Discourse and Society* 10 (April 1999): 147–48.

———. *Elite Discourse and Racism.* London: Sage, 1993.

———. "Introduction: Discourse Analysis in Mass Communication Research." In *Discourse and Communication: New Approaches to the Analysis of Mass Media Discourse and Communication,* ed. Teun A. van Dijk. 1–11. New York: Walter de Gruyter, 1985.

Vaughn, Alden T. *Roots of American Racism: Essays on the Colonial Experience.* New York: Oxford University Press, 1995.

Villard, Osborn Garrison. *John Brown, 1800–1859: A Biography Fifty Years After.* New York: Knopf, 1943.

Volkan, Vamik D. *The Need to Have Enemies and Allies: From Clinical Practice to International Relationships.* Northvale, N.J.: Jason Aronson, 1988.

Wade, Richard C. "The Vesey Plot: A Reconsideration." *Journal of Southern History* 30, no. 2 (1964): 143–61.

Walker, David. *Appeal, in 4 Articles, Together with a Preamble, to the Colored Citizens of the World, but in Particular, and Very Expressly to Those of the United States of America.* Baltimore: Classic Black Press, 1993.

———. *Appeal, in 4 Articles, Together with a Preamble, to the Colored Citizens of the World, but in Particular, and Very Expressly to Those of the United States of America.* Edited and with a new introduction and annotation by Peter P. Hinks. University Park: Penn State Press, 2000.

———. *Walker's Appeal and Garnet's Address: To the Slaves of the United States of America.* Salem, N.H.: Ayer, 1969.

Webster, Noah, "Effects of Slavery, on Morals and Industry." In *Racial Thought in America: From the Puritans to Abraham Lincoln, a Documentary History,* ed. Louis Ruchames,. Amherst: University of Massachusetts Press, 1969.

Wetherell, Margaret, and Jonathan Potter. *Mapping the Language of Racism: Discourse and the Legitimation of Exploitation.* New York: Columbia University Press, 1992.

Wilson, Edmund. *Patriotic Gore: Studies in the Literature of the American Civil War.* London: Hogarth Press, 1987.

Wood, Betty. *The Origins of American Slavery: Freedom and Bondage in the English Colonies.* New York: Hill and Wang, 1977.

Wyatt-Brown, Bertram. "From Piety to Fantasy: Proslavery's Troubled Evolution." In *Yankee Saints and Southern Sinners,* ed. Bertram Wyatt-Brown. 155–82. Baton Rouge: Louisiana State University Press, 1985.

————. "John Brown's Antinomian War." In *Yankee Saints and Southern Sinners*. 97–127. Baton Rouge: Louisiana State University Press, 1985.

————. "A Volcano beneath a Mountain of Snow: John Brown and the Problem of Interpretation." In *His Soul Goes Marching On: Responses to John Brown and the Harper's Ferry Raid*, ed. Paul Finkelman. 10–40. Charlottesville: University Press of Virginia, 1995.

Zelensky, Wilbur. *Nation into State: The Shifting Symbolic Foundations of American Nationalism*. Chapel Hill: University of North Carolina Press, 1988.

INDEX

abolitionist movement: abolitionist press, 38–40, 50–53, 149–52, 155, 163; alleged political ties of, 134–35; attributed to religious fanaticism, 86–91, 100; considered race betrayal, 91–99; early efforts, 9; early rationale against, 10–11; as moral position, 129, 137–40; pro-slavery reaction to, 69, 85–86, 107–9, 113; replaces black rebels as slavery's main enemy, 117, 120, 146–47

Adams, John, 8–9, 20, 92–93, 153

Adams, John Quincy, 29, 52

African Methodist Episcopal Church, 87–88

African Repository, 30

Alabama, 12, 147

Albany Argus, 114, 139. See also *Albany Atlas and Argus*

Albany Atlas and Argus, 133. See also *Albany Argus*

Albany Evening Journal, 154

Albany Journal, 96

American Colonization Society, 30–31, 50–51, 179n5, 179n13. *See also* Liberia

American Indians, 44, 113

Anderson, Osborne P., 61, 63, 65–66, 68, 107

André, Manuel (planter), 26–27, 105, 111–12; 177n77

Aptheker, Herbert, 92

Aristotle, 2

Associated Press, 67–68, 75–76, 114

Atlantic Monthly, 37–38

Augusta Dispatch, 144

Augustine, Saint, 2

Baltimore and Ohio Railroad, 66–67

Baltimore American, 68, 113

Baltimore Exchange, 107

Baltimore Sun, 68–69, 107–8, 113, 118, 146

Banneker, Benjamin, 9

Beddenhurst, Alexander, 21

Beecher, Henry Ward, 216n42

Bennett, James Gordon, 59, 67, 88, 95–96, 131, 134, 136, 155, 157. See also *New York Herald*

Bennett, Thomas (S.C. governor), 34, 37, 106, 117, 124–25, 144, 182n53, 216n43

Benton, Thomas Hart, 174n16

Bird, Sam, 21

Blumenbach, Johann Friedrich, 6

Bolner, James, Sr., 10

Boston Evening Transcript, 37, 47, 50, 69, 75–77, 93, 99, 127–28, 132, 134, 140, 147

Boston Recorder, 125, 138

Boston Statesman, 128, 151

Bowler, Jack (alias Ditcher), 21–22

Brown, Andrew, 93

Brown, Frederick, 62

Brown, John, xi, xiv, xvi, xvii, 12, 15–16, 20, 33, 35, 37, 39, 55, 57–58, 60–63, 65–74, 85, 87, 90–92, 94–98, 101–3, 106–8, 113–16, 118–22, 124, 128–36, 140, 143–47, 155–58, 161–62, 222n3; press coverage of trial and execution of, 74–80 . *See also* Harper's Ferry

Buchanan, James, 96, 133, 158

Bryant, William Cullen, 70, 133–34, 149, 155, 157. See also *New York Evening Post*

Buffon, Comte de, 6

CPSIA information can be obtained
at www.ICGtesting.com
Printed in the USA
LVOW11*0826271016

510415LV00002B/8/P